The Collected Courses of the Academy of European Law
Series Editors: Professor Gráinne de Búrca,
                Fordham Law School, New York;
                Professor Bruno de Witte, and
                Professor Francesco Francioni,
                European University Institute,
                Florence
Assistant Editor: Barbara Ciomei, *European University*
                Institute, Florence

VOLUME XVI/2
The Fundamentals of EU Law Revisited:
Assessing the Impact of the Constitutional Debate

The Collected Courses of the Academy of European Law
Edited by Professor Gráinne de Búrca, Professor Bruno de Witte,
and Professor Franceso Francioni. Assistant Editor: Barbara Ciomei

This series brings together the Collected Courses of the
Academy of European Law in Florence. The Academy's mission is to
produce scholarly analyses which are at the cutting edge of the two
fields in which it works: European Union law and human rights law.
A 'general course' is given each year in each field, by a
distinguished scholar and/or practitioner, who either examines the
field as a whole through a particular thematic, conceptual, or
philosophical lens, or who looks at a particular theme in the context
of the overall body of law in the field. The Academy also publishes
each year a volume of collected essays with a specific theme in each
of the two fields.

The Fundamentals of EU Law Revisited: Assessing the Impact of the Constitutional Debate

Edited by

CATHERINE BARNARD

Academy of European Law
European University Institute

OXFORD
UNIVERSITY PRESS

OXFORD
UNIVERSITY PRESS

Great Clarendon Street, Oxford OX2 6DP

Oxford University Press is a department of the University of Oxford.
It furthers the University's objective of excellence in research, scholarship,
and education by publishing worldwide in

Oxford New York

Auckland Cape Town Dar es Salaam Hong Kong Karachi
Kuala Lumpur Madrid Melbourne Mexico City Nairobi
New Delhi Shanghai Taipei Toronto

With offices in

Argentina Austria Brazil Chile Czech Republic France Greece
Guatemala Hungary Italy Japan Poland Portugal Singapore
South Korea Switzerland Thailand Turkey Ukraine Vietnam

Oxford is a registered trade mark of Oxford University Press
in the UK and in certain other countries

Published in the United States
by Oxford University Press Inc., New York

British Library Cataloguing in Publication Data

Data available

Library of Congress Cataloging in Publication Data

Data available

Typeset by Newgen Imaging Systems (P) Ltd., Chennai, India
Printed in Great Britain
on acid-free paper by
Biddles Ltd., King's Lynn

ISBN 978–0–19–922621–4 (Hbk.)
ISBN 978–0–19–922622–1 (Pbk.)

1 3 5 7 9 10 8 6 4 2

Contents

Table of Cases

EUROPEAN

NATIONAL

Table of Legislation

EUROPEAN

NATIONAL

Table of Treaties and Conventions

Notes on Contributors

Catherine Barnard is Reader in European Union Law, Jean Monnet Chair of European Union Law of the University of Cambridge and Fellow and Director of Studies in Law at Trinity College, Cambridge. She has written extensively on European Union law and employment law, including *EC Employment Law* (OUP, 2006, 3rd ed.) and *The Substantive Law of the European Union: The Four Freedoms* (OUP, 2004).

Enzo Cannizzaro is Professor of International Law and European Union Law at the University of Macerata, and has written extensively in both fields. He has recently edited two books in English: *The European Union as an Actor in International Relations* (Kluwer, 2003), and *International Customary Law on the Use of Force: A Methodological Perspective* (Martinus Nijhoff, 2005) (co-edited with Paolo Palchetti).

Angus Johnston is University Lecturer in Law at the University of Cambridge and Director of Studies in Law at Trinity Hall, Cambridge. His research focuses mainly upon European law (including comparative and EC law), with particular emphasis upon competition law, energy law and judicial and institutional aspects. His recent publications include (with Alan Dashwood, eds.) *The Future of the Judicial System of the European Union* (Hart Publishing, 2001), (with Basil Markesinis and Hannes Unberath) *The German Law of Contract: A Comparative Treatise* (Hart Publishing, 2006) and (with Piet Jan Slot) *Introduction to Competition Law* (Hart Publishing, 2006).

Dora Kostakopoulou is Jean Monnet Professor of European Law and European Integration, School of Law, University of Manchester. Her principal research interests are in European public law, European integration, in the intersection of European Union law and political theory, European citizenship and migration law and policy. She is author of *Citizenship, Identity and Immigration in the European Union: Between Past and Future* (Manchester University Press, 2001).

Paul Magnette is Professor of Political Sciences and Director of the Institute for European Studies at the Université libre de Bruxelles. He has written extensively in the field of constitutional law, including editing *La constitution de l'Europe* (Université de Bruxelles, 2000).

Sacha Prechal is full-time Professor of European Law at the Law Faculty of Utrecht University (Europa Institute), specializing in European administrative and constitutional law, and in the relationship between substantive and institutional law of the European Union. She has written numerous case notes and articles on EC law, in particular on EC equality law, on various aspects of the relationship and interaction between EC law and national law and on problems related to EC directives, including *Directives in EC Law* (OUP, 2005).

Andrew Williams is Senior Lecturer in Law at the University of Warwick, and is the author of *EU Human Rights Policies: A Study in Irony* (OUP, 2004) as well as numerous journal articles on the subject of human rights and the EU.

1

Introduction: The Constitutional Treaty, the Constitutional Debate and the Constitutional Process

CATHERINE BARNARD

INTRODUCTION

The rejection of the Constitutional Treaty by the voters of France and the Netherlands sent shock waves across the EU. The voters of these two countries—founding members of the European project—registered a strong message of their discontent. This shock was exacerbated by the lack of enthusiasm for the yes votes in other Member States. In the absence of a 'give reasons for your answer' box on the ballot paper, it is difficult to state with certainty why the voters turned against a text whose aims were, according to the Laeken declaration,[1] to respond to citizens' calls for a 'clear, open, effective, democratically controlled Community approach' and to bring citizens closer to the 'European design'. Nevertheless, surveys have indicated that, for those voters who actually voted on the European issues (as opposed to those using the referenda as an opportunity to give a bloody nose to the incumbent national government), their concerns ranged from specific fears generated by reading the text, in particular its perceived excessive market liberalism (ie it was 'too British'[2]), to more general concerns about the EU's expansion, both geographically and in terms of competence.

The Member States are now in a period of reflection,[3] giving them a chance to think about the possible ways forward. To date, little of substance has emerged, leading some commentators to suggest that the Treaty is dead, if not yet buried, or

---

[1] http://www.consilium.europa.eu/ueDocs/cms_Data/docs/pressData/en/ec/68827.pdf.

[2] Garton-Ash, 'What is to be done—Blairism is the answer to Europe's ills—but we need someone else to deliver it', *The Guardian*, 2 June 2005 describing the French perception of the Constitutional Treaty as 'too much enlarged to include new countries, too Anglophone, and too enamoured of liberal-free market economics'.

[3] Declaration by the Heads of State or Government of the Member States of the EU on the ratification of the Treaty establishing a Constitution for Europe, European Council, 16 and 17 June 2005.

at least in the deep-freeze,[4] although the German Presidency in 2007 is showing signs of trying to rescue it, at least in part. The chapters in this book, drawing on the content of the courses given at the Academy of European Law, Florence in 2005, take the chance offered by this period of reflection to reflect themselves on key aspects of EC and EU law. All take some part of the Constitutional Treaty as a prism through which to examine where the EU currently stands in the particular field, where it might go, and what effect, if any, the Constitutional Treaty might have. It is not, however, a book about the Constitutional Treaty itself.[5] Rather, all chapters come from the perspective that while the Constitutional Treaty, at least in its present form, may well be dying, it presents an important opportunity to examine the ongoing constitutional debate in the EU.

THE CONSTITUTION AND THE EUROPEAN COURT OF JUSTICE

Of course the term 'constitutional', applied in the EU context, is highly contested. Even before the adoption of the Treaty establishing a Constitution for Europe there was lengthy discussion in the literature as to whether the EU already had a Constitution. The European Court of Justice certainly thought that it did.[6] As the Court said in *Opinion 1/91*[7]:

[T]he EEC Treaty, albeit concluded in the form of an international agreement, nonetheless constitutes the *constitutional charter* of a Community based on the rule of law. The Community Treaties established a new legal order for the benefit of which the States have limited their sovereign rights and the subjects of which comprise not only Member States but also their nationals. The essential characteristics of the Community legal order which has thus been established are in particular its primacy over the law of the Member States and the direct effect of a whole series of provisions.

The Court of Justice itself has been at the forefront of this process of constitutionalization, transforming the original EEC Treaty—an international agreement binding at intergovernmental level—into a Constitutional Charter regulating the relations between individuals and the state, and between individuals *inter se*. While its remarks in *Opinion 1/91* suggest that the doctrines of direct effect and supremacy were integral parts of the original Treaty, it was, in fact, the Court that 'discovered' them in a series of cases beginning with *Van Gend en Loos*[8] in order to ensure the effectiveness of the operation of Community law. Yet, with a deft sleight of the

---

4 Walker, 'EU Constitutionalism and New Governance' in de Búrca and Scott (eds) *Law and New Governance in the EU and the US* (Hart Publishing, Oxford, 2006), 18.

5 A number of such books have already appeared. See for eg, Piris, *The Constitution for Europe: A Legal Analysis* (CUP, Cambridge, 2006).

6 Case 294/83 *Les Verts* [1986] ECR 1339, para. 23; Case C-2/88 *Zwartveld* [1990] ECR I-3365, para. 16; Case C-314/91 *Weber* [1993] ECR I-1093, para. 8.

7 [1991] ECR I-6084, para. 1.

8 Case 26/62 *Van Gend en Loos v Nederlandse Administratie der Belastingen* [1963] ECR 1.

judicial hand, these doctrines rapidly mutated into the key features of the EC's new legal order.[9] To these doctrines were added the judicially-recognized principle of effective judicial protection, the doctrine of implied powers, the recognition of fundamental rights, and citizens' rights.[10] When these developments are viewed together, the ECJ has already done much to constitutionalize the Community's legal order.[11] Certainly the judges, writing extra-judicially, thought so.[12] As Judge Mancini put it, 'the Court has sought to "constititonalize" the Treaty, that is to fashion a constitutional framework for a federal-type structure in Europe'.[13]

As Mancini himself recognizes, in constructing the constitutional architecture of the EC, the Court was not seeking to replicate constitutions of nation states—even federal states. Rather, it has created constitutional doctrines—federal tools if you like—appropriate to a hybrid polity such as the EC's, one from which the 'umbilical cord' connecting the Constitution and the nation state has been cut.[14] This hybridity has long been characteristic of the EU, an organization which has defied easy classification: there are those who see the EU as a (nascent) federal or confederal system, others consider it as merely a species of international organization.[15]

It is clear that the EU is more than an international organization (as reflected by the judicially recognized doctrines of supremacy, direct effect etc) but less than a federal state (no welfare state, insufficient resources, no army etc).[16] Dashwood's preferred description of the EU reflects these tensions. He describes the EU as a 'constitutional order of states',[17] thereby emphasizing both the constitutional nature

---

[9] cf Case 26/62 *Van Gend en Loos v Nederlandse Administratie der Belastingen* [1963] ECR 1: 'the Community constitutes a new legal order in international law . . .' with Case 6/64 *Costa v ENEL* [1964] ECR 585 'By contrast with ordinary international treaties, the *EEC Treaty* has created its own legal system . . .' (emphasis added).

[10] This story is told fully by Weiler 'The Transformation of Europe' (1991) 100 *Yale LJ* 2403, reprinted in *The Constitution of Europe. 'Do the New Clothes have an Emperor?' and Other Essays on European Integration* (CUP, Cambridge, 1999), ch. 1. See also Piris, 'Does the European Union have a Constitution? Does it Need One?' (1999) 24 *ELRev*. 557.

[11] Haltern, 'Pathos and Patina: The Failure and Promise of Constitutionalism in the European Imagination' (2003) 9 *ELJ* 14, 15.

[12] Mancini 'The Making of a Constitution for Europe' in *Democracy and Constitutionalism in the European Union: Collected Essays* (Hart Publishing, Oxford, 2000). See also Zuleeg, 'The European Constitution under Constitutional Constraints: the German Scenario' (1997) 22 *ELRev*. 19, van Gerven, 'Towards a Coherent Constitutional System within the European Union' (1996) 2 *EPL* 81. More generally, see Stein, 'Lawyers, Judges and the Making of a Transnational Constitution' (1981) *AMJ. of Int. law* 1.

[13] Above n.12, 2.

[14] de Witte, 'The Closest Thing to a Constitutional Conversation in Europe: The Semi-Permanent Treaty Revision Process' in Beaumont, Lyons and Walker (eds), *Convergence and Divergence in European Public Law* (Hart Publishing, Oxford, 2002), 39.

[15] See eg Wyatt, 'New Legal Order, or Old' (1982) 7 *ELRev*. 147, Hartley, *Constitutional Problems of the European Union* (Hart Publishing, Oxford, 1999), ch. 7 and the critique in Craig, 'Constitutions, Constitutionalism and the European Union' (2001) 7 *ELJ* 123, 126 ff.

[16] Piris describes it as a 'Partially Federal Union': *The Constitution for Europe: A Legal Analysis* (CUP, Cambridge, 2006), 192.

[17] Dashwood, 'States in the European Union' (1998) 23 *ELRev*. 201.

of the EU, as well as the fact that the states remain in the driving seat. His reference to 'constitutional order' underlines the fact that the EU has a (complex) set of rules governing its own operation and its relations with the Member States. Generally, the states respect these rules. Such a narrow approach would indicate that the EU has a constitution in much the same way as a golf club, as Jack Straw, the former British foreign secretary, once observed.[18] However, in his attempt to play down the significance of the Constitutional Treaty, Jack Straw's minimalist characterization of a constitution rendered the term 'constitution' devoid of any real substance.

Weiler also recognizes that the EU's constitution (both pre- and post- the Constitutional Treaty) is not of the 'thick' variety described by Raz[19] but Weiler's explanation for this is very different from Jack Straw's. He argues that Europe's constitutional principles (a hierarchy of norms, with Community norms trumping conflicting Member State norms), while materially similar to those of traditional federations (the US, Germany, Australia and Canada), are rooted in a framework which is altogether different[20] because Europe's constitutional architecture has never been validated by a European constitutional demos. He concludes that 'It is a constitution without some of the classical conditions of constitutionalism.'[21]

THE CONSTITUTION AND THE POLITICAL PROCESS

It took much longer for the political discourse on constitutionalization to catch up with the judicial developments. The Treaty of Rome, adopted in 1957, was not significantly amended, apart from by the various Accession Treaties, until the Single European Act in 1986. After that, Treaty amendments came thick and fast: Maastricht (1992), enlargement (1995), Amsterdam (1997), Nice (2000), enlargement (2004 and 2007). The resulting edifice—often described using the image of a Greek temple with three pillars ((1) the European Community pillar governed by the Community method,[22] (2) Common Foreign and Security Policy, and (3) Police and Judicial Cooperation', governed by a more intergovernmental method)—was complex and messy. The pillarization—so clear on paper—proved difficult to operate in practice.[23] To the outsider, understanding the new structures was as easy

---

[18] 'Strength in Europe Begins at Home' Speech by Jack Straw, Edinburgh, 27 August 2002, www.europa.eu.int/futurum, cited by Brand, 'Formalising European Constitutionalism: Potential Added Value or death by Constitution' in Inglis and Ott (eds), *The Constitution for Europe and an Enlarging Union: Unity in Diversity* (Europa Law Publishing, Groningen, 2005) who describes this conception of a constitution based on an approach of 'trivial minimalism'.

[19] Raz, 'On the Authority and Interpretation of Constitutions: Some preliminaries' in Alexander (ed) *Constitutionalism: Philosophical Foundations* (CUP, Cambridge, 1998), 153–154 discussed in Craig, 'Constitutions, Constitutionalism and the European Union' (2001) 7 *ELJ* 123.

[20] See further Magnette in this volume.

[21] Weiler, 'A Constitution for Europe? Some Hard Choices' (2002) 40 *JCMS* 563, 567.

[22] The Commission proposes; the Council/EP adopt and the resulting measure has precedence over national law.

[23] Case C-176/03 *Commission v Council (Criminal Penalties)* [2005] ECR I-7879.

as grasping jelly. These problems were recognized by the Laeken Declaration of December 2001 which, under the heading 'Towards a Constitution for European citizens', raised the question of how to simplify and reorganize the existing Treaties and how, if at all, to incorporate the Charter of Fundamental Rights. The Declaration, recognizing the possibility that the resulting simplification and reorganization might 'lead in the long run to the adoption of a constitutional text in the Union', put the constitutional question on the table, albeit a long way down the agenda. However, convening the 'Convention on the Future of Europe' suggested that a constitutional debate was nevertheless under way.

The resulting document was called a 'Treaty establishing a Constitution for Europe' (TCE). This title recognized the hybrid nature of the text—part Treaty, part Constitution. It contained, in Parts I, II and IV, a statement of values, a division of competences including the depillarization of the Treaties, a supremacy clause, the symbols of the Union and fundamental rights. This is the most 'Constitutional' part of the Constitutional Treaty and it may be the part that will be saved by the German and subsequent Presidencies. The more 'Treaty'-based,[24] and by far the largest part of the text, was Part III on the Policies and Functioning of the Union which, apart from a bit of light dusting, remained largely untouched from the EC Treaty version. Yet, it was this part of the text that most frightened the voters.[25]

However, the fact that the text was described as a Constitution generated its own problems, especially for readers coming from states with their own constitutions. The first problem concerned the sheer volume of the final document. With 448 Articles, 36 protocols and 2 annexes covering 560 pages (including the Euratom Treaty),[26] the Constitutional Treaty was a doorstop not a pocket book, and it bore little resemblance either physically or substantively to slim, brief national constitutions.[27] Now, of course there were good reasons for the length: if Part III had been removed, the text as a whole would have made little sense (for example, some would argue how can there be a categorization of competences in Part I without their contours being clarified in Part III?) and opponents would have complained that the Constitutional Treaty told only half the story. But nevertheless the Constitutional Treaty's size was a major hurdle.

The second problem concerned the substance. Traditionally the language of 'constitution' has been associated with the construction of a nation state. This raised fears in the minds of some that the final objective of the EU constitution was converting the EU into some type of federal state. This perception was exacerbated

---

[24] On the Constitution/Treaty debate, see Birkinshaw, 'Constitutions, Constitutionalism and the State' (2005) 11 *EPL* 31, 42–44. Schwarze, 'The Treaty establishing a Constitution for Europe—Some General Reflections on its Character and its Chances of Realisation' (2006) 12 *EPL* 199, 200.

[25] Editorial Comments (2005) 42 *CMLRev.* 905, 906.

[26] This is a considerable reduction form the present 2800 pages of primary law: see Piris, *The Constitution for Europe: A legal Analysis* (CUP, Cambridge, 2006), 58.

[27] See Sutherland, 'Editorial' *EU Constitution Newsletter*, The Federal Trust, July 2005: 'people are asked to vote on a long and complex document such as a Treaty, a Treaty wrongly described as a "constitution" and with little obvious damage following on from its non-adoption'.

by the grandiose language and symbols found in Part I. Politicians tried to reassure the voters by suggesting that the document actually preserved powers for the states, but this raised the question as to how a single text could, at one and the same time, be both the cornerstone of the future architecture of the EU and the protector of nation states.

THE CONSTITUTION AND THE PUBLIC

It is now clear that the EU has a constitution, at least in the narrow sense of the word—with or without the Constitutional Treaty—and that this constitution is in the process of constant evolution and contestation.[28] However, the EU has been criticised for the fact that this evolution has occurred largely in the absence of popular participation. The principal Treaty amendments have taken place through an inter-governmental process (mainly through an intergovernmental conference (IGC)), largely divorced from popular understanding and debate.[29] This was particularly the case with enlargement, perhaps the biggest constitutional change in the last decade or so[30] which, for many European citizens, represented a (potential if not actual) threat to their way of life, as the debate over Polish plumbers 'flooding' France has shown.[31] Yet, the EU citizens were not asked their views on the need for enlarge-ment. When changes have been put to a public vote, the result has often been negative (France came very close to rejecting the Maastricht Treaty, Denmark did actually reject it, and Ireland rejected the Nice Treaty first time round).

In terms of public debate, the negotiation of the Constitutional Treaty was more open and transparent.[32] The Convention process involved a wider range of actors,[33] the key documents were readily accessible, and there was more public debate about the Constitution's content. Yet, one of the strengths of the Constitution—that it was in part (75 per cent according to Peter Hain[34]) a tidying-up exercise reorga-nizing the text to make it more accessible to its citizens—was also its weakness. Unlike the Maastricht Treaty with its big idea (the single currency) which was easy to communicate, the Constitutional Treaty did not have a simple message to sell.[35]

---

[28] de Witte, 'The Closest Thing to a Constitutional Conversation in Europe: The Semi-Permanent Treaty Revision Process', in P. Beaumont, C. Lyons and N. Walker (eds.), *Convergence and Divergence in European Law* (Hart Publishing, Oxford, 2002), 39.

[29] Duhamel, 'Convention versus IGC' (2005) *EPL* 55.

[30] Weiler, 'A Constitution for Europe? Some Hard Choices' (2002) 40 *JCMS* 563, 564.

[31] See further the chapter by Barnard in this volume.

[32] José Menéndez, 'Between Laeken and the Deep Blue Sea: An Assessment of the Draft Constitutional Treaty form a Deliberative-Democratic Standpoint' (2005) 11 *EPL* 105.

[33] de Búrca, 'The Constitutional Challenge of New Governance in the European Union' (2003) 28 *ELRev.* 828. See also the table in the chapter by Johnston in this volume.

[34] Quoted in Gisela Stuart, *The Making of Europe's Constitution* (Fabian Society, London, 2003), 4. She adds that Hain later admitted that the remaining quarter was 'creating a new constitutional order for a new united Europe'.

[35] Editorial Comments (2005) 42 *CMLRev.* 905, 908.

In the end, the French and Dutch voters took the low-cost option of preserving the status quo and voted no.

Nevertheless, in some of those countries where a referendum was held there was a vibrant debate about the EU project as a whole.[36] For those looking for a silver lining, this was a positive feature of the recent constitutional debacle; at long last it engaged the 'people'. They shook off their indifference and took to the streets. However, the closer they looked, the less they liked what they saw. This makes it very difficult to see how the Treaty might ever be amended in the future. In his chapter, Angus Johnston makes some suggestions first as to what can be saved from the Constitutional Treaty without the need for a Treaty amendment (transparency and the subsidiarity mechanism) and second, how the EU and the Member States can seek to re-engage EU citizens with the EU project without which future reforms of the Treaty would be impossible.

THE CONTENTS OF THIS BOOK

If it is accepted that the EU has a constitution and that the EU is engaged in a process of constitutionalism then it is time to go back to reconsider the basic elements of the EU's constitutional provisions in the light of the constitutional debate. This is the principal aim of this book.

In her chapter, Sacha Prechal offers a detailed, careful analysis of the many and varied meanings of the principle of direct effect, uncertainties about the scope of supremacy and the 'radiation effect' of the reasoning and rationale of principles developed under the first pillar to the third pillar (PJC) resulting in a rapprochement between EC and non-Community EU law. This comes together in her detailed discussion of the case of *Pupino*,[37] a decision under the third pillar, where the Court ruled that the doctrine of consistent interpretation applies equally to Framework Decisions but limited by general principles of law and fundamental rights.

The importance of human rights is recognized in Andrew Williams' contribution. He argues that not only are human rights a prominent and explicit feature of the core values identified in Article I-2 TCE but they also help frame an array of implicit constitutional themes. From constructing an identity for the EU, legitimizing its operations, providing a bulwark against extremism and the abuse of power, to acting as a spur to 'closer union' between the peoples of Europe, human rights provide an iconic concept without respect for which the EU would lack moral and enduring substance. However, his interest lies in assessing, rather than cataloguing, the achievements to date. The question for him is: how can an effective analysis be carried out into the current state of human rights and the EU, and the

---

[36] Prechal notes that this was not the case in the Netherlands: she says that the debate in the Netherlands started far too late, it was at times almost hysterical on the part of the proponents and opponents, the government included which proved incapable of responding to the challenge posed by the Treaty's opponents.

[37] Case C-105/03 *Pupino* [2005] ECR I-5285.

proposed direction they may take whether or not the TCE (or its specific human rights related components) is enacted?

The rights theme continues in both my own and Kostakopoulou's chapters. We both note that one of the most important contributions of the Constitutional Treaty was the incorporation of the Charter of Fundamental Rights into Part II. Much has already been written about the importance of the means by which the Charter was negotiated in 2000, prior to its proclamation by the Heads of State at Nice, and the fact that economic and social rights were (ostensibly) put on an equal footing with civil and social rights.[38] Critics of the Charter's incorporation into the Treaty refer to the rather uncomfortable fit between the Charter and the Constitution, and the amendments made by the Constitutional Treaty to the final provisions of the Charter with a view to limiting any interpretative use of the Charter by the Courts. These were introduced despite the fact that the Charter broadly endorses the human rights jurisprudence developed by the Court of Justice, not only as a means of challenging the validity of acts of the Community institutions but also of the Member States, when implementing (and derogating) from Community law. This case law, now buttressed by the Charter, has done much to reorientate the EC Treaty away from being seen as an economic constitution towards a Constitution in the more full sense of the term.

These issues help frame the debate in my own chapter on social policy. I trace the evolution of EC social policy from its market-oriented origins in the 1957 version of the Treaty of Rome up until today when social policy has been used to give the EU a more truly 'social face'. I then take two of the values identified by the Constitutional Treaty—solidarity and equality/non-discrimination—and use them as a prism through which to examine the state of European social policy. The chapter then considers how the European Union has sought to deal with concerns about social dumping, taking the developments in the field of free movement of services, and the issue of posted workers in particular, as an illustration.

The interplay between the desire to protect human rights and the need for citizens to have 'freedom, justice and security' (FJS) is one of the themes in Dora Kostakopoulou's contribution. She tracks the development of FJS from its early incarnation in the Justice and Home Affairs Pillar, introduced by the Maastricht Treaty, through to the changes introduced by the Constitutional Treaty. She argues that the evolution of JHA and the present debate about the constitutional future of the EU are poignant reminders of the fact that EU constitutionalism is, essentially, an ongoing process of debate and engagement with the principles and terms of European governance and with institutional design.

The pillarization of the EC/EU's external relations is also a key feature of Cannizzaro's chapter. He takes the field of external relations to demonstrate

---

[38] See eg Kenner, 'Economic and Social Rights in the EU Legal Order: the Mirage of Indivisibility' in Hervey and Kenner (eds), *Economic and Social Rights under the EU Charter of Fundamental Rights* (Hart, Oxford, 2003), 3.

the internal fragmentation of the EU foreign relations power deriving from the distribution of competences between the EC and the EU. He then analyses the attempt to lend unity and coherence to the EU foreign relations power. He examines the new provisions on the EU's external action in the Constitutional Treaty, which have the express aim of establishing a comprehensive system of external action for the Union. This, he argues, requires the re-unification of the vast array of powers and prerogatives which are currently distributed in a disorderly and random bundle of competences.

CONCLUSIONS

The problems facing the EU recognized by the Laeken declaration have not gone away. For all the positive spin that has been put on the 'No' votes—that citizens are now engaged in the constitutional debate, that the referenda have energized the EU, that the 'no' votes have forced all actors to take a good look at themselves—the fact remains that the existing Treaty arrangements are cumbersome, the Nice Treaty compromises are uncomfortable, the national Parliaments feel alienated and the Charter of Fundamental Rights now occupies some strange, twilight world. Some of the solutions contained in the Constitutional Treaty were imaginative and/or useful (eg the catalogues of competence,[39] the introduction of the post of president of the Council, the subsidiarity mechanism). Others were incomprehensible and wholly user-unfriendly[40] (eg the hierarchy of norms and the reform of the *locus standi* provisions for judicial review of Community acts by non privileged applicants[41]). The French voters might have been right in their thinking that by voting 'no' to this text there might be a better one round the corner. The trouble is: what would make a 'better' text? This goes to the heart of the matter: what is the EU for?

In the early days of the EEC, its telos was clear: market integration (ie opening up national markets to goods, persons, services and capital from other Member States). This provided the Court with a clear steer as to how to interpret the Treaty provisions[42] and the free trade message was a reasonably easy one to sell to national electorates. The EU was being legitimated through growth and prosperity arising from free trade.

But the opening up of the market led to regulation, and regulation had to be enacted in a democratic and legitimate way by bodies ultimately accountable to the

---

[39] Goucha Soares, 'The Division of Competences in the European Constitution' (2005) 11 *EPL* 603.

[40] It was also a shame that some key provisions of the Treaty were not amended to take account of changing circumstances, in particular Art. 30 (Art. III-154) on the free movement of goods to recognize environmental protection and consumer protection as an express derogation and Art. 50 (Art. III-145) on services which suggests that services are a residual free movement category, although cf Case C-452/04 *Fidium finanz Ag v Bundesanstalt für finanzdleistungsanfsicht* [2006] ECR I-000, para 32.

[41] See further Dougan, 'The Convention's Draft Constitutional Treaty: Bringing Europe Closer to its Lawyers' (2003) 6 *ELRev.* 763, 793.

[42] Koopmans, 'Guest Editorial: In Search of Purpose' (2005) 42 *CMLRev.* 1241, 1243.

electorate. Increasingly, public law issues came to the fore. And, as the tentacles of integration expanded beyond the rather narrowly-defined group of economic actors—to include the less economically active such as tourists, students, work-seekers—the personal scope of the Treaty opened up to include citizens and citizens who have, or should have, human rights. Inevitably, the spillover effect of market integration forced the EU into ever new pastures, increasingly requiring it to equip itself with more power to accomplish its tasks. This inevitably put the EU on a collision course with some Member States and the EU's response has been to draw up a Constitutional Treaty setting out the rights and interests of the different parties. But what legitimizes this text, and the next stage of European developments? What are those developments to be? These issues lie at the heart of Magnette's chapter. Focusing on the question of democracy, he asks: how can we conceive a European democracy that is primarily transnational, but also has some vertical elements? He suggests that we should start by identifying the underlying principles and psychic frame of mind—on which European norms and institutions are buttressed—which might consolidate the EU's legitimacy if they were made more explicit.

In the last 15 years or so, the EU has resembled a whirligig, constantly in motion, constantly changing, with those in power keen to leave their mark[43] and to be remembered for posterity for their role in the construction of the EU. This has led to a number of big bangs (Maastricht, enlargement, the Constitutional Treaty) but little evidence of any pause for reflection and listening to discover what citizens actually want.[44]

At one level, the EU is a victim of its own success. The fact that there has been no war between the Member States since 1945 has shown that Jean Monnet's goals of peace through trade have been realized. But given that world war between the great powers does not raise fears in the minds of today's citizens, the EU needs to refocus on new priorities. Writing this as the war on terror comes ever closer to home, security is an obvious candidate but so is the need to combine security with religious freedom and tolerance. The EU might therefore benefit from extending its period of reflection while it works out its real priorities—and then gets on with them.

As to the Constitution, does the EU actually need a formal Constitutional text?[45] Can it not get by with the existing arrangements which can evolve to accommodate changing circumstances? One of the remarkable features of the deepening of the EU is that much has occurred organically. While the EU has acquired more

---

[43] See eg Silvio Berlusconi, the Italian prime minister, who was determined that the Constitutional Treaty be signed in Rome in the dying days of his government, at a time when he himself was mired in corruption charges.

[44] Weiler, 'Introduction: We will do, and hearken' in *The Constitution of Europe. 'Do the New Clothes have an Emperor?' and Other Essays on European Integration* (CUP, Cambridge, 1999), 4.

[45] For strong counter-arguments, see Brand, 'Formalising European Constitutionalism: Potential Added Value or death by Constitution' in Inglis and Ott (eds), *The Constitution for Europe and an Enlarging Union: Unity in Diversity* (Europa Law Publishing, Groningen, 2005).

powers, they have been exercised not only by the Community—through the Council and the comitology committees comprising representatives of the Member States—but also by the Member States at national and subnational levels. This unique system of multi-level governance is one of the strengths of the EU.[46] As Moravcsik puts it, the current constitutional settlement is defined by a stable balance between Brussels and national capitals and democratic legitimacy through indirect accountability and extensive checks and balances.[47] He adds that '[o]nce we set aside ideal notions of democracy and look to real-world standards, we see that the EU is as transparent, responsive and accountable and honest as its Member States'.[48]

As the British have long known,[49] the advantage of not having a written constitutional document is that the constitutional arrangements are sufficiently flexible to enable them to accommodate the vicissitudes of life. The Constitutional Treaty risks upsetting this delicate constitutional settlement. Although of course the new Constitutional Treaty aims to codify and clarify existing relationships, the very process of fixing has solidified what previously was fluid and flexible and removed the possibility for incremental evolution.

Catherine Barnard
Trinity College, Cambridge, August 2006

---

[46] See Ward, *A Critical Introduction to European Law* (2nd edn, Lexis Nexis Butterworths, London, 2003), 251.

[47] Moravcsik, 'A Category Error', *Prospect*, July 2005, 22, 22.

[48] ibid 24.

[49] Birkinshaw, 'Constitutions, Constitutionalism and the State' (2005) 11 *EPL* 31, 33; Weiler, 'A Constitution for Europe? Some Hard Choices' (2002) 40 *JCMS* 563, 566.

2

European Democracy Between Two Ages

PAUL MAGNETTE

Among the drafters of the constitutional treaty, the rejection of the EU's proposed constitution by voters in France and the Netherlands prompted bitter reactions. That the citizens rejected a treaty that aimed at curbing the EU's democratic deficit seemed to echo the paradox underlined by Tocqueville in *The Ancien Regime and the Revolution*: 'Experience teaches us that the most dangerous moment for a bad government is usually when it starts reforming itself'. Though the drafters' disappointment is understandable, the comparison is misleading. The constitutional treaty may have been a major step in the process of bringing EU issues, opened at Maastricht, into the public domain but it would be simplistic and erroneous to regard the pre-Maastricht form of EU government as non-democratic. In this chapter, we argue that the period opened by Maastricht, and of which the constitutional saga is the last step to date, is rather marked by the passage from a democratic logic to another one. The problem today is how to reconcile the liberal philosophy, extolling 'democracy among nations' that has nourished the EU since its origins, and the republican desire for the emergence of a 'continental democracy', a concept that has gained increasing momentum over the last 15 years.

DEMOCRACY AMONG NATIONS:
THE EU'S LIBERAL IMPETUS

Students of European integration have often been tempted to assess it by comparing it to other federal experiences, first and foremost to the development of the US. Provided such an approach is not aimed at erecting the US as a model that the EU should imitate, such a comparative analysis may be useful. The specificity of Europe's construction process is indeed clearly visible if we compare it with other models of political integration.

Historian Gordon Wood has shown that the events that spanned the period from the proclamation of independence in the 13 colonies in 1776 to the adoption of the federal constitution in 1787 were part and parcel of the same revolution. The Americans first focused their attention on the adoption of republican constitutions within each state. The formation of a Confederation was regarded as of secondary importance: 'in marked contrast to the rich and exciting public explorations of political theory accompanying the formation of the state constitutions, there was little discussion of the plans for a central government'[1] (Wood (2002), 70). But less than 10 years after, the two problems intersected. As the war of colonial liberation was dragging on, the weaknesses of the Confederation became increasingly obvious. At the same time, the 'populist drift' spreading across the 13 colonies led the elites to consider reforming the newly established republican constitutions. In the mid-1780s, the ruling classes thus came to the conclusion that both sides of the problem were closely linked: 'the reconstruction of central government was being sought as a means of correcting not only the weaknesses of the Articles (of Confederation) but also the democratic despotism and the internal political abuses of the states'.[2] As these two preoccupations—democratic consolidation in the states and the necessary reinforcement of the Confederation—were no longer differentiated, a federal constitution was adopted in the so-called 'spirit of Philadelphia' in 1787. In this seminal moment, the democratic issue was addressed at the level of both states and central government. The reference to 'We the people' and the doctrine of 'dispersed sovereignty' were to be the foundations of a new form of democracy in which state and federal authorities were intimately associated.

As we know, such was not the case in Europe. The political movements and organizations that had emerged from the Resistance period were used as instruments by post-war governments and were thus unable to take any durable initiative.[3] The Summit of The Hague in 1948, heralded as a moment of federal euphoria, only revealed the inner contradictions within the pro-European movements. As the great expectations attached to the creation of the Council of Europe were dashed on account of its complex and confused organization, it was clear from the start that Europe would not follow the American constitutional model. It was to be functional, based on international treaties negotiated *in camera* by government officials and diplomats. It was not to be a federation but a 'community'—a neologism that referred to a mix of classic intergovernmental procedures and a carefully measured dose of supranational incentives and controls. According to this scheme, the divide was clearly set between the democratic issue, a national prerogative, and inter-state affairs, partly dealt with within the framework of the Community. The federalist project—ie merging both agendas—never came true. Europe from then on would be a more modest and indirect form of government in charge of market regulation and commercial policies. The democratic issue was thus confined at state level—the locus of solidarity policies and political links.

---

[1] G. Wood (2002). *The American Revolution, A History*, (New York: The Modern Library), 70.

[2] ibid 152.

[3] Lagrou (2000), *The Legacy of Nazi Persecution. Patriotic Memory and National Recovery in Europe 1945–65*, (Cambridge: Cambridge University Press.

This does not imply that the EU had no relation to the democratic question. Indeed, if we approach the question of democracy in a framework such as the EU's in terms of national democracy, we are bound to come to the conclusion that it is not, and is unlikely to become, a democracy. An alternative conceptual approach to assessing how democratic a political entity is would be to come back to the very concept rather than compare it with given historical forms of democracy. We may agree that the EU will never look like a continental democratic state, and yet consider that it embodies a peculiar form of democracy. The concept of democracy, Bobbio reminded us, echoes the idea of autonomy, defined in opposition to both anarchy (the absence of norms) and heteronomy (a set of imposed norms). In this sense, international democracy may be apprehended in a different way, not as the reproduction of state mechanisms on a wider scale, but rather as the diffusion of mutually negotiated norms in inter-state relations.[4] If we accept the idea that the building of national democracy has meant that the rule of law and negotiations have progressively replaced power struggle between social groups, we may contend that democracy will spread in international and transnational relations through the replacement of force by law and peaceful negotiations among equal states. A contrario, what we need to understand is how the exclusive conception of national sovereignty, inherited from the early stages of modernity, has hindered the development of universal fundamental rights and binding legislation; and how the persistence of *Machtpolitik* has fuelled a feeling of mistrust between nations, thus making any form of cooperation almost impossible. Bobbio did not study the EU, but those who, like him, take their inspiration from Kant's cosmopolitanism, have all stressed that, in actual fact, the formation of the EU is a long process of legalization of conflicts and substitution of 'civilized' negotiations to power relations, and this amounts to an extension of the democratic principle to the inter-state order.[5]

Repudiating the Hegemonic Principle

The first feature of the EU which makes it a democratic inter-state order is its regime, the way power relations are organized by the treaties, which can be read as an attempt to avoid any form of hegemony. Contrary to all the historical examples of multinational entities throughout European history (the Austro-Hungarian Empire, the German Reich, the United Kingdom, the Soviet Union and Yugoslavia), the EU has never been dominated by any majority ethnic group. From its very origin, it has been based on a 'balance of unbalances', to quote the definition given by Stanley Hoffmann (1996), a balance that has been regularly confirmed by the successive enlargement processes. The six founding Member States were composed of three larger states and three smaller ones, with various configurations: some were

---

[4] N. Bobbio (1995), 'Democracy and the International System' in D. Archibugi and D. Held (eds) *Cosmopolitan Democracy*, (Cambridge: Polity Press).

[5] J. -M. Ferry (2000), *La question de l'Etat européen* (Paris: Gallimard); P. Magnette (2000), *L'Europe, l'Etat et la démocratie, Le Souverain apprivoisé* (Bruxelles: Complexe); F. Cheneval (2005), *La Cité des Peuples* (Paris: Cerf); J. -M. Ferry (2005), *Europe: la voie Kantienne* (Paris: Le Cerf).

rural while others were essentially urban and industrialized; some had won WWII, others had been defeated; some were old centralized states and others were younger and more fragile; some were colonial powers and others, states without any empire; some were countries of immigration and others, countries of emigration; some had export market activities while others had more protectionist policies, . . . There were enough intersecting differences between the states to make the creation of stable fronts very unlikely.

Of course, France enjoyed a predominant position in Europe, as divided Germany was racked with guilt from its Nazi past, Italy painfully recovering from the ruins of Fascism and the three Benelux states too small to set their own pace. The great achievement of the 'Community method' was to overcome the reluctance of some countries that feared the hegemony of France or of the Big Three by suppressing any potential risk of solitary leadership. Suspected *a priori* of being France's Trojan horse, the High Authority—and the Commission that replaced it—was quickly perceived by the other Member States as a means of achieving common leadership. By transferring the monopoly of initiative to a third party whose independence was guaranteed, the most ambitious and influential states were thus denied the power of fixing the European agenda. Likewise, the system of rotating presidency in the Council of Ministers symbolized inter-state equality. The qualified majority voting system, based on a subtle system of weighing votes, put the Big Three on an equal footing and gave the three smaller states a capacity of obstruction—provided they worked in collaboration—nearly on a par with any of the other larger countries—much greater in any case than their respective demographic power would have enabled them to have. Unlike other international organizations in which inter-state equality remained a virtual principle, the EU thus efficiently prohibited the possibility for a state to occupy a hegemonic position.[6] With time, negotiations based on mutual respect became the rule and spread in every part of the institutional system, even in the bureaucratic and diplomatic spheres which were the foundation of the EU's political system.[7]

The most remarkable aspect of such a development process is that the EU—contrary to what happened in federal regimes—was not obliged to establish a new hegemonic centre, that would rule *super partes* in order to achieve the repudiation of hegemonic relations among states. Unlike the American, German or Swiss federal models, the EU did not set up a central executive power or a single jurisdiction prevailing over national law. The EU's political regime remains essentially headless.[8]

---

[6] This is also the reason why negotiations were so tough and difficult over the adaptation of this subtle balance of power to an enlarged Europe. The spectre of the potential hegemony of the larger states over the smaller ones—and vice versa—may explain the governments' stubborn defence of their respective power in the new European mechanisms.

[7] C. Joerges and J. Neyer (1997), 'From Intergovernmental Bargaining to Deliberative Political Processes: The Constitutionalisation of Comitology', *European Law Journal*, 3/2: 273–299; J. Cohen and C. Sabel (1997) 'Directly Deliberative Polyarchy', *European Law Journal*, 3/4: 313–340.

[8] P. Magnette (2005) *What is the European Union? Nature and Prospect* (Basingstoke: Palgrave).

Of the two contracts which makes Hobbes' state, the EU only knows the first—the *pactum societatis*, but not the *pactum subiectionis*.[9] As opposed to the model of a central executive power set up in federal systems and legitimized by the vote of a unified people, the successive European treaties have provided for shared executive functions between the Commission and the Council—and the Council being made up of state representatives is itself an instance of shared leadership. Although they often resort to blame-shifting, the Member States cannot in fact claim they are under the influence of a higher executive power since they are equally represented at all institutional levels, even in the supranational institutions—the Commission, the ECJ and the European System of Central Banks.[10]

A Community of Democracies

The EU's second democratic pillar relates to the political regimes of the Member States. The EU has been a community of democracies since its very beginning. Unlike other international organizations set up in Europe at the same time (OECD and NATO), there have only been democracies within the Union.[11] This 'democratic' condition was not explicitly mentioned in the founding treaties and the reasons why the Europe of the Six never started actual membership negotiations with authoritarian regimes have not been thoroughly studied. In that matter, the geopolitical context obviously played a key role. East-European countries— prevented by Moscow from receiving aid from the Marshall Plan—remained cut off from the European project as early as 1947. Commercial reasons may have also accounted for Europe's decision not to open membership negotiations with Spain and Portugal.

Nevertheless, the reasons why the EU refused to open up to autocracies were not merely material. Indeed the Six were from the start caught in their own rhetoric. Acting as the 'free West' champions in their struggle against communism, they could not cooperate with autocratic regimes without contradicting themselves. For the very same reasons they could not either reasonably refuse to incorporate the new Southern European democracies in the 1980s or the post-communist regimes in Central Europe after the fall of the Berlin wall. Moreover, the lessons of the interwar period had been drawn and learnt. After WWI, the creation of the League of

---

[9] In Hobbes' terminology, through the 'pactum societatis' the individuals mutually agree to reject violence among themselves, while through the 'pactum subiectionis' they then erect an impartial authority and agree to abide by its rule.

[10] The non-centralized dimension of the EU is not formally challenged by the EU's legal order either. European law has supremacy over national law but such a pre-eminence is only conditional, as stated in the respective national constitutions, and the states argue that they may opt out if they consider the EU violates their fundamental constitutional rights.

[11] The Council of Europe, whose provisions set the democratic nature of a country as the condition *sine qua non* of being a member, has not always been so demanding. The Council of Ministers had indeed considered excluding Greece in 1969, after the Colonels' coup d'état, which was not necessary as Greece decided to withdraw, but showed much less reservation when it decided to open up to Eastern Europe, and especially to Russia.

Nations—European nations in fact—had seemingly been the crowning achievement of Europe's democratic transition. President Wilson's Kantianism had seemed to govern the new Europe, when for a few years the democratic process seemed the harbinger of a new inter-state order to come, based on cooperation and litigation. Until the late 1920s, the 'spirit of the League of Nations' had fostered hopes for peaceful and legal relations between European democracies. But the collapse of the young parliamentary regimes in Southern and Eastern Europe had crushed these hopes and Munich was some time later to symbolize the impossible cooperation between democracies and authoritarian regimes. The European experience confirmed Montesquieu's theory—taken up by Rousseau—according to which a federative league could exist only between republics, ie regimes founded on the principles of the separation of powers and civic representation.[12]

Whereas the democratic nature of political regimes may be perceived as the condition *sine qua non* for an international order based on cooperation, the reverse relation also holds true. Belonging to the EU is also supposed to consolidate democracy within states. The prospect of becoming a member of the EU seemingly reinforces the camp of the 'modernizers' in their fight against those who look back nostalgically to the *Ancien Regime*; it also facilitates the implementation of some hard but necessary reforms in the name of the superior objective of becoming a member of this exclusive club. In the long term, peaceful interstate relations are thought to weaken the power of the armed forces and the prominent role played by the executive, thus contributing to reducing the two major dangers to democratic regimes.

We must admit that these are only plausible hypotheses which have hardly been confirmed by empirical analysis. The 2000 'Austrian crisis' showed that the European 'community of values' was not as strong as it looked and that the positive effects of being a member of the EU were far from being univocal. The 1997 Treaty of Amsterdam had codified the democratic nature of a state as a necessary condition for EU membership—thus echoing one of the oldest claims from the federalist movements—and accompanied it with the creation of a multilateral surveillance mechanism.[13] The 'constitutionalization' of this process intended to consolidate

---

[12] Both authors put forward two explanations which may, *mutatis mutandis*, apply to the EU today. They first stressed that monarchies, whose legitimacy mainly rested on external power, were by nature more bellicose than representative regimes, and thus more reluctant to accept the federal model—an idea which was taken up by the Founding Fathers of the American Republic, and systematized by Kant. They then contended that a federation of states could only survive if there was no potential risk of internal and fundamental opposition between its members—notably on the nature of the regime—that might lead them to resort to force. This thesis was upheld by Tocqueville when he explained that the strength of the US could be accounted for by the fact that they shared the same philosophy of government. Such an explanation may apply to the EU: if it can endure without any centralized executive power, it is, in large part, because the common stock of the Member States is strong enough to prevent the emergence of any conflict over its fundamental principles.

[13] The treaty of Amsterdam symbolically mentioned the democratic principles before 'the respect of the states' national identities', thus reversing the order established in the Maastricht treaty.

national democracies and prevent any authoritarian drifts was first perceived with suspicion because it coincided with the opening of membership negotiations with Central and Eastern European countries. Some went as far as to regard it as reminiscent of Brezhnev's doctrine of 'limited sovereignty'. First activated on the occasion of the formation of a government coalition that included Jorg Haider's FPÖ in Austria, this constitutional arrangement revealed the ambivalence of the mechanism of democratic interference. The sanctions adopted by the other 14 states against Austria were seen by some as the sign Europe was confirming its role as 'a community of values', based on the rule of law and entitled to pass judgment in matters of national domestic policies. But there was no real consensus on such a vision. Others were shocked by what they regarded as pure interference or criticized the counter-productive consequences of such a move. In their views these sanctions could lead to the re-emergence of national pride and potential nationalistic drifts.[14] The Austrian crisis gave rise to much scepticism as divisions among Europeans— solidarity for Haider's FPÖ as expressed by conservative milieus from Italy and Southern Germany, the eventual lifting of the sanctions after only seven months on the recommendations of a group of 'Wise Men'—created a feeling of confusion and disorder.[15] The longer term effects of the constitutional arrangement remain uncertain. The increasing number of 'interference cases'[16] has contributed to trivializing this mutual surveillance, and forced the Europeans to widen their conception of their own national history. The question remains whether such a new trend will lead to some form of national hostility, as a reaction to 'foreign criticisms', or will help abandon the most narcissistic and exclusive forms of national political cultures.[17]

Post-nationalist citizenship

The EU's third democratic pillar is related to the progressive emergence of the notion of citizenship of the Union. This notion had existed *in nuce* since the very beginning. The cardinal principle of the free movement of persons, together with the essential principle of non-discrimination on the ground of nationality, gave citizens new rights *vis-à-vis* the other member states. As they were allowed to settle and work in another Member State and were entitled to the same rights as the natives, the 'Union citizens' could not really be considered as foreigners in the country of residence. From then

[14] There was a parallel debate that pitted those who supported the political sanctions adopted by the governments, against those who wanted this mechanism to be given a more constitutional dimension. The latter eventually won the day as the Treaty of Nice further codified the procedure and associated the Commission and the European Parliament in the decision-making process.

[15] C. Lecomte (2004), *L'Europe Face an défi populiste* (Paris: PUF); and N. Levrat and J. Le Rider (eds) (2004), *La Crise autrichienne de la culture politique européenne* (Bern: Peter Lang).

[16] cf the criticisms expressed by Chancellor Schroeder against the formation of a coalition with the League of the North in Italy in 2000. The European institutions and many governments likewise expressed their deep concerns about the presence of Jean-Marie Le Pen in the second round of the French presidential elections in 2002. In 2004 the European Parliament voted a series of resolutions that called for the respect of pluralism in Italy's media.

[17] J. M. Ferry (2000), *La question de l'Etat européen* (Paris: Gallimard).

on, the concept of Union citizenship could progressively escape from its essentially functionalist origins.[18] These 'migrant workers' challenged national administrations in cases of discrimination based on nationality or required national courts to refer questions to the European Court in Luxembourg on the meaning of the principles of free movement and equal treatment. The Commission and the European Parliament urged the Council of Ministers to make these principles less functional, by broadening them to other categories of people and incorporating new rights other than those directly attached to the economic status. The principle of European citizenship, separated from its purely socio-economic dimension, was finally established with a few restrictions in the Treaty of Maastricht.

The meaning of the notion of 'Citizenship of the Union' is still blurred by the fact that it is often apprehended through the national prism, not least because national citizenship is a requirement for being an EU citizen. In other words, being a citizen of the Union is commonly related to the idea of a direct link between citizens and the Union, some form of legal and political vertical relation. But such a relation, though not absent in the European citizen's status, remains embryonic. As early as 1979, citizens were given the right to elect their representatives in the European Parliament, and were, some time later, granted the right of petition and appeal to the European Ombudsman. The Charter also endows them with further rights.[19] The direct link with the Union stops here, and the question of knowing if it is the foundation of a form of federal citizenship remains open.[20]

The horizontal dimension of European citizenship is much more substantial. From a legal point of view, the constant enhancement of the right to travel freely and the banning of any form of discrimination based on nationality have profoundly affected national law. Migrant citizens have been granted civil and social rights, economic freedom and even political rights they were denied before.[21] National legal systems are now expurgated of most references to 'national preferences' which once characterized them.[22]

---

[18] P. Magnette (1999), *La citoyenneté européenne* (Bruxelles: Editions de le l'université de Bruxelles).

[19] Most of these rights are given to all residents.

[20] O. Beaud (2004) 'Droits de l'homme et du citoyen et formes politiques. Le cas particulier de la federation' *Revue universelle des droits de l'homme*.

[21] In that respect, the Union has gone further that what Kant recommended. In his project for perpetual Peace, he only envisaged a 'right of access' for the citizens coming from the other states, but fell short of calling for any right of residence or equal treatment protected by law. This would have been the logical consequence of his vision of a Federation of Free States, but 'the gap between rational political order on the cosmopolitan level and the political possibilities visible to Kant must have been too wide for him even to suggest bridging it, as he did (. . .) for the state and international levels' E. Ellis (2005), *Kant's politics* (New Haven: Yale University Press), 95). His cautiousness may explain why he only called for a more modest institution—universal hospitality—which could 'retain the possibility of civil relations' (ibid.) between the citizens of a state and another state, thus opening the way to a genuine cosmopolitical right.

[22] The question whether the new rights given to nationals coming from other Member States creates a new frontier for third country citizens remains open. The latest development in European law

In today's EU, the enlargement of the notion of citizenship to the Other is not a mere legal issue. As Joseph Weiler rightfly noted, the changes of attitude implied by these legal dispositions are perceptible in social reality: 'it is most present in the sphere of public administration, in the habits and practices it instils in the purveyors of public power in European polities, from the most mundane to the most august'[23] and extends to the legislative and judiciary spheres where 'many policies in the public realm can no longer be adopted without examining their consonance with the interest of others'.[24] Beyond political, judiciary and bureaucratic practices, collective representations are also being transformed. The growing number of exchanges—professional migration, tourism, twinning programmes, agreements, networks, . . .—has helped lessen the feeling of mistrust that long prevailed in relations between Europeans,[25] facilitated better understanding and created some form of mutual curiosity. The lifting of legal and administrative discrimination practices has also contributed to arousing a community feeling among Europeans, but not as pronounced as the great 'melting pot' of the American model.[26] Public opinion polls show that national identities remain strong among people who are still attached to national habits and practices inherited from history, and often reflected in some apolitical form of nationalism, be it about food, sports or arts. But their attachment to the nation has become somewhat looser and less exclusive; it is complemented by similar attachment to Europe and greater interest for the culture of the other nations.[27]

It has often been noticed[28] that the three democratic aspects of the Union correspond to the three legal orders of a federation of states as identified by Kant: (i) relations between citizens and state as established by *ius civitatis*, (ii) relations between states as governed by *ius gentium*, and (iii) relations between nationals and a foreign state as defined by *ius cosmopoliticum*. Although the democratic foundations of European integration may have been more a matter of mere chance or purely functional necessity than the consequence of a comprehensive philosophical plan, hindsight makes it possible to see that they form a coherent whole. Each of

---

rather points to the extension of the principles of non-discrimination for all residents. As regards social representation, closer solidarity between European citizens may be regarded as some form of discrimination towards third countries, but it may well herald more tolerance among citizens on account of the 'denationalization' of the notion of citizenship.

[23] J. Weiler (2001), 'Federalism without constitutionalism: Europe's Sonderweg', in K. Nicolaïdis and R. House (eds), *The Federal Vision, Legitimacy and Levels of governance in the United States and the European Union* (Oxford: OUP), 68.

[24] ibid 69.

[25] H. Kaelble (2005), *La démocrate européenne* (Paris: Belin).

[26] K. Nicolaïdis (2004), 'We the Peoples of Europe . . .', *Foreign Affairs*, 83/6: 97–110.

[27] S. Duchesne et A.P. Frognier (2002), 'Sur les dynamiques Sociologiques et politiques de l'identification à l'Europe', *Revue Française de Science Politique*, 2002, 52/4: 355–374.

[28] J.M. Ferry (2002), *La question de l'Etat européen* (Paris: Gallimard); P. Magrette (2000), *L'Europe, l'Etat et la démocratie, Le Souverain apprivoicé*, (Bruxelles: Complexe); and F. Cheneval (2005), *La cité des peuples* (Paris: Cerf).

the three founding principles is indeed the necessary condition for the existence of the other two. (i) The requirement for each state to adopt and keep a democratic constitution (Kant's first condition) is the necessary condition to establish cooperative relations between states—the interwar period showed *a contrario* that such cooperation was impossible between democracies and 'dictatorships'—while also making the principle of non discrimination plausible—'dictatorships' have always regarded foreigners as their main victims. (ii) The 'federalism of free states' exemplified by the European legal and political mechanisms of non-hegemonic cooperation (Kant's second condition) consolidates the states' democratic foundations and forces them to respect the principle of non-discrimination. (iii) Such a principle that guarantees equal treatment between nationals and citizens of the other Member States (Kant's *ius cosmopoliticum*) consolidates democracies by protecting them against their own nationalistic drifts, while furthering peaceful relations between states (as potential diplomatic disputes over expatriates' status are avoided).

From a conceptual standpoint, the EU may thus be apprehended as a countervailing power that balances any potential excesses from democracies—very similar in a way to the institution of the rule of law. It draws its legitimacy from the lessons of the past. If they are left to themselves democracies may become xenophobic, nationalistic and bellicose. In the light of the experience of the twentieth Century, the project of European integration appears as 'an attempt to control the excesses of the modern nation-state in Europe'.[29] The twentieth Century evidenced the excesses of both nationalism and formalism. Indeed a modernist, bureaucratic and impersonal political system may well cause similar abuses or create a feeling of anomy that might eventually lead a country to withdraw into itself and have aggressive reactions. As stated by John Rawls, a European Union freed from the supervision of the nation states might well sacrifice in the name of profitability and legal standardization the rights enjoyed by citizens that stem from 'individual nation-states, each with their own political and social institutions, history, forms and traditions of social policy' which are so many 'achievements of great value for their citizens, (that) give sense to their lives'.[30] The constant confrontation between the two 'most elemental, alluring and frightening social and psychological poles of our cultural heritage'[31] is the greatest achievement of the federation of European states. European constitutionalism thus complements internal constitutionalism conceived in the nineteenth Century and instituted in the twentieth Century. In the internal order, the rule of law moderates the power of the majority without subduing it since the people retains its sovereign right to alter the constitution. In the external order, European federalism checks the excesses of national democracies, while allowing people to criticize it and potentially secede from it. In that respect the EU may be seen as a unique and original regime

---

[29] J. Weiler (1997) 'To be a European Citizen—Eros and Civilization', *Journal of European Public Policy*, 4/4: 495–519.

[30] J. Rawls (2003), 'Three letters on the Law of the Peoples and the European Union', *Revue de philosophie économique*: 7–20, 9.

[31] See n. 29 above.

that combines the best of both national democracies and supranational liberalism[32] while controlling their respective excesses.

THE AMBIVALENCE OF EUROPEAN PARLIAMENTARISM: EUROPE'S REPUBLICAN AMBITION

However attached we may be to the vision of the EU as a Federation of States inspired by Kant's cosmopolitanism we have to admit that such an interpretation fails to fully account for the political nature of the present-day EU. The desire to see democracy institutionalized at EU level, as expressed by large segments of the general public and highlighted by the recent constitutional reforms, calls for the emergence of a more vertical form of democracy in Europe.

From a legal and institutional point of view, the parliamentarization of the EU has been the most striking and enduring tendency in its long constitutional process.[33] Whereas the first Assembly was not elected directly, only convened for a few days every year, was granted some vague form of deliberative power and could theoretically exert the highly improbable right to censor the High Assembly, the European Parliament's prerogatives have been regularly extended under the provisions of the five treaties signed since the mid-1980s. The constitutional dimension of the treaties has confirmed this tendency. For the members of the Convention who drafted the constitutional treaty as well as for the government officials who negotiated it during an intergovernmental conference, the necessity of turning the EU into a parliamentary system was indeed the obvious and imperative response to Europe's alleged democratic deficit.

However, there was a persistent misunderstanding behind this superficial unanimity. Indeed the reasons invoked to call for a parliamentary Europe differed according to the interests and political views of the parties. Just as Europe has a 'constitution without constitutionalism',[34] it might just as well be a 'parliamentary regime without parliamentarism'. Indeed, some of the advocates of a directly-elected Assembly, with legislative, budgetary and monitoring powers equivalent to those of a national parliament, had a federalist vision. In their views, empowering the European Parliament meant furthering the emergence of a 'European ruling class' that would be the vector of integration dynamics. According to them, it also meant the consolidation of the Commission-European Parliament couple in order to minimize the Council's intergovernmental logic. The parliamentary scheme was intimately linked to the federalist scenario. But other actors defending a more

---

[32] R. Bellamy and D. Castiglione (1998), 'Between Cosmopolis and Community: Three Models of Rights and Democracy within the European Union', in D. Archibugi, D. Held and M. Kölher (eds), *Re-Imagining Political Community* (Cambridge: Polity).

[33] R. Dehousse (1995), 'Constitutional Reforms in the European Community: Are these alternatives to the majoritarian Avenue?; *West European Politics*, 18/3: 118–136.

[34] J. Weiler (1999), *The Constitution of Europe, Do the new Clothes have an Emperor? And other Essays* (Cambridge: Cambridge University Press).

intergovernmental vision of the EU, also supported the European Parliament.[35] As the European Parliament was elected through national elections, reinforcing its power might offer an extra channel for the representation of national interests and thus make it more difficult for the Commission to play its role. In addition, for states such as Germany who felt they were under-represented in the Council, such an option would strike a new balance of power—as the allocation of seats in the European Parliament was more proportional than the qualified majority voting system in the Council.

The misunderstandings over the meaning and final objective of European integration were not clarified by the constitutional process, on the contrary, they were hidden by the formalist nature of constitutional debates. The European heads of state and government who took part in the negotiations considered turning the EU into a parliamentary system as both necessary and natural.[36] But the core problems were not addressed. As in many other aspects of European constitutionalism, the EU parliamentary dimension has been a superficial consensus.

The fundamentally ambiguous dimension of European parliamentarism stems from this false consensus. For some the objective was to control the action and limit the powers of the EU institutions, according to a liberal logic. Since the Commission could exert some autonomous executive power—however limited it might be—it seemed essential that it should be accountable to the people's representatives. As a potential executive power it had to be controlled by parliament. Such was the implicit justification for the creation of an Assembly in the first treaty, the same argument being taken up by the ECJ to defend the European Parliament's prerogatives.[37] The role of an assembly is to bring to light the action of the executive in order to limit its independence and submit it to public scrutiny. We might say that it is the negative side of publicity—what would be called 'transparency' today—which aims at controlling power from the outside.[38]

There is also a more republican vision of the European Parliament's role, mainly supported by MEPs and federalist movements. It is based on a more demanding conception of publicity which means more than acting in public, making official documents accessible to the general public and enabling citizens to resort to judiciary or extra-judiciary action. Public deliberation, in this reading, requires that

[35] A. Moravcsik (1998), *The Choice for Europe* (NY/Ithaca: Cornell University Press).

[36] See n. 33 above; B. Kohler-Koch (2000), 'Framing': The bottleneck of constructing legitimate institutions, *Journal of European Public Policy*, 7/4: 513–531; and B. Rittberger (2001); 'Which institutions for post-war Europe? Exploring the institutional design of Europe'; *Journal of European Public Policy*, 8/5: 673–708.

[37] S. Ninatti (2003), 'How do our Judges conceive of Democracy? The democratic nature of the community decision-making process under scrutiny of the European Court of Justice', *Jean Monnet Working papers*, 10/03.

[38] Such a control does not amount to a mere ex post assessment, since a body, exposed as it is to the judgment of those it is supposed to represent, tends to anticipate their reactions and consequently adapts itself.

the current issues are formulated so that they may be understood by ordinary citizens—the condition *sine qua non* for them to be able to express their opinions on such topics.[39] Empowering the European Parliament necessarily means clarifying the political game, 'staging' it and opening it up to public criticism. Publicity is understood here as a necessary form of 'enlightened understanding', to use Robert Dahl's famous phrase. It means that the stakes should be made simpler, complex choices reduced to clearer alternatives, and that there should even be some personification process in the political game in order to attract public attention and facilitate understanding. Such requirements are all the more significant, it is argued, as the EU's competences have been extended. In such sensitive domains as domestic security, social protection, public spending, etc. the action of the national governments is limited by European regulations and the constraints imposed by co-ordination. In order to address the widespread feeling that citizens are being somewhat dispossessed of their rights by European legislation and coordination, it is necessary to invent new forms of deliberation that make matters intelligible to the people. The European Parliament can no longer content itself with supervising European institutions *a posteriori* and from the outside; it must find the means to shape collective will *ex ante*, and make it public. Many people believe that such an evolution means furthering constitutional mimetism, empowering the European Parliament, notably as regards the appointment of the Commission[40] and extending the EU's competences in order to incorporate fiscal and socio-economic policies which rank high among citizens' priorities.[41]

There is no clearly defined position in the constitutional treaty on such matters. The treaty may well have reinforced the powers of the European Parliament, but it has fallen short of turning the Assembly into the single source of political legitimacy, which in fact makes the EU a fundamentally semi-parliamentary regime.[42] The main victory for the 'parliamentary' side has been to impose the idea that 'law' must be the EU's central instrument and cannot be adopted in principle without European Parliament consent. MEPs' participation in policy-making used to be the

---

[39] A. Przeworski, S. Stokes, and B. Manin (eds) (1999), *Democracy, Accountability and Representation* (New york and Cambridge: Cambridge University Press).

[40] S. Hix (2005), *The Political System of the EU* (2nd ed, Basingstoke: Palgrave).

[41] P. Schmitter (2000), *How to democratize the EU and why bother?* (Lanham: Rowman and Littlefield); See n. 17 above; and J. Habermas (2001) 'Why Europe needs a constitution?' *New Left Review*, 11: 5–26.

[42] The EU regime as defined by the constitutional treaty is still marked by its intergovernmental origins. First, a wide range of European competences are still outside the legislative logic. In all the domains where the EU coordinates Member State policies rather than leads a real common policy, the European Parliament influence is negligible. In all matters in which there are a few or no EU regulations—whether it be in the policy areas regulated by intergovernmental procedures, as for instance the security and defence policy, or other areas under the more flexible coordination methods, economic and social policies for example—the contours of European Parliament power are still blurred. It is indeed very hard for the European Parliament to structure public deliberation on the EU foreign policy, the Stability and Growth Pact or the Lisbon Agenda, for lack of any real and binding powers.

exception before the adoption of the Single European Act; it should be the rule according to the constitutional treaty. According to this new logic, those who defend government prerogatives would have to prove that, in some specific domains, the European Parliament's role should be limited to that of a monitoring body. Turning the law into the instrument of reference and making the co-decision process the 'normal' legislative procedure amounts to inverting the burden of proof. This has been an indisputable victory for the parliamentary doctrine: the few remaining exceptions and obstacles to the co-decision process were regarded as constitutional anomalies which are bound to disappear.

There have also been a few symbolic changes that have accentuated such a conceptual evolution. It is significant that the European Parliament should be mentioned first in the chapter of the constitutional treaty devoted to the institutions, whereas the President of the Convention, along with some other personalities, wanted the European Council to have precedence over all others. Other linguistic and semantic changes are just as meaningful: the European Parliament is no longer supposed to 'approve' but to 'elect' the President of the Commission nominated by the European Council; moreover the European Parliament is no longer referred to as the representative of 'the peoples of the member states' but as that of 'the European citizens'. Such visible evolution in the type of language used shows the will of the treaty drafters to define the European Parliament as the first locus of the EU's common will and its main source of legitimacy.

The strength of parliamentary tropism is also implicit in the refusal by the constitution drafters to consolidate other democratic bodies that could have challenged the European Parliament. Contrary to the Madisonian tradition of 'dispersed sovereignty' according to which the executive, legislative and judiciary powers were conceived as complementary representations of the American people's will—the people also keeping some form of direct decision-making power—the underlying concept on which the European constitution is built is clearly of a representative type and confers a pre-eminent role to the European Parliament. In other terms, Europe is closer to the monist theories than to the pluralist conception defended by the *Federalist Papers*. While some wanted to give national parliaments their own representative body, or even grant them some form of electoral power,[43] the constitutional treaty merely codifies the means of control and obstruction they already enjoyed.[44] In the same vein, the idea of 'parliamentarizing' the consultative bodies—the Economic and Social Committee and the Committee of the Regions—and giving them more binding decision-making powers was quickly abandoned. The only breech in the European Parliament's monopoly of representation is to be found in

---

[43] President Giscard d'Estaing did not hide his wish to establish a 'Congress' of national parliaments that would have been in charge of electing the President of the Council, following the example of the US Electoral College.

[44] The new 'early warning' mechanism does not confer on national parliaments any new power: they might well make use of this opportunity in the absence of any constitutional arrangement.

the new right given to citizens to submit a request to the Commission in its capacity to take legislative initiatives. But this is a very limited concession, as the Commission has kept its discretionary power and the European Parliament and Council their co-decision power. It is a far cry from the Swiss or American style popular initiatives, or even from the power to abrogate as established by the Italian constitution.[45] The same prudence has also guided the constitution drafters in their approach to the ECJ's powers. Unlike the US Supreme Court, the ECJ is not entitled to make majoritarian rulings, nor will it accept appeals lodged directly by individuals. The 'commentaries' attached to the Charter of Fundamental Rights, destined to limit potential judiciary interpretation, confirm the governments' refusal to turn the Court into a means of political mobilization used to bypass the legislative process. In that respect the EU regime is clearly in the constitutional tradition of Europe.

Despite the weight of this parliamentary pattern, the ambivalence of the EU's parliamentary structure is visible in the general institutional architecture as established in the constitutional treaty. It is a well-known fact that the members of the Convention did not agree on a precise definition of 'EU government'. Some, in a federal and parliamentary tradition, advocated the pre-eminence of the Commission, that should be directly elected by the MEPs. Others favoured a more intergovernmental approach and were inclined to confer a prominent role on the President of the Council. In their views, following the example of France's semi-parliamentary 5th Republic, the permanent president of the European Council should be granted the power of political impetus and might speak in the name of the EU in the world. The compromise that was reached did not propose any definite answer. Indeed, by allowing the same person to be both President of the Commission and of the European Council, and by placing the Foreign Minister in-between these two poles, the treaty leaves all possible developments open. Some may consider that in the long term the Commission will progressively come under the influence of the President of the European Council, with the support of the national governments, while others hope that the President of the European Council will progressively 'communitize' it. Both schemes—federal-parliamentary and inter-governmental-presidential—are compatible with the flexible rules established by the treaty. In that respect, the compromise on which the constitutional treaty is based can be seen as an 'ambivalent agreement' ie an 'agreement based on preference differences and belief differences that cancel each other'.[46] Such compromises have the great advantage of making agreements possible in spite of persistent and fundamental differences of opinion. Their main drawback is to prolong the debate on the nature of the EU and on its political objectives, a debate the constitutional treaty was supposed to close.

---

[45] I. Papadopoulos (2005), 'Implementing (and radicalizing) art. I-47.4 of the Constitution: Is the addition of some (semi-) direct democracy to the nascent consociational European federation just Swiss folklore?', *Journal of European Public Policy*, 12/3: 448–467.

[46] Jon Elster (1998), 'Deliberation and constitution-making', in Jon Elster (ed) *Deliberative Democracy* (Oxford: Oxford University Press), 101.

THE CONSTITUTION AND THE FORMATION
OF A EUROPEAN CIVIC AREA

If this is where we are—somewhere between a federal-parliamentary notion of pan-European democracy, and a more transnational view of democracy among nations—the present problem is to think a coherent articulation of these two models. This has, so far, proved quite hard. In both academia and politics, the debate over the democratic development of the EU has turned into some kind of Columbus dispute: while some argue that a European democracy is unthinkable in the absence of a European people, others argue that the construction of a European democracy is precisely the pre-condition for the emergence of a European people.

For some the EU cannot become a European parliamentary republic because it will still lack the socio-cultural substratum of European democracies even if it adopts all the formal characteristics of a parliamentary regime. In other terms, Europe's parliamentary regime can only be an empty shell in the absence of a European people. Its linguistic diversity—protected by the constitution—is a major obstacle to the development of a European public area. Such an idea echoes the objection to multinational democracy that J. S. Mill made more than 100 years ago:

Free institutions are next to impossible in a country made up of different nationalities. Among a people without fellow-feeling, especially if they read and speak different languages, the united public opinion, necessary to the working of representative government, cannot exist. The influences which form opinions and decide political acts are different in the different sections of the country. An altogether different set of leaders have the confidence of one part of the country and of another. The same books, newspapers, pamphlets, speeches, do not reach them. One section does not know what opinions, or what instigations, are circulating in another. The same incidents, the same acts, the same system of government, affect them in different ways; and each fears more injury to itself from the other nationalities, than from the common arbiter.[47]

The advocates of federalism bow to Mill's opinion and call for the spreading of a common communication language—English—in addition to national languages, in order to facilitate the emergence of a common locus where opinions can be made.[48] Such an argument obviously fails to convince those who regard supranational democracy as illusory. From a national-civic perspective, this is not only a linguistic problem. It has more to do with the peculiarity of national cultures.[49] Nationality 'helps to foster the mutual understanding and trust that makes democratic citizenship possible'.[50] It helps create a feeling of solidarity that may reduce social inequalities in society. 'The Welfare state (. . .) has always been

[47] J. S. Mill (1991), *Considerations on representative government* (1862) (Oxford: Oxford University Press), 428–429.

[48] See Habermas n. 41 above; and P. Van Parijs (2004) 'Europe's Linguistic Challenge', *Archives européennes de sociologie*, XLV/I: 113–154.

[49] J. Lacroix (2002) 'For a European Constitutional Patriotism', *Political Studies*, 50/5; 944–958.

[50] D. Miller (1995) *On Nationality* (Oxford: Clarendon Press), 185.

national projects, justified on the basis that members of a community must protect one another and guarantee one another equal respect'.[51]

Those who uphold the idea of a continental democracy across Europe do not disagree with such a statement but advance the idea that what is considered by the national-civic advocates as a pre-requisite for the formation of a European political community is actually an historical process—which is precisely what should be undertaken in Europe. Jürgen Habermas, in his vibrant call for the constitutional-ization of the EU, thinks that the major mistake made by those who deem multinational democracy impossible is that they tend to forget 'the voluntaristic character of a civic union, the collective identity which exists neither independently of nor prior to the democratic process from which it springs'.[52] Being a 'full-blown' citizen requires symbols, representations and narratives that do not stem from race or history. They are the products of a political community. According to Habermas, the link between nationality and democracy is not conceptual but historical, which makes it possible to imagine the formation of a more composite social fabric. 'Why should this generation of a highly artificial kind of civic solidarity—a 'solidarity among strangers'—be doomed to come to a halt just at the borders of our classical nation-states?'. He contends that the history of national democracy is not a constraint but a resource in order to envisage the creation of broader civic links. 'The artificial conditions in which national consciousness came into existence recall the empirical circumstances necessary for an extension of that process of identity-formation beyond national boundaries'.[53] According to this constructivist method, Habermas states the necessary conditions for the formation of multinational democracy.

The drafting of a written text—a constitution—is an important founding moment as it may represent the 'symbolic crystallization' of a 'political act of foun-dation'.[54] The incorporation of the Charter of Fundamental Rights may highlight the existence of a common identity by recalling 'the painful learning process it has gone through' and 'the lasting memories of nationalist excess and moral abyss'.[55] Economic and social policies may help foster the development of a social commu-nity. In other terms, the constitution is needed because the necessary legal and political means to constitute a European people should be sought, contrary to those who think that the very absence of a European people makes it impossible to create a European democracy.

The saga of the European constitutional treaty reveals that this is a very precarious exercise. The Convention was supposed to address the problem of Europe's 'finalité', and associate as many citizens as possible in order to spread the 'idea of Europe' to every level of collective representation. With hindsight, it is hard to deny that this

---

[51] ibid 187.
[52] See Habermas n. 41 above, 18.
[53] ibid 16.
[54] ibid 6, 9.
[55] ibid 19.

has been an undeniable failure. The existential questions of Europe remain open. Should Europe set its own frontiers, or should it expand indefinitely? Should it codify its competences or should they be shaped by circumstances and power struggle? Should it affirm its ambition to become a global power or confirm its relation of subordination with the US? Should it adopt a parliamentary and federal regime or keep its somewhat baffling 'Community' logic? The constitution has not provided any clear answers to these questions. By conferring a constitutional status on these issues it may have exacerbated the general feeling of disarray among European citizens. It has also accentuated the polarization of the positions as expressed during the campaign, pitting the 'die-hards' who stubbornly defend the principle of the unity of the nation, with its traditions, its 'social model', its 'diplomatic doctrine', its 'democratic culture' and the deeply emotional values attached to national world visions, against those who see the EU as a new frame of civic identity.

The problem thus remains, as it was before the Convention, how can we conceive a European democracy that is primarily transnational, but also has some vertical elements. Admittedly the rejection of the European ideal is based on the difficulties citizens have to apprehend its very nature and objectives. It is therefore essential to focus on civic socialization (ie the process of acquiring civic competence). It is a well-known fact that unilateral information campaigns, such as the information campaigns conducted by the Commission with a view to promoting Europe, are insufficient, or even counter-productive. Institutional messages sent and relayed by bodies that suffer from a low degree of legitimacy are suspect *a priori*, in so far as these institutions give the impression that they mainly act out of self-defence, thus reinforcing the convictions of those who are already bent on criticizing them. In a post-traditional society, political socialization is only effective if set in a contradict-ory environment. It is only when they confront and compare diverging points of view that citizens can make their own.

The problem then is to determine the locus for such deliberation on the European issue. For some, the locus of democratic deliberation essentially remains at the national level.[56] If Europe was more often the topic of public debates—and not only during periods of systemic crisis, and if these debates were held in forums and with a rhetoric citizens are more familiar with, the fantasies and false ideas attached to Europe would disappear. If the European issue became a more common and banal topic, the EU would then be perceived as another level of power whose functioning and political logic would be more easily understood and accepted.

Nevertheless, there is a major downside to confining the European debate within national borders. The risk is to perpetuate diverging national perceptions of what Europe is and to fuel the original controversy over what it should be. If deliberation remains purely national, it might engender more radical forms of

---

[56] R. Bellamy (2006), 'Between Past and future: The democratic Potential of European Citizenship', in R. Bellamy, D. Castiglione and J. Shaw (eds), *Making European Citizens: Strategies of Civic Inclusion in Pan-European Civil Societies* (Basingstoke: Palgrave).

misunderstanding. According to the well-known principle of 'group polarization' in social psychology, orators who belong to the same groups tend to adopt even more radical positions as they endlessly debate among themselves. It is therefore necessary, if we want to go beyond the present point of misunderstanding and ambivalent agreements, to ponder on the possible ways and means in order to open up national spheres to the others and thus force the peoples of Europe to widen their points of view. We have to acknowledge the fact that the national civic sphere is today the only locus for any effective mass deliberation. But that does not mean that we may not conjointly think about the potential creation of a structured and common locus, and on the Europeanization of national arenas. This is not an easy task. The common stock of a society is obviously the first resource, but it is not enough. Europeans have increasingly converging values, aspirations, ways of life and world visions. If they were conscious of such a state of things, we might say about contemporary Europe what Tocqueville declared about America in 1835: people 'see a great many things from the same angle', and we might speak of a common 'civilization', based on a community of 'philosophical and moral opinions' which 'organize daily activities and regulate collective behaviour'.[57] But that remains a necessary but not a sufficient condition for the formation of a civic area.

In an attempt to define the foundations of a European civic culture that would ideally combine the plurality of national civic cultures and the singularity of the European legal and political architecture, we should start by identifying the underlying principles and psychic frame of mind—on which European norms and institutions are buttressed—which might consolidate the EU's legitimacy if they were made more explicit. In this view, Jean-Marc Ferry insists on the 'political predispositions for co-operation between Member States, (and) the peoples' symbolical dispositions for mutual recognition and for the acceptance of the principles that can federate them', which are discernable, in his eyes, in the political integration process across the European continent. He also quotes such public and common values as 'reciprocity, non discrimination, cooperation, tolerance, transparency, participation'.[58] If we want to draw any lesson from the failure of the constitutional treaty, we have to understand how people and nations may acquire and develop such dispositions and how they may accept Europe's complex political regime.

In this prospect, and by way of conclusion, we can try to sketch a reconstructive narrative of European integration, dwelling on the fragile emergence of these dispositions.

(a) First came the common market, which was more a necessity than a real choice, but which did not mean that the political dimension was abandoned. Indeed, the creation of a common market required the acceptance of the major principles of free movement and non discrimination. Such initial

---

[57] A. de Tocqueville (1985), *La démocratie en Amérique* (Tome I, Paris, Garnier-Flammarion), 492–493.

[58] J.-M. Ferry (2005), *Europe: la vote Kantienne* (Paris: Le Cerf), 206.

concessions led to the dismantling of protectionist laws, increased competition for national products and producers and brought about the abolition of the principle of 'national preference' associated with most citizens' rights.

We could contend *a posteriori* that the acceptance of such constraints marked *the relaxing of the traditional conception of national sovereignty*—what the French philosopher Marcel Gauchet calls 'Europe's silent cosmopolitan revolution'.[59]

(b) There is more to it than the market. From the very beginning, the EU has generated a series of coordination methods. The methods and procedures may have varied from one policy area to another: self-discipline is necessarily more of a requirement in such domains where there is a risk for a country to be in the minority or to be obliged to abide by decisions made by an independent supranational body—as in the case of monetary policy for instance—than in other fields still regulated by unanimity vote where national interests are thought to be better preserved—in matters of foreign policy for example. Yet, the acceptance of these constraints evidences two types of dispositions on the part of the European leaders. As a corollary of the relaxing of the conception of national sovereignty, it shows their *capacity to accept the institutionalized constraints of collective action*—the qualified majority voting system, the right of initiative of the Commission and the monitoring power of the ECJ were first accepted with the greatest caution—because the bitter experience of the inter-war period has proved how necessary such mechanisms are in order to ensure some form of effective international co-operation. For more than 20 years, these institutions were suspect in the eyes of many European leaders who repeatedly tried to abolish them. Then with time and experience, the actors came to realize that these measures protected their own interests. Their adhesion—which originally concerned specific institutions and was motivated by purely egoistic motivations—progressively extended and became more stable.

In addition to such 'vertical' trust, coordination also implies a high dose of *mutual trust*. In a cooperation system, fair procedures are not enough if the parties fear they might be twisted by some. To quote just an example, the Member States will only accept cooperation in criminal law matters when they trust the criminal norms and procedures of their partners.[60] Vertical trust and mutual trust form a coherent whole: the less Member States trust the others, the more necessary norms and institutional constraints are for effective cooperation, and *vice versa*.

(c) The EU is also, in embryo at least, an institution of transnational solidarity. The European budget, however meagre and submitted to the logic of 'fair return' it may be, has been from the very beginning an instrument of

[59] M. Gauchet (2005), *La condition politique* (Paris: Gallimard), 501.

[60] A. Weyembergh (2004), *L'harmonisation des législations: Condition de l'espace pénal européen et révélateur de ses tensions* (Brussels: Editions de l'Université de Bruxelles).

transnational redistribution that has benefited some regions or some socio-professional categories. This testifies to the existence—at least minimal—of a feeling of cross-border *solidarity*.

Such dispositions—the capacity to have a distanced apprehension of one's own national community, the acceptance of the constraints attached to collective action, mutual trust among partners and basic transnational solidarity—are the result of a slow process that can be seen, with hindsight, as a gradual—if not continuous—path. The lessons drawn from nationalist confrontation relieve the concept of sovereignty from the burden of its exclusivity and aggressiveness. Such a relaxation process makes it possible to accept the constraints of cooperation. The existence of mutually accepted norms fosters mutual trust. The acknowledgement of the Other as a trustworthy partner and growing awareness of a shared philosophy in international and transnational relations may eventually engender a feeling of solidarity.

In fact, such a process is neither linear nor univocal. We may find traces of progress, or stagnation—or even regression—in matters of cooperation, in today's EU. The most urgent question facing the EU today and brought to the fore by the constitutional crisis is the following one: how is it possible to spread the political leaders' favourable dispositions for cooperation to the citizenry at large? In their daily negotiations in Brussels or in Strasbourg, European leaders show that they can distance themselves from their national prejudices and accept the common rules of a game played by trustworthy partners. But at home, they cannot, or do not want to convince their own people that these common rules are fair and that the concessions made are legitimate. This explains in a great part the general feeling of mistrust ordinary citizens have towards the EU. There may admittedly be numerous signs that national prejudices or attitudes of exclusion—that can be assessed through public opinion polls and are perceptible in tourism or professional activities—tend to recede,[61] but vertical trust—a form of rational adhesion to the European regime and its compromise-based logic—remains negligible. Cross-border solidarity is, in that respect, hardly more developed.

The process of relinquishing some part of one's national identity and acknowledging the existence of the other, and the progressive passage from mutual recognition to solidarity are full of pitfalls. Challenging and questioning national certitudes may lead people to withdraw within themselves, exacerbate their sense of national identity and develop new forms of aggressive nationalism. Europe's current situation finds echoes in what Norbert Elias said about the difficulties attached to transition periods:

The difficulty is that, in most cases, intellectual comprehension that allows one to understand that more extended forms of integration would fit reality collides with the stubborn resistance of highly emotional representations according to which such an integration is perceived as a loss, a loss that one will mourn forever. In such situations one does not even wish to

---

[61] H. Kaelble (2005) *La démocratie européenne* (Paris: Belin).

come out of mourning. The main problem lies—as can be noted—in the specific nature of the passage from one level of integration to another one. In the transition period, one goes through a phase of evolution which is often prolonged, during which the inferior group loses, in the eyes of its own members, most of its value as a unit of the collective Us, without the superior group yet being able to assume this function and thus bring some similar form of emotional justification.[62]

The next generations will perhaps regret the slow pace we tend to adopt to come out of this transition period. They may also congratulate us for refusing to come out of it. It might be that the European integration process is singular as it does not fit into the integration scheme analysed by Elias, but remains durably, maybe definitively, in such a state of transition as described by the sociologist. If this is true, it remains to see whether we can recognize that perpetual doubt and experimentation, so visible in Europe's peculiar constitutionalism, are just as enthralling as certitudes and collective consciousness.

---

[62] N. Elias (1991), 'Les transformations de l'équilibre Nons-Je', in *La Société des individus* (Paris: Fayard), 292.

3

Direct Effect, Indirect Effect, Supremacy and the Evolving Constitution of the European Union

SACHA PRECHAL[*]

INTRODUCTION

One of the greatest achievements of the Constitutional Treaty was the merging of the three pillars, not least because this would have resulted in applying the principles of supremacy and loyalty for the whole body of EU law. Similarly, the Constitutional Treaty, by introducing one single set of legal instruments, would have resolved another problem, namely the explicit exclusion of direct effect from being invoked in respect of framework decisions and decisions in the Third pillar. On the other hand, the Constitutional Treaty still leaves us with the thorny issue of horizontal direct effect of directives.[1] With the prospect of the Constitutional Treaty coming into force in the near future—or perhaps even at all—being bleak, we have to fall back upon the traditional default option: the Court of Justice in partnership with European law practitioners and scholars. For the time being it is up to them to continue to construct, with their patient needlework, the constitutional legal order of the EU.

The relationship between European and national law has always been a classic theme of the 'transnational constitution', to borrow the famous expression of Eric Stein,[2] in the same way as the relationship between national and international law has been in any other, more traditional constitution. Yet, in European law, by contrast to national constitutional law, the principles governing this relationship turned out to be quintessential: first, in building the Community legal order and, more recently, in giving shape to a EU legal order.

---

[*] Professor of European Law, Europa Instituut, Utrecht University.

[1] Cf. the definition of framework laws. See on this Prechal, 'Adieu à la Directive?' *EUConst* (2005) 431.

[2] See 'Lawyers, Judges and the Making of a Transnational Constitution', *Am. J. of Int. Law* (1981) 1.

Although, for a while, it seemed that direct effect and supremacy were the dominating concepts determining the relationship between Community law and national law, developments in jurisprudence make it clear that the relationship is much more complex. The following issues can be mentioned as examples: the acknowledgement of state liability for violations of Community law, independently of direct effect; the emergence of legality review, which was seen as a form of direct effect by some, but according to others, it was rather an expression of supremacy; the obligation to interpret national law in such a way as to render it compatible with Community law and, therefore, give effect to that Community law (also called indirect effect or consistent interpretation[3]); and the problematic scope of supremacy, its relationship with direct effect and with the protection of fundamental rights. A complicating element in the case law is also the acceptance that provisions from international treaties can work their way into national legal systems through Community law and they can do so independently of the way in which states have provided for their relationship to international law in their constitutions.

Many of these phenomena have been described and analysed in great detail in legal writing, and the principles continue to evolve. To all this, a new dimension has to be added: the presence—or absence—of these characteristic constitutional features in the Second and Third pillar. This topic is vital not only from the perspective of protection of individuals, one of the well-established *Leitmotifs* of Community law (but which is not yet fully present in the non-Community part of EU law), but also for the building of a single *constitutional* framework for the EU. It is submitted that such a single constitutional framework requires, *inter alia*, a number of *common* principles which govern the relationship between national law and EU law, both Community and non-Community law.

In the present chapter I will explore whether such principles exist. I will start with a brief description of a discrete model which, in my view, represents reasonably well the state of the art in relation to direct effect, indirect effect, supremacy and their mutual relationship. The next section focuses more closely on the most important limits to these 'instruments', which are used to give effect to Community law, namely fundamental rights and general principles of law. I will then look into the question whether there exists supremacy without direct effect. This exercise is highly relevant for the subsequent discussion, a sort of *pièce de résistance*, namely the ECJ's judgment in the case of *Pupino*.[4] The constitutional significance of this judgment can hardly be overestimated. What *Van Gend & Loos*[5] did for the First pillar, *Pupino* has done for the Third. An analysis of the judgment should enable us to identify constitutional principles which at least the First and Third pillar have

---

[3] 'Indirect effect' is in fact slightly confusing. It can, for instance, also be used to indicate the effects which an application of a directly effective provision might have *vis-à-vis* third parties or any other effects produced by Community law other than 'direct effect'. I preferred to use it in the title mainly for aesthetic reasons.

[4] Case C-105/03 *Pupino* [2005] ECR I-5285.

[5] Case 26/62 *Van Gend & Loos* [1963] ECR 1.

in common. Finally, I will draw some conclusion as to the question of what this all means in terms of constitutional development in the EU.

DIRECT EFFECT, CONSISTENT INTERPRETATION, SUPREMACY: THE BASI(C)S

The principles of direct effect, consistent interpretation and supremacy may be widely known, but the debate on their meaning, limits and implications has not abated. On the contrary, a string of cases decided in the last few years continue to nourish the discussion. In the present Chapter, I am not going to describe the evolution of these principles again. I prefer to build upon the description given by Bruno de Witte of the nature of direct effect and supremacy,[6] and complement it by a definition of consistent interpretation. Instead, I will confine myself to a few remarks on the basis of these principles since, in my view, this is important for a proper understanding of what is going on in the Third pillar.

Direct effect was (and sometimes still is) defined as the capacity of a Community law provision to create rights for individuals. However, as has been pointed out by various scholars, direct effect may also be understood as *a broader concept* than the mere creation of rights. Community law provisions can be invoked or relied upon for a wide variety of purposes, for example as a defence in criminal proceedings or as a standard for review of the legality of a Member State's action in administrative proceedings, including the control of the use of discretion by the Member States—national courts are required to review whether national legislative measures or even individual decisions of national authorities do not transgress the limits laid down in Community law.[7] In other words, there has been an important shift, now also accepted by the ECJ, from a narrow understanding of direct effect to a broad one, meaning that direct effect may be understood as the capacity of Community norms to be invoked by individuals in national courts which are bound to apply them. However, the term 'to invoke' or 'to rely upon' can give rise to a good deal of confusion. An individual may rely on Community law in order to ask the national judge to interpret national law in conformity with that Community provision, or in the context of state liability. In some cases a national court may apply the relevant provisions of its own motion. Therefore, invocability as a central element of the definition is not entirely satisfactory. The most important feature of direct effect would seem to be the obligation of the national court to apply the provisions at issue. And since there are also dicta of the Court that administrative authorities too are under the obligation to apply directly effective Community law provisions, the definition may run as follows: *Direct effect is the obligation of a court or another*

---

6 Cf. De Witte, 'Direct Effect, Supremacy, and the Nature of the Legal Order', in Craig and De Búrca, *The Evolution of EU Law*, (Oxford University Press, Oxford, 1999), which is still one of the best and at the same time concise discussions of the main developments of the doctrines of direct effect and supremacy.

7 Cf. Case C-72/95 *Kraaijeveld* [1996] ECR I-5403 and Case C-127/02 *Landelijke Vereniging tot Behoud van de Waddenzee* [2004] ECR I-7405.

authority to apply the relevant provision of Community law, either as a norm which governs the case or as a standard for legal review. In brief, the core of direct effect is 'an obligation to apply'.

Supremacy can be defined as the capacity of Community law rule to take precedence over inconsistent norms of national law. At least, this holds true where such an inconsistency appears in a procedure before a national court.[8] The national court is then, as a rule, requested to set aside the conflicting provisions of national law. In other words, supremacy corresponds to 'an obligation to disapply' as a method to resolve the conflict. However, domestic courts may also try to resolve it through consistent interpretation. In other terms, supremacy entails the obligation to resolve the conflict in favour of the Community law provision, either by setting aside the conflicting rule of national law, or by national law being consistently interpreted with Community law.

This duty of consistent interpretation—'an obligation to interpret'—was added later. Only in 1984 did the Court make clear that national courts were under a legal duty to interpret and apply national law and, in particular, legislation adopted for the implementation of the directive, in conformity with the latter.[9] From later cases we learn that the obligation to interpret national law in conformity with Community law is an obligation of a more general nature: it relates to any norm of Community law and not only to directives.[10]

What constitutes the basis of direct effect, supremacy and consistent interpretation? A proper theoretical underpinning of these doctrines has always been a matter of controversy, if not a flaw in the foundation of the Community legal order itself, at least from a doctrinal point of view. The Court's case law is pragmatic, building on the paradigm of the Community as an independent—autonomous—legal order of a new kind.[11] Autonomous refers here to the fact that law creation and the effects of this law are decided by that legal order itself, independently from national (constitutional) law. Community law is here also considered as common internal law of the Member States. This means that the whole body of Community law is, as such, incorporated into the national legal orders—it is, as such, valid and applicable. This is why individuals can rely on provisions of Community law before national courts and why the latter must take them into consideration and apply them. Here again, pragmatism is rampant. In principle, legal rules are designed to be applied in practice and are intended to operate effectively. For this reason, the so-called 'principle of useful effect' or '*effet utile*' is brought to the fore as a basis of direct effect. It must be noted, however, that useful effect is not a substantive principle. It is merely a rule of interpretation which requires that 'preference should be given to the

---

[8] For some other implications see below, p. 54–56.

[9] Case 14/83 *Von Colson* [1984] ECR 1891.

[10] Cf. Case C-165/91 *Van Munster* [1994] ECR I-4661 or Joined Cases C-300/98 and C-392/98 *Parfums Christian Dior* [2000] ECR I-11307.

[11] For a detailed discussion see Barents, *The Autonomy of Community Law*, (Kluwer Law International, Den Haag—London—Boston, 2004).

construction which gives the rule its fullest effect and maximum practical value'.[12] In some judgments the Court added Article 10 EC as an additional argument to reinforce this line of reasoning. In the *Moormann*[13] case the Court expanded the legal basis of direct effect of directives by combining Article 249 EC (the binding effect which that Article ascribes to directives) with Article 10.[14]

As to consistent interpretation, first, the Court's case law obliging national authorities and, in particular, national courts to interpret national law in conformity with Community law can more readily be understood if one accepts that Community law is an integral part of the legal systems of the Member States. Second, a central argument in the foundation of consistent interpretation is Article 10 of the EC Treaty. While, initially the obligation to interpret national law in conformity with a directive was based on the binding nature of Article 249(3) and Article 10, the reference to Article 249(3) had to disappear in those cases which concerned primary Community law or international treaty obligations. Third, the Court's concern to make provisions of Community law as effective as possible is also fully present in this area. This was made plain explicitly in *Pfeiffer*,[15] where the Court linked the obligation of consistent interpretation to the responsibility of the national court to provide effective legal protection to individuals and to ensure that Community law is fully effective. Since consistent interpretation helps national courts to fulfil their 'mission' to protect rights and safeguard full effectiveness of Community law, it is considered by the Court as a matter which 'is inherent in the system of the Treaty'.

The idea that Community law is integrated into the legal systems of the Member States says nothing as such about its position *vis-à-vis* other national rules. However, as is well-known, ever since *Costa v ENEL*[16] the Court has constantly affirmed the supremacy of Community law over national law. It based this supremacy on the special nature and autonomy of the Community legal order which, in turn, was again rather pragmatically based on the objective of the EEC Treaty, the Common Market. It is striking that nowadays the initial, very close, link between this objective, the institutional rules and principles and substantive law is often neglected. The establishment and proper functioning of the Common Market as *one single market* requires a system of common rules and principles which safeguards its unity. Any unilateral interference with these rules by the Member States or other actors has to be excluded.

Thus, one of the leading substantive principles for the interpretation of Community law is, in this respect, the concept of market unity. Its institutional

---

[12] Kutscher, Methods of Interpretation as Seen by a Judge at the Court of Justice, *Judicial and Academic Conference, 27–28 September 1976*, Luxemburg (1976) at 41.

[13] Case 190/87 *Moormann* [1988] ECR 4686.

[14] As to the link of principle of loyalty with the principle of estoppel as another alleged basis for direct effect of directives, see Prechal, *Directives in EC Law*, (OUP, Oxford, 2005) 218–226.

[15] Joined Cases C-397/01 to C-403/01 *Pfeiffer* [2004] ECR I-8835.

[16] Case 6/64 [1964] ECR 585.

counterpart is the principle of unity of Community law.[17] The latter requires uniform interpretation and application of that law and therefore also its supremacy.[18] From a procedural point of view, the unity of Community law is underpinned by the Article 234 preliminary reference procedure. In fact, as is widely recognized, the existence of this mechanism has proved to be quintessential: interpretation and effects of Community law are matters that are decided centrally and national courts are told what to do.[19]

The relationship between the unity of the Common Market, the unity of Community law and the principle of supremacy was rather sharply formulated by the ECJ in *Hauer*, when it addressed the question as to whether Community law provisions can be tested against fundamental rights as laid down in national constitutional law: '. . . the introduction of special criteria for assessment stemming from the legislation or constitutional law of a particular Member State would, by damaging the substantive unity and efficacy of Community law, lead inevitably to the destruction of the unity of the Common Market and the jeopardizing of the cohesion of the Community'.[20]

The origins of the special nature and autonomy of the Community legal order, with its characteristic features of direct effect, consistent interpretation and, in particular, supremacy can as such be explained from the concept of the Common Market. The nature is above all underpinned by pragmatic considerations, with the proper functioning of the Common Market as a leading principle. Despite various doctrinal criticisms and misgivings about the theoretical foundation of the autonomous nature of the legal order and its constitutional principles, it can hardly be denied that these developments constituted a sort of intellectual big-bang, with remarkable consequences. This is particularly true when we look at what happened next.

The Community evolved into an entity far beyond the Common Market. This tendency has been reinforced by the creation of separate legal bases and by adding new objectives to the EC Treaty itself. Although, for a part, a number of domains and legal rules can still be linked to the concept of the Common Market (eg certain parts of environmental law, labour law and consumer law)[21] the relationship is getting weaker and weaker. Another example of this process is the evolution of EU citizenship, 'from market citizenship to Union citizenship'.[22] In some instances the efforts to present these developments as still being a matter of the Common

---

[17] Cf. Mertens de Wilmars, *De grondslagen van het recht van de Europese Gemeenschappen*, (R&R, 1986) 28–41.

[18] Which, as such, does not exclude differentiation, but the decision on that must be taken at EU level. Cf. Barents, *supra* n. 11, 213 and 215.

[19] Cf. De Witte, n. 6, 181.

[20] Case 44/79 *Hauer* [1979] ECR 3727, para 14.

[21] Before the Maastricht Treaty, often Art 235 EEC (now Art 308 EC) was used.

[22] Cf. *inter alia* Case C-209/03 *Bidar* [2005] ECR I-2119.

Market are ridiculous.[23] On the other hand, it would seem that the Community is increasingly segregated into various parallel legal (sub-)orders, each with its own rationality and set of values,[24] as was for instance recently highlighted in *Commission v Council* (protection of the environment through criminal law).[25] The recognition of a Community, ie First pillar competence to prescribe criminal sanctions in the area of environmental law is in this case closely linked to the fundamental and self-standing nature of environmental protection as an essential objective of the EC. It is the combating of serious offences against the environment as such that matters and that justifies Article 175 EC as legal basis instead of the Third pillar. Yet, this emancipation from the Common Market did, by no means, imply that the rules governing these more or less 'independent' areas would lose their Community law character, including features like direct effect and supremacy. No serious argument was ever made about, for instance, the Bathing Water Directive (Directive 76/160)[26] or Directive 2003/4 (public access to environmental information)[27] or Regulation 2580/2001 (specific restrictive measures directed against certain persons and entities with a view to combating terrorism)[28] not having direct effect or primacy. Apparently, while the Common Market was a crucial notion for establishing the special character of Community law, this law maintained this character, irrespective of whether the link with the Common Market was still real or not.

As I will discuss below on pages 58–64, in relation to the Third pillar similar, rather pragmatic, arguments were used by the ECJ to establish comparable 'special features' in Third pillar law. The Court reached this conclusion despite the fact that the objectives of the EU are much less well-articulated as those of the Common Market.

A THREE STEP MODEL OF APPLICATION OF COMMUNITY LAW

The Three Obligations in Concrete Context

What do the obligation to apply, interpret and disapply mean in a concrete case? How do they operate in practice? Taking the risk of oversimplifying judicial activity, which is certainly much less principled in everyday life, it is possible to give a three

---

[23] This was, for instance the case with Regulation 881/2002 'specific restrictive measures directed against certain persons and entities associated with Usama bin Laden, the Al-Qaeda network and the Taliban', OJ 2002, L 139/9. According to its recitals, the measures required, in particular the freezing of funds, were said to fall within the scope of the Treaty and Community legislation had to be adopted 'notably with a view to avoiding distortion of competition'. Cf. Case T-306/01 *Yusuf* [2005] ECR II-3533, para 138–150. Similarly, in case C-60/00 *Carpenter* [2002] ECR I-6279, the relationship between the freedom to provide services (and thus the Common Market) and the right of residence of Ms Carpenter is rather tenuous, to say the least.

[24] See Chalmers, 'The Single Market: From Prima Donna to Journeyman' in: Shaw & Moore (eds), *New Legal Dynamics of European Union*, (Clarendon Press, Oxford, 1995) 55, at 69–71.

[25] Case C-176/03 *Commission v Council* [2005] ECR I-7879.

[26] OJ 1976, L 31/1.

[27] OJ 2003, L 041/26.

[28] OJ 2001, L 344/70.

step model of application of Community law in which direct effect, consistent interpretation and supremacy play the central role.[29]

The first step is to compare the relevant provisions of national law and Community law and to establish their compatibility. In other words, Community law is used here as a standard for legality or other forms of compatibility review of national provisions in the broadest sense of the term,[30] including, where appropriate, also the exercise of discretion by national authorities. This is 'obligation to apply I'.

If the first step results in a conclusion that the national provisions are at variance with Community law, there are basically two options: the exclusion of inconsistent national law—thus the obligation to disapply—comes into the picture. Alternatively, one may try to resolve the apparent incompatibility through consistent interpretation ('obligation to interpret I'). The courts will often use this technique in order to avoid an outright choice of one of the conflicting rules.

If consistent interpretation at this stage is possible, it is the 'adjusted' version of national law that will be applied in the case. If the result of step two is disapplication, then there are several options open. Much depends on the purpose for which an individual is relying on Community law and what national law lays down, and how it is drafted. In some cases the mere setting aside will be sufficient. This will, for instance, be the case in proceedings where Community law is relied upon by means of an exception of illegality in criminal or administrative proceedings. In criminal cases, the charges are deprived of their legal basis: the relevant national provisions, defining the criminal offence remain inapplicable. In administrative law proceedings, the basis for a decision of the administration, for instance a tax assessment or a refusal to grant a licence, may be discarded in this way. The same holds true *mutatis mutandis* where the applicant merely seeks a declaration, that, for example, a Member State acted contrary to Community law. In certain cases it may suffice to disapply a derogation to the main rule which is, as such, compatible with Community law and it is the derogation which amounts to a violation. Again, in other cases, the setting aside may imply that a 'default provision' may become operative and that this suffices to achieve the result prescribed by Community law.

This way of using Community law in the context of a national proceedings, precluding the application of national provisions which are contrary to Community law, is often called 'exclusionary effect'. In some cases, it will, however, not bring the case to a satisfactory solution, in particular where the disapplication results in a gap. At this point we turn to step three.

Here, in the first place, a domestic court may consider to apply the provisions of Community law *instead of* the national provisions, by way of *substitution*. The same will happen if, for some other reason, the claim is based directly on the Community

---

[29] A caveat seems appropriate here: this model is inspired by a continental way of thinking and is not always easy to grasp by lawyers and law students from a common law tradition.

[30] Including the different forms of both direct challenge of the validity of a national provision and indirect challenge, for various purposes, as they exist in national law.

law provisions, for instance because there are no national legal provisions at all. This corresponds to the 'obligation to apply II'. In the second place, and as an alternative to this, the court may also consider proceeding with consistent interpretation of the remaining national law, ie national law that could still apply despite the fact that the contrary rules were set aside. After all, according to the Court: '. . . the principle of interpretation in conformity with Community law [. . .] requires the referring court to do whatever lies within its jurisdiction, having regard to the whole body of rules of national law, to ensure that [Community law] is fully effective.'[31] This can be named 'obligation to interpret II'. A final option—or rather non-option—is that nothing can be done. Here, state liability may bring some relief.

This basic scheme shows how interrelated the operation of direct effect, consistent interpretation and supremacy is in legal practice and how the one takes over when the other leaves off. It also illustrates the relevance of the distinction between exclusionary and substitution effect. This distinction, which is mainly inspired by ideas of French or French-speaking scholars,[32] is also important in at least two other respects. In the first place, it makes a difference for the assessment of the classical conditions of direct effect, namely that the provision at issue must be unconditional and sufficiently clear. In principle it is understood that the terms and content of the relevant provisions must provide a manageable standard for the courts.[33] However, the assessment will differ whether a court wants to apply the norms by way of substitution or merely uses the Community law provisions as a gauge for the review of legality or compatibility. Some have argued that in the latter case, in particular there where exclusionary effect brings the appropriate solution, it was not necessary at all to verify the unconditional and sufficiently precise nature of the Community rules concerned.[34] A second important point is that some scholars, and in some cases it seems also the Court, are prepared to accept exclusionary effect in horizontal relationships.[35] As is well-known, this is particularly problematic in the case of directives.

[31] Joined Cases C-397/01 to C-403/01 *Pfeiffer* [2004] ECR I-8835, para. 118.

[32] Cf. for instance Simon, *Le système juridique communautaire*, (3rd edn., PUF droit, Paris, 2001), at 441 and 445 and Wathelet, 'Du concept de l'effet direct à celui de l'invocabilité au regard de la jurisprudence récente de la Cour de Justice', in Hoskins and Robinson (eds), *A True European. Essays for Judge David Edward*, (Hart Publishing, Oxford, 2004). This distinction corresponds to an important extent also with the German distinction '*Wirkung als Maßstabsnorm*' (Community law as a gauge for legal review) and '*unmittelbare subjektive Wirkung*' (direct effect, used in the sense of creation of individuals rights). Cf also A-G Kokott, Opinion in Case C-127/02 *Landelijke Vereniging tot Behoud van de Waddenzee* [2004] ECR I-7405 and A-G Léger in his Opinion in Case C-287/98 *Linster* [2000] ECR I-6917.

[33] Cf. A-G Van Gerven in his Opinion in Case C-128/92 *Banks* [1994] ECR I-1209, at point 27.

[34] Cf. A-G Léger in his Opinion in Case C-287/98 *Linster* [2000] ECR I-6917 and Whatelet, op. cit. n. 32, at 374.

[35] Stuyck and Wytinck, for instance, have baptized this use of directives as 'passive horizontal effect'. See Stuyck and Wytinck, 'Comment on case C-106/89 *Marleasing*', CMLRev. (1991) 205. For a brief discussion and further references see Prechal, 'Comment on Joined Cases C-397/01 to C-403/01 *Pfeiffer*', CMLRev. (2005) 1445.

Broad Or Narrow Reading of Direct Effect?

The three step model follows a broad definition of direct effect. Traditionally, direct effect has been a crucial vehicle for bringing Community law into the domestic courts. If non-directly effective provisions are treated as having no relevance in a concrete dispute before a national court, it is easy to understand why the jurisprudential broadening of the concept into the notion of 'invocability' and the corresponding 'obligation to apply I' was so important. However, there is also another side to this shiny coin.

First, somewhat paradoxically, with the explicit exclusion of direct effect of framework decisions and decision under the Third pillar, there is quite some interest in defining direct effect very narrowly, leaving as much scope as possible for other methods of giving effect to EU law, such as consistent interpretation, state liability and perhaps also the exclusionary effect. Second, if direct effect is understood as the 'obligation to apply I', then the almost unavoidable conclusion must be that in every case where the national court compares the national and Community law provision, as a rule in order to establish their compatibility, there is always direct effect, irrespective of what follows next (ie setting aside, consistent interpretation, substitution of Community law provisions for national rules or perhaps even state liability).

In this respect, it would, at least, make sense to distinguish between direct effect in the broad sense and direct effect in the narrow sense. Alternatively, we could consider going back to the narrow, orthodox, understanding of direct effect, namely that the relevant Community law provisions must provide an *'Alternativ-Normierung'*: wherever national rules are set aside or where there are no national rules at all, the Community law provisions must be applied instead. In the same vein, Lenaerts and Corthaut have proposed bringing 'direct effect back to its true proportions', ie considering direct effect as 'the technique which allows individuals to enforce a subjective right, which is only available in the internal legal order in an instrument that comes from outside that order, against another (state or private) actor'.[36] In fact, the authors make an effort to dispel the myth that individuals can only rely on directly effective provisions. Other provisions can also be relied on, but the rationale for that is, in their view, a matter of supremacy and not direct effect.[37]

The consequence of this would certainly be that effects other than enforcing individual rights of framework decisions and decisions in the Third pillar will not be excluded. This proposal also has the merit that the legality control in domestic law procedures for judicial review cannot be precluded if the norm of reference has no direct effect in the classic sense of being intended to confer rights on individuals and being, to that effect, sufficiently clear, precise and unconditional. To this one may also add the possible impact of this approach for the problems discussed

---

[36] Lenaerts and Corthaut, 'Towards an internally consistent doctrine on invoking norms of EU law', research paper for the Binding Unity and Divergent Concepts in EU Law, Utrecht, 12–13 January 2006, at point 39. Papers can be obtained at www.tilburguniversity.nl/budc-conference.

[37] Cf. also an abridged version of this paper, 'Of birds and hedges: the role of primacy in invoking norms of EU law', ELRev. (2006) 287.

in more detail below, pertaining to the issue of 'obligations for individuals'. As is widely known, directives cannot, as such, impose obligations upon individuals. Where direct effect is considered as a mechanism to enforce individual rights directly based on a directive, the counterpart to this is usually an obligation imposed upon another. In this perspective, the narrowing down of direct effect may also help to narrow down the understanding of a 'genuine' imposition of obligations, which is prohibited, and the existence of obligations as a reflex of, for instance, setting aside.

'Bringing direct effect back to its true proportions' goes pretty far in the same direction as questioning, at this stage of development of Community law, the usefulness of direct effect altogether, at least in the relationship between Community law[38] and national law of the Member States.[39] After all, Community law is part of the national legal orders of the Member States—all Community law, not just directly effective provisions. National courts should therefore handle Community law provisions in the same way as national law, ie without making the formalistic and obsolete preliminary inquiry into unconditionality and sufficient precision *as a precondition* for the use of Community law provisions in a case before them.

Yet, there are certain drawbacks to these proposals. First, linking direct effect and individual rights[40] implies a considerable risk that what might perhaps be gained with distinguishing direct effect and other forms of 'invocability', is immediately lost in terms of coherence and clarity due to the ambiguities surrounding the notion of rights in Community law context.[41] To this one may add that the experience in certain Member States, for instance Germany, has taught us that coupling direct effect and 'subjective' rights is not the most felicitous option: where no subjective rights, according to the rather strict German parameters, could be established, the persons concerned were left empty-handed and could not rely on Community law at all.[42] This brings me to the next, closely-related argument. In many jurisdictions direct effect means that the provisions at issue may be employed in a court case. Non-directly effective provisions are then perceived as provisions, which are not judicially cognisable at all, or only cognisable for purposes of interpretation.

The ultimate consequence of this is that the courts are not even able to establish whether there is an incompatibility between the national and Community law provisions, which, in the familiar scheme of supremacy, leads to the setting aside of the national provision. In terms of liability, this would imply that the fulfilment of one of the preconditions, namely that there is a breach of Community law, cannot be established either. In this context it is worth mentioning that, before the judgment

---

[38] Non-Community EU law needs perhaps also a more cautious approach.

[39] Cf. Prechal, 'Does Direct Effect still Matter?' CMLRev. (2000) 1047.

[40] I use here 'individual rights' as an alternative for the continental law notion of 'subjective rights' which does not make much sense in English but nevertheless appears from time to in both legal writing and judgments of the ECJ, also in the English version.

[41] Cf. Prechal, op. cit. n. 14, at 97–130.

[42] Cf. Ruffert, 'Rights and Remedies in European Community Law: a comparative view', CMLRev. (1997) 307.

in *Francovich*,[43] it was by no means clear whether a breach of a non-directly effective provision could lead to state liability.[44] Similar arguments had been put before the Luxembourg courts, in particular in the context of EU institutions' liability for breaches of obligations under international law, even after the judgment in *Francovich*. Since the WTO provisions at issue were not directly effective, the breach of these rules could not lead to liability of the institutions.[45] In other words, no direct effect in terms of 'obligation to apply I' would mean, in this line of reasoning, that liability could not be established either.

Clearly, there is something infinitely paradoxical to all this. Under the broad meaning, direct effect is used as a device to persuade courts (and other lawyers, where appropriate) to give effect to the 'obligation to apply I', which is necessary in order to take the next step: set aside, to proceed with consistent interpretation or sometimes also with liability, a mechanism *par excellence* to provide judicial protection where direct effect was said to be impossible.[46] For the time being, such a broad understanding of direct effect should be preferred to a narrow reading, not least for pragmatic reasons. In my view, the approach based on hierarchy of norms[47] is not yet a sufficiently safe device for guaranteeing that appropriate effect is given to Community law in national legal orders. Furthermore, the 'hierarchy way' of thinking is not equally obvious in all Member States, as it is, for instance, in France or Belgium. If the concept of direct effect is narrowed down, the somewhat pathological fixation on that concept will not do justice to other possible effects of EC law. With 10 new Member States, with mainly a dualistic tradition, the legacy of not taking international law into consideration in courts at all and a rather reserved position towards application of Community law and its supremacy,[48] a broad meaning of direct effect should be preferred to the narrow one. The same holds true for doing away with direct effect altogether. At least, not yet.

When opting for a broad definition of direct effect, one thing is vital. One has to bear in mind that the 'obligation to apply I' is different in nature from 'obligation to apply II' and is governed by different conditions—if any at all. In fact, 'obligation to apply I', ie the use of Community law as a standard for the review of compatibility of national provisions with that law, is presumed. For 'obligation to apply II', ie the

---

[43] Joined Cases C-6/90 and C-9/90 *Francovich* [1991] ECR I-5357.

[44] There are cases in which domestic courts have decided that in such a situation liability is excluded. In the Netherlands, for instance, the proceedings which concerned the so-called 'Roosendaal-method' of expulsion of aliens and which were at the end of the day settled by the Hoge Raad, judgment of 11 June 1993, AB 1994, nr. 10.

[45] Cf. Case T-18/99 *Cordis* [2001] ECR II-913 and, more recently, Case T-383/00 *Beamglow* [2005] ECR II-0000.

[46] But that is direct effect in the sense of 'obligation to apply II'.

[47] In this context, by hierarchy of norms I refer to the idea that there is a ranking order of sources of law which implies, *inter alia*, that an act must be examined as to its compatibility with all superior rules of law. So here 'hierarchy' is used to resolve conflicts between competing norms.

[48] Cf. Kühn, 'The Application of European Law in the New Member States: Several (Early) Predictions', German Law Journal (2005) 563.

application of the provisions of Community law *instead of* the national provisions, usually in order to fill the gaps, it may be necessary to check more often whether the traditional conditions of direct effect are satisfied or not. Moreover, the conditions differ. That means, *inter alia*, that the exclusion of direct effect in the sense of 'obligation to apply II' by no means implies that 'obligation to apply I' would not work.[49]

THE FRAMEWORK OF FUNDAMENTAL RIGHTS AND GENERAL PRINCIPLES OF LAW

The three step model may help us to understand how Community law may, or perhaps should, operate in concrete cases. However, the model itself functions within a framework of fundamental rights and general principles of law. These provide the limits to the various obligations and their legal effects.[50] I will discus this framework while taking the case law on directives as a point of departure.

As relatively recent case law shows, the 'obligation to disapply' does not work if the Community act involved is a directive and the relevant provision of national law has to be set aside either *in disputes between individuals*[51] or where it would have as effect the *determination or aggravation of the liability in criminal law*[52] for the person concerned.

The rationale of this limitation is the well-known and hotly debated denial of horizontal direct effects of directives or inverse vertical direct effect,[53] respectively—a directive cannot, of itself, impose obligations on an individual and cannot therefore be relied on as such against that individual.[54] There are three main arguments in the case law for this finding: (a) textual one—according to Article 249 EC directives are binding upon the Member States and therefore not upon private individuals; (b) a constitutional one—the acceptance of horizontal direct effect of directives would amount to recognizing 'a power in the Community to enact obligations for individuals with immediate effect, whereas it has competence to do so only where it is empowered to adopt regulations'[55]; and (c) one pertaining to legal certainty—'the principle of legal certainty prevents directives from creating obligations for individuals.'[56]

---

[49] As far as the Third (and arguably Second) pillar is concerned, I will argue a specific approach. See below, p. 60–64.

[50] Additional limitation, which is not discussed here, may result from national procedural and remedial autonomy, sometimes in combination with certain constitutional principles. See, for instance, the Dutch *Waterpakt* case, where the national court refused to give an order to legislate. For a discussion of this case in English see CMLRev. (2004) 1429 (by Besselink).

[51] Joined Cases C-397/01 to C-403/01 *Pfeiffer* [2004] ECR I-8835.

[52] Joined Cases C-387/02, C-391/02 and C-403/02 *Berlusconi* [2005] ECR I-3565.

[53] The situation in which a Member State relies on a provision against a private individual, while horizontal effect means that the relevant provision can be invoked and enforced by an individual *vis-à-vis* other individuals.

[54] Joined Cases C-397/01 to C-403/01 *Pfeiffer* [2004] ECR I-8835, para. 108.

[55] Case C-91/92 *Faccini Dori* [1994] ECR I-3325, para. 24.

[56] Case C-201/02 *Wells* [2004] ECR I-723, para. 56.

The principle of legal certainty is, no doubt, most pressing in criminal law. In *Berlusconi*,[57] in contrast to Advocate-General Kokott, the Court did not accept that an Article of the First Company Directive could have the effect of setting aside national provisions at issue,[58] providing for more lenient penalties, with the effect that a manifestly more severe criminal penalty should apply. This would be incompatible with the Court's well-established case law, according to which 'a directive cannot, of itself and independently of a national law adopted by a Member State for its implementation, have the effect of determining or aggravating the liability in criminal law of persons who act in contravention of the provisions of that directive'.[59] This finding is a direct consequence of the principle of legality (ie *nullum crimen sine lege* and *nulla poena sine lege*) in criminal proceedings, as laid down in Article 7 of the European Convention on Human Rights.[60]

The Court's dicta about the determination or aggravation of an individual's liability in criminal law explained above, does not only hold true for the setting aside scenario, like in *Berlusconi*, or in case of 'genuine' inverse vertical effect. In fact, the arguments were initially developed in the context of consistent interpretation, ie the 'obligation to interpret'. Cases like *Kolpinghuis* and *Arcaro* were criminal cases in which the scope of the obligation to proceed with consistent interpretation was at issue.[61] Apparently, in criminal cases, Article 7 ECHR extends to almost all the possible obligations from the three step scheme.[62] Yet, the relevance of fundamental rights does not stop here.

In its judgment in *Pupino*, the Court decided, that the obligation of consistent interpretation applies in relation to a framework decision under the Third pillar.[63] Mrs Pupino, a nursery school teacher, was accused of maltreatment of children aged less than five years by such acts as regularly hitting them and putting sticking plasters over their mouths. In the criminal proceedings that were initiated against her, the prosecutor asked the judge to take the testimony of a number of children by the use

---

[57] Joined Cases C-387/02, C-391/02 and C-403/02 *Berlusconi* [2005] ECR I-3565.

[58] The national provisions were probably as such incompatible with the Community requirements on effective, dissuasive and proportionate sanctions. Cf. on this in particular the Opinion of A-G Kokott.

[59] Joined Cases C-387/02, C-391/02 and C-403/02 *Berlusconi* [2005] ECR I-3565, para. 74. These are, according to para. 77 'the limits which flow from the essential nature of any directive'.

[60] Joined Cases C-74/95 and C-129/95 *X* [1996] ECR I-6609 and C-60/002 *X* [2004] ECR I-651. Cf. also Case C-58/02 *Commission v Spain* [2004] ECR I-621, where the Court pointed out that the interpretation of the Spanish criminal code in accordance with the Directive cannot fill the gaps in implementation without breaching the principles of legality and legal certainty. The more general—constitutional—principle of legality is clearly echoed in *Faccini Dori* (Case C-91/92 [1994] ECR I-3325), in the sense that any intervention by the public authorities at the detriment of individuals needs a valid legal basis. Directives alone cannot constitute such a basis.

[61] Case 80/86 *Kolpinghuis* [1987] ECR 3969 and Case C-168/95 *Arcaro* [1996] ECR I-4705. Cf. also the more recent Case C-384/02 *Grøngaard* [2005] ECR I-9939.

[62] Though not to 'obligation to apply I' as such: a review is allowed but the consequences of that review for the accused are mitigated by that Article.

[63] Case C-105/03 *Pupino* [2005] ECR I-5285. For a more detailed discussion of that aspect of the case see below, p. 58–64.

of a special procedure for recording evidence provided for by an Italian law. Under this procedure, the children would have been interviewed in a non-confrontational setting, instead of being subjected to cross-examination by the school teachers' lawyers. The main problem was, however, that the relevant provisions of Italian law did not cover the offences in question. Although, under national law alone, the application would have to be dismissed, the national judge wondered whether this law was compatible with the Framework Decision on the standing of victims in criminal proceedings.[64] This Framework Decision provides for special arrangements for taking evidence from victims, particularly the 'vulnerable' ones. Therefore, the judge sought a preliminary ruling on the scope of that Framework Decision.

The interesting feature of this judgment for the purposes of the present Section is that the case did not concern the extent of the criminal liability of the person concerned but the conduct of the proceedings, the means of taking evidence and, in particular, the protection of vulnerable victims from the effects of giving evidence in open court. In other words, it was not the criminal liability of Ms. Pupino as such, which was at stake; the consistent interpretation did not concern a behavioural norm the accused had to comply with, nor did it concern the imposition of a sanction. Therefore, the national court could in principle proceed with the consistent interpretation of the procedural rules. However, here again a limitation lay in the protection of the defendant's rights: 'the national court [had] to ensure— assuming use of the Special Inquiry and of the special arrangements for the hearing of testimony under Italian law is possible in this case, bearing in mind the obligation to interpret national law in conformity with [the Framework Decision[65]]—the application of those measures is not likely to make the criminal proceedings against Mrs Pupino, considered as a whole, unfair within the meaning of Article 6 of the Convention, as interpreted by the European Court of Human Rights.'[66]

In so far as *Pupino* may be understood as introducing explicitly fundamental rights as a limit to consistent interpretation, there is indeed nothing very surprising about it. After all, all interpretation, application or disapplication of EU or, where appropriate, national law must take place within the boundaries of fundamental rights.[67] In other words, the whole operation of the three step model must be

---

64 Framework Decision 2001/220/JHA on the standing of victims in criminal proceedings, OJ 2001 L 82/1.

65 In various paragraphs of the judgment the English version uses erroneously the terms 'in conformity with Community law'.

66 Case C-105/03 *Pupino* [2005] ECR I-5285, para. 60.

67 Cf., for instance Joined Cases C-20/00 and C-64/00 *Booker Aquaculture and Hydro Seafood* [2003] ECR I-741. In Joined Cases C-387/02, C-391/02 and C-403/02 *Berlusconi* [2005] ECR I-3565, it was the principle of the retroactive application of the more lenient penalty that put the limits. Somewhat paradoxically, fundamental rights may also function as a 'sword': In Case C-144/04 *Mangold* [2005] ECR I-9981, after having established that the principle of non-discrimination on grounds of age is a general principle of Community law, the Court held, that the national court must set aside any provision of national law which may conflict with Community law, in the particular case at hand with the general principle of non-discrimination. This way the Court circumvented its own refusal to allow for setting aside in disputes between individuals.

squared with the fundamental rights requirements and, arguably, also other general principles of law. Moreover, fundamental rights and general principles of law as limits are by no means restricted to the operation of directives and framework decisions but also apply to any other provision of EU law.[68]

Much depends also on the subject area. It would seem that in criminal law cases in particular, fundamental rights increasingly play a central role in limiting the potential effects of directives or, more generally, other EU law instruments. In *Berlusconi*, the setting aside did not work because of the principle of legality in criminal proceedings. Consistent interpretation would not have worked either, for the same reasons. By contrast, in *Pfeiffer*, a civil law case, the Court first denied the setting aside option as a matter of Community law. However, it achieved the same result through consistent interpretation: national methods of construction were supposed to serve as a vehicle for the *de facto* disapplication of national provisions which were incompatible with the directive. In other words, consistent interpretation may be burdensome and result in obligations for individuals, as long as this is possible as a matter of national law and due account is taken of the principle of legal certainty[69] and fundamental rights. Obviously, fundamental rights concerns, like Article 7 ECHR, are a less weighty argument in civil law than in criminal law.

The above considerations lead me to a final observation. In my opinion, and in the light of the discussion above, the claim based on the EC Treaty text that directives cannot of itself impose obligations on an individual should be construed as relating to 'obligation to apply II', ie to a situation where a directive is used as a direct basis for a claim—in civil, criminal or administrative law—against an individual. In a situation where an 'obligation to disapply' or an 'obligation to interpret' are the central issues, sufficient safeguards are provided by fundamental rights, legal certainty or other general principles of law. In those two situations it is not the directive as such that imposes the obligation, but national law. On top of that, additional mitigation of harsh effects may be provided by national law provisions or principles. The consequences of 'setting aside' is a matter governed by national law. The national court is then only required to apply those procedures and remedies which are appropriate for protecting the individual rights at issue and to observe the principle of equivalence and effectiveness.[70] In this national law context the effects of setting aside can be toned down on grounds of national rules,

---

[68] Cf., for instance, Case C-60/002 *X* [2004] ECR I-651 and Case C-108/01 *Parma* [2003] ECR I-5121, which both concerned a regulation. Concerns relating to fundamental rights or general principles of law may also arise in respect of other provisions of Community law where the obligation to disapply provides an alternative in cases where the 'full' horizontal direct effect or direct effect as such are a disputed matter, such as Arts 12 and 28 EC or the principles of precaution and prevention enshrined in Art 174 EC.

[69] Legal certainty also explains why there is no obligation to interpret national law *contra legem*, as the Court has explicitly confirmed in *Pupino* (para. 47). However, if *contra legem* interpretation is possible as a matter of national law, the domestic court is allowed to proceed with it and, arguably, under the principle of equivalence, also obliged to do so.

[70] Joined Cases C-10–22/97 *IN.CO.GE* [1998] ECR I-6307.

such as rules in national contract law that aim at making the severity of a sanction more proportionate to the defect, or other considerations, such as general principles of law or notions of reasonableness and equity.[71]

SUPREMACY BEYOND DIRECT EFFECT

Is there supremacy without direct effect? In the first place, much depends on how direct effect is understood. If it covers both, 'obligation to apply I' and 'obligation to apply II', direct effect and supremacy would seem to be intrinsically linked, in the sense that 'obligation to apply I' always precedes supremacy and the obligation to disapply. If direct effect is construed in the narrow sense, as creation of rights, the 'obligation to apply I' is then often based on supremacy itself, thus independently of direct effect. In exceptional, probably rather theoretical, cases it may also be the other way around: application of Community law provisions without supremacy coming to the fore, namely there, where there are no national provisions whatsoever that would govern the case.

In the second place, the answer may also depend on how supremacy itself is understood. Without plunging into a detailed discussion of the concept of supremacy it may be useful to recall a number of points that arise in that context. In some legal systems and scholarly writing a distinction is made between primacy and supremacy. Sometimes the terms are used to designate two different kinds of primacy, namely primacy in application and primacy in validity. This distinction is often made in, *inter alia*, German legal writing, following the dicta of the *Bundesverfassungsgericht* and *Bundesverwaltungsgericht* which use the concepts *Anwendugsvorrang* and *Geltungsvorrang*.[72] The former is the expression of priority in application. The latter term refers to the idea of a hierarchy of rules within a legal system and is closely linked to the question of what is the validating norm of all rules in the legal system concerned. One of the more practical effects is that in case of incompatibility, the higher norm invalidates the norm of lower ranking. This is indeed a far more drastic consequence than priority in application.

The Spanish Constitutional Court also uses the distinction 'primacía' and 'supremacía' in its Declaration of 13 December 2004 on the 'European Constitution'. It comes, *inter alia*, to the conclusion that since Article I-6 of the Constitutional Treaty refers to primacy and intends to reflect no more than the existing case law of the ECJ,[73]

---

[71] Cf. Case C-159/00 *Sapod* [2002] ECR I-5031. For comparable considerations, see also Tridimas, 'Black, White and shades of Grey: Horizontality of Directives Revisited', *YEL* (2002) at 336–340 and Prechal, 'Direct effect reconsidered, redefined, rejected', in Prinssen & Schrauwen (eds), *Direct Effect. Rethinking a Classic of EC Legal Doctrine*, (European Law Publishing, Groningen, 2002) at 39–40.

[72] For a discussion see, for instance, Niedobitek, 'Kollisionen zwischen EG-Recht und nationalem Recht', Verwaltungs-Archiv (2001) 58, with further references.

[73] Article I-6 provides: 'The Constitution and law adopted by the institutions of the Union in exercising competences conferred on it shall have primacy over the law of the Member States'. The Declaration on Article I-6 states: 'The Conference notes that Article I-6 reflects existing case law of the Court of Justice of the European Communities and of the Court of First Instance.'

the Treaty is on this point compatible with the Spanish constitution.[74] It would have been otherwise if the Treaty had imposed EU law as rules which are superior in the hierarchy of the Spanish legal system and would determine the validity of the rules applicable in that legal system. However, according to the Constitutional Court this was not the case, despite the recognition of primacy in Article I-6. The validity of the rules in Spain derives ultimately from the Spanish constitution.

A comparable reasoning is followed by the French *Conseil constitutionnel*.[75] On the point of primacy it stated that the Constitutional Treaty does not affect the place of the French constitution at the summit of the internal legal order. The same considerations can be found in the judgment of the Polish Constitutional Tribunal on the constitutionality of Poland's accession to the EU,[76] where the superiority of the Constitution within the Polish legal system was confirmed, but did not interfere as such with the accession to the EU.

What these decisions have in common is that the supremacy of EU law over national law is based on the respective national constitutions.[77] This concerns, in the first place, supremacy over 'ordinary'—non-constitutional—domestic law provisions. It may also imply supremacy over national constitutional provisions, but this is only possible within the limits that the constitution itself allows for that. In other words, supremacy in the sense of a conflict rule, or in the sense of priority in application, is accepted, though within the limits defined by national constitutions. By contrast, supremacy in the sense of highest rule in the ranking of norms valid in the domestic legal order is not accepted. This place is reserved for the national constitutions themselves.

Up until now, the ECJ has not claimed a hierarchical relationship between Community law and national law in the terms of the German *Geltungsvorrang*. On the contrary, it would seem that a form of supremacy which results in invalidity of national rules is primarily a scholarly construction. Here the theoretical underpinning of the principle of supremacy, ie the conception of an autonomous Community legal order involving a transfer of powers to the Community and consequent limitation of Member States' sovereign rights is sometimes taken to the conclusion that national legal rules which are contrary to Community law cannot apply or cannot validly be adopted,[78] since they are *ultra vires*.[79]

[74] Schutte, Tribunal Constitucional on the European Constitution, Declaration of 13 December 2004—Case Note, EuConst (2005) 281.

[75] Decision No. 2004–505 DC of 19 November 2004, discussed in English in, *inter alia*, CMLRev. (2005) 871 (by Azoulai and Ronkes Agerbeek).

[76] Judgment of 11 May 2005, with a summary in English available at http://www.trybunal.gov.pl/eng/index.htm.

[77] Indeed, here they follow other constitutional courts, like Denmark and Italy, with as a solitary exception The Netherlands. For an extensive discussion see Claes, *The National Court's Mandate in the European Constitution*, dissertation Maastricht 2004, (also published by Hart, Oxford, 2005).

[78] Terms used in Case 106/77 *Simmenthal* [1978] ECR 629, para. 17.

[79] Cf. Kapteyn and VerLoren van Themaat, *Introduction to the Law of the European Communities*, (edited by Gormley), (3rd edn, Kluwer, Deventer, 1998) at 85–87.

However, when the Commission argued on this basis in *IN.CO.GE. '97* [80] that Italy had no power whatsoever to adopt certain fiscal provisions and that those provisions therefore had to be considered as not existent, the Court disagreed. It merely pointed out that the national court had to disapply the national provisions concerned and apply those procedures and remedies which were appropriate for protecting the individual rights at stake, while observing the principle of equivalence and effectiveness. In other words, it was up to the national courts to decide about the legal consequences of the setting aside. The choice of any of the possible concepts—non-existence, invalidity, absolute or relative nullity, illegitimacy, voidness, loss of force, or whatever classifications there may exist in national law—as well as their meaning and scope, are left to the national legal system. The ECJ's choice for disapplication also means that Community law does not invalidate national rules which are incompatible with it. It limits the effects in the sense that the setting aside applies to the concrete case and only to the extent of the inconsistency. For the rest, the rule may continue to be applied. This is particularly true for situations which do not fall within the scope of Community law.

On the other hand, even if one accepts that the principle of supremacy was and should not be conceived as a mechanism that differentiates between legal rules of a lower order (national rules) and higher order (Community rules)[81] and, by doing this, introduces a new hierarchy of norms into the national legal order, in *practical* terms, the construction often amounts to giving Community law a higher ranking status in the national legal systems. This is, in particular, the case because supremacy has the effect of setting aside national law, and the parallel obligation of the Member States to take all the necessary measures to bring the breach to an end. To maintain incompatible national rules in force constitutes a breach of Community law obligations. The solution of the ECJ, leaving it up to national law to draw the most appropriate consequences, makes it possible to temper the rigour of the supremacy rule and accommodate it within national law.

The understanding of supremacy as a mere conflict rule[82] entails, in the first place, that direct effect and supremacy are often coupled, both in legal writing and by the European and national courts. The reason for this is that, as a rule, national courts encounter supremacy each time an individual relies on a directly effective provision of Community law in order to have contrary provisions of national law set aside and, where necessary, to have the Community provision applied instead. This is why supremacy is considered to be a corollary of the doctrine of direct effect.[83]

---

[80] Joined Cases C-10–22/97 *IN.CO.GE* [1998] ECR I-6307.

[81] Cf. Kapteyn and VerLoren van Themaat, op. cit. n. 79, at 87. As to the relationship between supremacy and hierarchy of norms, see also Gautron, 'Un ordre juridique autonome et hiérarchisé', in Rideaux (ed), *De la Communauté de droit à l'Union de droit. Continuité et avatars européens*, [L.G.D.J., Paris, 2000].

[82] This is also how I use it in the present Chapter. Moreover, I do not distinguish between primacy and supremacy but use the terms rather interchangeably.

[83] Cf. for instance Arnull, *The European Union and its Court of Justice* (OUP, Oxford, 1999) at 95.

However, in my view, the supremacy net should be cast wider, in the sense that the principle goes beyond this function of a basic conflict rule for the courts in a situation where domestic law is confronted with directly effective provisions of Community law. Supremacy also means that a national court may not review the validity of Community acts in the light of national provisions of (constitutional) law.[84] In such a case the individual does not rely on the provisions of Community law in the sense indicated above. On the contrary, the person argues that the Community act is invalid, for instance for reasons of incompatibility with his constitutionally guaranteed rights. As the *Tobacco* case of 2002 made clear, individuals may, for instance, question the *validity* of the directive before the period for its implementation has expired. Obviously, direct effect is not playing a role here at all, yet the validity will be assessed in the light of Community law standards and not in the light of national provisions. In the same vein, national implementing measures may not be tested against national—fundamental rights or otherwise—standards in so far as this would imply that it is, in fact, the Community law provisions that are *indirectly* reviewed.[85] Here again, it is the 'higher ranking' Community (or international) law rule that is the valid point of reference. Similarly, it is submitted, the national courts may not construe the Community law provision in accordance with national legal rules. On the contrary, the obligation of consistent interpretation can be understood as a corollary of the principle of supremacy.[86]

This is not perhaps a universally shared view. Often consistent interpretation by the courts may stem from the presumption that an enactment of a statute was intended to meet the government's obligation resulting from a treaty[87] or from the idea that the courts should proceed to such an interpretation with a view to helping their state comply with its international law obligations and avoiding their state's liability.

On the other hand, quite some efforts have been made in legal writing to link consistent interpretation to supremacy. Interestingly, in Germany, for instance, a parallel is often drawn between consistent interpretation and the '*verfassungskonforme Auslegung*', ie interpretation in conformity with the Constitution, rather than between the former and the '*vertragskonforme Auslegung*', ie interpretation of national law inconformity with an international treaty. Under the technique of the

---

[84] Cf. Case 11/70 *Internationale Handelsgesellschaft* [1970] ECR 1125.

[85] This was basically the approach of the *Conseil constitutionnel* in its decision of 10 June 2004 (e-commerce). See CMLRev. (2005) at 863–864 (comment by Dutheil de la Rochère). For another parallel see Case T-306/01 *Yusuf* [2005] ECR II-3533, in relation to indirect review of a Security Council Resolution.

[86] Cf. Lenaerts and Corthaut, op. cit. n. 36 , at point 12, A-G Van Gerven in Case C-106/89 *Marleasing* [1990] ECR I-4135 and Simon & Magnon, La Jurisprudence communautaire du Conseil constitutionnel (Juin 2004–Novembre 2004), CDE (2005) at 252, n. 111.

[87] For instance, for a long time this was the only possibility available to the French courts for resolving a conflict between a statute and a prior treaty as they were not permitted to review the former in the light of the latter. The judgments in *Jacques Vabre* and *Nicolo* changed this.

'*verfassungskonforme Auslegung*', if the wording of a norm, the genetic history, the coherence of the rules concerned and their sense and purpose allow several interpretations, the court has to follow that method of interpretation which brings the rule to be construed into conformity with the Constitution.[88] It is accepted that the latter form of interpretation is supremacy driven: 'Das höherrangige Recht setzt sich durch, ohne daß es zu einer Kollision kommt'.[89] A school in the German doctrine defends a 'double thesis': first, consistent interpretation as such is underpinned by supremacy and, second, it also entails national canons of construction having to yield to interpretation in conformity with Community law.[90] In my opinion, it is exactly this latter aspect—the obligation to choose for Community law consistent interpretation and not to choose for another interpretation—that distinguishes consistent interpretation under Community law from the international law friendly interpretation that exist in relation to conventional international public law norms.

Supremacy is also said to be inherent to state liability.[91] One of the conditions for liability is that there must be a breach of a Community law provision. This is, in principle, a breach of a higher ranking rule and that makes the Member State action unlawful, which sounds in liability. State liability for the breach of a lower ranking rule does not make much sense, at least not when one approaches the problem of state liability from this perspective. In France for instance, the administrative court in Clermont-Ferrand accepted liability of the state for breach of the EC Treaty as a consequence of the supremacy of the Treaty over national law, as provided by Article 55 of the French Constitution.[92]

Summing up, from the point of view of the courts and, arguably, also from the point of view of national administration,[93] supremacy can be conceived as a conflict rule, entailing, in the first place, the 'obligation to dissapply'. As such it is often coupled with direct effect. But, it does not stop there. Supremacy is also closely linked to the obligation of consistent interpretation and state liability. For the legislator, the principle of supremacy has more the effect of blocking the enactment of unilateral and contrary national measures[94] and that national legal provisions must be brought in line with Community law.[95] Despite its practical effects, however, supremacy is not accepted as implying a hierarchical relationship between

---

[88] Cf. Alexy & Dreier in MacCormick and Summers (eds), *Interpreting Statutes*, (Darthmouth, Aldershot-Brookfield, 1991) at 101 and Jarass, Richtlinienkonforme bzw. EG-rechtskonformen Auslegung, EuR (1991) at 214.

[89] Zuleeg, Deutsches und europäisches Verwaltungsrecht-wechselseitige Einwirkungen, in VVDStRL (1994), at 166.

[90] For a discussion see Brechmann, *Die richtlinienkonforme Auslegung*, (Beck, München, 1994) Ch 5.

[91] Cf. A-G Mischo in his Opinion in Joined Cases C-6/90 and C-9/90 *Francovich* [1991] ECR I-5357, at point 65.

[92] Case *SA Fontanille*, 23 September 2004, AJDA 2005, 385.

[93] Cf. Case 103/88 *Costanzo* [1989] ECR 1839.

[94] Cf. Case 106/77 *Simmenthal* [1978] ECR 629; national provisions which are not in conflict with Community law are however allowed: see Case C-143/91 *Van der Tas* [1992] ECR I-5045.

[95] Cf. Case C-197/96 *Commission v France* [1997] ECR I-1489.

national law and Community law in the sense that it is Community law itself that validates the rules within the national legal order. Despite some scholarly efforts, this conclusion cannot be drawn from the case law of the ECJ which, moreover, leaves the necessary space to the national legal systems to accommodate Community law provisions.[96]

DIRECT EFFECT, CONSISTENT INTERPRETATION AND SUPREMACY OF EU LAW

Between Maastricht and Pupino

Ever since the entry into force of the EU Treaty in 1993 the nature of the non-community EU law instruments of the Second and Third pillar and their potential normative force and effect in the Member States were a rewarding subject of speculation. While it was recognized, certainly in the early 'post-Maastricht' days, that the instruments were primarily to be considered as conventional public international law instruments, in particular as they belonged to the intergovernmental realm of those two pillars, this perception changed rapidly, at least in some quarters. This was mainly due to the fact that legal research and everyday practice made clear that the relationship between EC and the EU was more complex and closer than was initially believed.[97] The EU appeared to be able to develop from a loose structure into an international organization of its own right. A crucial factor in this process was the Treaty of Amsterdam, which has reinforced the institutional structure of the EU and the interdependence between the pillars. It has introduced, *inter alia*, a number of 'community method inspired' elements into the non-community parts of the EU, such as Article 6 EU, providing for the respect of the principles of liberty, democracy, fundamental rights and the rule of law and limited jurisdiction for the ECJ in the Third pillar. The legal or policy instruments were clarified and further defined.

Since the three pillars became increasingly intertwined, the question was raised in how far the core principles, which characterize the Community legal order, could spread to the Second and Third pillar? While a 'simple' transposition of these principles is not believed to be possible due to the difference in nature between the First pillar, on the one hand, and the Second and Third on the other, nevertheless, the '*Reflexwirkung*' (radiation effect) might exist.[98] The elements supporting this

---

[96] The nature of supremacy as a somewhat expanded conflict rule fits also better to the upcoming pluralist conceptions of the relationship between legal orders instead of views based on the Kelsenian pyramid. See on this, for instance, Kumm, 'The Jurisprudence of Constitutional Conflict: Constitutional Supremacy in Europe before and after the Constitutional Treaty', European Law Journal (2005) 262.

[97] See, for instance, Curtin & Dekker, 'The EU as a "Layered" International Organisation: Institutional Unity in Disguise', in: Craig & De Búrca (eds), *The Evolution of EU Law* (CUP, Oxford, 1999) 83.

[98] Cf. Timmermans, 'The Constitutionalization of the European Union', *YEL* (2002) 1, Claes, op. cit. n. 77 at 81 and 89; and for the Second pillar, in particular, Corthaut, 'Doorwerking van het tweede pijlerrecht van de EU in de Belgische rechtsorde—de Belgische rechter als doe-het-zelver in GBVB-aangelegenheden?' in Wouters & Van Eeckhoutte (eds), *Doorwerking van het internationaal recht in de*

view are the single institutional structure in which the same actors act, though in slightly different capacities, the common principles on which the EU is based and the common objectives the EC and the EU aim at.[99] Another vital element is that the EU as a whole is subjected to the respect of human rights and the rule of law. These commonalities would favour a similar, or at least a comparable, approach to the question of the internal effects of the various EU instruments, and, as far as relevant, Treaty provisions. However, it is also recognized that not all the elements from the *Van Gend & Loos* and *Costa/ENEL* case law, on which the ECJ based its findings about the separate, autonomous legal order of the EEC, are equally present in the non-Community pillars.[100] Besides some other intergovernmental features, the most important stumbling blocks seem to lie in the explicit denial of direct effect of decisions and framework decisions in the Third pillar and the incomplete system of judicial protection and law enforcement through the ECJ.

Apart from the efforts to extend—by radiation or otherwise—certain characteristics from the Community pillar to the other two, some commentators have argued that the Second and Third pillar law might well have an effect in the national legal orders as a matter of *national* constitutional law.[101] This should certainly hold true for those instruments which do not contain any indication as to their effects, such as conventions under Article 34(2) EU Treaty. Moreover, it has even been submitted that, on the basis of national constitutional law, it is even possible to overcome the express exclusion of direct effect of decisions and framework decisions under Title VI.[102] Reference is made in this respect to cases in which the ECJ pointed out that direct effect is merely a 'minimum guarantee'[103] and where it allowed for further-reaching effects and protection of individuals, as a matter of national law. For example, in *Dior* the ECJ allowed individuals to rely on Article 50(6) of TRIPS despite the fact that, under Community law, the provision was not directly effective.[104] In two German cases the ECJ accepted that certain equal pension claims were allowed with retroactive effect under German law while, as a matter of Community law, such a retroactive effect was excluded through the Court's case law.[105] It would therefore seem that self-standing constructions of national courts which allow more judicial protection are, as such, not prohibited by EU law. Yet,

---

Belgische rechtsorde. Recente ontwikkelingen in een rechtstakoverschrijdend perspectief, (Antwerpen, Intersentia (2006, forthcoming)).

[99] Art. 2 EU and Art. 2 EC.

[100] The assessment of this differs. Cf. Timmermans, op. cit. n. 98, Corthaut, op. cit. n. 98. See also Eeckhout, *Does Europe's Constitution Stop at the Water's Edge?*, (European Law Publishing, Groningen, 2005), at 17–20.

[101] Corthaut, op. cit. n. 98 and Jans & Prinssen, 'Direct effect: Convergence or Divergence? A Comparative Perspective', in Prinssen & Schrauwen (eds.), *Direct effect of European law*, (European Law Publishing, Groningen, 2002), at 122–124.

[102] Jans & Prinssen, op. cit. n. 101, at 122.

[103] Joined Cases C-46/93 and C-48/93 *Brasserie du Pêcheur* [1996] ECR I-1029, para. 20.

[104] Joined Cases C-300/98 and C-392/98 *Dior* [2000] ECR I-11307.

[105] Joined Cases C-270/97 and C-271/97 *Sievers & Schrage* [2000] ECR I-929.

on the other hand, one may wonder whether domestic courts will ever arrive at such a conclusion, in particular where direct effect is *expressis verbis* excluded. After all, one of the rules of thumb when deciding issues of direct effect is the will of the contracting parties.

Pupino

In the case of *Maria Pupino* the ECJ got its first opportunity to address a number of the issues under discussion as to the effects of non-Community EU law.[106] The case concerned the question of a framework decision and consistent interpretation. The ECJ endorsed the claim that an obligation to proceed with such an interpretation exists as a matter of EU law, in the same way as it exists in relation to directives (and other EC law). It came to this conclusion on the basis of two main arguments: the *binding character* of the framework decision, which is defined in Article 34(2)(b) EU in almost the same way as a directive in Article 249 EC, and the existence of an implied *duty of loyal cooperation in the EU context*, thus parallel to Article 10 EC. The ECJ construes this unwritten principle of EU-loyalty on basis of Article 1 of the EU Treaty which 'marks a new stage in the process of creating an ever closer union among the peoples of Europe' and that describes as the task of the Union 'to organise, in a manner demonstrating consistency and solidarity, relations between the Member States and between their peoples.' To this a second argument is added, the effectiveness of the cooperation under Title VI of the EU Treaty. According to the Court:

it would be difficult for the Union to carry out its task effectively if the principle of loyal cooperation, requiring in particular that Member States take all appropriate measures, whether general or particular, to ensure fulfilment of their obligations under European Union law, were not also binding in the area of police and judicial cooperation in criminal matters, which is moreover entirely based on cooperation between the Member States and the institutions, ...[107]

Like the discovery of the principle of EU-loyalty, the parallelism with directives was further substantiated by an *effet utile* argument: the recourse, in the EU Treaty, to legal instruments with effects similar to those provided for by the EC Treaty, was fully comprehensible since it contributes effectively to the pursuit of the EU's objectives. It reached this conclusion irrespective of the degree of integration envisaged by the Treaty of Amsterdam. A combined reading of the judgment and the opinion of A-G Kokott makes clear that this point responds to the submission of a number of governments, which argued that framework decisions were different to directives and that, despite the similarities in definition, they should not be interpreted identically. In particular, the exclusion of direct effect would clearly indicate a lesser degree of integration within the scope of the EU Treaty when compared to the EC Treaty.

[106] Case C-105/03 *Pupino* [2005] ECR I-5285.
[107] Ibid para. 41.

In addition to the two main arguments, the Court also observed that its own limited jurisdiction in the Third pillar and the incomplete system of actions and procedures designed to ensure the legality of the acts of the institutions in the context of Title VI, did not change its findings. In particular, it stated that its jurisdiction to give preliminary rulings under Article 35 EU would be deprived of most of its useful effect if individuals were not entitled to invoke framework decisions in order to obtain a conforming interpretation of national law before the courts of the Member States.[108]

Obviously, the Court's reasoning can be—and, indeed, has been—criticized,[109] especially when the arguments are taken separately. The Court is blamed for disregarding the 'intergovernmentalist' intentions of the authors of the EU Treaty and for creating the principle of EU-loyalty out of the blue. However, for those used to the Court's teleological interpretation, with *effet utile* as a purposive argument par excellence, the judgment does not come as much of a surprise. Apart from the fact that the Court has never been too sensitive about the intention of the authors of the Treaties—something that is closely related to the very idea of an autonomous legal order—it is legitimate to wonder how seriously the initial intention to set up two intergovernmental pillars should weigh after the changes by the Amsterdam and Nice Treaties, such as introducing certain institutional guarantees from the First pillar to the Third pillar, giving jurisdiction to the ECJ over certain measures, and in the light of the legal practice in these pillars themselves. This has all resulted in bringing the Third pillar closer to the Community structures, a process which would have culminated in the merger of the pillars by the Constitutional Treaty. In any case, a 'lesser degree of integration' does not necessarily correspond to intergovernmental cooperation. Moreover, it is debatable what the Member States exactly wanted to exclude when they provided for no direct effect of framework decisions.[110]

In addition to the issue of the obligation of national law having to be interpreted in conformity with framework decisions, three more points must be briefly addressed in the judgment. The first one is the alignment of preliminary procedure of Article 35 EU to the 'traditional' preliminary procedure under Article 234 EC. Without any ado the Court transposes its case law on the admissibility of preliminary references from the First pillar to the Third pillar. The preliminary procedure of Article 234 EC is the point of departure. Article 35 is to be understood as laying down a number of specific—additional—conditions.

Second, the well-established case law on the limits to consistent interpretation, including those which lie in the general principles of law,[111] apply fully in relation

---

[108] Indeed, this is very close to the reasoning in Case 26/62 *Van Gend & Loos* [1963] ECR 1.

[109] See, for instance, Fletcher, 'Extending "indirect effect" to the third pillar: the significance of *Pupino*?' ELRev. (2005) 862, Hillgruber, 'Unionsrecht und nationales Recht—der Fall Pupino', JZ (2005) 841, Kristen & Simmelink, 'Europese integratie door de rechter: kaderbesluitconforme interpretatie', DD (2005) 1058.

[110] See also below, p. 62–63.

[111] See above, p. 47–51.

to the duty of framework decision consistent interpretation of national law. From general principles of law, it is a small step to the third, rather vital, element in the judgment, namely the protection of fundamental rights. Indeed, fundamental rights, like the principle of legality in criminal proceedings, constitute in themselves a limit to consistent interpretation, as was already discussed above. However, the Court went further. When interpreting the framework decision at issue itself, the Court used Article 6(2) of the EU Treaty as a stepping stone to import its own *fundamental rights acquis* from the First pillar into the Third pillar: The framework decision on the standing of victims in criminal proceedings must be interpreted in such a way that fundamental rights are respected. This is also an obligation for the national court, so that there is not only an obligation to framework decision consistent interpretation of national law, but when doing this, the national judge must also make sure that the fundamental rights are respected. It is submitted that what is transposed here from the First pillar into the Third pillar is the Court's case law according to which Member States are bound by fundamental rights whenever they are implementing Community law[112] or when they act within the field of that law.[113]

Beyond Pupino: an Appraisal

The significance of the judgment in *Pupino* obviously goes further than the issue of consistent interpretation. Despite the arguments brought forward by several governments as to the intergovernmental character of the cooperation under the Third pillar, the Court has not opted for a reasoning that would correspond to the alleged traditional international law nature of the pillar. It rather drew upon the *acquis* from the Community law pillar in various respects, construing similar principles. It did not rely on international law principles, like *pacta sunt servanda*, in order to construe a framework decision friendly interpretation, as was suggested by a number of governments. It also did not accord much weight to the intentions of the authors of the EU treaty. Instead, it opted for a rather orthodox approach, by fully using the *effet utile* interpretation method and the effectiveness of Third pillar law as the leading argument. It linked, as it had done in the past, the substance—police and judicial cooperation in criminal matters—to institutional principles. It would seem that, in addition to this cooperation, the new reference point became the relations between the Member States and their peoples which are organized in a consistent way and based on principle of solidarity.[114]

The Court has also transformed a horizontally framed principle of cooperation between the Member States and the EU institutions into a vertical one, the principle of EU-loyalty. The recognition of the principle of EU-loyalty may have a wide

---

[112] Cf Case C-5/88 *Wachauf* [1989] ECR 2609 and Joined Cases C-20/00 and 64/00 *Booker Aquaculture* [2003] ECR I-7411.

[113] Case C-260/89 *ERT* [1991] ECR I-2925, Case C-60/00 *Carpenter* [2002] ECR I-6279; and Case C-112/00 *Schmidberger* [2003] ECR I-5659.

[114] This despite the fact that these aspirations are considerably less sharp than the notion of the Common market. Cf. on this Koopmans, 'In search of purpose', CMLRev. (2005) 1241.

range of far-reaching implications, certainly if one compares the role of Article 10 in the context of Community law. It may require that measures contrary to Community law are withdrawn or annulled. It reinforces the existing obligations under the Treaty and may in some cases serve as a basis for 'new' obligations. It has provided a basis for the Member States to act as agents where the Council could not reach an agreement.[115] Incidentally, it has served as an additional basis for direct effect and, perhaps more importantly, is the basis of the obligation of national courts to ensure the protection of the rights which individuals derive from Community law,[116] of effective enforcement of Community law by national authorities and, in the line of that, of the effectiveness of sanctions.

In the same vein, state liability for breaches of Third pillar law can also be construed on the basis of the principle of EU-loyalty,[117] together with the need for effective judicial protection, which is not only 'inherent in the system of the Treaty',[118] but which also follows from fundamental rights, which are part and parcel of EU law.

Another significance of the principle of loyalty lies in the fact that it may apply beyond the analogy with the First pillar instruments, thus, for instance, as basis for consistent interpretation of common positions or conventions. Last but not least, it applies irrespective of the acceptance of Court's jurisdiction under Article 35(2) EU.[119]

The Court's 'Community law inspired' approach, focusing on the full effectiveness of the EU and, in particular, Third pillar rules, leads, in my view, inevitably to the conclusion that supremacy should be accepted as a characteristic feature of at least the Third pillar and, arguably, all of non-community EU law. Even if we assume that in the Third pillar there exists 'a lesser degree of integration',[120] and that the pillar does not comprise fully all the elements of the Community autonomous legal order, there are nevertheless sufficient reasons for accepting supremacy. Consistent organization of the relations in the EU and, *a fortiori*, effectiveness in police and judicial cooperation, which forms an important building block of the Area of Freedom, Safety and Justice, need like the Common Market

---

[115] Case 804/79 *Commission v United Kingdom* [1981] ECR 1045.

[116] Cf. Case 33/76 *Rewe* [1976] ECR 1989 and Case 45/76 *Comet* [1976] ECR 2043 and subsequent case law.

[117] Cf. Joined Cases C-6/90 and C-9/90 *Francovich* [1991] ECR I-5357.

[118] Cf. Joined Cases C-6/90 and C-9/90 *Francovich* [1991] ECR I-5357, in connection with liability and Joined Cases C-397/01 and C-403/01 *Pfeiffer* [2004] ECR I-8835 in connection with consistent interpretation.

[119] To this I would like to add that, in my view, the consensual jurisdiction of the ECJ in relation to the preliminary procedure in the Third pillar must be interpreted restrictively, as meaning that the domestic courts from the Member States concerned are not allowed to make a reference. This does, however, not mean that interpretation of Third pillar law or decisions as to its validity can be disregarded in those Member States.

[120] The indicators for this are, for instance, no direct effect of decisions or framework decisions and no full jurisdiction of the ECJ when compared to the First pillar.

in the past a system of common rules and principles and cannot allow for unilateral deviation by the Member States. Similarly, by virtue of the rule of law, laid down in Article 6(1) EU, Member States cannot, by unilateral acts under domestic law change their EU law obligations. In practical terms this means that in case of conflict, EU rules must prevail.

The obligation of consistent interpretation, as construed by the ECJ in *Pupino*, indicates such supremacy. As was explained above, consistent interpretation is a tool to safeguard supremacy of non-community EU law when there is a conflict between an EU and a national norm. In my view, there is no valid reason to believe that other manifestations of supremacy should also not hold true. These comprise, *inter alia*, the prohibitions to review the validity of EU acts in the light of national provisions of (constitutional) law or to do the same with national implementing measures in so far as this would boil down to an *indirect* review of the EU norms at issue. Similarly, the legislator must refrain from enacting unilateral and contrary national measures, etc.

This raises the question whether the Court should, in the Third pillar allow for the disapplication of national law as a means of giving effect to supremacy?[121] As we have already seen, it is this particular manifestation of supremacy that is often coupled to direct effect. It seems appropriate in this context to ask what direct effect in Article 34(2) EU means. What did the Member States want to exclude in relation to framework decisions and decisions? The answer may seem simple: the possibility for an individual to rely on the framework decision[122] in order to have contrary national rules set aside and to have the provisions of the framework decision applied. The proviso cannot be understood as excluding all forms of reliance on framework decisions and preventing the national courts from taking these into consideration when applying the law.[123] The very existence of the preliminary procedure makes this clear: the parties before the domestic courts must be able to raise arguments based on the framework decision or to question the validity of a framework decision.[124] The presumption that domestic courts would look into the EU law of their own motion is naive and would show little sense of reality. That a framework decision may be relied upon for purposes of consistent interpretation has now been confirmed in *Pupino*. However, this already presupposes a comparison of the

---

[121] This was probably one of the points when the UK claimed that EU-law cannot claim the same primacy as Community law. See the Opinion of A-G Kokott in *Pupino*, at point 37.

[122] Indeed, same considerations apply to Third Pillar decisions as well.

[123] It was argued that by excluding direct effect, the Member States wanted to exclude all the possible ways in which EU law can be given effect. Cf. Hillgruber, op. cit. n. 109, at 842. For a more thoughtful approach see Monjal, 'Le droit dérivé de l'Union européenne en quête d'identité', RTDeur (2001) 357. It might be that in the EAW judgment, by referring to 'unmittelbare Anwendbarkeit' instead of to 'unmittelbare Wirksamkeit' the German Constitutional Court wanted to exclude the invocability in general. On this judgment, see below. For a brief discussion of the terminology see Prechal, op. cit. n. 14, at 227 with further references.

[124] Cf. the reference of the Belgian Court of Arbitration on the validity of the EAW framework decision, Case C-303/05 *Advocaten voor de Wereld*, OJ 2005, C 271/14.

national and EU norms, which will often amount to a review of compatibility of the former with the latter. Should it then be understood as excluding only direct effect in the sense of 'substitution effect', ie the 'obligation to apply II' discussed above? Interestingly, this was what the French government argued in the *Pupino* case.[125]

Can framework decisions be used, at least, as a standard for legality review? The adherence to the rule of law would plead in favour of this since the rule of law implies that public authorities, the Member States included, may be called to account before a impartial judiciary. An additional argument for a strict interpretation of the scope of direct effect in Article 34(2) EU may lie in the fact that it is an exception to the main rule and to the effectiveness of EU law provisions. In my opinion, the application of a framework decision as a standard for review of national provisions as such should be allowed. What really matters is what happens next. That may be consistent interpretation or disapplication. As was argued above, setting aside as such may still allow for finding the solution for the problem before the domestic court within the limits of national law and by applying national above law. Moreover, as was also discussed, there exist additional guarantees against consequences of the disapplication option which are too harsh, namely fundamental rights and general principles of law. These considerations apply fully in the Third pillar. All this leads to the conclusion that there should be no obligation to set aside national rules which are contrary to a framework decision wherever fundamental rights or general principles oppose such a disapplication, or where the proper solution of the case would require the application of the framework decision to the facts of the case, substituting national law.[126]

The discussion here has primarily focussed on the framework decisions and the Third pillar. The underlying principles, established in the *Pupino* judgment however apply also, quite naturally,[127] to other acts in the Third pillar, including conventions which are governed by EU law and not by traditional international law.[128] The next rather obvious question is whether the findings can also be extended to the Second pillar. The 'ingredients' in the Second pillar are different to the Third. For instance, there is no jurisdiction of the ECJ at all on the one hand, but, on the other, there is a more explicit 'embryonic' principle of EU-loyalty in Article 11(2) EU. The common provisions of Title I EU are shared by all three pillars. The possible special characteristics certainly have consequences for the Member States' authorities. Yet, without the jurisdiction of the ECJ they are less spectacular, since in the past it was often the ECJ which made plain the sometimes rather far-reaching

---

[125] Para. 24.

[126] Indeed, a partial limitation here will also lie in the very prohibition of inverse vertical direct effect of directives which applies per analogiam to framework decisions.

[127] In certain cases also more easily since the proviso as to direct effect is limited to framework decisions and decisions.

[128] Some debate as to the character of these conventions is possible. See, however, also Case 288/82 *Duijnstee* [1983] ECR 3663.

consequences of EC law. Even though an authoritative judgment of the ECJ on the Second pillar is unlikely for the time being, this does not exclude the possibility that national courts may be called upon to apply Second pillar law.[129]

Consistent Interpretation and Supremacy in the Third Pillar in the 'European Constitutional Dialogue'

Reading Community method principles into the Third pillar is one thing, the acceptance of this by constitutional—or other 'highest'—courts in the Member States is another. It may be useful to briefly recall the—what has been called—'two dimensionality' of supremacy.[130] Not only does the Court of Justice make an effort to accommodate its own and Member States' constitutional or other highest courts' views on the acceptance of supremacy in a kind of ongoing constitutional dialogue in the EU, but these national courts also make a contribution. In principle, the normative force and precedence of EU law over 'ordinary' national law (and sometimes even the constitution) are accepted, but within certain limits. These pertain to the scope and extent of the transfer of powers to the EU, which, in turn, may find its limits in the status of a Member State as a sovereign state,[131] constitutionally protected fundamental rights,[132] other supreme principles of the national legal order,[133] the principle of democracy[134] or the prohibition of changing the federal structure of the state.[135] In France, after having abandoned the criterion of the 'essential conditions for the exercise of national sovereignty which may not be undermined', the *Conseil constitutionnel* introduced a new—rather vague—proviso, the '*disposition expresse contraire de la Constitution*'.[136] Comparable considerations can also be found in the judgment of the Polish Constitutional Tribunal on the Accession Treaty, which makes a reference to 'results contradicting the explicit wording of constitutional norms', which are not allowed.[137] Moreover, in relation to France it should not be excluded that the *Conseil constitutionnel* will relate the acceptance of supremacy to the existence and scope of jurisdiction of the ECJ which must be in a posititon to review the use of the powers by the EU bodies.[138]

[129] Cf. Corthaut, op. cit. n. 98.

[130] Weiler, 'The Community System: the Dual Character of Supranationalism', *YEL* (1981) 267.

[131] The judgment of the Polish Constitutional Tribunal of 11 May 2005, with a summary in English available at http://www.trybunal.gov.pl/eng/index.htm.

[132] German Constitutional Court, decision of 12 October 1993 (Maastricht Treaty).

[133] Italian Constitutional Court, decision 232/89 of 21 April 1989 (Fragd).

[134] German Constitutional Court, decision of 12 October 1993 (Maastricht Treaty) and Polish Constitutional Tribunal, judgment of 11 May 2005.

[135] German Constitutional Court, decision of 12 October 1993 (Maastricht Treaty).

[136] Decision of 10 June 2004 (e-commerce). For a discussion in English, see CMLrev. (2005) 859 (by Dutheil de la Rochère).

[137] For a brief discussion, see Komárek, 'European Constitutionalism and the European Arrest Warrant: Contrapunctual Principles in Disharmony', *Jean Monnet Working Paper 10/05*, in particular at p. 7.

[138] Cf. Schutte & Reestman, 'Het Europees Grondwettelijk verdrag en beginsel van voorrang van Europees recht in Frankrijk en Spanje. Lessen voor Nederland?', *SEW* (2006) 145.

How will these national courts receive the ECJ's findings in the *Pupino* judgment? On the one hand it should be noted that in their respective decisions on the EU Constitutional Treaty, the French *Conseil constitutionnel* and the Spanish *Tribunal Constitutcional* both accepted Article I-6, which lays down supremacy of all EU law. It has been argued that this Article is merely declaratory, in particular since the Member States stated that this Article merely reflected the existing case law of the ECJ and the CFI and therefore did not mean anything new.[139] Understood in this sense, both the *Conseil* and the *Tribunal* are said to accept something that already exists. Seen from this perspective, *Pupino* should not pose many problems. However, two remarks should be made here. First, these constitutional judges accepted 'their own reading' of Article I-6 and the Declaration.[140] Second, the 'existing case' law related, until *Pupino*, to the inherent characteristics of *Community* law and was, as such, not unambiguous either.[141]

Other indications as to the appraisal of Pupino-like constructions of Third pillar law can be found in the judgments of the Polish Constitutional Tribunal and the German Constitutional Court concerning the European Arrest Warrant (EAW).[142] The German judgment did not concern the EAW decision as such, neither directly nor indirectly,[143] when the Constitutional Court reviewed the German European Arrest Warrant Act. However, it made a number of important dicta about the nature of Third pillar law and the framework decision in particular. The Constitutional Court denied in fact the parallel between a directive and a framework decision. It stressed that if the framework decision was not directly effective (*unmittelbar wirksam*), in order to become law valid in the Member States, it had to be implemented first (the issue of *innerstaatliche Gültigkeit*). By excluding direct 'applicability' (*unmittelbare Anwendbarkeit*), the Member States wanted to prevent the Court's case law on direct effect (the Court uses the term *Anwendbarkeit*: applicability) of directives from being extended to framework decisions.[144] This points very much to a direction of not accepting the justiciability of a framework decision whatsoever, not even

---

[139] Cf. Lenaerts and Corthaut, op. cit. n. 37, at 289.

[140] Cf. above. See also Simon & Magnon, op. cit. n. 82.

[141] Cf. discussion and speculation above, p. 51–56.

[142] *BverfG*, judgment of 18 July 2005, available at www.bverfg.de, Polish Constitutional Tribunal, judgment of 27 April 2005, translation in English available at www.trybunal.gov.pl. Similar case is pending in Spain. Cf. Komárek, op. cit. n. 137, at 4. The Czech Constitutional Court gave its decision on 5 May 2006, see below. See also Case C-303/05 *Advocaten voor de Wereld*, pending, a reference of the Belgian Cour d'Arbitrage, questioning the validity of the EAW Framework Decision.

[143] It has been noted, however, that it challenged the philosophy of the Third pillar measures, namely the principle of mutual trust. See Komárek, op. cit. n. 137, at 4.

[144] This position of the BverG must be placed against the background of a discussion as to the nature of the framework decision: Is it an instrument of international law, which needs, in the German legal system, always transposition in order to become law valid in that Member State, or is it rather something akin to a directive, which is to be considered as law valid in the Member States, despite the fact that it needs in principle transposition? Cf. Herrmann, comment on the *Pupino*, in *EuZW* (2005) 437 (with further references).

the 'softer' modalities of justiciability. The Constitutional Court also stressed that despite the progress in integration, Third pillar law is to be considered as international law and not as supranational law. The arguments for this lie in the fact that framework decisions are adopted by unanimity in the Council, they must be implemented by the Member States, they cannot be enforced in judicial proceedings (*gerichtlich durchsetzbar*) and the European Parliament is only heard in the decision-making process relating to a framework decision.[145] It is hard to imagine a greater contrast with the *Pupino* case, decided a month earlier. In a dissenting opinion, Justice *Gerhardt* pointed at this discrepancy and blamed the majority of the German Court for not trying to avoid conflict between constitutional and EU law.

The Polish Constitutional Tribunal, apart from having decided the case in a much more Europe-friendly manner,[146] did not exclude the possibility of extending the duty of consistent interpretation from the First to the Third pillar.[147] However, it must be noted that the Tribunal did not hesitate to proceed with constitutional review of the implementing measures, rejecting the view that this should be excluded since measures at issue were implementing the EAW framework decision. This seems to imply that an indirect constitutional review of a framework decision should not be *a priori* excluded. Interestingly, from the judgment of the Polish Constitutional Tribunal it can be deduced that, relatively speaking, it has much confidence in the protection of the fundamental rights in criminal proceedings in other EU Member States.[148] This again contrasts with the German Constitutional Court, which showed considerable distrust of the protection of fundamental rights in the criminal justice systems of other Member States and did not want to accept the very existence of Article 6(1) EU as a sufficient basis for mutual trust in extradition matters.

The Czech Constitutional Court[149] left the issue of supremacy and the nature of framework decisions explicitly open, stating that the judgment in *Pupino* did not decide this issue and that the case law of the ECJ is still developing in this respect. It would seem, however, that the Constitutional Court is willing to follow the avenue of consistent interpretation. The alleged conflict between the national implementing measures of the EAW Framework Decisions and the national constitution was resolved by the Constitutional Court through a EU-friendly interpretation. On basis of Article 1, Section 2, of the Czech Constitution,[150] read together with the

---

[145] Points 80 and 81.

[146] By creating a prospective temporal limitation of the effects of its decision and allowing the constitutional legislator to amend the Constitution. Cf. also Kowalik-Bańczyk, 'Should We Polish It Up? The Polish Constitutional Tribunal and the Idea of Supremacy of EU Law', *German Law Journal* (2005) 1355.

[147] The judgment dates from before the ECJ judgment in *Pupino* but the Opinion of A-G Kokott was already available. However, consistent interpretation could not work here since it would go beyond the limits set out by ECJ. It is understood that also the Cypriot Supreme Court, in its decision of 7 November 2005, followed a comparable reasoning.

[148] Cf. Komárek, op. cit. n. 137, at 14.

[149] Decision of 5 May 2006, available at www.concourt.cz.

[150] 'The Czech Republic shall observe its obligations resulting from international law.'

European principle of loyalty, the main Article at issue[151] had to be interpreted in harmony with the principles of European integration and cooperation between the Community and national organs. The interpretation which makes possible to meet the obligations under EU law must prevail.

On the basis of these national decisions it is far from certain whether the ECJ's extension of Community method elements to the Third pillar will be smoothly accepted in the national systems. The ingredients which are required for such an acceptance—sufficient rule of law guarantees at EU level, protection of fundamental rights through courts, review of use of competences by courts and a sufficient degree of democratic influence—are not yet fully present in the Third pillar.

CONSTITUTIONAL IMPLICATIONS

The evolution of the EU remains a fascinating phenomenon. Since 1992, it developed from a loosely structured setup to an international organization. It managed to absorb a number of 'satellite arrangements', like the *Schengen acquis*. It comprises various regimes and sub-regimes on the one hand, but, on the other, it also displays a certain degree of internal cohesion. Due to Treaty changes and legal practice the regimes became much less disconnected than the initial template of the EU suggested. In addition to the common provisions of the EU Treaty, an important factor of potential cohesiveness is the spreading of substance over two or three different institutional regimes.

The Area of Freedom, Security and Justice (AFSJ) is the best example here. It is spread over the Third pillar, the particular regime of Title IV of the First pillar, and also in the 'ordinary' First pillar, so certain aspects of the fight against racism such as Directive 2000/43 (equal treatment between persons irrespective of racial or ethnic origin)[152] is based on Article 13 EC. Despite the various *loci* in the Treaties, there are also several connecting points between the sub-areas of the AFSJ, such as Article 2 EU, the objectives of the EU, which overlap, at least partly, certain principles of the EC Treaty,[153] the cross-references in Article 61(1) EC and the close relationship between the Title IV and Third pillar measures.[154] Another example is, indeed, the *Yusuf* case,[155] in which the CFI linked the objectives pursued under the CFSP with Articles 60, 301 and 308 EC, which, when taken in isolation, did not provide sufficient legal basis for the EC legislation at issue.

---

[151] Article 14, Section 4, of the Charter of Fundamental Rights and Freedoms, stating in its second sentence: 'No citizen may be forced to leave his homeland'.

[152] OJ 2000, L 180/22.

[153] See, in particular, Article 3(1) ((c) and (d)) and Article 14 EC.

[154] Directive 2004/81 (residence permit for victims of trafficking in human beings), OJ 2004, L 261/19, and framework decision 2002/90 (combating trafficking in human beings), OJ, 2002, L 203/1.

[155] Case T-306/01 *Yusuf* [2005] ECR II-3533.

The spreading of substance over more institutional regimes tends to blur the institutional differences.[156] However, it also calls for a minimum of common principles that safeguard as much as possible inner coherence of the law that applies to the areas concerned. The judgment in *Pupino* fits into this approach of looking for a common framework and it helps to develop it, in spite of what is perceived as a lesser degree on integration. The present Chapter has addressed the evolution of a number of principles, which govern the relationship between the European and national orders. Traditionally, these principles are considered as central features of the constitutionalization in the EC, including the process in which supremacy and justiciability of Community law and the respect for fundamental rights and the rule of law are attained. The discussion in previous sections illustrates how the process of constitutionalization has moved beyond the First pillar into the Third pillar. It is submitted that a common constitutional framework is emerging within the EU. The common principles are there, although their application and concrete effects may differ, according to the areas concerned and depending on specific provisos which govern them.[157]

Summing up the findings from previous sections, the main 'constitutional building blocks' which emerge are, in the first place, the principle of EU-loyalty, with potentially sweeping consequences. A second—implicitly—accepted principle is supremacy and with supremacy also the monist relationship between national law and non-Community EU-law.[158] In other words, non-Community EU-law must also be considered as an integral part of the legal systems of the Member States. A third constitutional feature present is the invocability of non-Community EU-law provisions. For certain acts this invocability may have limited effects only. This may lie in their very nature, as in the case of common positions and joint actions which are legally binding, but wherever they are politically sensitive, the courts will practise a hands-off policy.[159] Another reason may be the explicit exclusion of direct effect. I have, argued that the most sensible interpretation of this proviso in Article 34(2) is the direct effect in the sense of 'obligation to apply II', ie the application of the Third pillar instruments by way of *substitution*. This means that the provisions at issue may be relied upon for purposes of legality control, in the sense of a check whether the Member States measures are compatible with EU-law provisions, with—next—various options: State liability, consistent interpretation or setting aside.

I do not believe that this leads to a nightmare scenario, as some have suggested.[160] Although perhaps supremacy may, in principle, entail the obligation to dissapply,

---

[156] This may also to an extent hold true for Case C-176/03 *Commission v Council* [2005] ECR I-7879.

[157] Within one single pillar, like Title IV of the EC Treaty and in the three pillars taken separately.

[158] The issues of monism precedes logically the question of supremacy.

[159] This may result in a very restraint review or in taking refuge to doctrine, like the political question etc.

[160] Cf. Dashwood, 'The Relationship between the Member States and the European Union/European Community', CMLRev. (2004), at 379–380.

there are various factors which tone down the consequences of this, as I have argued above. These are national law techniques to deal with consequences of the setting aside of a norm, there are general principles of law and fundamental rights requirements. And arguably, since we are dealing with criminal law, situations which would lead to a gap which cannot be 'filled' by EU law by way of substitution should be avoided, partly for reasons of legal certainty and protection of the persons concerned and partly for reasons of effective prosecution of criminal offences which, after all, need a basis in the law.

Finally, the transfer of the case law on the fundamental rights and general principles of law into the area of non-Community EU law is of great significance. Not only because they form the framework within which this law must be applied in the Member States, as indicated above, but also because they will function as a standard for review and a guiding principle for interpretation of the EU-law provisions themselves. All this was perhaps already present in Article 6 EU. However, now it is clear that fundamental rights and general principles of law are fully operative standards for both Member State and EU institutions' action.

This implies, in turn, two consequences. First, it seems to entail the Court extending its law-making function and power of autonomous interpretation based on Article 220 EC Treaty into the realms of non-Community EU-law.[161] Such an extension or, at least, analogous application of this Article, read together with the reference to the respect for the rule of law in Article 6 EU, may serve as a basis for a broad interpretation of jurisdictional and other issues in order to compensate for the limitations in the system of judicial protection in the Third pillar. This seems the more indispensable as long as the democratic deficit in that pillar continues to exist.[162]

Second, adequate protection of fundamental rights in the Third—and arguably also the Second—pillar is vital in the context of the dialogue with national constitutional (or other highest) courts. Concern about the level of protection of fundamental rights is one of the central issues brought before national constitutional courts in cases on the implementation of the EAW framework decision.[163] It is not difficult to imagine that, due to the very nature of the subject-matter of the Third pillar, the same concerns emerge in relation to many other pieces of EU legislation.[164] A lot of additional patient needle work will be needed in convincing national courts to accept a single *constitutional* framework for the EU, with *common* principles, which govern the relationship between national law and EU law. The dialogue could prove to be much more tougher than it was in relation to traditional EC law.

[161] Cf. Barents, comment on the *Pupino* case, *SEW* (2006) at 76.

[162] In the Second pillar both are lacking.

[163] Not only in general but also in an individuals case. This is, indeed, not so much a problem of the standard itself but rather about its actual application. As is well known, the other two concerns of the Constitutional courts relate to effective judicial control of exercise of competence by the EU and the democratic deficit.

[164] In the Second pillar same problems exist, but the protection is left to national courts. The big question mark here is how effectively these will proceed.

4

Respecting Fundamental Rights in the New Union: A Review

ANDREW WILLIAMS*

INTRODUCTION

In the beginning was silence. Sometimes it is easy to forget this. When the European Economic Community was established in 1957, human rights did not figure in the political or legal landscape constructed by the Treaty of Rome. Their presence was at best subliminal.[1] The subsequent construction of a discourse by the European Court of Justice, the Commission, the Council and now all institutions of the EEC/European Community/European Union that human rights were fundamental in the creation of the European Project is a myth. Not an unhealthy one perhaps, but still a myth.

The appearance of a Treaty establishing a Constitution for Europe (TCE)[2] is a moment when fundamentals need to be revisited, even mythic ones. And, given the institutional practice that has developed over the past 30 or more years, few self-consciously governing discourses can be more important than that associated with human rights and the EU's future. Not only are human rights a prominent and explicit feature of the core values identified in Article I-2 TCE but they also help frame an array of implicit constitutional themes. From constructing an identity for the EU, legitimising its operations, providing a bulwark against extremism and the abuse of power, to acting as a spur to 'closer union' between the peoples of Europe, human rights provide an iconic concept without respect for which the EU would lack moral and enduring substance. This remains true regardless of the future of the Constitution.[3]

---

* School of Law, University of Warwick. Address for correspondence: A.T.Williams@warwick.ac.uk

[1] Armin von Bogdandy reminds us that the creation of the EEC was 'legitimated by goals that were to a large extent neutral with regard to constitutional issues'. These include respect for fundamental or human rights. See von Bogdandy, 'Doctrine of Principles' Jean Monnet Working Paper 9/03 at 9 available at http://www.jeanmonnetprogram.org/papers/03/030901–01.html

[2] See Treaty Establishing a Constitution for Europe available at http://europa.eu.int/eur-lex/lex/JOHtml.do?uri=OJ:C:2004:310:SOM:EN:HTML

[3] The rejection of the TCE by both France and the Netherlands in 2005 seems to have sealed its fate. However, this does not mean that aspects of its provisions, for instance the incorporation of the

Given the importance of a review of this key component of the EU's constitution, how should we go about the exercise? What should be our method of analysis? On a superficial level we might argue that in order to assess how human rights might develop in the ever-evolving EU, some consideration of trajectory is needed. To assess where we might be heading, we have to understand where we are and how we came to be here. That is of course a major task, one beyond the constraints of this chapter. However, a more focused and preliminary concern is to consider how such an enterprise might be conducted, and which criteria we might use to assess any trajectory. In other words, what principles should we look for when we engage in acts of judgement on this subject? What are the standards we need to apply? Such analytical guidance has been in short supply to date either from the EU's institutions (at least as regards its processes of self-assessment) or commentators in general.[4] How then can an effective analysis be carried out into the current state of human rights and the EU, and the proposed direction they may take whether or not the TCE (or its specific human rights related components) is enacted?

In response, this chapter aims to reconsider the nature of the purported founding principle and those attendant virtues that might provide the basis for an appreciation of human rights in the EU. Although we do not have a ready universal template against which any institutional adherence to human rights can be fully judged (either conceptually or practically), except perhaps those human rights standards themselves, (and we know how fluid they can be given their diverse national, regional and global development) we might not have to look too far-afield for inspiration in this endeavour. The EU has identified a whole cohort of standards that might be applied. They may be rarely directed at itself but when analysing the records of third countries the EU has adopted and clarified notions of the rule of law and good governance, both of which place human rights at their heart, which are equally pertinent to its own structure and practice. If we couple these with more objective criteria that have been fashioned in discourses of governance in a post-Cold War era, we might be confident in constructing the means for assessing both the EU's history in the field of human rights and its potential future.

With this core purpose in mind, the chapter has been divided into two parts. The first examines the nature of the operative principle that applies to human rights. Without making such identification, critical analyses of fundamental rights in the EU become aimless. Examining both the existing formulation of principle and those changes evident from the TCE we can then determine the axis around which judgement can be made. This takes us beyond the application of integration theory as

---

EU Charter of Fundamental Rights and accession of the Union to the ECHR, will not be instituted through some other treaty arrangement.

   [4] The noble attempt by Philip Alston *et al* to evaluate the EU from a human rights perspective for all its qualities still could not provide a means of assessment either in general or particular. Rather the reviews are by their nature disparate and thus unfocused. See Alston *et al* (eds) *The EU and Human Rights* (Oxford: OUP, 1999).

a means of explaining what the EU has done in this field. It assumes that the fundamental principle ascribed to respect for human rights is just that, fundamental.[5]

However, identifying the principle cannot be the end of the story. The extent to which the principle is realised must also be reviewed. This is not simply a matter of outlining a number of indicators or desired outcomes and gauging the EU's actions against them. The nature of human rights and certainly the nature of respecting them warrant more flexibility. The second part of this chapter therefore looks to establishing the basis for a scheme to review the EU's behaviour on human rights. Calling upon the notion of 'virtue' to encompass the qualities that might be expected of an institution endeavouring to respect human rights, a template is provided of virtues against which the EU can be judged. Three categories are noted: virtues of governance; executive virtues; and virtues of justice.

The concentration on virtue is a self-conscious adoption of an ethical belief that justice requires just means as well as just ends. Of course that could be contested but given the history of the EU it is hardly stretching a point to suggest that the EU has some role as either a primary or secondary agent of justice in Onora O'Neill's terms.[6] The former, O'Neill describes as agents with the capacity to 'determine how principles of justice are to be institutionalized within a certain domain'.[7] They have the power to direct and assign responsibilities and to some degree control the actions of secondary agents, whom O'Neill suggests 'contribute to justice mainly by meeting the demands of primary agents, most evidently by conforming to any legal requirements they establish'.[8] No doubt originally the Member States would have been viewed as the primary agents and the EU only capable of being a secondary agent. However, the EU has gradually assumed the characteristics of a primary agent through the steady assumption or designation of powers although this clearly remains a hotly disputed subject.[9] Either way, with such agency, whether primary or secondary, come responsibilities. These at least can be focused on the way in which the EU acts in human rights matters thereby reflecting the extent to which human rights are indeed 'respected' by the Union. The purpose therefore in looking to the virtues displayed by the EU is to assess the depth of its commitment to the fundamental principle.

Even though the seemingly usual caveat for any assessment based on human rights in the Union must apply, namely that lack of space forbids any claims to

---

[5] There is of course scope for a whole work to examine whether or not human rights *are* fundamental to the EU in practice and indeed to determine what 'fundamental' can mean in a complex political and economic institution such as the EU. This lies outside the aims of this chapter.

[6] Onora O'Neill, 'Agents of Justice' in Andrew Kuper (ed) *Global Responsibilities* (London: Routledge, 2005) 37–52.

[7] Ibid at 38.

[8] Ibid.

[9] The supremacy of EU law attests to the possibility of primary status where the EU is granted competence. Although the EU does not have general competence to enact human rights measures it nonetheless has specific powers that have human rights dimensions. Thus, in some areas the EU can operate as primary agent even with the principle of subsidiarity hovering above all action.

completeness, the analysis provides a flavour of the main areas of concern. Hopefully, it will give rise to a renewed interest not only in the technical construction of human rights initiatives (one could hazard a guess that the creation and operation of the Fundamental Rights Agency alone will otherwise suck the lifeblood of debate on human rights in the EU for the next year or so) but also the often taken-for-granted ethical bases for the EU's operations in this area *in toto*.

ESTABLISHING THE PRINCIPLE

There always seems to be a preliminary question one must deal with when it comes to assessing the nature of the EU's role in any particular area. The whole ethos of subsidiarity perhaps reflects this state of affairs, suggesting as it does that commentators and actors must engage in an assessment of both the authority and suitability of the EU to act in any particular field. In our case the preliminary question is simple: should the EU have a role to play in the governance of human rights in Europe? This question, however, may well be otiose. For good or ill the EU *has* assumed a role in the promotion and pursuit of human rights as well as in the self-assessment of its constituent parts, including the Member States to some degree.[10] Thus, whether or not the EU *should* be concerned with human rights work beyond avoiding its own violations is something of a *passé* question. The reality is that the EU operates in the field of human rights, explicitly accepts this fact, and actively pursues initiatives designed to demonstrate its commitment to respect and promote human rights regionally and globally as well as institutionally. We need look no further than its record in development policy, in its establishment of agencies designed to monitor human rights in Member States, in its approach to states applying to become a part of the Union, and in its commitment to address specific rights (such as the right not to be discriminated against on the grounds of race).

We might argue that this should not be the case. We might argue that the EU should only be concerned with the efficient organization of a free trade area and not involve itself with matters of human rights *tout court* at all, that these are issues for the Member States alone or at best in tandem with the regional human rights organization based in the European Court of Human Rights and perhaps other international bodies. But there seems little to be gained in undertaking this debate. Even if we left aside the arguments of collective responsibility that might be presumed through the universalization of human rights in international law, the EU on its own initiative can be seen to have established the point of departure. After three decades and more of legal and political action that has placed respect for human rights firmly within the realm of the EU, the principle has been established. The gap between the rhetorical acceptance of this state of affairs and the actual practice may continue to inform critique but arguments of principle seem to relate

---

[10] We examine the extent of the assessment of Member States below.

more to the *extent* of the commitment to human rights rather than whether or not they have a legitimate place in the EU's constitutional framework.

Nevertheless, we still have to establish what the scope of this principle might be. To begin with we do not perhaps need to be too contentious or look too far. Article 6 TEU provided the constitutional moment of solidifying the principles that had already attained legal or political recognition through the jurisprudence of the ECJ and/or statements and actions of the institutions. As von Bogdandy rightly suggests, 'this provision almost requires that it be developed into a general doctrine of principles against which all areas of Union law and in particular the older layers of Community law must be assessed.'[11] For our specific purposes Article 6(1) TEU tells us that the EU 'is founded on the principles of . . . respect for human rights and fundamental freedoms'. Article 6(2) then requires that 'the Union shall respect fundamental rights' as guaranteed by the ECHR and the common constitutional traditions of the Member States.

These combined statements of principle are not wholly harmonious. Certainly the former as a pre-conditional and almost historical assertion is complemented by the latter, which dictates immediate and future action. Tension is nevertheless apparent between the 'human' and 'fundamental' labels attached to the subject-matter of the principle. Why the distinction? Does it suggest a difference in substance? On a super-ficial level we might note that the term 'fundamental' appears reserved for internal consumption. The 'human' epithet attaches more readily to the external, an interpret-ation made plain when the Commission neatly transformed the proposal for a 'Human Rights Agency' put forward by the Council into a 'Fundamental Rights Agency'. As the latter has adopted a largely internal function, the correspondence between 'internal' and 'fundamental' and 'external' and 'human' has been reinforced.[12]

Most commentators have found it easier, however, to suggest that the two terms are interchangeable, providing us with no residual legal or philosophical problems. It is probably best to accede to this line of reasoning for the moment. The difference may only be a reflection of loose drafting based on equally vague jurisprudence. But the suspicion remains that there is intended to be a distinction. It is just not clear what that might be.

[11] von Bogdandy *supra* n. 1 at 15. Interestingly, von Bogdandy does not discuss respect for human rights as a specific founding principle except in the context of and as a subsidiary element of the prin-ciple of liberty that appears first in the list of principles contained in Article 6(1) TEU. To my mind this is an interpretation that is not wholly justified by rules of interpretation. Rather the activities devel-oped by the EU in relation to human rights suggest that the individual nature of liberty accorded to the principle by von Bogdandy is not without qualification. In particular, the support for certain group rights in external affairs might suggest that respect for human rights has a more independent meaning than von Bogdandy assumes.

[12] We can see the same dichotomy played out with the Charter for Fundamental Rights on the one hand (primarily a document for internal consumption although some attempt to apply it to the external has been made, albeit unsuccessfully) and the European Initiative for Democracy and Human Rights on the other, a project designed by the Commission for 'third countries' (see http://europa.eu.int/comm/europeaid/projects/eidhr/index_en.htm for details of the latter).

Instead of focusing on the differences we can perhaps focus on the connections. What can be extracted from the constitutional provision that is Article 6? Clearly, the underlying requirement and common denominator is 'respect'. Whatever conception we have of the subject-matter, the principle is to 'respect' it/them. The definition of the verb 'to respect' should not be beyond us. It would surely encompass the following: to consider, to take into account, to refer to, to treat with consideration, to refrain from violating, to show deference to, to honour rather than to 'realize', 'promote' or 'enforce' (those other applicable terms that have been traditionally associated with human rights). Such would be the range of ordinary definitions that give rise to a number of possible active and passive options. To honour for instance might well place the principle in the realm of the rhetorical, engaging no greater demands upon the institution than an obligation to reiterate the importance of human rights as a general concept. But such a restrictive interpretation would surely be disingenuous given the preponderance of and importance ascribed to both the declaration *and* active protection of human rights in international law and community.

What then are the realistic implications of identifying 'respect' as the operative institutional command? Does it imply a responsibility to act as a moral agent in relation to human rights, dictating an active or positive obligation?[13] Or does the principle merely possess a passive or negative nature, one that forbids the EU from violating human rights itself but does not impose upon it a greater duty to promote and enforce human rights? Perhaps here we find the basis for an ethical struggle, a central tension that lies at the heart of human rights policy construction. In EU terms Olivier de Schutter has rightly suggested that the adoption of fundamental rights in the Union was the result of a negative response, one which sought to protect interests that might be harmed by the actions of the EU. The case law of the European Court of Justice might be seen as taking the same line. In particular, in *Opinion 2/94 on Accession by the Community to the ECHR* the Court famously, if not ambiguously, noted that '[n]o Treaty provision confers on the Community institutions any general power to enact rules on human rights'.[14] Nonetheless, it did acknowledge the declaratory importance of respect for human rights in the EU and noted that 'fundamental rights form an integral part of the general principles of law'[15] and that 'respect for human rights is . . . a condition of the lawfulness of Community acts.'[16] But de Schutter also points out that the adoption of this approach has placed fewer limits on the EU's human rights activities than one might expect. Indeed, the development of a wide spectrum of fundamental rights texts,

---

[13] The possibility of institutions generally adopting a sense of collective moral agency is explored in some detail, although not as regards the EU specifically, in Toni Erskine (ed) *Can Institutions Have Responsibilities? Collective Moral Agency and International Relations* (Basingstoke: Palgrave, 2003).

[14] *Opinion 2/94 on Accession by the Community to the ECHR* [1996] ECR I-1759 para. 27. The statement was ambiguous because it did not articulate what the EU *could* do with regard to human rights. It certainly did not preclude the adoption of *specific* rather than general legislative measures.

[15] Ibid para 33.

[16] Ibid para 34.

legislative rules, institutional practices, supported agencies, and applied resources testify to a broader and deeper conception of the commitment to 'respect' than a negative connotation would allow. It might even represent recognition of a responsibility that progresses from (and encompasses) an *ex post* to *ex ante* condition; *ex post* in the sense of being held accountable for one's actions, *ex ante* in the sense of a continuing obligation to ensure that violations are prevented and the substance of rights fulfilled.[17] Should the assumption of responsibility in practice indeed extend across these positions then this would suggest an institution bound to devote its energies to the attainment of human rights without geographical or jurisdictional constraints and not merely to prevent violation by its own hands.

But here we come across a crucial dilemma in the assignment of responsibility, not only for the EU in terms of human rights but also as regards its whole character. For in assessing the EU, are we concerned with the actions of an institution that possesses independent collective responsibility (or 'political' responsibility in Hannah Arendt's terms), to be judged according to moral and ethical demands that might attach to any institutional 'primary' agent? Or are we dealing with a creation of the Member States as purely a secondary agent, a legally constructed entity whose parameters for action and thus responsibility are strictly confined by its legal constitution, leaving little room for valid independent initiative? This lies at the heart of the question regarding the supranational or intergovernmental nature of the EU which we do not need to pursue here.

Nonetheless, the former designation of a collective primary responsibility would clearly suggest that the term 'respect' entails a wide interpretation so that the scope of commitment extends not only to avoiding direct harm but also actively to realizing human rights *wherever possible*. This last injunction embraces a sense of 'imperfect obligation' in Kantian terms, those ethical demands that are not accompanied by legal prescription and which thus require judgement as to both the opportunities and capabilities that the EU possesses to respect human rights. Similarly, judgement about the level of respect would not be restricted to observance of particular legal texts. We might well have to examine those '*ultimate* moral concerns' and choices that exist whether or not specific texts are enacted.[18] By comparing the resulting institutional choices, perhaps after 'public reasoning' in a Rawlsian sense, with those objectively determined opportunities and capacities, we would thus be able to see just how far the assumption of responsibility has developed.[19] Then we might be able to assess whether the EU's commitment to

---

[17] For a discussion of the terms *ex post* and *ex ante* responsibility see Dieter Birnbacher 'Philosophical Foundations of Responsibility' in Ann Elisabeth Auhagen and Hans-Werner Bierhoff (eds) *Responsibility: the Many Faces of a Social Phenomenon* (London: Routledge, 2001) 9–22.

[18] See Thomas Pogge, 'Human Rights and Human Responsibilities' in Andrew Kuper (ed) *Global Responsibiities* (London: Routledge, 2005) 3–36 at 10.

[19] Amartya Sen has discussed the desirability of such analysis that involves not only internal review based on local values but also appreciation of other notions of justice from a 'certain distance' (deploying Adam Smith terminology). See, 'Elements of a Theory of Human Rights' 32(4) *Philosophy and Public Affairs* (2004) 315–356.

human rights extends to a form of what Thomas Pogge calls 'moral' or 'institutional' cosmopolitanism, reflecting a Union intent on pursuing a form of global justice that incorporated within its understanding of human rights the relief of poverty or impoverishment.[20] Whether or not we can make such a claim, Pogge notes the essential role the EU has in the 'eradication of poverty and starvation' and sees hope in the influence of the 'moral convictions of citizens',[21] a possibility that might be sustainable should participatory processes of the EU ever mature.

However, it is not within the scope of this chapter to carry out a survey that would determine the point (if that were ever possible) one way or the other. It might nevertheless be useful to make brief reference to some of the evidence for a wide ranging interpretation of responsibility. Leaving aside the ubiquitous rhetoric in support of human rights, it encompasses standard setting, the establishment of monitoring systems and the adoption of meaningful enforcement measures all seemingly inspired (albeit reflected in legal provision) by the assumption of concern for human rights. So we can see that standards have not only been reinforced through the Charter but have also emerged from less 'normative-judicial' sources (in Gráinne de Búrca's term, which refers to human rights principles and standards that emanate from court decisions or legal texts).[22] The guidelines produced on human rights dialogues, for instance announce 'issues' for discussion that incorporate not only the 'implementation of international human rights instruments' but also more generally 'the role of civil society' 'promotion of the processes of democratisation and good governance and the prevention of conflict.'[23] Similarly, the Council highlighted its intention to support work that addressed 'a wide range of human rights concerns, such as . . . international justice including the ICC, the fight against the death penalty and support to democracy, good governance and the rule of law'.[24] These practical initiatives tend to emerge in the external sphere where there is greater scope perhaps for the assumption of a responsibility to respect fundamental human rights that is not constrained so easily by legal norms introduced by agreed texts. They testify to a broader interpretation of human rights and the circumstances in which they should be considered, promoted, and/or enforced. Whether that suggests the move towards a sense of global justice one would have to doubt, if only for the dubious nature of that concept.[25]

---

[20] See Thomas Pogge, 'World Poverty and Human Rights' (Cambridge: Polity Press, 2002).

[21] Ibid 211.

[22] Gráinne de Búrca, 'Beyond the Charter: How Enlargement has Enlarged the Human Rights Policy of the European Union' 27 *Fordham International Law Journal* (2004) 679–714 at 681.

[23] European Guidelines on human rights dialogues Council 2001.

[24] Council Conclusions on the implementation of EU human rights policy 2004 available at ue.eu.int/cms3_fo/showPage.asp?id=822&lang=EN&mode=g

[25] See Thomas Nagel, 'The Problem of Global Justice' 33(2) *Philosophy and Public Affairs* (2005) 113, for the contention that global justice might only be possible ironically through the creation of supranational institutions 'that do not aim at justice but that pursue common interests and reflect the inequalities of bargaining power among existing states' and are initially 'tolerable to the interests of the

Even though the EU appears to adopt broad notions of the respect for human rights in the external realm, similar support exercised internally cannot be discounted. The potential rights-based approach to social policy might well configure an understanding of responsibility that sought to delve deep within the traditionally exclusive territory of the Member States. Particularly with regard to an understanding of citizenship that extended beyond the basic rights granted therein and towards a condition of non-discrimination and equality, we can see an intent to advance a social model that has significant scope.[26] Whether or not a chimera, this does not necessarily detract from the presumption that the principle of 'respect' possesses expandable boundaries.

The forces pressing for the alternative more restricted designation of responsibility, however, should not be dismissed. Based on the theory of intergovernmental agreement and the interpretation of treaties, a different picture comes to the fore. What that might be could be determined by familiar interpretative techniques suggested by the Vienna Convention on the Law of Treaties. This would entail an examination of the 'ordinary meaning to be given to the terms of the treaty in their context and in the light of its object and purpose',[27] the intentions of the parties (the Member States),[28] and 'any subsequent practice in the application of the treaty which establishes the agreement of the parties regarding its interpretation'.[29] Of course the latter element would draw in those initiatives I have already alluded to as evidence of the assumption of a collective responsibility. Nevertheless, the starting point would be the references to human rights in the Treaties and other major texts or decisions that determined the governance of the EU.[30] There we would find the most important argument for a restricted and restrictive reading of the human rights principle particularly with regard to the relationship between the Union and its Member States.

So we can observe that the ECJ has established that it only has jurisdiction to review actions of Member States when they implemented European law, or, more contentiously, when they derogated from Union rules. The EU Charter on Fundamental Rights confirmed that stance, more or less, through Article 51, which declared that the Charter provisions were addressed 'to the Member States only

most powerful current nation-states'. If this suggests that justice must proceed on the hope of some transformation through existing and functioning power structures then the EU might well fit Nagel's requirements.

[26] See for instance Deborah Mabbett, 'The Development of Rights-Based Social Policy in the European Union: the Example of Disability Rights' 43(1) *JCMS* (2005) 97–120.

[27] Art 31(1) Vienna Convention on the Law of Treaties 1969.

[28] Ibid Art 31(4).

[29] Ibid Art 31(3)(b).

[30] The reference to human rights in the Treaties only became significant with the Treaty of Maastricht, which introduced human rights considerations into Art 177 EC Treaty in relation to development cooperation. The Treaty of Amsterdam then made a more solid and general reference in the amended Art 6 TEU. For a useful review of this subject and the ECJ's response, see Koen Lenaerts, 'Fundamental Rights in the European Union' 25 *ELRev* (2000) 575–600.

when they are implementing Union law'.[31] The Commission's proposal for a
Fundamental Rights Agency has similarly limited its remit to the 'situation of
fundamental rights in the European Union and in its Member States when implementing Community law'.[32] The language is consistent. And the legal dimension
seems to be clear; the EU's responsibility remains focused on its own institutional
actions as regards any negative impact on human rights. Any positive obligations
are reserved for external activity and those internal areas which are specifically identified through Treaty provision or other legislative measure.[33]

   Of course it can never be a simple choice between the two forms of responsibility described above in determining a complete understanding of the principle of
'respect'. That is where the tension arises. On the one hand the EU, howsoever it
may have been created, has developed into a polity that possesses independent legal
personality and institutions which are capable of making and implementing
decisions and establishing a *praxis* without slavish reference to its founding text. On
the other hand, constraints are imposed by the treaties. The reality must therefore
lie somewhere between these positions leaving significant scope for political and
legal debate. Thus, the institutions may be seen to have *assumed* responsibility as
regards human rights that combine elements of a duty to act to respect human rights
wherever possible whilst casting an eye towards its legally established parameters.

   A prime example of this tension can be found in the approach taken to Article 7
TEU. Establishing a mechanism for enforcement (thus adhering to one of de Búrca's
requirements for a 'functioning international human rights system')[34] that enables the
EU to respond to a 'serious and persistent breach' of Article 6(1) principles or even a
'clear risk of serious breach', Article 7 as instituted through the Treaty of Nice suggested a Treaty recognition of *political responsibility*. Thanks to Article 46(e) TEU
the measure is explicitly non-justiciable save for its procedural provisions. And yet the
Commission has declared that Article 7 helped 'equip the Union institutions with
the means of ensuring that all Member states respect' the principles set out in Article
6(1).[35] On the strength of this it acceded to the European Parliament's suggestion that
some form of monitoring of Member States' human rights records, irrespective of
whether they relate to the implementation of Union law or not, was a precondition
for Article 7 and established the Independent Network of Experts on Fundamental

   [31] The Charter's wording did not dispel the debate concerning whether the principle would extend
to derogation. However, case law continues to adopt an inclusive approach. See, for instance, Case
C-60/00 *Carpenter v Home Secretary* [2002] ECR I-6279.
   [32] See Art 3(3) Proposal for a Council Regulation establishing a European Union Agency for
Fundamental Rights COM(2005)280.
   [33] It should be remembered that even in the external realm, specific regulatory authorisation was
required for the Commission to allocate significant resources in the pursuit of human rights. See
Regulations 975 and 976/1999 as amended.
   [34] de Búrca *supra* n. 22.
   [35] Communication form the Commission to the Council and the European Parliament on Article 7
of the Treaty on European Union: Respect for and promotion of the values on which the Union is based;
COM(2003) 606 final at 3.

Rights to produce the necessary regular reports. But these actions have not resolved the tension. There remains the institutional acknowledgement that Article 7 is a purely political measure and as such does not represent an expansion of the EU's competence in human rights. The recent proposal for a Fundamental Rights Agency would seem to confirm this.[36] It now ensures that scrutiny of Member States under Article 7 is not to be incorporated within that Agency's remit. The Impact Assessment that accompanied the proposal has also introduced the notion that there is *no* requirement for constant monitoring in terms of Article 7, given that sufficient extra-Union systems already exist to carry out this function.[37] Consequently, the possibility for Article 7 to be the basis for an enhanced interpretation of human rights responsibilities for the Union has been curtailed somewhat.

It is clear, therefore, that the limits of the principle to respect human rights remain highly contested. Paradoxically, this can both undermine *and* support the maturation of the EU's human rights policy. While suggesting a failure to establish a clear approach as to how the Union is to go about fulfilling its requirement to respect human rights, it also provides important room for political—if not legal—manoeuvre.

We might find here an echo of the struggle that has appeared generally in Western notions of human rights. Theories of natural and positive rights also display conflict in relation to how obligations might flow from human rights articulations. Natural rights theories suggest that states should be obliged to respect human rights regardless of their status in any legal system. Positivists only recognize obligations flowing from rights that are enshrined into a state's law. Is the EU playing out similar theoretical debates on the nature of its principle, trying to determine whether it has an obligation to look beyond its formal duties set down in the Treaties towards a broader sense of its human rights responsibilities? Perhaps in practice it is adjusting itself to, what Sen calls, an 'ethical understanding of human rights' that moves away from a 'law-centred approach' to seeing human rights as 'if they are basically *grounds* for law, almost "laws in waiting" '.[38] Thus, human rights might be treated as relevant and influential regardless of the constraints currently placed on the EU through its constitutional framework. The practical effect may be paradoxical. On the one hand there may be a tendency to both restrict the application of human rights (by ensuring they only apply in specific contexts determined by the legal texts) *and* allow for their wider promotion through incremental, perhaps even ad hoc or informal, institutional measures that emerge through practice.[39]

---

[36] Commission Communication on Fundamental Rights Agency, COM(2004) 693, Brussels, 25 October 2004.

[37] Preparatory Study for Impact Assessment and Ex-ante Evaluation of Fundamental Rights Agency Final Report (2005) available at http://europa.eu.int/comm/justice_home/doc_centre/rights/doc/study_epec_fund_rights_agency_en.pdf.

[38] Sen *supra* n. 19 at 326.

[39] Whether this creates a politics of human rights that is confused and confusing or is to be applauded for its capacity to respond to the ever-changing specifics of human rights is considered further below.

I will return to this theme later, but it is within this context that we should consider whether the TCE points to a change in direction with regard to the 'respect' principle, perhaps providing a solution to the tensions that evidently subsist. Would the TCE suggest that the Member States and the institutions were prepared to clarify the responsibility to respect human rights? Article I-2 modifies slightly the Article 6(1) formula by providing that the 'Union is founded on the values of respect for human dignity, freedom, democracy, equality, the rule of law and respect for human rights, including the rights of persons belonging to minorities'. The crux of the principle of respect thus remains intact albeit with a potentially unnecessary addition. However, a small change in attitude might be inferred from the operative Article I-3, which states that the 'Union's aim is to promote peace, its values and the well-being of its peoples'. This suggests that 'promotion' of human rights *is* an acknowledged and legitimate aim of the EU, providing the Union with the authority to develop its human rights policy. The additional intentions for the EU to 'recognize' the EU Charter on Fundamental Rights and to accede to the ECHR, all contained in Article I-9, lend further credence to this argument that the commitment to respect human rights is spreading rather than receding. But the central tension between deepening its human rights work and keeping it within the parameters of Union law with regard to the Member States remains. The slightly revised Charter as it appears in part II of the TCE still dictates that it has application only as regards the implementation of EU law. And the proposals for a Fundamental Rights Agency, as we have seen, will have as one of its tasks the monitoring of Member States' human rights records again only in relation to the application of EU law. Thus, it seems clear that the TCE and recent initiatives have reinforced the confusing and confused nature of the Union's response to its stated principle.

Even though the TCE has failed to resolve the tension it does at least confirm that we need to assess the practice of human rights policy in the Union from more directions than abstract principle. If we are to do justice to a review of fundamental rights in the Union we must also consider a framework for critical analysis that looks to the practical dimension of its human rights activities. We need to construct the basis for judgement that will help evaluate the scope of the EU's practice. This is the task of the following section.

FROM PRINCIPLE TO VIRTUES

Identifying a central principle is an essential first step in the process of judgement. But it is not enough. A mere rhetorical observation that an institution 'respects human rights' is patently insufficient. We need to look further for guidance. What concerns us is *how* the principle is or is not fulfilled. In other words, the principle is not the last word in values. We must also consider the means by which it is brought into effect. Only then can an effective evaluation be made as to the extent to which the principle has been and is realized.

One approach would be to rely on the fairly recent 'science' applied to human rights indicators.[40] Todd Landman, a commentator on the production of methods of assessment for human rights, identifies three areas for examination: (1) *rights in principle*: in other words formally declared commitments to human rights standards through the ratification of conventions; (2) *rights in practice*: records that indicate the breadth of violations of those conventions; (3) *policies and outcomes*: indicators that suggest the fulfilment or failure for human rights realization therefore looking to the impact of policies with regard to general and specific human rights standards.[41] Such indicators do provide the basis for a forensic examination, but the focus is limited. The emphasis is upon *violation* and tends to favour civil and political rights, which possess qualities that make them easier to assess with regard to their abuse than economic, social and cultural rights, let alone 'people's' rights that apply to groups (such as linguistic minorities) rather than individuals. There is small scope in this scheme to evaluate the depth of commitment to an expressed and constitutional undertaking to 'respect' human rights by an institution such as the EU, which clearly may have significant possibilities for influencing the development of human rights locally if not globally but does not have a monopoly of action in the field. Thus, indicators showing that the EU has not ratified any conventions, that it has not committed any significant violations of accepted standards, and that indicators of development in the Union are generally good, do not therefore assist in evaluating the success and impact of the EU's adherence to a principle of respect. We must look further then for inspiration.[42]

The philosophy of ethics, as well as law, seems well suited to this context. The discourse of virtue ethics implies that we are as much concerned with the practical way in which a principle is observed and fulfilled as we are with the end attained. This is all the more relevant for the realization of human rights, which by their nature are always and forever capable of violation and therefore must always and forever be subject to review.

Inherent in this analysis is the understanding that adherence to (or at least non-contravention of) certain virtues is necessary if an ethical principle is to be realized in practice. And therefore it is against these generalized virtues that any institutional behaviour can be assessed if not measured. But what specifically should we look for and what should we be looking at when we try to assess the means by which respect may be realized? Is it possible to construct a non-exhaustive list of institutional traits

---

[40] For a general review of this particular subject, see Michael Kirby, 'Indicators for the Implementation of Human Rights' in Janusz Symonides (ed) *Human Rights: International Protection, Monitoring, Enforcement* (Aldershot: Ashgate, 2003) 325–346.

[41] Todd Landman, 'Measuring Human Rights: Principle, Practice and Policy' 26 *Human Rights Quarterly* (2004) 906–931 at 927.

[42] As an aside, it is unfortunate that the impact assessment exercise for the creation of the FRA has not adopted a similarly critical approach to the value of indicators. Those suggested as useful for assessing adherence to the Charter of Fundamental Rights are unimaginatively narrow and if adopted by the Agency will provide little scope for evaluating the depth of human rights realization in the EU.

and virtues against which an assessment of both enunciation and practice of human rights in the EU can be made? This is, of course, fraught with danger. Determining the nature of virtue cannot be a purely objective enterprise. What is seen as a positive attribute, say certainty in the law, might also be viewed as detrimental for a conception of human rights that values flexibility and the ability to respond to particular contexts and cultural perspectives. Nevertheless, even with this proviso some potential guidance can surely be identified. It might be that any process of judgement would then dismiss one particular quality as worthy of assessment, or even weigh some significantly more than others. Equally, we might find that desirable virtues could conflict in certain circumstances, again as an example the need for certainty in interpreting a human right on the one hand and the desire to respect cultural diversity on the other.[43]

This is not to say that a *checklist* of virtues can or should be provided. The aim is not to establish a set of rules that can be said to determine how an institution purportedly committed to respect human rights should look and behave. Rather, the aim would be to suggest an analytical framework around which a process of 'practical judgement' can then be enacted in line with the responsibility to respect human rights that the EU has assumed.[44] As Onora O'Neill notes, when we examine the way in which societies are and should be ethically bound, we look, in essence, for 'design criteria' that 'constitute a set of constraints and standards which cannot all be met perfectly, but which also cannot always or perhaps generally be traded off against one another'.[45] In short, 'the real task of practical judgement is simply to seek ways of acting that respect multiple obligations'.[46] We might add that the delineation of criteria or virtues would never be fixed but rather contingent on differing and evolving conditions.

The EU does in fact carry out this task of virtue designation. But it does so predominantly in the external sphere, when it looks to third countries and how *they* manage and apply human rights norms. It is reasonable to suppose therefore that if the EU and its Member States have identified certain criteria as essential in terms of assessing the quality of human rights governance in others then they should be relevant for self-application. As a starting point for analysis this would make sense. This does not mean we should lose sight of other conceptions of virtue that relate to the creation of a just society, a society intent on achieving justice commensurate with respect for human rights. Theories of governance as they relate to the rule of law and justice as well as to those predominantly functional matters of proper administration must therefore have relevance in our assessment.

---

[43] It would not accept however an equation that allowed for the 'interests of the Union' to hold sway in any particular conflict, if respect for human rights were to be a principle fundamental in nature rather than merely desirable.

[44] In this respect one might follow Onora O'Neill's conception of 'practical judgement' described in *Bounds of Justice* (Cambridge: Cambridge University Press 2000). O'Neill describes practical judgement as focusing on 'types of possible action (policies, attitudes)' at 56.

[45] Ibid at 61.

[46] Ibid.

We might start the process by identifying clusters of virtue. Three come to mind: virtues of governance, executive virtues and 'justice virtues'.[47] These are by no means exhaustive but they give a flavour of the breadth of criteria that are both deployed by the EU in some of its affairs and might be inferred from the general discourse of ethics. They can be represented simply (but incompletely) by the grid in *figure 1*. One might immediately note from such a list that its foundations lie in administrative law, ethics, good governance and jurisprudence amongst other fields. In some respects they reflect accounts of values that are occasionally referred to in public law terms.[48] But the identification of virtue as opposed to value is designed to embrace the practical as well as theoretical aspects for assessment of a regime (or policy) of human rights under construction. At the very least, I contend, one would have to produce a valid argument *in human rights terms* if these virtues are to be dismissed either singularly or in total. That is if one holds with the view (as it would appear

Governance Virtues	Executive virtues	Justice virtues
Clarity of human rights conception	Sufficient and timely allocation of resources for human rights	Non-discrimination and tolerance of cultural distinctions
Capacity for human rights evolution	Qualified and competent personnel in human rights	Participatory processes in human rights work
Competence to make decisions and to act on human rights	Efficient human rights related decision making	Access to justice for citizens or other injured parties
Capacity to monitor and enforce human rights standards	Transparency in human rights matters	Consistent application of human rights standards
Coherence in human rights	Capacity for effective enforcement of human rights	Certainty of application of human rights
		Accountability

Figure 1 *The virtues for respecting human rights.*

[47] 'Virtues of justice' is a phrase used by Onora O'Neill and it is not intended to accept her formulation *in toto* when talking about justice virtues. However, considerable reliance has been placed on O'Neill's identification of virtues in this context as I indicate where appropriate. See O'Neill, *Towards Justice and Virtue* (Cambridge: Cambridge University Press, 1996).

[48] See for instance Peter Cane, 'Theory and Values in Public Law' in P.P. Craig and R. Rawlings (eds) *Law and Administration in Europe: essays in Honour of Carol Harlow* (Oxford: OUP, 2003) 1–21, who lists the immanent values in UK public law as including accountability, equality before the law, access to courts, executive authority, transparency and participation (amongst others) that are reflected in my schema.

the EU does externally) that the realization of human rights requires attention to the detail of their promotion, implementation and protection.

Some of the virtues listed are specific, requiring evaluation that relies upon data or quantitative information: the speed of decision-making, for instance; also the means by which a procedure for judicial review might be accessible to an individual.[49] Others require a qualitative assessment, one that creates a value orientation (thus involving the notion of value as well as virtue) determining the nature and scope of adherence to that virtue. The depth of participation in the construction of policy, the commitment espoused by the institution, are some examples. Regardless, we need to look at the extent to which any particular virtue is embraced, thus illuminating the depth of reverence for the central principle. Such a task is a massive one and not within the scope of this chapter.[50] Nonetheless, it is possible to demonstrate the *feasibility* of the task by taking examples from the criteria and applying them to crucial aspects of the EU's practice. With these specific purposes in mind let us examine briefly each cluster and some of their representative virtues which I suggest are particularly important in assessing the degree of 'respect' for human rights in the EU. This will hopefully give a flavour of my analytical scheme.

Governance Virtues

The designation of virtues of governance for human rights might appear to echo the general rhetoric of 'good governance' but in my terms they have more specific meaning.[51] They relate to the means by which an institutional framework can cope both with the complexity of the discourse of human rights and the difficulties of their implementation. Essentially this must be considered in the knowledge that the normative standards that human rights have come to represent are Byzantine in character and that processes of implementation are complicated by the interaction between state, region and supranational institution.

The virtues I have assigned to this category relate therefore to how such a situation of complexity ideally might be governed. As one can see from *figure 1* this includes the capacity to conceptualize rights in the EU context; the capacity to evolve such conceptualization in response to changing social conditions (including perhaps changes in membership through enlargement), the competence, capacity and authority to act in order to realize the principle of respect, and the administration of a coherent approach to all these aspects. Such virtues of governance are essential in the

---

[49] It is here that human rights indicators might have specific relevance.

[50] To a great extent we only have the mammoth work overseen by Philip Alston *et al supra* n. 4, which although remaining relevant is now significantly out of the date. This chapter cannot attempt to supplant that work but it does suggest the parameters within which a new evaluation might be conducted.

[51] The internal EU rhetoric primarily emanates from the Commission and its, 'European Governance: A White Paper' COM (2001) 428, 25 July 2001. This proposed five principles for good governance: openness, participation, accountability, effectiveness, and coherence. This was a reasonable attempt to simplify the aims but not necessarily reflective of the range of virtues that might be considered in relation to human rights.

practical realization of the central principle. And it is against them that some evaluation can be made as to the *ability* of the EU to fulfil (and the extent to which it does so fulfil) its institutional promise to respect human rights.

Certainly, the key aspect in this respect might be that of competence. The identification of this as a virtue is not to suggest there is a definable standard against which any institution could be measured in this respect. Rather, it is to indicate that the scale of competence assumed or assigned will shed light on the commitment to do more than merely speak of respecting human rights. It is perhaps unsurprising therefore that the issue of competence has been central to the debate concerning the role of human rights in the EU. We have already observed that the institutions, the ECJ and the Member States alike have concurred that such competence is to be limited. Individual institutions, particularly the Parliament although the Commission also has a role here, might well push at the boundaries of such constrained competence, and academics might argue for interpreting the Treaties as favourably as possible but the governing attitude is restrictive. The right of the Member States to be the primary point of reference for human rights promotion, monitoring, and enforcement both within the EU and outside remains crucial in this limiting environment.

However, given that this issue has been the subject of intense review elsewhere,[52] it is perhaps more useful to consider a closer examination of two of the other virtues I have identified, particularly in view of the current constitutional proposals. These would be first, clarity of conception and second, capacity for evolution.

Clarity of conception

Human rights conception has already been discussed when addressing the nature of the general principle. But it is necessary to re-emphasize that a primary attribute of a meaningful human rights policy would surely be clarity of the subject-matter or at least clarity in the processes by which such a conception can be determined or perhaps, in some circumstances, altered. For, is it possible to construct a policy on human rights that failed to define what they entailed or how they might be identified? This might seem something of a straightforward issue. How can human rights be invoked and acted upon without an understanding of the nature and extent of those rights? As already indicated, the mere statement that an institution 'respected human rights' would rarely be, if ever, effective in itself. Preconditional, perhaps, but sufficient, never. There are too many instances of a textual commitment to human rights being accompanied by state practice of violation to rely solely on such constitutional pronouncements. Indeed, recent analysis by Oona Hathaway goes so far as to suggest that even the ratification of specific human rights treaties by 'individual countries appear more likely to offset pressure for change in human rights

---

[52] See for instance, Olivier De Schutter, *The Implementation of the EU Charter of Fundamental Rights through the Open Method of Coordination* Jean Monnet Working Paper 2005 http://www.jeanmonnetprogram. org/papers/04/040701.html

practices than to augment it'.[53] In other words, the public textual commitment to international normative standards might be counter-productive to their attainment at least where this is not accompanied by effective monitoring and enforcement systems. One might make an even stronger case when considering the rhetorical adherence to 'respect' for human rights.

Even accepting such a critique, one would struggle to argue that a human rights policy could exist effectively without something of an identifiable catalogue of rights, or at least an institutional adherence to a definable content. This might even be considered necessary and a *sine qua non*. Even then the presence of a catalogue might not be sufficient condition to establish clarity. A brief examination of the history of human rights tells us that a rigid list rarely encompasses the totality of rights-meanings assumed by a society at any given time. The evolution of international and national discourse and textual development, as well as judicial, social and political interpretation, ensures that human rights instruments and concepts tend to be always in a state of flux at least in their application. Even the Universal Declaration of Human Rights (UDHR), which has achieved iconic status without ever appearing complete, has failed to provide a wholly fixed position. Through the development of various 'generations' of human rights, each building on previous manifestations without eradicating their predecessors, one can testify to the changeable nature of the subject. Equally, the process of interpretative judgement on specific rights in differing contexts can have a profound and continuing effect on acceptable conceptions. Although working on generally settled ideas, those margins of appreciation or discretion accorded to national decision-makers, and changing social and moral environments act consistently to shape the meaning of human rights. Reference to a simple list, however accessible, will not therefore be sufficient to judge clarity of conception, particularly if the list has not or cannot remain constant in practice. Even taking a positivist stance, where rights are only recognized when written into legislative acts, the scope for interpretation and development can be broad.[54]

Consequently, in looking for clarity of conception we must also examine how an institution embraces change, how it has constructed processes by which change can be effected whether through politics or law, and how indeed it manages the development of the notions of human rights that it is devoted to respecting. In other words, what the institution does in practice, how it settles conflicts between rights, which rights it chooses to monitor, promote or enforce, and who makes those decisions, will all reflect on the institutional conception. The virtue sought then would be clarity that provided an understanding of the evolutionary nature of human rights and embraced the possibility and reality of change through processes of governance.

---

[53] Oona Hathaway, 'Do Human Rights Treaties Make a Difference?' 111 *Yale Law Journal* (2002) 1935–2026 at 2025.

[54] The right to life, for instance, provokes significant debate and political controversy when considered in relation to 'mercy killings', abortion and 'collateral damage'.

Looking to the EU, Piet Eeckhout recognizes that if the Union 'is to develop a meaningful human rights policy ... a sufficiently clear and enforceable basic human rights document is indispensable'.[55] A feeling of some progress towards such clarity has been evinced since the creation of the EU Charter on Fundamental Rights. Gráinne de Búrca, although sceptical about the restrictions of application imposed within the Charter, acknowledges that its adoption 'and the likelihood of its being incorporated into a constitutional text in the near future is one important step' in the direction of a working 'judicial-normative dimension' to an EU human rights system.[56] Eeckhout goes further to suggest that the Charter represents 'a common law of fundamental rights protection in the European Union and its Member States', a common law "discovered" from the ECHR and the Member States' constitutional traditions, which sets it apart from the ECHR system.[57] Certainly one could argue that the Charter does indicate an institutional assurance that the human rights the EU is committed to respect transcend the ECHR, which would be the most natural textual focus, given its history in the region and its importance in European judicial reasoning. By eschewing the Council of Europe as a site for the construction of rights of whatever hue, and identifying those to which the Union desires to give expression, an institutional statement of intent has been made: namely that the EU has the *right* to devise or rather describe its own conception of human rights, a conception that stands on the foundations of traditions familiar to Europe but has its own identity.

Is this too grand a claim for the Charter? Christopher McCrudden has reflected upon its possible futures and counsels against being too immodest in one's hopes for the document.[58] But if, as Eeckhout suggests, the Charter could 'become a force for some degree of harmonization of human rights law in the European Union' then there surely has to be some faith in its ability to foster respect. To do that effectively it must possess sufficient clarity to enable both Courts and policy-makers to embrace its contents with confidence.[59] On the face of it, the Charter assists in producing an accessible list of rights that is easy to read and presumably to understand. But there remains a problem concerning the scope of the Charter's application. It is in this context that its potential for clarity may have been undermined by the TCE. Even if the TCE is not adopted this may still be the case as it

---

[55] Piet Eeckhout, 'The EU Charter on Fundamental Rights and the Federal Question' 39 *CMLR* (2002) 945–994 at 990.

[56] de Búrca *supra* n. 22 at 713.

[57] Eeckhout *supra* n. 55 at 992.

[58] Christopher McCrudden 'The Future of the EU Charter of Fundamental Rights' UACES Online Reflection Papers No.1 2002 http://www.uaces.org/.

[59] There is an argument to be made that such confidence has already been shown through the occasions in which the Advocates-General have referred to the Charter as a source of inspiration in concluding their opinions on certain fundamental rights issues before them. The ECJ has been less willing to take that approach one would suspect because of the Charter's current lack of legal basis. For a review of recent cases citing the Charter, see Eeckhout *supra* n. 55.

indicates the institutional design for the Charter. For in the process of redrafting for adoption within the Constitution, thus making the rights therein justiciable, certain amendments were made both to the main document and the accompanying explanatory text that might suggest confusion rather than clarity.

In particular, Article 51 now restates the established formula that the fundamental rights in the Charter are addressed to the EU institutions and the Member States only when implementing EU law. But it also adds that such parties must 'therefore respect the rights, observe the principles and promote the application thereof in accordance with their respective powers'. Fairly innocuous one would have thought. But Article 52(5) has been added to provide that 'those provisions of the Charter which contain principles may be implemented by legislative and executive acts taken by institutions, bodies, offices and agencies of the Union, and by acts of Member States when they are implementing Union law, in the exercise of their respective powers'. It then goes on to state, '[t]hey shall be judicially cognisable only in the interpretation of such acts and in the ruling on their legality.' The Explanatory Declaration re-emphasizes (thus giving a good understanding of the limits of the Charter) that 'subjective rights shall be respected whereas principles shall be observed'. In seeking to clarify this seeming attempt to distinguish between the textual content of the Charter it continues to note that principles 'become significant for the Courts only when such acts are interpreted or reviewed'. '[T]hey do not give rise to direct claims for positive action by the Union's institutions or Member States authorities.'

Examples are helpfully provided of some of these 'principles'. Article 25, for instance, provides that the 'Union recognises and respects the rights of the elderly to lead a life of dignity and independence and to participate in social and cultural life.' Article 26, declares that 'the right of persons with disabilities to benefit from measures designed to ensure their independence, social and occupational integration and participation in the life of the community' is to be recognized and respected. Article 37, provides that a 'high level of environmental protection and the improvement of the quality of the environment must be integrated into the policies of the Union and ensured in accordance with the principle of sustainable development'.

Of course critics could argue that it is hard to understand why such 'principles' should be included into a Charter of fundamental rights when they are not to be conceived of as rights at all. They might also question the value in seeming to promise 'respect' for a particular social condition whilst ensuring that such promise would only lead to an enforceable claim if further action were taken. They might conclude that the vapidity of a statement that provides no avenue for judicial review in itself was tantamount to a sleight of hand that did discredit to the notion of a putative declaration of rights. However, the presence of rights-related statements, such as those regarding the elderly, the disabled and the environment, do provide a focal point for further EU activity. And, at least as regards the disabled and elderly, when taken with the general prohibition of discrimination, there is recognition of policy goals that might be framed in human rights terms.

This latter interpretation suggests an ambiguity towards the nature of the Charter's contents that has negative as well as positive connotations. If we are seeking clarity in our conception of human rights in the EU then the principle/right device does little to assist. Alternatively, if we wish for an approach towards rights that embraces their aspirational character, and recognizes the practical limits to what might be a desired but currently unattainable condition, then the device identifies where we might strive for further and specific legislation. Does this reflect the well-trodden philosophical difference between perfect and imperfect obligations (the latter suggesting desired results but no commitment—the former legally enforceable duties)? Sen talks freely about the differences suggesting that both fit within the corpus of human rights articulations although producing varying individual and institutional reactions.[60] If that were the motivation then we might be witnessing the development of a conceptual approach to human rights in the EU that is quite sophisticated.

But another interpretation is possible, particularly given the relative lack of theoretical analysis offered by the Union's institutions regarding the Charter. It is that the EU has been unable to construct a viable concept of fundamental rights that would provide sufficient guidance for the institutions to frame a human rights policy. For all the Charter's efforts in providing a working text for the EU, something implicitly acknowledged through the intention to incorporate it into the TCE, it does not produce satisfactory clarity. Perhaps that was always going to be an impossible task but the adoption of a distinction between principle and right certainly gives support to a critical rather than approving stance.

We should not pass over here the recognition that the Charter, with all its ambiguity and imperfections, does *not* represent the sum of the EU's approach to human rights. Internally it may be the fullest expression we have to which the EU is happy to see itself aligned. But externally the Charter remains a very peripheral if not ephemeral document. It does little to frame the activities of the Union in human rights terms. Those Regulations 975 and 976/1999 that determined the scope of activities which may be financially supported by the EU institutions, provide better indicators of the extent to which human rights should be respected. In particular, the EU commits itself to 'promote human rights' rooted in 'the general principles established by the Universal Declaration of Human Rights, the International Covenant on Civil and Political Rights and the International Covenant on Economic, Social and Cultural Rights.'[61] More specifically the activities envisaged include 'support for minorities, ethnic groups and indigenous peoples' that appears at least to cast an eye towards the notion of group rights that the Charter successfully avoids.[62]

---

[60] Sen, *supra* n. 19 at 319.

[61] Paragraph (6) Preamble Council Regulation 976/1999.

[62] The absence of specific minority rights, for instance, prompted significant concern. It is debatable whether the TCE would have resolved this concern through Article I-2 and its reference to respect for minority rights.

On balance therefore the textual discrimination between principle and right and the varying approach to rights adopted in practice between the external and internal realms creates uncertainty about fundamental rights within the Union. The TCE does little if anything to affect this judgement, throwing into question the extent to which this virtue may be observed in the future.

Capacity for evolution

The seriousness with which an institution places respect for human rights is dependent significantly on its capacity or power to fulfil the attendant constitutional promise of change through action. It is all very well to have clear provisions and expressions of intent but if this is to be more than empty rhetoric the words would have to be accompanied by the capacity to act on and evolve both its policies and its human rights understandings.

In this context, we should not be looking merely to a constitutional statement of competence. That might be the point of departure but certainly not of conclusion. Instead an examination of practice would be needed, one that considered processes of norm creation, conflict mediation, and human rights monitoring, promotion and enforcement, all of which would be components of the principle in evolution. The extent to which an institution had forged a competence in practice as well as in law would be a vital matter of structural principle. As a part of this assessment, inevitably an issue for law in the first instance but also for institutional practices that have been adopted that have not been tested as *ultra vires*, we would look to the behaviour of individuals as well as organizations. This might be a matter of anthropological study as well as institutional legal structure.

But what is the cornerstone of the EU's current capacity? Article 6(1) and (2) TEU provide, as already discussed, the basic principle but they do not determine the scope of action available. Here we must split the issue between internal and external matters. In the former, the EU is 'bound' by parameters that are extremely porous. It is fairly common, if contested, ground that the EU has no general power to enact legislation on human rights: Opinion 2/94 determined that.[63] But if we are considering a human rights *policy* the imposition of legislation is not a necessary condition. Gráinne de Búrca has pointed to the need for any human rights regime to possess a normative-judicial capacity, a monitoring capacity and an enforcement capacity.[64] Do such capabilities inhere in the Union?

For the first of these, the normative-judicial, the EU suffers from comparison with other international human rights regimes. Although we have a Court of Justice that is capable of determining whether fundamental rights have been breached either by the EU institutions or the Member States when implementing (or to some degree derogating from) Union law, it has not been assigned the task of deciding the depth and breadth of meaning of any particular human right. Unlike the European Court

---

[63] *Supra* n. 14.
[64] de Búrca *supra* n. 22 at 681–682.

of Human Rights, the ECJ is constrained. It is obligated to consider rights in the context of their construction through other means, namely international instruments (particularly but not exclusively the European Convention on Human Rights) and the constitutional traditions of the Member States.[65] It has little capacity to explore how these rights might be evolved in the context of the EU's socio-political environment.

Similarly, the EU currently possesses no coherent structure for exploring the boundaries of human rights meanings. It does not possess a commission provided with a proactive mandate enabling a thematic or even geographic focus on any particular rights issue. There is nothing to match the United Nations Commission for Human Rights structure that overseas a *rapporteur* and working group system. The EU only has limited capacity to instigate investigations into allegations of human rights abuses and has little in the way of a framework for the examination and discussion of the meaning of human rights in general or in particular. When compared with the proposed requirements for national human rights institutions advocated by the UN's General Assembly Resolution on National Institutions for the Promotion and Protection of Human Rights,[66] the EU appears to preside over an incoherent and chaotic number of disparate initiatives. So we have, for instance, the EU Monitoring Centre on Racism and Xenophobia, which may well have undertaken some monitoring tasks regarding racism and xenophobia in EU Member States but which has been battling to make any meaningful impression upon the understanding of the phenomena or induce a change in either institutional or social response to these serious matters of human rights abuse.[67]

We also have such bodies as the Network of Experts on Fundamental Rights, created by the Commission as an independent actor, and the Parliamentary Committee on Civil Liberties. Both undertake a monitoring function although the former has also begun to address thematic issues.[68] Similarly, in the external realm we have various departments of the Commission applying their minds to human rights matters. Throughout there is no sense of a fully recognized institutional construction *capable* of coping with (re-)definition or (re-)examination of human rights in any context.

Would the virtue of capacity to evolve human rights have been enhanced by the TCE proposals? Certainly the accession to the ECHR would have exposed the EU

[65] Article 6(2) now enshrines this criteria developed initially through case law ECJ.

[66] UN GA Res 48/134 1993.

[67] One only has to look at the way in which the Eurobarometer and the European Social Survey of 2003 record public attitudes to those of other races and we can see the depth of the problem. More than 20% of respondents in the original 15 Member States prior to enlargement 'favoured repatriation for legal migrants'. More than 50% perceived a 'collective ethnic threat'. See Eurobarometer 2003 as well as the EUMC's Annual Report 2005 available at http://eumc.eu.int/eumc/material/pub/ar05/AR05_p2_EN.pdf and more specifically *Policing Racist Crime and Violence Report* 2005 available at http://eumc.eu.int/eumc/material/pub/PRCV/PRCV-Final.pdf.

[68] It has done so through the issuance of opinions. See http://europa.eu.int/comm/justice_home/cfr_cdf/list_opinions_en.htm for details.

institutions to the direct gaze of the European Court of Human Rights, a body much more used to developing human rights notions than the ECJ. But would it have caused the EU to embrace in any meaningful way the work of the Council of Europe and its various human rights related committees? No fusion between the two great European institutions would have taken place, and it is unlikely that the EU could have assumed the work of such bodies as the Committee of Experts for the Development of Human Rights and its siblings as well as more generally the Steering Committee for Human Rights in any of its own work. Rhetorical acknowledgement of such discursive adventures as the call for 'freedom from poverty' to be labelled a 'right'[69] and the more intrusive actions regarding the prevention of torture[70] and the protection of national minorities[71] were possible before the TCE. Accession would have done nothing to change that state of affairs. It would certainly not have revolutionalized the EU's ability to contemplate the future of human rights within its domain. Nor would it have settled the greater charge of incoherence levelled by Philip Allott against the EU. He maintained that there 'is no integrative concept at the Community level to resolve [the] multiplicities and divergences' that arise from the simultaneous operation of the national, ECHR and the EU's human rights regimes.[72] By acceding to the ECHR this environment would not have been simplified. If anything it may have complicated the position.

Perhaps then a Fundamental Rights Agency would be able to act as a conduit for effective evolution? Much will depend, however, on its willingness to act as a proactive institution, one determined to progress beyond a role as a repository for human rights data and one able to influence the EU institutions and Member States alike.

In conclusion, therefore, it is difficult to believe that the EU has assumed a capacity to evolve human rights understandings within its own domain. This might be a conscious choice given a possible desire not to intrude on such a task otherwise within the scope of the Member States or the Council of Europe or conceivably the UN human rights organs. But there are sufficient examples to suggest that the EU does not wish to be so constrained. Its work at the UN (notably regarding the right to development), its interests in equality, its involvement in social policy, all speak to a willingness for the EU to adopt a proactive position vis-à-vis human rights evolution. But what is lacking is coherence in this endeavour, something the FRA may or may not resolve.

---

[69] See Message from the Council of Europe Deputy Secretary General on the occasion of the World Day to Overcome Extreme Poverty, 17 October 2005 at http://www.coe.int/T/E/Com/Files/Events/2005–10-misere/20051017_disc_sga.asp

[70] Under the European Convention on the Prevention of Torture 1987.

[71] See the Framework Convention for the Protection of National Minorities 1995.

[72] Philip Allott, 'Epilogue: Europe and the Dream of Reason' in J.H.H. Weiler & Marlene Wind (eds) *European Constitutionalism Beyond the State* (Cambridge: Cambridge University Press, 2003) 202–225 at 217.

Executive Virtues

Onora O'Neill describes executive virtues as 'manifested in deciding on, controlling and guiding action, policies and practices of all sorts'.[73] On the face of it this would suggest matters of governance. However, they should be seen as distinct from those covered by my previous category. They speak more to a *style* of governance, the character of the agents, rather than the substance of governance. O'Neill calls this the 'means to [effective] action'.[74] So, she identifies 'self-control', 'decisiveness', 'courage', 'endurance', 'efficiency', 'carefulness', and 'accuracy' as representative of executive virtues, matters that traditionally have more personal than institutional connotation. In terms of those fundamental facets of human rights work, in other words norm creation, monitoring and enforcement, they do take on an institutional relevance. It is the extent to which the EU displays these traits, or enables them to flourish, replicating personal qualities in the collective realm, which might contribute to our determination of the depth of commitment to respect human rights.

We can say at the outset that there is an institutional recognition that such traits are appropriate in its assessment of external regimes. An 'effective executive enforcing the law' is a specific requirement of the Commission when examining third states and their observance of good governance criteria.[75] Similarly, an 'effective and accessible means of legal recourse' in the face of human rights violation is seen as a prerequisite.[76] A legitimized system for monitoring governance and the enhancement of the capacity of officials to protect human rights are specifically deemed suitable for 'consolidating democracy' and respecting human rights.[77]

Given the acceptance of these executive virtues we might ask how they could be, or are, applicable to the EU itself?[78] Two particular areas are dealt with below: the capacity for enforcement and transparency in decision-making.

Capacity for enforcement

Do we have an effective executive enforcing the law of human rights in the EU? Fundamentally this is absent, perhaps significantly, because we do not have in place a certain list of human rights and because there has been either unwillingness for or incapacity of EU institutions to take on the role of enforcer. Any such self-assessment is always problematic, of course, but can we point to any agency that

---

[73] O'Neill *supra* n. 47 at 187.

[74] Ibid. O'Neill qualifies the phrase to include 'effective' without addressing the subjective nature of the meaning of 'effective'.

[75] Commission Communication to the Council and Parliament 1998 COM (98) 146.

[76] Ibid.

[77] Ibid.

[78] I have avoided any consideration of external enforcement in this regard. As we are concerned with the commitment to *respect* human rights it would be strange to rely upon an external policing role as somehow obviating the need to judge the EU's internal approach as a primary issue. There is an argument that the external dimension speaks to the EU's global commitment to human rights and this should not be ignored but it remains a subsidiary ethical question here.

might assume such a role? Similarly, do we have an executive that sees to the enforcement of human rights in the Member States?

As regards the actions of the EU institutions a number of institutional safeguards have emerged. The European Ombudsman provides an avenue for some recourse in relation to the administrative failings of the institutions. But to regard it as at the forefront of ensuring the respect of fundamental rights would be stretching the argument too far. At an individual level such action is of course not to be underestimated. But it is superficial when considered in relation to the totality of possible human rights interference, promotion, scrutiny, enforcement that might accompany an institution of the scope and power of the EU. We need to look further therefore.

The Commission is the obvious place to start. But even the most optimistic reviews of the Commission's human rights enforcement activities would have to recognize the bias placed on attention to the external rather than internal realm. Unlikely to pursue any strategy against itself, without the powers to challenge the actions of the Council, the Commission is reduced to self-assessment, at least at a pre-legislative stage. The advent of impact assessment, scrutinizing proposals to ensure that any violation of human rights might be kept to a necessary minimum, indicates a willingness to pre-empt criticism.[79] Similarly, the adoption of a process of mainstreaming human rights suggests a determination to make the respect for rights central to everything the Commission instigates.[80] But these are matters of prevention rather than enforcement. Although they may be praised for advancing the status of human rights, they do not qualify as an 'effective' executive *enforcement* of the law. Rather they only qualify as safeguards in relation to future legislation. They are not designed to deal with institutional practice.

Similarly, there is precious little evidence that the executive will enforce against the Member States. Although, the ECJ offers a route for challenging states when they breach human rights in the enactment of EU law, such activity is rare and largely to be avoided by all concerned. Even for a subject as raw and crucial to the EU's moral standing as anti-racism legislation, the process adopted is either slow (in the case of forcing Member States to enact the Racial Equality Directive[81]) or non-existent (in the case of failure by a significant number of Member States to address the issue of race discrimination in a coherent and meaningful way[82]).

---

[79] See Commission Communication 'Compliance with the Charter of Fundamental Rights in Commission legislative proposals: Methodology for Systematic and Rigorous Monitoring' COM(2005)172.

[80] For a review of this strategy, see De Schutter, 'Mainstreaming Human Rights in the European Union' in Philip Alston and De Schutter (eds) *Monitoring Fundamental Rights in the EU* (Oxford: Hart, 2005) 37–72.

[81] Report on the protection of minorities and anti-discrimination policies in an enlarged Europe A6–0140/2005FINAL(2005/2008(INI)) Committee on Civil Liberties, Justice and Home Affairs *The shortcomings in the Member States' responses to the measures based on Article 13 TEC.*

[82] See EUMC Annual Report 2005 which points to many instances of Member State failure in this regard. The report is available at http://eumc.eu.int/eumc/material/pub/ar05/AR05_p2_EN.pdf

The relative lack of practical enforcement possibilities available to the executive caused some to identify the enactment of Article 7 TEU in the Amsterdam Treaty and its subsequent amendment at Nice, as a significant opportunity to fill that gap.[83] The insertion of this provision instituted a mechanism for enforcing, *inter alia*, the principle of respect for human rights should any Member State appear about to or actually contravene seriously and persistently that principle. Alston and Weiler commented after the Amsterdam Treaty that there was a need to develop the methodology and guidelines for dealing with such circumstances to avoid 'leaving the provision as a virtual dead-letter to be resuscitated only after a crisis has erupted'.[84] Although the Commission has attempted to create such guidelines with its Communication to the Council and the Parliament,[85] the initiative has stalled. First, the Council has failed to reply to the Commission's proposals and second, the creation of a Fundamental Rights Agency (FRA) *does not* incorporate within its remit any ongoing review of Member States for the purposes of Article 7 monitoring. Thus, although the Preparatory Study for the Impact Assessment on the FRA noted the argument that 'given the seriousness of implications of evoking Article 7 procedures, the basis for [identifying events attracting concern] should be a regular, systematic and independent monitoring of respect for common values in all Member States'[86] and suggested that 'an Agency capable of providing the Council with reliable, systematic and independent information relating to common values and fundamental rights would be useful'[87] the final Impact Assessment made clear that a limited remit for the FRA was preferred.[88] It suggested that the cost would be excessive to police Article 7 conditions. It preferred to rely upon an understanding that any Article 7 'crisis would be identified without any specific mechanisms at the EU level'.[89] The hope, therefore, that consistent institutional monitoring of Member States' human rights records as a means of persuasive enforcement would be embraced by the EU has been severely undermined.

The impact of this decision has been to reduce the opportunities for the EU to transform its current enforcement capacities. The diplomatic and political pressure

[83] See for instance, Madeleine Colvin and Peter Noorlander, 'Human Rights and Accountability after the Treaty of Amsterdam' 2 *EHRLR* (1998) 191–203.

[84] Alston and Weiler, 'An "Ever Closer Union" in Need of a Human Rights Policy' in Alston *supra* n. 4 3–66 at 40.

[85] Communication form the Commission to the Council and the European Parliament on Article 7 of the Treaty on European Union: Respect for and promotion of the values on which the Union is based; COM (2003) 606 final.

[86] Preparatory Study for Impact Assessment and Ex-ante Evaluation of Fundamental Rights Agency, February 2005 at 42.

[87] Ibid at 43.

[88] Commission Staff Working Paper Impact Assessment Report 30 June 2005 COM (2005) 280 final.

[89] See http://europa.eu.int/comm/justice_home/fsj/rights/fsj_rights_agency_en.htm for details of the public consultation undertaken. Details of the Impact Assessment are available at http://europa.eu.int/comm/justice_home/doc_centre/rights/doc/sec_2005_849_en.pdf

that would have been possible through an FRA able to monitor the Member States' human rights records, would have presented this executive virtue as considerably well-developed.[90] Similarly, the decision not to provide the new FRA with any powers of enforcement for itself suggests that matters of enforcement directed at the Member States are going to remain at a relatively low level. Instead we will have another institution that is highly unlikely to contribute to the effective enforcement of the law of human rights. It will follow the pattern set by its predecessor, the EUMC, which was the subject of previous criticism for its failure to come to grips with its tasks in an efficient manner.

Is it too harsh to say, therefore, that the EU does not and will not value the virtue of effective human rights enforcement within its own borders and through its own measures? We know the political constraints that have guided the legal response to enforcement; states are exposed to existing domestic and international systems that do enough to protect human rights and do not require another organization such as the EU interfering in these matters. Although this argument is generally approved by the EU institutions it is subject to marginal qualification. Processes have been instituted that might suggest an attempt to redeem the relative absence of this virtue of capacity for enforcement. A brief review will give a flavour of the extent to which this is effective.

First, one might point to the Network of Experts on Fundamental Rights as an example of enforcement through scrutiny. But how long will this initiative last? The creation of a FRA has been mooted as rendering the Network redundant, an odd conclusion given that the Network's current remit is to consider the human rights behaviour of both the institutions and the Member States even when the latter are not implementing EU law. Indeed, the Network has seen its role as acting as something of an early warning system in Article 7 terms. Its incorporation within the FRA would have the likely effect of removing its broader concerns and focusing its work (assuming it even survives such incorporation) on the FRA's more restricted terms of reference. If this does not happen then there is some hope that the Network will provide something of a monitoring service that encompasses all aspects of human rights within the Union. That it does not have the resources to do this effectively or comprehensively, and that there are few if any methods by which its findings can lead to greater enforcement certainly tells against its overall ability to shoulder the enforcement processes within the EU. But it could be the basis of virtue realization in the future, depending on the support it received.

Outside the Network there remains limited scope for effective enforcement as part of the EU's remit. Of course, one has to acknowledge that the political opposition to the EU being involved in enforcement *per se* is acute. By pointing to the other existing international and domestic means of securing peoples rights within the Member States, a case has been made to preclude intervention by any

---

[90] For a review of Article 7 TEU and the FRA, see Andrew Williams, 'The Indifferent Gesture; Article 7 TEU, the Fundamental Rights Agency and the UK's Invasion of Iraq' 31(1) *ELR* 3–27.

other body, least of all one supported or operated by the EU. The argument against creating yet another level of assessment has been strongly put by Armin von Bogdandy.[91] If correct, this view ensures that the EU will always struggle to convince as an institution that ensures effective enforcement of human rights.

Transparency

Do we need transparency in decision-making in relation to human rights measures? Is all we require an end result that accords with our perceptions of justice as perhaps determined by competent courts charged with the protection of an established body of norms? Ethically it is not clear whether transparency in this respect is a virtue or not. Some have argued that it should be considered a central 'value' of public law but perhaps we do not have to go this far in order to identify transparency as a quality worthy of note in assessing the depth of respect for human rights.[92]

Nonetheless, if we followed Amartya Sen, transparency should be a condition of human rights in so far as it enables any reviewer to determine whether choices made between competing rights or interests are done so 'sensibly' and 'reasonably'.[93] In other words judgements (made in the name of human rights) and the processes by which they are reached should be open to scrutiny. Thus, so the argument might go, it is possible to review reasoning and the means by which interests are weighed against each other in order to demonstrate that justice is being done.

Such a perspective is echoed by the EU. Article 255 EC Treaty (as introduced in the Treaty of Amsterdam) established the individual's right to documentation produced by the Parliament, Council and Commission. Subsequent regulations have specified the extent to which this obligation should be met by the Council, Commission and Parliament.[94] The TCE sought to reinforce this benefit. Article I-46(2) committed the institutions to 'maintain an open, transparent and regular dialogue with representative associations and civil society'.[95] Article I-49 went further to suggest that 'in order to promote good governance and ensure the participation of civil society, the Union institutions, bodies, offices and agencies shall conduct their work as openly as possible'. Interestingly this notion of good governance had already been well established in the EU's external requirements when dealing with developing states, in so far as 'transparent and accountable management' was expected of states who wished to receive the largesse of the Union.[96] Although no doubt considered in terms of the management of public

---

[91] Armin von Bogdandy, 'The European Union as a Human Rights Organization? Human Rights and the Core of the European Union' 37 *CML Rev* (2000) 1307–1338.

[92] Peter Cane has suggested transparency is a value to be aspired to in public law terms but Paul Craig argues against such an elevation. For a review of this argument in the UK, see Martin Loughlin 'Theories and Values in Public Law: An Interpretation' *Public Law* (2005) 48–66.

[93] Sen *supra* n. 19.

[94] Regulation 1049/2001.

[95] This aspect is covered in more detail later under the virtue of participation.

[96] Commission Communication to the Council and Parliament 1998 COM (98) 146.

resources, it takes little imagination to apply that condition to human rights-related decisions, many of which will have considerable bearing over the allocation of public funds and in making choices in government policy.

The question then is to what extent the EU is embracing this need for transparency with regard to its human rights practices? Although several initiatives suggest heavy reference to this quality, scepticism must intervene. We may well have the rhetoric and legislation of transparency related to the technical availability of documentation on the internet but to what extent are the *means* by which decisions are reached, made public?

The matter has received explicit attention recently through the Commission's communication on attaining compliance with the EU Charter of Fundamental Rights in its legislative proposals.[97] A most significant development in this respect is the introduction of impact assessments and explanatory memoranda as a way of assessing that compliance. For here is a method for intensive review of the possible implications, from a human rights perspective in part, of any Commission prompted legislation. The results of such reviews are published and therefore can be scrutinized to determine the extent to which human rights considerations have been addressed. Thus, matters of human rights importance might be made transparent suggesting a willingness to make this virtue a vital aspect of the Union's human rights activities.[98]

But how does this operate in practice? Although there has been an upsurge in the availability of documentation, including minutes of meetings and notes that might shed light on particular decisions, there is no specific requirement (other than that which might follow a decision that could affect an individual directly, in which case the requirements of Article 6 ECHR and the right to fair trial might apply) to provide the reasons for any decision. Indeed, should such disclosure be considered to 'seriously undermine the institution's decision-making process' then it will not be provided to the public.[99] The issue then is transparency of reasoning rather than transparency of documentation.

An extremely apt demonstration of this is happily available to us. The impact assessment for the proposal to construct a Fundamental Rights Agency (FRA) one would think might provide an exemplar from which one can discern the scope of commitment to transparency in human rights matters.[100] On the face of it, there is clear indication of a willingness to make public the means by which the final form of the FRA was determined. Reports were provided of the public consultation

[97] Commission Communication 'Compliance with the Charter of Fundamental Rights in Commission legislative proposals: Methodology for Systematic and Rigorous Monitoring' COM(2005)172.

[98] For a comprehensive review of this strategy see Helen Toner, 'Impact Assessments and Fundamental Rights Protection in EU Law' (2006) 31(3) *ELR* 316–341.

[99] Regulation 1049/2001, Art 4(3).

[100] See http://europa.eu.int/comm/justice_home/fsj/rights/fsj_rights_agency_en.htm for details of the public consultation undertaken. Details of the Impact Assessment are available at http://europa.eu.int/comm/justice_home/doc_centre/rights/doc/sec_2005_849_en.pdf.

launched in 2004 and the views expressed by a wide range of interested parties from NGOs to the Member States. Interestingly, however, on matters of decision the tendency to be less than open manifests itself. Although the Impact Assessment Report referred to the 'divergent views' in relation to the proposal that the FRA should be given monitoring status for the purposes of Article 7 TEU, the final decision to accept the 'prudent' views of the Member States, rather than the more bullish stance of NGOs, was accompanied by no explanation of why the former should hold sway. Despite the fact that 'shortcomings in EU screening mechanisms for the purposes of Article 7' were identified as one of the 'possible problems and needs of observing fundamental rights in the Union'[101] (thus giving rise to the desire for a monitoring Agency in the first place) no detailed analysis of the rationale for avoiding Article 7 scrutiny was provided. Of course, at some stage a decision would have had to have been made. But the key aspect of transparency of reasoning is that it necessitates providing not only the details of the issues that are the subject of judgement but also details of the reasoning deployed to choose one course rather than any other. Such is the implicit requirement, I suggest, lying behind O'Neill's sense of 'practical judgement' referred to previously.

In this sense, transparency has to involve a greater commitment to openness than demonstrated by merely making documentation accessible. As Joseph Stiglitz has suggested the 'basic right to know, to be informed about what the government is doing *and why*' (emphasis added) is of fundamental importance.[102] At present the political nature ascribed to human rights decisions that involve Member States seem to reside in the field of politically sensitive issues. Paradoxically, this makes understandable reasoning more important and less easy to access at the same time. Such a condition currently affects the Union in its human rights dealings but, as Francesca Bignami suggests, 'the negotiations and political deals . . . are coming under pressure, albeit still limited, from the European right to transparency'.[103] The problem is that the pressure is mainly directed against limited targets. How meaningful, for instance, is the urge to tackle transparency in those areas that affect the wider constituency, in lobbying processes by corporations, in the Union's dealings with third states? The EU's activities in these fields may well have significant human rights impacts but the willingness to provide reasons for any specific decision, and perhaps more poignantly the failure to make a decision, remains elusive.

Justice Virtues

It could well be said that the greatest test for determining the depth of the EU's commitment to respect human rights lies in its pursuit of justice. But what does

[101] Impact assessment p. 5.

[102] Joseph Stiglitz, 'On Liberty, the Right to Know, and Public Discourse: The Role of Transparency in Public Life' in Matthew J. Gibney (ed) *Globalizing Rights* (Oxford: OUP, 2003) 115–156 at 115.

[103] Francesca Bignami, 'Creating European Rights: National Values and Suprantional Interests' 2005 Duke Law School Working Paper Series available at http://lsr.nellco.org/duke/fs/papers/2 at 64.

justice mean in this context? If we simply use the term as a euphemism for 'respect for human rights' our search for suitable evaluative criteria will be largely circular and thus redundant. Where else then should we look? O'Neill provides some limited help when she outlines a basic vision of justice virtues that might be applicable to institutions as well as individuals. Even then her first virtue is 'justice itself'.[104] In the context of the EU we perhaps therefore need to construct a relevant under-standing of justice that is both *of* human rights and *for* human rights.[105] In other words, we are looking to evaluate an institution that pursues the 'aims' of human rights and does so in a manner consistent with human rights norms. O'Neill admittedly touches upon some of these when she continues to list 'justice virtues' to include 'varied forms of fairness, of toleration and respect for others, of fidelity and probity, and of truthfulness and honesty'.[106] Such traits are often difficult to translate to such a complex institutional construct as the EU but certain basic elements can be extracted. These I have listed in *figure 1* as including tolerance and non-discrimination, participatory processes, access to justice for citizens or other injured parties, consistent application of standards, certainty of application, and accountability. Again these demand greater attention than is possible within this chapter. Nonetheless, I have chosen to highlight one that warrants particular attention; namely participation.

So, to what extent can the virtue of participation be relevant to respect for human rights? The starting point for answering this question is to recognize the clear link-age between freedoms of expression and association (as well as the right 'to take part in the conduct of public affairs')[107] to contemporary notions of participation in public governance. But this is a very textual rights-based approach that relies on established limitations to participatory processes, limitations fixed by the standard human rights instruments. Perhaps ironically these fail to cope with a fuller sense of justice implied by wider visions of participation. We can think here perhaps of Sen's idea of democratic structures that create a dialogue of human rights,[108] or indeed a Habermasian 'legal institutionalization of citizens' communication', a 'communicative context' that may be formed through 'a civil society encompassing interest associations, nongovernmental organizations, citizens' movements etc'[109] to take two examples. In these contexts, we can excavate a notion of 'civic virtue' that might conceivably warrant public participation with fewer restrictions, encompass-ing debate *and* decision-making within the EU. These are the additional dimensions that set the possible parameters for the virtue of participation.

[104] O'Neill *supra* n. 47 at 187.

[105] This echoes Upendra Baxi's politics *of* and politics *for* human rights in his *The Future of Human Rights* (New Delhi: OUP, 2002).

[106] O'Neill *supra* n. 47 at 187.

[107] Article 25 International Covenant on Civil and Political Rights 1966.

[108] Sen *supra* n. 19.

[109] Jurgen Habermas 'Does Europe Need a Constitution?' in *The Inclusion of the Other: Studies in Political Theory* (London: Polity Press, 1999) 155–161 at 160.

My immediate concern then is not to examine the depth to which the Union respects any right, howsoever defined, associated with participation. Such evaluation, as with all articulated rights in the EU context, is a necessary endeavour. But of prior interest is the nature of participation as a virtue rather than a specific and severable right. To this end we might consider two further dimensions of participation in relation specifically to human rights matters. First, the deliberative dimension, whereby consultation with a wider constituency than that related to bureaucratic or political creatures. Second, the emancipatory, more radical in nature that points to people's active involvement in the creation, development and fulfilment of human rights.

Referring to these dimensions should not be taken as suggesting that the EU *should* or even could embrace such participatory manifestations. Rather it is to describe the possible scope of the concept and thus provide a gauge for determining how far along the participation route the EU has been willing to go in human rights related matters.

So looking to these possible dimensions, we can point to the emerging determination of the Commission to engage in 'dialogue' with civil society.[110] We can point to Article I-47 TCE as setting the basis for a constitutional principle of participatory democracy by giving 'citizens and representative associations the opportunity to make known and publicly exchange their views on all areas of Union action'. And we can point to the willingness to involve civil society in human rights norm creation through consultation processes.[111] The involvement of NGOs in decision-making and, more generally, public consultation are the hallmarks of this approach. These can be taken in turn.

The Commission's discussion paper on 'the Commission and Non-Governmental Organisations: Building a Stronger Partnership'[112] in 2000 signalled the intention to enable NGOs to become more involved in EU work, including the human rights field. This was for the stated purposes of strengthening participatory democracy, ensuring the representation of the views of specific groups of 'citizens', and allowing NGOs to contribute to policy-making, project management and 'European integration'.[113] Such bold aims recognize the importance of acquiring some kind of public acceptance of the EU's actions generally as well as specifically in human rights matters. However, it is not open-ended. The Commission recognized that not all

---

[110] For a comprehensive review of this tendency see Francesca Bignami *supra* n. 99.

[111] I am thinking here of the process by which the EU Charter on Fundamental Rights came into being. However, I would exclude the Convention for the future of Europe, at least with regard to human rights, given that the Working Group which set the task of reviewing the role of human rights in a future constitution was precluded from re-opening the substance of the rights in the Charter. For a critique of this latter process, see Andrew Williams, 'EU Human Rights Policy and the Convention on the Future of Europe: a Failure of Design?' 6 *ELR* (2003) 794–813.

[112] COM (2000) 11, http://europa.eu.int/comm/secretariat_general/sgc/ong/docs/communication_en.pdf accessed 9 October 2005.

[113] Ibid.

such organizations had the *right* to participate in its decision-making processes. Some kind of selection was necessary during which attention would be paid to each NGO's 'structure and membership', the 'transparency of their organization and the way they work', any 'previous participation in committees and working groups', their 'track record as regards competence to advise in any specific field', and 'their capacity to work as a catalyst for exchange of information and opinions between the Commission and the citizens'.[114] As the Commission stated, '[i]t is important for NGOs and groupings of NGOs to be democratic and transparent as regards their membership and claims to representiveness.'[115] Thus, the Commission 'encourages organisations to work together in common associations and networks at the European level since such organisations considerably facilitate the efficiency of the consultation process.'[116] Many would accept such limitations as necessary for the efficient construction of dialogic processes. But one must question the degree to which it leads to the institutionalization of public deliberation, allowing established and 'acceptable' NGOs into the decision-making fold, as it were, whilst casting doubt on those less formalized groupings that do not appear to have the resources to act as a 'catalyst' for the Commission. Clearly this cries out for in-depth research into the role of NGOs in human rights matters, a study that to my knowledge has yet to be undertaken. In the meantime although we might applaud the intentions we have to wait and see how deep the commitment to dialogue becomes.

If we then turn to consultation we encounter more concerns about the depth to which the virtue of participation is realized. Undoubtedly there is now a commitment to imbed consultation into the workings of the EU. The Commission's initiative 'Your Voice in Europe' may have the feeling of a gimmick but it does record the broader approach to consultation that has developed over the last 10 years.[117] How deep this is needs to be considered, albeit briefly.

Let us therefore take the example of development policy. Here we have a policy area that regularly undergoes review by the EU in order to assess priorities and practices. In 2005 such a review was commenced with a consultation procedure. Three methods were employed: '(a) an internal dialogue within the Commission and between the Commission and key players in the EU policy making cycle (ie, Member States, European Parliament, Economic and Social Committee); (b) a series of meetings and workshops with other stakeholders (eg, civil society, governments, academia, social partners); and (c) an 'electronic debate centred on an online questionnaire'.[118]

[114] Ibid.

[115] Ibid at 9.

[116] Ibid at 9.

[117] See 'Your Voice in Europe' website at http://europa.eu.int/yourvoice/index_en.htm

[118] EC Commission Report on the Public Consultation Procedure on the Future of EU development Policy 2005 at 4, available at http://europa.eu.int/comm/development/body/tmp_docs/consultation_report_en.pdf#zoom=100.

The Commission may well have worked hard to engender some interest in the process and used various lines of communication to provoke a response. But the inevitable target of these procedures could only be the upper echelons of those societies addressed. Simply placing the paper on the internet and then sending many emails to organizations thought to be interested could never reach the wider constituency.[119] The fact that the process only provoked 346 responses indicates the massive dislocation of those affected and those reached.

But what could one expect? Surely it would be impossible to access the millions if not billions of people who might be the subject of the development policy that the EU eventually adopts. The impoverished are just too numerous to include in such deliberations. Besides, the policy represents an ethical decision for the Union *not* the recipients of any aid or trade relationships. Or at least these might be the responses advanced by realists. But what if we recall that the virtue of participation has been identified as one related to 'justice'? Does this change the perspective? Does this imply greater attention to the aims of participation rather than its means?

If justice is the determining factor in participation then of course we must have a reasonable idea of what we mean by justice. Certainly, this might change depending on the policy area involved. Let us return to development policy as our example. The Commission suggested that consultation was, in part, to take soundings on what should be the objectives of this policy. The Issues Paper that provided the focus for comment identified a number of possibilities, including the eradication of poverty and meeting the aims of the Millennium Declaration (which is slightly tautological given that the eradication of poverty is the primary aim of the Declaration).[120] This is a matter of justice, global justice if preferred but justice nonetheless. In such a context, has sufficient attention been paid to more active participatory methods, those which might actually give some sense of 'justice' to the notion of participation that my identification of it as a virtue would suggest? Ironically, one of the issues raised in the Issues Paper was the matter of ownership and participation, particularly with a view to help 'promote bottom-up development approaches'.[121] This on the back of an acknowledgement by the Commission that 'Civil Society participation in the development process facilitates the overarching poverty reduction objective.'[122] Similarly, the Commission has recommended

---

[119] Ibid at 24. The Consultation Paper reflected respondents who criticized the process on the grounds that, (a) it was too short in duration (60 days); (b) the debate was limited; and (c) the use of a questionnaire was too rigid. Such criticism did not seem to suggest to the Commission, however, that the process was flawed in any way.

[120] See Consultation on the Future of EU Development Policy Issues Paper 7/1/2005 available at http://europa.eu.int/comm/development/body/theme/consultation/doc/Issues_Paper_EN.pdf#zoom=100

[121] Ibid at 11.

[122] See Commission 'Guidelines on Principles and Good Practices for the Participation of Non-State Actors in the development dialogues and consultations' 2004 available at http://europa.eu.int/comm/development/body/organisation/docs/guidelines_principles_good_practices_en.pdf#zoom=100 at 5.

that 'special attention should be given to small and grassroots organizations' in any consultation or dialogue that is organized.[123] Given this recognition it is surprising that the overall policy consultation should be so weak in this respect. This might lead us to question both the understanding that underlies the principle of participation as well as the EU's commitment to it.

Any identification of participation with justice, as I propose, would therefore necessitate a theoretical engagement with both concepts. We may well look to a practical rationalization for participation (as the best means of achieving acceptance of a policy or particular project) but this might not suffice when faced with complex circumstances that require amendments to standard processes. For instance, a determination to engage with civil society does not alone take into account structures of inequality that might undermine the principle of participation. Gender distortions in certain dialogues with established social patriarchal structures are a case in point already recognized in development discourse and eventually adopted by the EU in project and policy construction.[124] Other differentiating factors, however, do not necessarily receive the same attention: language, race, class, caste, minority status, and access to resources (or poverty) all will be negative influences for any participatory process if not addressed, making it not only flawed but even a contributor to inequality. By adopting a consultation process that favours advanced technologies, meetings of invited groups, and time limits that are extremely short, it seems unlikely that the prospect of such contribution to injustice can be removed.

Nonetheless, we must acknowledge that the Union is at least aware of some of the justice implications of participation. We can see that it is attempting to institute processes that do some justice to that virtue. But what is still missing is a coherent policy *and* theory of participation for both internal and external constituencies, particularly in human rights matters. In the external realm it is difficult to see a meaningful engagement with what Santos calls 'the right to create rights'.[125] As he warns, '[i]nadequate representation or even exclusion from membership, lack of meaningful political participation, repression of organization and demobilization are different dimensions of the same deficit of democracy that foster the violations of human rights and guarantee their impunity.'[126] The Union does not have the best record with regard to such a deficit and a failure to treat participation seriously and sensitively will continue to reinforce that reputation rather than change it.

---

[123] Ibid at 11.

[124] Many critiques of participatory development practices appear in B. Cooke and U. Kothari (eds), *Participation: the New Tyranny?* (London: Zed Books 2001).

[125] Boaventura de Sousa Santos *Towards a New Legal Common Sense* 2nd edition (London: Butterworths, 2002) 300–301. Note the fact that in foreign and security policy and in enlargement, areas with significant human rights considerations, no consultations have been publicized, indicating the limited acknowledgement of the scope of participation.

[126] Ibid at 301.

CONCLUSION

Where once there was silence there is now cacophony. Human or fundamental rights feature across the Union's landscape impacting upon everything it does. At a time when there is still a concern to set the constitutional parameters of the EU there is sore need for a systematic and comprehensive appraisal of its human rights commitment. This chapter has therefore attempted to review the current state of fundamental rights in the EU by suggesting a method for carrying out such a review. Although this might sound unnecessarily tautological my underlying purpose is to talk about human rights in this context by outlining *how* we may talk about them. By first identifying the central principle to be reviewed and then compiling framework criteria for assessing the extent to which that principle has been attained, we will surely be better placed to start the process of making sense of human rights policy in the Union. In adopting this approach I have inevitably provided analysis of some key developments in the EU's human rights practices along the way. Ultimately more work needs to be done, particularly now that the Constitutional Treaty is moribund if not dead. The absence of a constitutional text that embraces many human rights aspects, as I have shown, means that the analysis I propose becomes even more urgent. A failure to deploy a systematic review of both principle and virtue is likely to miss subjecting the EU's activities in this area to critique and thus understanding the nature of the human rights regime now and in the future.

Whatever the outcome of such a review, there is clearly going to be constant revision and re-negotiation of the Union's involvement in human rights for many years to come, if indeed it will or should ever end. The Constitutional Treaty would have clarified some issues but it would have also opened new avenues for policy construction and thus debate. Its burial does not mean that such initiatives will no longer be possible. At the very least it has provided an insight into some of the institutional thinking about the possible direction of the EU's human rights policy. The need to monitor and subject the proposals that will emerge in this area over time is acute.

5

Social Policy Revisited in the Light of the Constitutional Debate

CATHERINE BARNARD
Trinity College

INTRODUCTION

In the beginning there was next to no social policy in the EEC Treaty. By the time of the Constitutional Treaty, social policy had become firmly established as an important dimension of the European Union. The rejection of the Constitutional Treaty by French and Dutch voters, and the long pause for reflection, have inevitably put the Constitutional Treaty on the back burner for the meantime, and possibly forever. However, for the purposes of this book, I should like to argue that the Constitutional Treaty is still significant in terms of its ability to identify just how far the EU has travelled along the path of recognizing the European Union's social face. In this chapter, I shall argue that the paltry social provisions found in the original (misnamed) Title on social policy in the EEC Treaty were broadly justified by market-making ideals of removing distortions of competition and thus prevent social dumping. Only later did market correcting/social justice notions come into play. By contrast, the Constitutional Treaty is more obviously premised on values traditionally associated with social policy, notably human rights, non-discrimination, solidarity and equality. Yet, paradoxically one of the reasons given for the rejection of the Constitutional Treaty, particularly by the French voters, is that the Treaty was perceived as not doing enough to preserve the European social model and to prevent social dumping.

This chapter takes two of the values identified by the Constitutional Treaty—solidarity and equality/non-discrimination—and uses them as a prism through which to examine the extent to which the European Union now has a true 'social' face. The chapter then considers the extent to which the European Union has sought to deal with concerns about social dumping, taking the developments in the field of free movement of services, and the issue of posted workers in particular, as an illustration. However, we begin by examining the social provisions found in the European Economic Community Treaty at the time of its adoption in Rome in 1957 and those in the Treaty establishing a Constitution for Europe adopted in Rome in 2004.

SOCIAL POLICY AND THE ROME TREATIES

The EEC/EC Treaty

The Treaty of Rome

(a) The original treaty provisions
The European Economic Community (EEC) Treaty was primarily about the realization of the four freedoms (goods, person, services and capital). The view was that economic integration—the removal of artificial obstacles to the free movement of labour, goods and capital—would in time ensure the optimum allocation of resources throughout the Community, the optimum rate of economic growth and thus an optimum social system.[1] This would lead, according to the Preamble, to the 'constant improvement of the living and working conditions of their peoples'. So, as the original Article 117 EEC spelled out, an improvement in working conditions would '*ensue* not only from the functioning of the Common Market . . . but also . . . from the approximation of provisions laid down by law, regulation or administrative action'.[2] In other words, improved working conditions would be the consequence of market integration, not a prerequisite to it. Viewed from this perspective, there was little need for the EEC to have a social dimension.

This perspective was shaped by the influential Spaak report,[3] drawn up by the foreign ministers prior to the signing of the Treaty of Rome, which also envisaged only limited action in the social field to ensure the functioning of the Common Market. Spaak, in its turn, relied heavily on the earlier Ohlin report of ILO experts.[4] This report had argued for the transnational harmonization of social policy in some areas, such as equal pay, but, invoking the economic theory of comparative advantage, rejected a general role for harmonization of social policy. It argued that differences in nominal wage costs between countries did not, in themselves, pose an obstacle to economic integration because what mattered was unit labour costs, taking into account the relationship between nominal costs and productivity. Because higher costs tended to accompany higher productivity, differences between countries were less than they seemed. This explained why there was no need for harmonization.

Although opposed to general intervention in the social sphere, the Spaak committee did say that action should be taken to correct or eliminate the effect of specific distortions which advantage or disadvantage certain branches of activity. By way of example, the authors cited a list of areas including working conditions of labour such as the relationship between the salaries of men and women, working

---

[1] Shanks, 'Introductory Article: The Social Policy of the European Community' (1977) 14 *CMLRev.* 14.

[2] Emphasis added.

[3] Rapport des Chefs de Délègations, Comité Intergouvernemental, 21 April 1956, 19–20, 60–1.

[4] International Labour Office, 'Social Aspects of European Economic Cooperation' (1956) 74 *International Labour Review* 99.

time, overtime and paid holidays, and different policies relating for credit. The French government strongly endorsed this view that there was a need for federal intervention in these areas. With its strong legislation on equal pay for men and women, and its more generous rules on paid holidays, France was concerned that the additional costs borne by French industry would make French goods uncompetitive in the Common Market.[5] By contrast, Germany insisted that social policy was a matter for the nation state and would not countenance EEC intervention.

These different perspectives were reflected in the ragbag of provisions contained in the so-called Title on Social Policy. Articles 117 and 118 EEC (new and amended Articles 137 and 140) on the need to improve working conditions and co-operation between states, even if textually broad, were legally shallow, reflecting the Spaak (and also German government) preference for laissez-faire,[6] while Article 119 (new Article 141) on equal pay and Article 120 (new Article 142) on paid holiday schemes and the third protocol on 'Certain Provisions Relating to France' on working hours and overtime,[7] were specific provisions designed to protect French industry.[8]

The essentially protectionist function of these provisions was recognized by Advocate General Dutheillet de Lamothe in *Defrenne (No 1)*.[9] He said that although Article 141 had a social objective it also had an economic objective:

for in creating an obstacle to any attempt at 'social dumping' by means of the use of female labour less well paid than male labour, it helped to achieve one of the fundamental objectives of the common market, the establishment of a system ensuring that 'competition is not distorted'.

He continued that 'This explains why Article [141] of the Treaty is of a different character from the articles which precede it in the chapter of the Treaty devoted to social provisions'.

---

[5] These arguments are considered more fully in Barnard, *EC Employment Law* (3rd edn., OUP, Oxford, 2006), ch. 1.

[6] Forman, 'The Equal Pay Principle under Community Law' (1982) 1 *LIEI* 17.

[7] This provided that the Commission was to authorize France to take protective measures where the establishment of the Common Market did not result, by the end of the first stage, in the basic number of hours beyond which overtime was paid and the average rate of additional payment for overtime industry corresponding to the average obtaining in France in 1956. It does not seem that France has called upon this safeguard clause: Budiner, *Le Droit de la femme l'Égalité de salaire et la Convention No. 100 de l'organisation internationale du travail* (Librairie Générale de Droit et de Jurisprudence, Paris, 1975).

[8] According to the French Advocate General Dutheillet de Lamothe in Case 80/70 *Defrenne (No. 1) v SABENA* [1971] ECR 445, 'It appears to be France which took the initiative, but the article [119] necessitated quite long negotiations'. However, the content of Art. 119 was strongly influenced by ILO Convention No. 100 on equal pay. See Hoskyns, *Integrating Gender* (Verso, London, 1996) and Arnull, *The European Union an its Court of Justice* (OUP, Oxford, 2006), 534–540.

[9] Case 80/70 [1971] ECR 445. In Case 69/80 *Worringham and Humphreys v Lloyd's Bank* [1981] ECR 767, Advocate General Warner again referred back to Advocate General Dutheillet de Lamothe's statement in *Defrenne (No. 1)* that the first purpose of Art. 119 was to 'avoid a situation in which undertakings established in Member States with advanced legislation on the equal treatment of men and women suffer a competitive disadvantage as compared with undertakings established in Member States that have not eliminated discrimination against female workers as regards pay'.

The Court echoed these sentiments in its landmark judgment in *Defrenne (No 2)*[10]:

Article [141] pursues a double aim. *First*, . . . the aim of Article [141] is to avoid a situation in which undertakings established in states which have actually implemented the principle of equal pay suffer a competitive disadvantage in intra-Community competition as compared with undertakings established in states which have not yet eliminated discrimination against women workers as regards pay.

However, having recognized the economic purpose of Article 141, the Court then continued:

Second, this provision forms part of the social objectives of the Community, which is not merely an economic union, but is at the same time intended, by common action to ensure social progress and seek the constant improvement of living and working conditions of their peoples . . . This double aim, which is at once economic and social, shows that the principle of equal pay forms part of the foundations of the Community.

In other words, it was the Court that recognized the 'social' dimension of the social policy provisions, in a way that the original Treaty drafters did not, and the Court has since played a key role in fleshing out the meaning of the social policy provisions and giving them a 'social' as opposed to economic perspective.

(b) The 'social policy' title

Although included in a Title entitled 'social policy', it is in fact misleading to use this terminology to describe the social provisions in the EEC Treaty. The 'social policy' Title made no provision for what is generally agreed to be the central core of social policy: social insurance, public assistance, health and welfare services, education and housing policy.[11] There was also no evidence of the creation of a European welfare state to replace the national welfare states, and certainly no evidence of cradle-to-grave protection. This conception of social policy reflects the social justice/social cohesion or *market correcting*[12] function of social policy. In Marshall's words, social policy involves the use of 'political power to supersede, supplement or modify operations of the economic system in order to achieve results which the economic system would not achieve on its own, . . . guided by values other than those determined by market forces'.[13] These values include the need to redistribute income and resources in order to promote social inclusion and cohesion, thereby

---

[10] Case 43/75 [1976] ECR 455. This was emphasized in Case C-50/96 *Deutsche Telekom v Schröder* [2000] ECR I-743, paras. 53–55.

[11] Majone, 'The European Community: Between Social Policy and Regulation' (1993) 31 *JCMS*. 153, 158.

[12] Streeck, 'From Market Making to State Building? Reflections on the Political Economy of European Social Policy', in Leibfried and Pierson (eds) *European Social Policy: Between Fragmentation and Integration* (Brookings Institution, Washington DC, 1995) 399.

[13] Marshall, *Social Policy* (Hutchinson, London, 1975) 15.

ensuring political stability. This was not the original conception of EC social policy. Rather, in Streeck's words, the Treaty of Rome charged the Community with:

developing *a new kind of social policy*, one concerned with *market making rather than market correcting*, aimed at creating an integrated European labour market and enabling it to function efficiently, rather than with correcting its outcomes in line with political standards of social justice.[14]

In other words, the existing body of EC employment-related social policy represents regulation in support of creating a free or common market to ensure, in the words of Article 96, that the conditions of competition are not distorted. This has been the most influential of the justifications for social policy. The market-making thesis comprises two limbs: first, the creation of a 'European-wide labour market',[15] by removing obstacles to the mobility of workers, and secondly, removing distortions to competition by, on the one hand, seeking to harmonize costs on firms and, on the other, preventing social dumping by firms and a race-to-the-bottom by States.

The expansion of community competence and changes in the method of governance

(a) Changes in the scope of community competence

As is documented elsewhere,[16] subsequent Treaty amendments significantly expanded the Community's competence in the social sphere to include, initially, a broader range of employment matters (for example, health and safety, working conditions, worker representation, unfair dismissal) and then, at Nice, social policy measures in more traditionally 'social' fields such as the combating of social exclusion and the modernization of social protection systems, albeit that only softer measures of policy coordination (improving knowledge, developing exchanges of information and best practices, promoting innovative approaches) were envisaged in these fields. The Nice Treaty restructured and consolidated the social provisions in the EC Treaty, most importantly Article 137, the principal Article in this field. Nevertheless, it is important to emphasize that broader issues of the welfare state (such as healthcare and pensions) still remained firmly outside the scope of the EC's legislative competence and that EC social policy competence, while broader than in 1957 is by no means comprehensive.

(b) Changes in methods of governance

Methods of rule making also changed with successive Treaty amendments. Originally, legislation had to be adopted by the Council acting unanimously; following the amendments introduced by the Single European Act 1986 more measures could

---

[14] Streeck, 'From Market Making to State Building? Reflections on the Political Economy of European Social Policy', in Leibfried and Pierson (eds) above n. 12, 399.

[15] Streeck, above, n. 12, 397.

[16] Barnard, *EC Employment Law*, (3rd edn., Oxford, OUP, 2006), Chs 1–2.

be adopted by qualified majority voting but setting only minimum standards. Maastricht introduced new institutional actors into the legislative process—the social partners (sectoral and intersectoral)—who were permitted to negotiate collective agreements which could be extended to all workers by a Council Directive or which could be implemented by national collective agreement. While there was initial enthusiasm for this method of legislating in the social field, a number of questions have been raised about its legitimacy and about the representativity of the social partners.[17]

Amsterdam witnessed a further reorientation: the shift from the creation of employment law to the creation of employment policy, with the introduction of the Employment Title characterized by its emphasis on intergovernmental cooperation through the open method of coordination (OMC) in the European Employment Strategy (EES). While the epithet OMC was not used by the Amsterdam Treaty, the tools of OMC (guidelines, benchmarking, peer review) were very much to the fore. This was reinforced by the launch of the Lisbon Strategy at the Lisbon summit in March 2000,[18] where the Union set itself a new and ambitious strategic goal 'to become the most competitive and dynamic knowledge-based economy in the world capable of sustainable economic growth with more and better jobs and greater social cohesion'.[19] The strategy has three, mutually interdependent limbs: an economic limb (making the EU more competitive while sustaining a stable economy), an environmental limb (especially sustainable development), and a social limb (modernizing the European social model, investing in people and combating social exclusion).

This strategy was designed to enable the Union to regain 'the conditions for *full employment*' (not just a high level of employment as laid down by Article 2 EC), and 'strengthening regional cohesion in the European Union'. It was to be achieved by 'improving existing processes, introducing a new open method of coordination at all levels coupled with a stronger guiding and coordinating role for the European Council'.[20] The Lisbon Presidency conclusions described the Open Method of Coordination as the means of spreading best practice and achieving greater convergence towards the EU's main goals by helping Member States develop their own policies.[21] In particular, the Lisbon and subsequently Stockholm European Council set the EU the ambitious (unrealistic?) objective of reaching an overall employment

[17] Case T-135/96 *UEAPME* [1998] ECR II-2335.

[18] Presidency Conclusions, 24 March 2000.

[19] Para. 5.

[20] Para. 7. The Commission's social policy agenda goes further. The Commission says that it does not 'seek to harmonise social policies. It seeks to work towards common European objectives and increase coordination of social policies in the context of the internal market and the single currency' (COM(2000)379, 7).

[21] Lisbon European Council, 23 and 24 March 2000, para. 37. See also the definition of OMC offered in the Final report of Working Group XI on Social Europe: 'It is a new form of coordination of national policies consisting of the Member States, at their own initiative or at the initiative of the Commission, defining collectively, within the respect of national and regional diversities, objectives and indicators in a specific area, and allowing those Member States, on the basis of national reports, to improve their knowledge, to develop exchanges of information, views, expertise and practices, and to promote, further to agreed objectives, innovative approaches which could possibly lead to guidelines or recommendations.'

rate of 70 per cent by 2010, an employment rate of over 60 per cent for women and employment rate among older men and women (55–64) of 50 per cent.[22] However, in the 2005 mid-term review of the Lisbon strategy by the Brussels European Council, it was recognized that there were significant delays in reaching these targets, and in the Lisbon relaunch the 2010 deadline is down-played.

The Nice Treaty also gave greater prominence to OMC techniques. While Article 137(1) lists the areas of Community competence, Article 137(2) then details what form action in these fields might be taken. Part (a) provides that the Council may 'adopt measures designed to encourage *co-operation* between Member States . . . excluding any harmonisation of the laws and regulations of the Member States'; the power to adopt Directives appears only in part (b).

(c) Charter of Fundamental Rights
From the perspective of this chapter, by far the most significant development at Nice was the solemn proclamation of the Community Charter of Fundamental Rights which contained, in a single document, the fundamental rights and freedoms and basic procedural rights guaranteed by the European Convention on Human Rights as well as some of the economic and social rights contained in the European Social Charter and the Community Social Charter 1989.[23] It also contained a mixture of rights (essentially a catalogue of individual, negative rights) and principles (which allow for the progressive realization of rights).

The principal provisions relating to 'social matters' can be found in Title III entitled 'Equality'[24] and Title IV, 'Solidarity',[25] although two key rights, the right to freedom of association and of assembly and the freedom to choose an occupation and right to engage in work, are found in Title II 'Freedoms' and the prohibition of slavery and forced labour is found in Title I, 'Dignity'. The provisions in these chapters are essentially about rights in the classic sense of the word but, especially in the solidarity Title, the rights are carefully delimited by reference to national and Community law. For example, controversial Article 28 of the Charter (Article II-88 of the Constitution) provides that:

---

[22] Stockholm European Council, 23 and 24 March 2001, para. 9.

[23] For a discussion of the significance of having both first generation (civil and political) and second generation (economic and social) rights in the same document, despite the fluidity of these terms, see De Búrca, 'The Future of Social Rights Protection in Europe' in de Búrca and de Witte (eds), *Social Rights in Europe* (OUP, Oxford, 2005).

[24] Art. 20 lays down the principle of equality before the law; Art. 21 contains a non-exhaustive list of prohibited grounds of discrimination; Art. 22 talks of cultural, religious, linguistic diversity and Art. 23 concerns equality between men and women.

[25] E.g., Art. 27 concerns information and consultation within the undertaking; Art. 28 the right of collective bargaining and collective action; Art. 30 on protection in the event of unjustified dismissal and Art. 31 fair and just working conditions including, in Art. 31(2), 'the right to limitation of maximum working hours, to daily and weekly rest periods and to an annual period of paid leave'; and Art. 33 family and professional life. O'Leary describes this combination of rights as 'a heterogeneous mishmash of the predictable and the unexpected' ('Solidarity and Citizenship Rights in the Charter of Fundamental Rights of the European Union' in de Búrca, *EU Law and the Welfare States. In Search of Solidarity* (OUP, Oxford, 2005), 60).

Workers and their employers, or their respective organisations, have, *in accordance with Union law and national laws and practices*, the right to negotiate and conclude collective agreements at the appropriate levels and, in cases of conflicts of interest, to take collective action to defend their interests, *including strike action*.[26]

This provision does not grant a right to strike because the Charter contains 'General Provisions Governing the Interpretation and Application of the Charter'. These so-called 'horizontal provisions' provisions include Article II-111(2)[27] which states that '[t]his Charter does not extend the field of application of Union law beyond the powers of the Union or establish any new power or task for the Union, or modify powers and tasks defined in other parts of the Constitution' and Article II-112(2)[28] which provides that '[r]ights recognised by this Charter for which provision is made in other Parts of the Constitution shall be exercised under the conditions and within the limits defined by these relevant parts'. In particular, Article 137(5) (III-210(6) of the Constitutional Treaty) expressly excludes Community competence in respect of strike action under Article III-210137.[29] Thus, the Charter does not empower the Community to create a right to strike, nor does it require the Member States to create a right to strike. In this way the Charter preserves national autonomy.[30] The provision could, however, be used to ensure that where strike action taken in a Member State interferes with the free movement of goods or services, this interference—which is potentially unlawful—is balanced against the fundamental right to strike.[31]

The Solidarity Title also contains a number of principles which are not intended to be justiciable.[32] Hepple[33] subdivides the 'principles' category into (1) those rights

[26] Emphasis added.

[27] Prior to the Constitutional Treaty, the relevant Article was Art. II-51(2), albeit rather differently worded.

[28] Art. 52(2) of the Charter.

[29] For criticism, see Weiss, 'The Politics of the EU Charter of Fundamental Rights' in Hepple (ed), *Social and Labour Rights in a Global Context* (CUP, Cambridge, 2002).

[30] Hepple, *Rights at Work: Global, European and British Perspectives* (London, Sweet & Maxwell, 2005), 30, subject to the Court respecting that autonomy: cf Case C-71/02 *Karner* [2004] ECR I-3025. See also Case C-109/01 *Akrich* [2003] ECR I-9607.

[31] For an example of this balancing exercise, see Case C-112/00 *Schmidberger* [2003] ECR I-5659 and also Art. 2 of Reg. 2679/98 ([1998] OJ L337/8).

[32] Art. II-112(5), formerly Art. II-52(5) provides: 'The provisions of this Charter which contain principles may be implemented by legislative and executive acts taken by Institutions, bodies, offices and agencies of the Union, and by acts of the Member States when they are *implementing* Union law, in the exercise of their respective powers. They shall be judicially cognisable only in the interpretation of such acts and in the ruling on their legality'. Thus, ostensibly, the Charter does not apply to the Member States when they are derogating from EC Law: cf Case C-260/89 *ERT* [1991] ECR I-2925. Yet the Praesidium explanations (drawn up as a way of providing guidance in the interpretation of the Charter and to which due regard has to be given by the courts of the Union and of the Member States (Article II-112(7))) refer to both Case 5/88 *Wachauf* [1989] ECR 2609 (which concerns implementation) and *ERT* (which concerns derogations) by way of explanation for the rule. See generally, Arnold, 'From Charter to Constitution and beyond: Fundamental Rights in the New European Union' [2003] *Public Law* 774, 780.

[33] *Rights at Work: Global, European and British Perspectives* (Sweet & Maxwell, London, 2005) 35.

which the EU/Member States must 'respect' (ie EU and Member States must refrain from any action which would undermine the rights) and those rights which they must recognize (ie EU and Member States must protect these rights including preventing action by third parties who might interfere with the rights); and (2) those rights which the EU and the Member States are under a duty to 'ensure'. This latter category imposes a positive obligation and requires real resources. Article II-94 (Article 34 of the Charter) on social security and social assistance is confined to 'recognise and respect'. It provides that 'The Union recognises and respects the entitlement to social security benefits and social services providing protection in cases such as maternity, illness, industrial accidents, dependency or old age, and in the case of loss of employment' in accordance with Union and national laws and practices.

Even though the Charter is not legally binding—albeit that is has been cited by a number of Advocates General and the Court of Justice,[34] the Court of First Instance,[35] the European Court of Human Rights[36] and national courts[37]—its greatest significance may prove to lie in the fact that, in the social field at least, it will help provide some counterweight to the neo-liberal orientation of the Treaty,[38] providing the Court with a firmer foundation to reconcile social and economic rights. For the other Community institutions and the Member States, the Charter will provide a stark reminder of the EU's social rights agenda at a time when aspects of the EES have a deregulatory edge[39] and states, deprived of the traditional tools for managing their economies, might look to removing social rights as a way of gaining a competitive advantage.

Some signs of this reorientation can be detected in judgments of the Court of Justice. Even before the 2000 Charter was adopted, but after the Community Charter of Social Rights 1989, the Court said in *Albany*[40] that:

[I]t is important to bear in mind that, under [Article 3(1)(g) and (j)] of the EC Treaty, the activities of the Community are to include not only a 'system ensuring that competition in the internal market is not distorted' but also 'a policy in the social sphere'.

The European social model

The developments in the social field have enabled the Community institutions to recognize that there is now such a thing as the European social model, albeit that

---

[34] See, e.g. AG Jacobs' Opinion in Case C-50/00 *Unión de Pequeños Agricultores v Council of the European Union* [2002] ECR I-6677; AG Geelhoed's Opinion in Case C-224/98 *D'Hoop v Office National d'Emploi* [2002] ECR I-6191; ECJ in Case C-540/03 European Parliament v. Council [2006] ECR I-000

[35] E.g. Case T-177/01 *Jégo Quéré et Cie SA v European Commission* [2002] ECR II-2365, Case T-54/99 *Max Mobil Telekommunikation Service GmbH v European Commission* [2002] ECR II-313.

[36] *Godwin v UK* [2002] 35 EHRR 18.

[37] *R (on the application of Robertson) v Wakefield MDC* [2002] QB 1052, 170.

[38] Cf Giubboni, *Social Rights and Market Freedom in the European Constitution* (CUP, Cambridge, 2006), 61.

[39] Hepple, *Rights at Work* (Sweet & Maxwell, London, 2005) 36–37.

[40] Case C-67/96 [1999] ECR I-5751, para. 54.

its content is not always easy to identify. At the Nice European Council in 2000, the Heads of State said[41]:

The European social model has developed over the last forty years through a substantial Community acquis. . . . It now includes essential texts in numerous areas: free movement of workers, gender equality at work, health and safety of workers, working and employment conditions and, more recently, the fight against all forms of discrimination.

The European Council continued that this social model also includes the agreements between the Social Partners in the law-making process, the Luxembourg EES and the open method of coordination on the subject of social exclusion and greater cooperation in the field of social protection.[42]

These observations on the European Social Model (ESM) highlight the patchwork of rules covered by the ESM umbrella, the multiple actors involved in realizing the ESM, operating at different levels, and the multiple techniques for delivering it. What is clear is that the EU does not aspire to, and has never aspired to, replicating national social policy. Rather, it has a sufficient social face to help legitimize the EU's peculiar federal-like polity. But the repeated reference to the *European* Social Model, also serves to make the EU and its polity distinctive from rival systems, notably the US.

Subsequently, at the Barcelona European Council meeting in 2002,[43] the heads of state emphasized the link between economic and social success. It said that 'The European Social Model is based on good economic performance, a high level of social protection and education and social dialogue'. In other words, unlike the Spaak report and the original Article 117 EEC which saw social progress at being the consequence of economic success, by the turn of the century, social rights were seen as an input into that formula for success. The Commission spelt this out clearly in its own Social Policy Agenda adopted in June 2000. It said that 'growth is not an end in itself but essentially a means of achieving a better standard of living for all. Social policy underpins economic policy and employment has not only economic but also a social value'.[44] Against this backcloth, said the Commission, is the 'promotion of quality as the driving force for a thriving economy . . . quality of work, quality in industrial relations and quality of social policy'.[45]

One of the distinctive features of the EU's system is the common set of shared values. This was emphasized by the European Council in its Nice Social Policy Agenda[46]:

The European social model, characterised in particular by systems that offer a high level of social protection, by the importance of the social dialogue and by services of general interest

---

[41] Para. 12.
[42] Para. 11.
[43] http://www.consilium.europa.eu/ueDocs/cms_Data/docs/pressData/en/ec/71025.pdf, para. 22.
[44] COM(2000) 379, 13.
[45] Ibid.
[46] Para. 10. Emphasis added.

covering activities vital for social cohesion, is today based, beyond the diversity of the Member States' social systems, on a common core of *values*.

The reference to values serves to underline the extent to which the economic skin of the original Treaty has, apparently, been sloughed. In its White Paper on Social Policy,[47] the Commission articulated more fully the shared *values* around which the 'European Social Model' was based:

These include democracy and individual rights, free collective bargaining, the market economy, equality of opportunity for all and social welfare and solidarity. These values . . . are held together by the conviction that economic and social progress must go hand in hand. Competitiveness and solidarity have both been taken into account in building a successful Europe for the future.

This helped shape the values in the Constitutional Treaty.

Social Policy and the Constitutional Treaty

The express recognition of the values on which the Union is based is one of the most striking features of the Constitutional Treaty.[48] There is considerable overlap between the values identified by the European Commission in its White Paper on Social Policy and those listed in Article I-2:

The Union is founded on the values of respect for human dignity, freedom, democracy, equality, the rule of law and respect for human rights, including the rights of persons belonging to minorities. These values are common to the Member States in a society in which pluralism, non-discrimination, tolerance, justice, solidarity and equality between women and men prevail.

Further, Article I-3(3) includes, as one of the Union's objectives:

a highly competitive social market economy, aiming at full employment and social progress, and a high level of protection and improvement of the quality of the environment. . . . It shall combat social exclusion and discrimination, and shall promote social justice and protection, equality between women and men, solidarity between generations and protection of the rights of the child.

The reference to 'full employment' constitutionalizes what had already been agreed at Lisbon. The reference to the 'social market economy' is intended to emphasize the symbiosis between economic and social success recognized, in particular, by the European Commission in its Social Policy Agenda of 2000.[49] The reference to 'social justice'—the first time the phrase has been used in an EC/EU Treaty—underlines the market correcting function of social policy. However, in the minds of some, particularly the French, the reference in Article I-3(2) (repeating the contents of

---

[47] COM(94) 333, para. 3.

[48] For a full discussion of the changes introduced by the Constitutional Treaty, see Kenner, 'The Constitution that never was: is there anything worth salvaging from the wreckage?' (2005) 36 *IRJ* 541.

[49] Joerges and Rödl, '"Social Market Economy"' *EUI Working Paper*, Law 2004/8.

Article 3(1)(g) of the original EC Treaty) to 'an internal market where competition is free and undistorted' demonstrated what the EU was really about: in the words of Jacques Chirac 'ultraliberalism'.[50]

Article I-3(5) concerns competence. It says that 'The Union shall pursue its objectives by appropriate means commensurate with the competences which are conferred upon it in the Constitution'. Article I-14(2)(a) then identifies social policy, for the aspects defined in Part III, as an area of shared competence. Article I-12(2) explains that shared competence means that 'the Union and the Member States may legislate and adopt legally binding acts in that area'. The Member States shall exercise their competence to the extent that the Union has not exercised, or has decided to cease exercising, its competence'. The first two sections of Chapter Three 'Policies in Other Areas' are devoted to Employment (Section I) and Social Policy (Section 2). These provisions of the Constitution incorporate the content of the Employment and Social Policy Titles of the existing EC Treaty with only minor technical amendments.

In respect of the employment provisions, Article I-15 identifies employment policies as an area of 'coordination'. In particular, Article I-15(2) states:

The Union shall take measures to ensure coordination of the employment policies of the Member States, in particular by defining guidelines for those policies.

It is noticeable that OMC, such an influential an idea in recent years, is not actually mentioned by name. The Social Europe Working Group was divided on the issue, as was the Convention Praesidium.[51] However, Part III of the Treaty provided for the application of key features of OMC to a number of areas including social policy. Article III-213, which closely followed the wording of Article 140 EC, contains the addition that the Commission shall act in close contact with the Member States 'in particular in initiatives aiming at the establishment of guidelines and indicators, the organisation of exchange of best practice, and the preparation of the necessary elements for periodic monitoring and evaluation'.[52] In a nod towards concerns about the lack of democratic oversight of the procedure, Article III-213 adds that 'The European Parliament shall be kept fully informed'.

The other new method of governance introduced by the Maastricht Treaty is also formally recognized in the Constitutional Treaty. Article I-48 entitled 'The social partners and autonomous social dialogue' provides:

The Union recognises and promotes the role of the social partners at its level, taking into account the diversity of national systems. It shall facilitate dialogue between the social partners, respecting their autonomy.

The Tripartite Social Summit for Growth and Employment shall contribute to Social Dialogue.

---

[50] Kenner, above n. 48, 543.

[51] Ibid.

[52] Declaration 18 confirms that policies described within this Article 'fall essentially within the competence of the Member States'. Measures to provide encouragement and promote coordination to be taken at Union level shall be of 'a complementary nature'. They shall 'serve to strengthen cooperation between Member States and not to harmonise social systems'.

The lack of radicalism in the social provisions of the Constitutional Treaty can be explained in part by the limited attention paid to social issues by the Convention on the Future for Europe. Initially there was no specific Working Group on Social Policy because 'Giscard [d'Estaing] had little time for social policy'.[53] Social issues were instead referred to the Working Group on Economic Governance whose inability to reach consensus triggered petitions for a new specific Working Group on Social Policy.[54] This was eventually set up but, according to Norman, its large size (60 members, twice the number of previous groups) was seen by some as a ploy to limit its effectiveness.[55] Further, its remit was confined to whether Article 2 (values) and Article 3 (objectives) properly reflected Social Europe, whether competences in social matters should be modified and how far QMV and co-decision should replace unanimity. As Closa notes, the formalist approach of the Working Group meant that it did not even consider whether the Union should have fully fledged redistributive policies or whether it should have a full fiscal policy entailing fiscal obligations of citizens.[56]

Given that the social policy provisions of the Constitutional Treaty broadly retained the status quo,[57] they should not have scared the horses—even French ones. On the contrary, the combined effect of the incorporation of the Charter and the heavy reliance on values of social justice should have done much to reassure. When compared to the original Treaty of Rome and its focus on the market-making aspect of social policy, the second Treaty of Rome emphasizes market-correcting and social justice, values which the Court of Justice itself has already recognized in its case law. In the next section I take two of the values given prominent place in the Constitutional Treaty, solidarity and equality, and consider the extent to which they have already been recognized in the existing jurisprudence and thus will continue to have force, whatever the fate of the Constitutional Treaty.

THE VALUES

Solidarity

Solidarity in the treaties

Social solidarity, a tradition on which Europe prides itself,[58] is a concept which originated in the social welfare systems of the Member States, particularly those of France, Belgium, and Germany. It embraces universal healthcare coverage, free

[53] Norman, *The Accidental Constitution: The Making of Europe's Constitutional Treaty* (Eurocomment, Belgium, 2005), 104.

[54] PES MEP Anne van Lancker was a central figure in these moves: Shaw, 'A Strong Europe is a Social Europe' *Federal Trust Online Paper* 05/03, 2.

[55] Ibid., 105.

[56] 'Constitution and Democracy in the Treaty Establishing a Constitution for Europe' (2005) 11 *EPL.* 145, 157.

[57] Piris, *The Constitution for Europe: A Legal Analysis* (CUP, Cambridge, 2006), 188.

[58] Weiler, 'A Constitution for Europe? Some Hard Choices?' (2002) 40 *JCMS* 563, 569. See generally, Stjernø, *Solidarity in Europe: The History of an Idea* (CUP, Cambridge, 2004).

education from nursery to university, and generous welfare for the less fortunate.[59] In the light of this tradition, Advocate General Fennelly defined solidarity in *Sodemare* [60] as the 'inherently uncommercial act of involuntary subsidization of one social group by another'.[61] Thus, solidarity means that in large aggregates (territorial or community groupings, states, insurance schemes, etc) members of one social group are willing to subsidise another.[62] In the national system it has meant that national taxpayers pay their taxes to help look after their fellow nationals who need assistance. This sense of solidarity is derived in part from a shared nationality, in part from a shared sense of identity.

'Solidarity' has a prominent place in the Constitutional Treaty: it appears in the Preamble of both the Constitutional Treaty[63] and the Charter of Fundamental Rights[64] and again in the statement of the Union's values.[65] also appears in the list of Union's objectives in Article I-3 where the term is used in three different ways: first, Article I-3 talks of 'solidarity between generations'[66]; secondly, it talks of 'solidarity among Member States',[67] an idea which is given more concrete expression in Article I-43 which requires the Union and its Member States to 'act jointly in a spirit of solidarity if a Member State' is the victim of terrorist attack or natural or man-made disaster[68]; and thirdly, it refers to 'solidarity and

---

[59] Ibid.

[60] Case C-70/95 *Sodemare SA, Anni Azzurri Holding SpA and Anni Azzurri Rezzato Srl v Regione Lombardia* [1997] ECR I-3395.

[61] Para. 29. The meaning of solidarity in the EU context is considered further in C.Barnard, 'EU Citizenship and the Principle of Solidarity' in Dougan and Spaventa (eds), *Social Welfare and EU Law* (Oxford, Hart, 2005), upon which this section draws.

[62] O'Leary, 'Solidarity and Citizenship Rights in the Charter of Fundamental Rights of the European Union' in de Búrca, *EU Law and the Welfare States. In Search of Solidarity* (OUP, Oxford, 2005), 55.

[63] 'Believing that Europe, reunited after bitter experiences, intends to continue along the path of civilisation, progress and prosperity, for the good of all its inhabitants, including the weakest and most deprived; that it wishes to remain a continent open to culture, learning, and social progress; and that it wishes to deepen the democratic and transparent nature of its public life, and to strive for peace, justice and solidarity throughout the world'.

[64] 'Conscious of its spiritual and moral heritage, the Union is founded on the indivisible, universal values of human dignity, freedom, equality and solidarity'.

[65] Art.I-2: The Union is founded on the values of respect for human dignity, liberty, democracy, equality, the rule of law and respect for human rights, including the rights of persons belonging to minorities. These values are common to the Member States in a society in which pluralism, non-discrimination, tolerance, justice, solidarity and equality between men and women prevail'.

[66] Article I-3, para. 3 provides 'It shall combat social exclusion and discrimination, and shall promote social justice and protection, equality between women and men, solidarity between generations and protection of the rights of the child.' This usage was earlier recognized by the Court of Justice in Case C-50/99 *Podesta v CRICA* [2000] ECR I-4039, para. 21, in respect of those in employment and those in retirement.

[67] Article I-3, para. 3 continues: 'It shall promote economic, social and territorial cohesion, and solidarity among Member States'.

[68] See also Council Regulation 2012/2002 establishing the European Union Solidarity Fund (OJ 2002 L311/3) which has been used in cases of the storm and flooding in Malta in Sept 2003, the forest fire in Spain in the summer of 2003 and the flooding in Southern France in December 2003: see EP and Council December 2004/323/EC ([2004] OJ L104/112).

mutual respect among peoples' in respect of the Union's relations with the outside world.[69]

However, the reference to solidarity is not new: solidarity was expressly recognized in the first of the foundation Treaties, the ECSC Treaty of 1951. Its Preamble provided that:

Recognising that Europe can be built only through real practical achievements which will first of all create *real solidarity*, and through the establishment of common bases for economic development.

Reference to the principle of solidarity was also made in the Preamble to the EEC Treaty of 1957. This provided:

INTENDING to confirm the *solidarity* which binds Europe and the overseas countries and desiring to ensure the development of their prosperity, in accordance with the principles of the United Nations,

However, 'solidarity' was not mentioned in the text of the Treaty itself until 1992 when it was included in Article 2 EC under the heading of Community tasks.[70] At the same time it was also included in the Preamble to the Treaty on European Union which provides:

DESIRING to deepen the *solidarity* between their peoples while respecting their history, culture and their traditions,

Solidarity also appears in Article 1 TEU as a task of the Union 'to organise, in a manner demonstrating consistency and *solidarity*, relations between the Member States and between their peoples'.

Given the obvious connection between solidarity and social policy in the broadest sense, it is surprising that no connection was made between the two in the Social Title of the original Treaty of Rome. This tends to reinforce the view that the 'social' provisions of the original Treaty were there to serve market-making rather than market-correcting purposes. It was in fact the Court of Justice that began to make the link between solidarity and the broader social goals of the Community.

Solidarity and the Court of Justice

While the Court of Justice has long recognized the principle of solidarity in the context of restructuring in particular sectors, especially agriculture and steel,[71] it took some time before the Court realized that it had a role in the social field. At

---

[69] Article I-3, para. 4 states: 'In its relations with the wider world, the Union shall uphold and promote its values and interests. It shall contribute to peace, security, the sustainable development of the Earth, solidarity and mutual respect among peoples, free and fair trade, eradication of poverty and protection of human rights and in particular the rights of the child, as well as to strict observance and to development of international law, including respect for the principles of the United Nations Charter'.

[70] 'The Community shall have as its task . . . the raising of the standard of living and quality of life, and economic and social cohesion and solidarity among Member States'.

[71] See further Barnard, 'Solidarity and New Governance in the Field of Social Policy?' in De Búrca and Scott (eds) *New Governance and Constitutionalism in Europe and the US* (Hart, Oxford, 2006).

first, the Court's use of the principle was negative: to defend national social systems against attacks from the Community rules on the internal market. Subsequently, the Court used solidarity more positively, to impose obligations on the host state in respect of their obligations towards migrant citizens.

(a) Negative use of the solidarity principle
In a line of cases concerning challenges to pension or sickness schemes organized by employers on the grounds that they breach the Community rules on anti-competitive behaviour the Court has used the principle of solidarity[72] to justify arguing that where the activity is based on national solidarity, it is not an economic activity and therefore the body concerned cannot be classed as an undertaking to which Community competition rules apply.

This approach was first adopted in the case of *Poucet and Pistre*[73] where the Court held that certain French bodies administering the sickness and maternity insurance scheme for self-employed persons engaged in non-agricultural occupations and the basic pension scheme for skilled trades, were not to be classified as undertakings for the purpose of competition law. The schemes provided a basic pension.[74] Affiliation was compulsory. The pension scheme was a non-funded scheme: it operated on a redistributive basis with active members' contributions being directly used to finance the pensions of retired members; and the schemes had a social objective in that they were intended to provide cover for the beneficiaries against the risks of sickness or old age regardless of the individuals' financial status and state of health at the time of affiliation. The principle of solidarity was embodied in the *redistributive* nature of the pension scheme: contributions paid by active workers served to finance the pensions of retired workers. It was also reflected by the grant of pension rights where no contributions had been made and of pension rights that were not proportional to the contributions paid. Finally, there was solidarity between the various social security schemes, with those in surplus contributing to the financing of those with structural difficulties. The Court said:

It follows that the social security schemes, as described, are based on a system of compulsory contribution, which is indispensable for the application of the principle of solidarity and the financial equilibrium of those schemes.

. . . [O]rganisations involved in the management of the public social security system fulfil an exclusively social function. That activity is based on the principle of national solidarity

---

[72] T. Hervey, 'Social Solidarity: a Buttress against Internal Market law?', in Shaw (ed.) *Social Law and Policy in an Evolving European Union*, (Hart, Oxford, 2000). In a different context, and outside the scope of this Chapter, but in a similar vein, is the view expressed in *La Cinq SA v Commission* [1992] ECR II-1, para. 58. that: 'If commercial broadcasting undertakings were admitted as active members of the European Broadcasting Union alongside public-service broadcasting organisations, the Europe visions programme-exchange system itself could not remain what it is: a system of solidarity between organisations of the same nature indirectly supporting the weakest members'.

[73] Joined Cases C-159/91 and C-160/91 *Poucet and Pistre v AGF and Cancava* [1993] ECR I-637.

[74] These are helpfully summarized by Advocate General Jacobs in his Opinion in Case C-67/96 *Albany* [1999] ECR I-5751, para. 317.

and is entirely non-profit-making. The benefits paid are statutory benefits bearing no relation to the amount of the contribution. Accordingly, that activity is not an economic activity . . .

However, in *FFSA*[75] the Court 'clarified' its case law. The case concerned a French supplementary retirement scheme for self-employed farmers.[76] The Court noted that in *FFSA* membership of the scheme was optional, that the scheme operated in accordance with the principle of capitalization, rather than on a redistributive basis as in *Poucet*, and that the benefits to which it conferred entitlement depended solely on the amount of contributions paid by the recipients and the financial results of the investments made by the managing organization. It concluded that the managing body therefore carries on an economic activity in competition with life assurance companies and so the Community competition rules, in particular Article 81, applied. On the question of solidarity the Court said that 'the principle of solidarity is extremely limited in scope' and noted that while the scheme had solidaristic elements that was not sufficient to take the scheme outside Article 81.

The Court reached much the same conclusion in *Albany*,[77] another case involving a capitalization scheme. It said that a pension fund charged with the management of a supplementary pension scheme set up by a collective agreement to which affiliation was compulsory by the public authorities for all workers in that sector, was an undertaking within the meaning of Article 81. However, it did say that the solidarity elements[78] justified the exclusive right of the fund to manage the supplementary scheme under Article 86(2) and so there was no breach of Articles 82 and 86(1) respectively.

Although the Court's initial enthusiasm for the principle of solidarity seemed to have rather cooled after *FFSA* , the principle was successfully invoked in *Sodemare*[79] to allow Italy to insist that only non-profit-making private operators could

---

[75] Case C-244/94 *Fédération Française des Sociétés d'Assurances* [1995] ECR I-4013, discussed by Laigre, 'L'intrusion du droit communautaire de la concurrence dans le champ de la protection sociale' [1996] *Droit Social* 82.

[76] Case C-67/96 *Albany v Stichting Bedrijfspensioenfonds Textielindustrie* [1999] ECR I-5751, para. 325.

[77] Case C-67/96 [1999] ECR I-5751, para. 87.

[78] The solidarity was reflected by the obligation to accept all workers without a prior medical examination, the continuing accrual of pension rights despite exemption from contributions in the event of incapacity for work, the discharge by the fund of arrears of contributions due from an employer in the event of the latter's insolvency and by the indexing of the amount of the pensions in order to maintain their value. The principle of solidarity was also apparent from the absence of any equivalence, for individuals, between the contribution paid, which is an average contribution not linked to risks, and pension rights, which are determined by reference to an average salary. Such solidarity makes compulsory affiliation to the supplementary pension scheme essential. Otherwise, if 'good' risks left the scheme, the ensuing downward spiral would jeopardize its financial equilibrium (para. 75). This would increase the cost of pensions for workers, particularly those in small and medium-sized undertakings with older employees engaged in dangerous activities, to which the fund could no longer offer pensions at an acceptable cost (para. 108).

[79] Case C-70/95 *Sodemare v Regione Lombardia* [1997] ECR I-3395.

participate in the running of its social welfare system. The Italian rules did not breach Articles 43 and 48 on freedom of establishment because, as the Court noted, the system of social welfare, whose implementation is in principle entrusted to the public authorities, is based on the principle of solidarity, as reflected by the fact that it is designed as a matter of priority to assist those who are in a state of need.[80] Thus, in *Sodemare* the Court used the principle of solidarity to reinforce its view that Community law is not just about unrestricted access for all economic operators to the market in other Member States.[81]

Since *Sodemare* the Court has carefully examined the facts of the individual cases to consider whether there is a sufficient degree of solidarity to justify a finding that the activity is not economic, so falling outside the scope of Community law or insufficient solidarity and so Community law applies. For example, in *AOK*[82] the Court found that the sickness funds in the German statutory health insurance scheme were involved in the management of the social security system where they fulfilled 'an exclusively social function which is founded on the principle of national solidarity and is entirely non-profit-making'.[83] Since the funds were obliged by law to offer their members essentially identical benefits, irrespective of contributions, that they were bound together in a type of community founded on the basis of solidarity which enabled an equalization of costs and risks between them and they did not compete with one another or private institutions,[84] the Court considered they fell on the *Poucet and Pistre* side of the line and so their activity could not be regarded as economic in nature. On the other hand, in *Wouters*[85] the Court said

---

[80] Ibid Para. 29. See also Case C-192/05 *Tas Hagen* [2006] ECR I-000, paras. 34–34.

[81] In the context of free movement of goods, cf Case C-267/91 *Criminal proceedings against Keck and Mithouard* [1993] ECR I-6097.

[82] Joined Cases C-264/01, C-306/01, C-354/01 and C-355/01 *AOK Bundesverband, Bundesverband der Betriebskrankenkassen (BKK), Bundesverband der Innungskrankenkassen, Bundesverband der landwirtschaftlichen Krankenkassen, Verband der Angestelltenkrankenkassen eV, Verband der Arbeiter-Ersatzkassen, Bundesknappschaft and See-Krankenkasse v Ichthyol-Gesellschaft Cordes, Hermani & Co.* (C-264/01), *Mundipharma GmbH* (C-306/01), *Gödecke GmbH* (C-354/01) *and Intersan, Institut für pharmazeutische und klinische Forschung GmbH* (C-355/01) [2004] ECR I-2493. See also Case C-218/00 *Cisal di Battistello Venanzio & C.Sas v Istituto nazionale per l'assicurazione contro gli infortuni sul lavoro* [2002] ECR I-691, concerning compulsory insurance against accidents at work and occupational diseases; Case C-355/00 *Freskot AE v Elliniko Dimosio* [2003] ECR I-5263; Case T-319/99 *FENIN v Commission* [2003] ECR II-357, concerning the bodies which run the Spanish national health system); Joined Cases C-266/04 to C-270/04 *Nazairdis v Caisse nationale de l'orgaisation autonome d'assurance viellesse des travailleurs non salariés des professions industrielles et commerciales (Organic)* [2005] ECR I-9481, para. 54 (old age insurance schemes for self-employed persons in the craft sector). See Sciarra, 'Market Freedom and fundamental social rights' in Hepple (ed), *Social and Labour Rights in a Global Context* (CUP, Cambridge, 2002).

[83] Para. 51.

[84] Paras. 51–53.

[85] Case C-309/99 *Wouters, Savelbergh, Price Waterhouse Belastingadviseurs* BV *v Algemene Raad van de Nederlandse Orde van* Advocaten [2002] ECR I-1577, para. 58. See also Case C-55/96 *Job Centre Coop. Arl* [1997] ECR I-7119.

that because a professional regulatory body such as the Bar of the Netherlands was neither fulfilling a social function based on the principle of solidarity nor exercising powers which were typically those of a public authority, it did engage in an economic activity and so was subject to Community law.

(b) *The positive use of the solidarity principle*

More radically, the Court has taken the principle of solidarity and used it to require host states to offer social welfare benefits to migrants in certain circumstances. This can be seen in *Grzelczyk*.[86] Grzelczyk, a French national studying at a Belgian university, supported himself financially for the first three years of his studies but then applied for the minimex (the Belgium minimum income guarantee) at the start of his fourth and final year. While Belgian students could receive the benefit, migrant students could not.[87] As a result, Grzelczyk suffered (direct) discrimination contrary to Article 12.[88] The Court said that Grzelczyk, a citizen of the Union, could rely on Article 12 in respect of those situations which fell within the material scope of the Treaty,[89] which included those situations involving 'the exercise of the fundamental freedoms guaranteed by the Treaty and those involving the exercise of the right to move and reside freely in another Member State, as conferred by Article [18(1)] of the Treaty'.[90]

The Court then considered the limits laid down in the Residence Directives, in particular the limits imposed by Article 1 of the Students' Directive 93/96 (now Directive 2004/38) which requires migrant students to have sufficient resources when exercising the rights of free movement. The Court said that while a Member State could decide that a student having recourse to social assistance no longer fulfilled the conditions of his right of residence and so could withdraw his residence permit or decide not to renew it,[91] such actions could not be the automatic consequence of a migrant student having recourse to the host State's social assistance system.[92] The Court continued that beneficiaries of the right of residence could not become an 'unreasonable' burden on the public finances of the host State.[93] Therefore, the Belgian authorities had to provide some temporary support (the minimex) to the migrant citizen, as they would to nationals, given that there existed 'a certain degree of financial solidarity' between nationals of a host Member State and nationals of other Member States.[94] In other words, due to this 'certain degree of financial solidarity' between the Belgian taxpayer and the French migrant student, derived from

---

[86] Case C-184/99 [2001] ECR I-6193.
[87] Ibid Para. 29.
[88] Ibid Para. 30.
[89] Ibid Para. 32.
[90] Ibid Para. 33, citing Case C-274/96 *Bickel and Franz* [1998] ECR I-7637.
[91] Ibid Para. 42.
[92] Ibid Para. 43.
[93] Ibid Para. 44.
[94] Ibid.

their common (EU) citizenship, the student could enjoy the social benefit but only for so long as the student did not become an unreasonable burden on public finances. In *Bidar*[95] the Court built on the ruling in *Grzelczyk* to justify finding that the UK was obliged to treat legally resident migrants equally with nationals in respect of access to maintenance grants and loans. However, the Court said that the UK would be justified in imposing a three year residence requirement before the individual could claim maintenance grants and loans.

The solidarity principle also helps to explain *Baumbast*.[96] Baumbast was a German national who had been working in the UK and continued residing there with his family once his work in the EU had ceased. While he had sufficient resources for himself and his family, his German medical insurance did not cover emergency treatment in the UK, as required by Directive 90/364 on persons of independent means.[97] For this reason the British authorities refused to renew his residence permit. The Court said that he could rely on his directly effective right to reside under Article 18(1) but this right had to be read subject to the limitations laid down in the Residence Directives (now Directive 2004/38).[98] It then qualified this remark by adding that the limitations and conditions referred in Article 18(1) had to be applied 'in compliance with the limits imposed by Community law and in accordance with the general principles of that law, in particular the principle of proportionality'.[99] It concluded that, given neither Baumbast nor his family had become a financial burden on the state, it would amount to a disproportionate interference with the exercise of the right of residence if he were denied residence on the ground that his sickness insurance did not cover the emergency treatment given in the host Member State.[100] When viewed through the lens of solidarity, it could be argued that there was a sufficient degree of solidarity between Baumbast and the British taxpayer to justify him (and his family) receiving emergency medical treatment on the NHS.

---

[95] Case C-209/03 *R (on the application of Danny Bidar) v London Borough of Ealing, Secretary of State for Education and Skills*, [2005] ECR I-2119.

[96] Case C-413/99 *Baumbast and R v Secretary of State for the Home Department* [2002] ECR I-7091. See also the reference in para. 44 of *Grzelczyk* to Directives 90/364 and 90/365 which, like Directive 93/96, 'accepts a certain degree of financial solidarity'. See also Advocate General Geelhoed's comments in *Bidar*, para. 31: 'The notion of "unreasonable burden" is apparently flexible and, according to the Court, implies that Directive 93/96 accepts a degree of financial solidarity between the Member States in assisting each other's nationals residing lawfully in their territory. As the same principle is at the basis of the conditions imposed by Directive 90/364, there is no reason to presume that this same financial solidarity does not apply in that context too.' See further, Dougan and Spaventa, ' "Wish You weren't Here . . ." New Models of Social Solidarity in the European Union' in Dougan and Spaventa (eds), *Social Welfare and EU Law*, (Hart, Oxford, 2005).

[97] Ibid Para. 88. See also Case T-66/75 *Hedwig Kuchlenz-Winter v Commission* [1997] ECR II-637, paras 46–47.

[98] Ibid Para. 90.

[99] Ibid Para. 91.

[100] Ibid Para. 93.

The reliance on the solidarity principle to justify imposing additional financial obligations on the host state in respect of EU migrants is a remarkable development. As Ward puts it, 'Without democracy, without rights even, it is unreasonable to expect Europe's citizens to feel the sense of "social solidarity" which is necessary to any genuine sense of citizenship and belonging'.[101] Nevertheless, the Court has superimposed this sentiment of solidarity on an unsuspecting population. There is, of course a chicken and egg argument: what comes first—the creation of EU citizenship or the sense of solidarity which fosters that sense of commonality. But the real problem lies in the fact that while social solidarity may be a fundamental European identity marker, the essential features of the welfare state still lie with the Member States and, as Weiler puts it, Europe should not 'constitutionally promise and guarantee that which it cannot deliver, or is not its to deliver'.

This raises the question of whether solidarity can be invoked by all EU migrants, including those who have recently arrived in the host state, especially those seeking education.[102] *Bidar* suggests that the answer is no: that only those who enjoy a certain degree of integration in the host state can expect equal treatment in respect of certain benefits like maintenance grants and loans. In paragraph 56 the Court referred to the need for Member States to show 'a certain degree of financial solidarity with nationals of other Member States' in the organization and application of their social assistance systems. It then continued in paragraph 57 that:

In the case of assistance covering the maintenance costs of students, it is thus legitimate for a Member State to grant such assistance only to students who have demonstrated a *certain degree of integration* into the society of that State.[103]

The Court then makes clear that length of residence is a key indicator of integration[104]:

. . . the existence of a certain degree of integration may be regarded as established by a finding that the student in question has resided in the host state for a certain length of time.

---

[101] Ward, *A Critical Introduction to European Law* (2nd edn, Butterworths, London, 2003), 266.

[102] See Advocate General Geelhoed's opinion in Case C-413/01 *Franca Ninni-Orasche v Bundesminister für Wissenschaft, Verkehr und Kunst* [2003] ECR I-13187, where he referred to the need for a minimum degree of financial solidarity towards those residents who are students but holding the nationality of another Member State and concluded that a resident like Mrs. Ninni-Orasche with a 'demonstrable and structural link to Austrian society' could not be treated in Austria 'as any other national of a third country' (para. 96). This is particularly so in the field of education where, as Advocate General Geelhoed noted in Case C-224/98 *D'Hoop* [2002] ECR I-6191, para. 41, European integration has created an environment conducive to transnational education. Inter-state education is, moreover, viewed as an important instrument in promoting mutual solidarity and tolerance as well as the dissemination of culture throughout the European Union.

[103] Emphasis added.

[104] Para. 59. See also AG Geelhoed's remarks in Case C-413/01 *Ninni-Orasche v Bundesminister für Wissenschaft* [2003] ECR I-13187, paras. 90–91. For an emphasis on the contextual approach which takes account of length of residence and degree of integration, see AG Ruiz-Jarabo Colomer's opinion, in Case C-138/02 *Brian Francis Collins v Secretary of State for Work and Pensions* [2004] ECR I-2703, paras. 65–67.

Thus, *Bidar* emphasizes a 'quantitative' approach[105]: the longer migrants reside in the Member State, the more integrated they are in that state and the greater the number of benefits they receive on equal terms with nationals. The corollary of this is that in respect of newly arrived migrants there is insufficient solidarity between them and the host state taxpayer to justify requiring full equal treatment in respect of social welfare benefits. This was the view taken by Advocate General Ruiz-Jarabo Colomer in *Collins*.[106] Collins, who was Irish, arrived in the UK and promptly applied for a job-seeker's allowance (JSA) which was refused on the grounds that he was not habitually resident in the UK. The Advocate General distinguished the facts of *Grzelczyk*[107] (and the Court's reference to solidarity) and concluded that Community law did not require the benefit to be provided to a citizen of the Union who entered the territory of a Member State with the purpose of seeking employment while lacking any connection with the state or link with the domestic employment market.[108] The Court decided the case on a different basis but reached the same conclusion.

The Court's reliance on the principle of solidarity is, depending on your perspective, a radical step towards the creation of European social citizenship or an unwarranted extension of Community competence into areas where it should not legitimately go.

Equality/non-discrimination

Equality and the Treaties

So solidarity is firmly entrenched but its dynamic use is of more recent vintage. This stands in sharp contrast to equality which has been a central tenet of European Community law since its inception. The principle of equality, and its legal manifestation, non-discrimination, were recognized in the original EEC Treaty where it featured in a number of contexts including the prohibition of non-discrimination on the grounds of nationality in Article 12, non-discrimination between producers and consumers in Article 40 and, most importantly for our purposes, non-discrimination between men and women on grounds of pay in Article 141. In the social field the Treaty provisions have been supplemented by comprehensive equality secondary legislation first in the field of sex equality, most notably Directive 75/117 on equal pay[109] and Directive 76/207 on equal treatment[110] (both Directives now consolidated

---

[105] This idea is developed further in Barnard, *Bidar* (2005) 42 *CMLRev.* forthcoming.

[106] Case C-138/02 *Brian Francis Collins v Secretary of State for Work and Pensions* [2004] ECR I-2703.

[107] Para. 66.

[108] Para. 76.

[109] [1975] OJ L45/19.

[110] Council Directive 76/207/EEC, [1976] OJ L39/40. The Directive was based on Art. 235 [new Art. 308]. Member States had 30 months to implement the Directive from the date of notification. In addition, they had four years to revise discriminatory laws designed to protect one group whose justification is no longer well founded (Art. 9(1)).

and amended by Directive 2006/54[111]), Directive 79/7 on equal treatment in social security,[112] and subsequently prohibiting discrimination on other grounds (Directive 2000/43 prohibiting discrimination on the grounds of race and ethnic origin[113] and Directive 2000/78 prohibiting discrimination on the grounds of sexual orientation, disability, age, religion and belief).[114]

Looking particularly at its usage in the 'social' context, equality has gone from its lowly days as a one-Article provision in the Social Title of the 1957 EEC Treaty to becoming a significant constitutional principle even before the Constitutional Treaty was agreed in 2004. The Constitutional Treaty itself places much emphasis on the principle of equality. Non-discrimination and equality between men and women are identified as Union values in Article I-2 and as Union objectives in Article I-3.[115] In addition, Article I-45 requires the Union, in all its activities, to observe the 'principle of the equality of its citizens'. Article III-116 adds that in all the activities referred to in Part II, 'the Union shall aim to eliminate inequalities, and to promote equality, between women and men'. Article III-118 goes further and contains the important horizontal statement on mainstreaming. This provides that:

In defining and implementing the policies and activities referred to in this part, the Union shall aim to combat discrimination based on sex, racial or ethnic origin, religion or belief, disability, age or sexual orientation.

Equality also forms one of the Titles of the Charter of Fundamental Rights found in Part II of the Constitution which, according to Article I-9(1), the Union must recognize. Title II opens with the classic assertion that 'Everyone is equal before the law'.[116] Article II-81(1) (Article 21 of the Charter) then contains a specific, but non-exhaustive, list of the grounds of discrimination which are prohibited 'sex, race, colour, ethnic or social origin, genetic features, language, religion or belief, political or any other opinion, membership of a national minority, property, birth, disability, age or sexual orientation'. This list differs in certain key respects from the (shorter) list of prohibited grounds in Article 13. However, while Article 13 provides the legal power for the Community to act, Article II-81(1) (Article 21(1) of the Charter) addresses discrimination by the institutions and bodies of the Union themselves,

---

[111] [2006] OJ L204/23.

[112] [1979] OJ L6/24.

[113] [2000] OJ L180/22.

[114] [2000] OJ L303/16.

[115] The objectives must be taken into account in respect of the policies and activities referred to in Part III: Art. III-115. For a full discussion, see Bell, 'Equality and the European Union Constitution' (2004) 33 *ILJ*. 242.

[116] Art. II-80 (Art. 20 of the Charter). The numbering in the original Charter, adopted at Nice in 2000, is different. There are also minor textual difference between the original version of the Charter and the version incorporated into the Constitutional Treaty. Since the discussion of the Charter occurs within the section on the Constitutional Treaty, the Constitution's numbers will be used.

and by Member States when they are implementing Union law.[117] Article II-83(1) (Article 23(1) of the Charter) requires equality between men and women in 'all areas, including employment, work and pay'. Article II-83(2) (Article 23(2) of the Charter) contains the positive action provision. It specifies that the principle of equality 'shall not prevent the maintenance or adoption of measures providing for specific advantages in favour of the under-represented sex'.[118]

Equality and the case law of the Court of Justice

(a) Introduction
The Court has taken the principle of equality and non-discrimination seriously. Two strands of use can be detected in the 'social' case law.[119] On the one hand there is, what might be termed the 'programmatic' use of equality and, on the other, the constitutional use of equality. We shall look at these in turn.

(b) Programmatic use of equality
In this context equality takes the form of prohibiting non-discrimination on a number of grounds laid down by Directive (sex, race, age, disability, sexual orientation, religion or belief).[120] The various directives adopt a broadly common format: they prohibit direct discrimination which can be saved only by express derogations and indirect discrimination which can be objectively justified. They also make some provision for positive action. While many pages have been devoted to analyzing the detailed technical aspects of the Community rules on non-discrimination,[121] to which I cannot hope to do justice here, what I would like to highlight is the increasing shift from a formal approach to non-discrimination to a more substantive one.

The formal approach to equality requires that people should be treated according to their own merits and characteristics; irrelevant factors such as gender or race should not be taken into account. In law, this perspective is embodied in the concept of direct discrimination. The strength of this approach is that it assumes that men and women/ethnic minorities and whites, etc are equal and so should be paid the same and treated in the same way, irrespective of any dissimilarities they possess. This approach also characterizes what Deakin and Morris describe as 'equality within the market order'. According to this concept, the principal aim is to do what is necessary

---

[117] Art. II-111. See also the Praesidium explanation accompanying the article which must be given 'due regard by the Courts of the Union and of the Member States' (Art. II-112(7)).

[118] For a full discussion, see Costello, 'Gender Equalities and the Charter of Fundamental Rights of the European Union' in Hervey and Kenner (eds), *Economic and Social Rights under the EU Charter of Fundamental Rights* (Hart, Oxford, 2003).

[119] For broader discussion outside the field of social policy, see Tridimas, *General Principles of Law* (OUP, Oxford, 2006).

[120] See in particular the Consolidated Directive 2006/54 on the implementation of the principle of equal opportunities and equal treatment of men and women in matters of employment and occupation; and the Article 13 Directives: Directive 2000/43 (OJ [2000] L180/22); Directive 2000/78 (OJ [2000] L OJ L303/16.

[121] See, for example, Barnard, *EC Employment Law* (3rd edn, Oxford, OUP, 2006), chs 6–10.

to ensure free and equal competition in the labour market, but to regulate outcomes in terms of the distribution of economic and social resources as little as possible.[122] This approach is particularly resonant in the EU, with its origins in the creation of a common, now single, market.

However, the downside of the concentration on formal equality is that it assumes that the comparator groups are actually similarly situated and able to compete equally when, in fact, their social circumstances may mean that in practice they are not. This leads some to advocate a more substantive approach to equality, one aimed at achieving equality of outcome or results.[123] Positive action—and more radically positive discrimination—provide perhaps the best example of measures intended to achieve substantive equality, often at the price of formal equality. The original Article 2(4) of Directive 76/207 permitted positive action and it was relied on by the Court in *Marschall*[124] to uphold the state's law which gave preference to a woman in a tie-break situation, subject to a saving clause operating in favour of the man. The Court said that this national rule was compatible with (the original) Article 2(4) because:

even where male and female candidates are equally qualified, male candidates tend to be promoted in preference to female candidates particularly because of prejudices and stereotypes concerning the role and capacities of women in working life and the fear, for example, that women will interrupt their careers more frequently, that owing to household and family duties they will be less flexible in their working hours, or that they will be absent from work more frequently because of pregnancy, childbirth and breastfeeding.[125] For these reasons, the mere fact that a male candidate and a female candidate are equally qualified does not mean that they have the same chances.[126]

This case is not an isolated example. On a number of occasions the Court has said, as in *Thibault*,[127] that 'the result pursued by the Directive [76/207] is substantive,

---

[122] *Labour Law* (Hart, Oxford, 2005) 581.

[123] In Case C-136/95 *Caisse Nationale d'Assurance Vieillesse des Travailleurs Salariés (CNAVTS) v Évelyne Thibault* [1998] ECR I-2011, the Court claimed that the result pursued by the Directive was substantive, not formal, equality (para. 26).

[124] Case C-409/95 *Marschall v Land Nordrhein-Westfalen* [1997] ECR I-6363. Cf Case C-450/93 *Kalanke v Stadt Bremen* [1995] ECR I-3051.

[125] See also the views of the Federal Labour Court when the *Kalanke* case returned to it (Nr 226), Urteil of 5 Mar. 1996–1 AZR 590/92 (A). It said that it was impossible to distinguish between opportunity and result, especially in the case of engagement and promotion because the selection itself was influenced by circumstances, expectations and prejudices that typically diminish the chances of women.

[126] Paras. 29 and 30.

[127] Case C-136/94 [1998] ECRI-2011, repeated in Case C-207/98 *Mahlburg v Land Mecklenburg-Vorpommern* [2000] ECR I-549, para. 26; Case C-284/02 *Land Brandenburg v Sass* [2004] ECR I-11143, para. 34. See also Case 109/88 *Handels- og Kontorfunktionærernes Forbund i Danmark v Dansk Arbejdsgiverforening, acting on behalf of Danfoss (Danfoss)* [1989] ECR 3199, where the Court ruled that a criterion rewarding employees' mobility—their adaptability to variable hours and places of work—may work to the disadvantage of female employees who, because of household and family duties, are not as able as men to organise their working time with such flexibility. Similarly, the criterion of training may

not formal, equality'. This change in approach may in turn reflect something of a change in the European Union's self perception from being a European *Economic* Community to a Union based on solidarity and social inclusion[128] where attempts need to be made to accommodate those—particularly women with caring responsibilities—who have so far been excluded from the labour market.

(c) The Constitutional use of equality

The discussion so far has focused on what might be termed the programmatic use of the equality principle. We turn now to the 'Constitutional' use of equality.[129] In this context, the Court takes the view that equality requires consistent treatment ('equality as consistency')—or in the Aristotelian formulation 'like must be treated with like'.[130] Equality in this context is shorn of the detailed elaboration of the principles of direct and indirect discrimination which seem to apply only to the more programmatic field of non-discrimination law. The 'Constitutional' use of the general principle of equality (or non-discrimination) can be found in three contexts: (1) as a ground for challenging the validity of Community acts of a general legislative nature as well as specific acts in respect of the EU's own staff; (2) as a value against which other Community measures are interpreted; and (3) as a ground to challenge the acts of the Member States when acting in the sphere of Community Law. We shall consider these situations in turn.

The use of the principle of equality to challenge the validity of Community acts

General principles of law can be invoked to challenge the validity of *Community* legislative acts on the ground that they breach the principle of equality. In this context, the principle of equal treatment requires that 'comparable situations must not be treated differently and that different situations must not be treated in the same way unless such treatment is objectively justified'[131] Usually, the Court finds that the two situations are not comparable, or that the differences can be objectively justified. Therefore, in the *Alliance* case[132] the Court found that the distinction drawn by the Directive between those substances which had already been approved

---

work to the disadvantage of women in so far as they have had less opportunity than men for training or have taken less advantage of that opportunity. In both cases the employer may only justify the remuneration of such adaptability or training by showing it is of importance for the performance of specific tasks entrusted to the employee.

[128] Collins, 'Human rights; Employment Discrimination, equality and social inclusion' (2003) 66 *MLR* 16. See also Hepple, 'Race and Law in Fortress Europe' (2004) 67 *MLR* 1.

[129] See further Barnard, *EC Employment Law*, (3rd edn, Oxford, OUP, 2006), ch. 6.

[130] I am grateful to Dagmar Schiek for discussion on this point. See also McCrudden, 'Equality and Non-Discrimination' in Feldman, *English Public Law* (OUP, Oxford, 2004).

[131] Joined Cases C-184/02 and C-223/02 *Spain and Finland v Parliament and Council* [2004] ECR I-7789, para. 64.

[132] Joined Cases C-154/04 and C-155/04 *R v Secretary of State for health, ex parte Alliance for Natural Health* [2005] ECR I-6451, para. 116.

when the Directive was adopted, which were automatically added to the positive list, and those which had not already been approved which had to go through an onerous approval process, did not breach the principle of equality because the two situations were not comparable.

The principle of equal treatment can also mean non-discrimination on a prohibited ground. In this context, employees of the Community institutions have used the principle to challenge discriminatory rules and practices, and they have enjoyed somewhat more success than other applicants wishing to challenge a Community legislative act for breaching the principle of equality more generally. Thus, in *Razzouk and Beydoun*[133] the Community's staff regulations which distinguished between the treatment of widows and widowers for the purpose of a survivor's pension breached the principle of equal treatment on the grounds of sex.[134]

However, in *D v Council*,[135] the Court adopted a cautious approach to discrimination on the grounds of sexual orientation. The case concerned the EU's refusal to pay a household allowance, which would have been payable to a married employee, to a homosexual employee who was in a stable partnership registered under Swedish law. While the Court appeared to recognize that the principle of non-discrimination extended to sexual orientation[136] it found that the principle had not been breached on the facts of the case. The Court said that the principle of equal treatment could apply only to persons in comparable situations, and so it was necessary to consider whether the situation of an official who had registered a partnership between persons of the same sex was comparable to that of a married official.[137] The Court then noted that because there was a wide range of laws in the Member States on recognition of partnerships between persons of the same sex or of the opposite sex and because of the absence of any general assimilation of marriage and other forms of statutory union,[138] it concluded that the situation of an official who has registered a partnership in Sweden could not be held to be comparable, for the purposes of applying the Staff Regulations, to that of a married official.[139]

Equality as a vehicle for interpretation
The Court of Justice has also used the general principles of law to interpret potentially ambiguous provisions of Community law. The significance of this can be seen

---

[133] Joined Cases 75 and 117/82 *Razzouk and Beydoun v Commission* [1984] ECR 1509.

[134] Paras. 17–18. See also Case 2121/74 *Airola v Commission* [1975] ECR 221. For a successful challenge to an indirectly discriminatory measure, see Case 20/71 *Sabbatini v European Parliament* [1972] ECR 345.

[135] Case C-125/99P [2001] ECR I-4319.

[136] At para. 47 the Court said 'as regards infringement of the principle of equal treatment of officials irrespective of their sexual orientation, it is clear that it is not the sex of the partner which determines whether the household allowance is granted, but the legal nature of the ties between the official and the partner'.

[137] Para. 48.

[138] Para. 50.

[139] Para. 51.

in *P v S*.[140] The case concerned the dismissal of a male to female transsexual on the grounds of her gender reassignment. The question referred to the Court of Justice was whether the word 'sex' in the phrase there should be 'no discrimination what-soever on the grounds of sex' in the Equal Treatment Directive 76/207 was broad enough to include 'change of sex'. Drawing on the general principle of equality, the Court said that the Equal Treatment Directive was 'simply the expression, in the relevant field, of the principle of equality, which is one of the fundamental prin-ciples of Community law'.[141] This enabled the Court to conclude that the scope of the Directive could not be confined simply to discrimination based on the fact that a person is of one or other sex and so would also apply to discrimination based on gender reassignment.[142]

This was a quite remarkable decision. It seems that a strong opinion on the part of the Advocate General was highly influential. He declared:

I am well aware that I am asking the Court to make a 'courageous' decision. I am asking it to do so, however, in the profound conviction that what is at stake is a universal fundamental value, indelibly etched in modern legal traditions and in the constitutions of the more advanced countries: the irrelevance of a person's sex with regard to the rules regulating relations in society. . . . I consider that it would be a great pity to miss this opportunity of leaving a mark of undeniable civil substance, by taking a decision which is bold but fair and legally correct, inasmuch as it is undeniably based on and consonant with the great value of equality.[143]

The guiding hand of the principle of equality—and another impassioned opinion by the Advocate General, this time Ruiz-Jarabo Colomer[144]—seems also to have helped a transsexual couple in *KB*.[145] The case concerned a decision by the NHS Pensions Agency not to award a widower's pension to KB's transsexual partner on the grounds that they were not married. KB was a woman who lived with R. R had been born a woman but, following gender reassignment, had become a man. Under English law, a birth certificate could not be amended to reflect this change in gender. This meant that the couple could not marry under English law because the Matrimonial Causes Act 1973 required marriage to take place between a man and a woman; according to their birth certificates KB and R were both female. As a result, R was not entitled to a survivor's pension, should KB predecease R, because under the NHS pension scheme a survivor's pension could be paid only to a spouse and R was not—and could never be—a spouse.

---

[140] Case C-13/94 [1996] ECR I-2143.
[141] Para. 17.
[142] Para. 20.
[143] Para. 24.
[144] Case C-117/01 *KB v National Health Service Pensions Agency* [2004] ECR I-541., AG's Opinon esp. paras. 79–80.
[145] Case C-117/01 *KB v National Health Service Pensions Agency* [2004] ECR I-541 discussed by Cantor (2004) 41 *CMLRev.* 1113. See also Case C-423/04 *Richards v Secretary of State for Work and Pensions* [2006] ECR I-000.

The Court began by finding that there was no discrimination on the grounds of sex because, for the purposes of awarding the survivor's pension, it was irrelevant whether the claimant was a man or a woman.[146] However, the Court then changed tack.[147] It noted that there was inequality in treatment, not in respect of the right to the pension itself, but in respect of one of the conditions for the grant of that right: the capacity to marry.[148] As the Court explained, while a heterosexual couple always has the option of getting married (and thus benefit from the survivor's pension), a couple such as KB and R, where one of the partners had undergone gender reassignment, could never marry. The Court of Justice then noted that the European Court of Human Rights had already condemned the UK for not allowing transsexuals to marry a person of the sex to which they once belonged.[149] This enabled the Court of Justice to conclude that British legislation which, in breach of the ECHR, prevented a couple such as KB and R from being able to marry and thus to benefit from part of KB's pay, had to be 'regarded as being, in principle, incompatible with the requirements of Article 141 EC'.[150] However, the Court then added that since it was for the Member States to determine the conditions under which legal recognition was given to the change of gender of a person in R's situation it was for the national court to determine whether a person in KB's situation could rely on Article 141 to gain recognition of her right to nominate her partner as a beneficiary of a survivor's pension.

The use of the principle of equality to challenge the acts of the Member States when acting in the sphere of community law

So far we have concentrated on the Court of Justice's approach to reviewing the validity of Community acts and interpreting of Community acts in the light of the principle of equality. However, the Court of Justice has not limited itself to using general principles in this way. It has also said that when *Member States* are acting within the sphere of Community law (ie when they are implementing Community law[151] and when they are derogating from Community law[152]), their actions must also be compatible with fundamental rights, including equality. In future, as a result of the remarkable decision in *Mangold*,[153] the validity of *national* acts in the sphere

[146] Para. 29.

[147] Para. 30.

[148] Ibid. Cf. Joined Cases C-122/99P and C-125/99P *D v Council* [2001] ECR I-4319, para. 47, a case concerning the refusal by the EU Council to pay a household allowance payable to married couples to an employee in a stable homosexual partnership registered under Swedish law, the Court said '. . . as regards infringement if the principle of equal treatment of officials irrespective of their sexual orientation, it is clear that it is not the sex of the partner which determines whether the household allowance is granted, but the legal nature of ties between the official and the partner'.

[149] *Goodwin v UK* (2002) 13 BHRC 120 and *I v UK* [2002] 2 FCR 613.

[150] Para. 34.

[151] Case 5/88 *Wachauf* [1989] ECR 2609, para. 19 and Case C-2/92 *Bostock* [1994] ECR I-995, para. 16.

[152] Case C-260/89 *ERT* [1991] ECR 2925.

[153] Case C-144/04 *Mangold v Helm* [2005] ECR I-9981.

of Community law may also be subject to challenge on the grounds of the principle of equality.

Mangold concerned the German law implementing the Fixed Term Work Directive 99/70.[154] According to this law, a fixed term employment contract could be concluded only where there were objective grounds for so doing. However, until December 2006 (when the age discrimination provisions of the Framework Directive 2000/78[155] came into force) the need for objective justification did not apply to fixed term contracts for workers aged over 52. The Court of Justice upheld Mangold's challenge to this rule that it was discriminatory on the grounds of age. Even though the age discrimination provisions of the Directive had not yet come into force, the Court said the source of the principle of non-discrimination found in the Framework Directive was various international instruments and in the constitutional traditions common in the Member States.[156] It continued: 'The principle of non-discrimination on grounds of age must thus be regarded as a general principle of Community law'[157] and the observance of this general principle could not be made conditional of the expiry of the transposition date of the Framework Directive.

Most striking of all, the Court indicated that general principles of law could be directly effective and enforceable in the national courts. The Court said that:

> In those circumstances it is the responsibility of the national court, hearing a dispute involving the principle of non-discrimination in respect of age, to provide, in a case within its jurisdiction, the legal protection which individuals derive from the rules of Community law and to ensure that those rules are fully effective, setting aside any provision of national law which may conflict with that law.[158]

Thus, national courts had to provide a genuine and effective remedy to enforce a general principle of Community law which applied in a horizontal situation.[159]

The reorientation of the principle of equality

Equality in the 'Social Policy' Title started life as a defensive mechanism against social dumping. As we have seen, in the intervening years, the perspective on equality has changed, enabling the Court to declare in *Deutsche Post*[160] in 2000 that, in view of the case law recognizing that equality was a fundamental right:

> . . . it must be concluded that the economic aim pursued by Article [141] of the Treaty, namely the elimination of distortions of competition between undertakings established in

---

[154] [1999] OJ L175/43.

[155] [2000] OJ L303/16.

[156] Para. 74.

[157] Para. 75.

[158] Para. 77.

[159] See also AG Tizzano's opinion, para. 99ff. Cf AG Geelhoed's Opinion in Case C-13/05 *Chacón Navas v Eurest Colectividades SA* [2006] ECR I-000.

[160] Joined Cases C-270/97 and C-271/97 *Deutsche Post v Sievers and Schrage* [2000] ECR I-929, para. 57.

different Member States, is *secondary* to the social aim pursued by the same provision, which constitutes the expression of a fundamental human right.[161]

A complete volte face has occurred and this has been recognised by the prominent role given to equality in the Constitutional Treaty.

THE CONTINUED RESONANCE OF THE SOCIAL DUMPING DEBATE

Introduction

With the express recognition of such strong, resonant principles as solidarity and equality, why was the Constitutional Treaty rejected by those—especially the French—who feared it gave the green light to social dumping? In part, the French rejection of the Constitutional Treaty can be explained by a selective reading of the Treaty (a copy of which was sent to all voters) where provisions such as Article I-3(2), with its reference to competition being 'free and undistorted', alarmed a number of voters. This reinforced already grave concerns over the excessive market liberalism of the Treaty, concerns exacerbated by contemporaneous discussions of the Bolkestein directive on the opening up of the market in services. The French concerns were summed up in the idea of the 'Polish plumber' who, for many, had assumed 'bogeyman status as low cost, low standard, Eastern European Labour'[162] flooding onto the French market and undercutting French labour. It is to this issue of free movement of services and its ramifications for labour law that we now turn.[163]

Posted Workers

The Treaty Provisions on Services and the Case Law of the Court of Justice

In order to understand the nature of the French concerns, we need to go back to the 1990 case of *Rush Portuguesa* and the Court's interpretation of the Treaty provisions (Articles 49 and 50 EC) on the free movement of services and the effect on the transnational subcontracting. This decision enabled companies established in one state, having been awarded a contract in another Member State (the host state), to relocate their employees to the host Member State to fulfil the contract. For the successful tendering company and, ultimately, for the home state from which they come, the company's success in winning the contract means more revenue and more employment. For the host state, securing the services of a cheaper out-of-state service

---

[161] Emphasis added. See also Joined Cases C-234/96 and C-235/96 *Deutsche Telekom AG v Vick and Conze* [2000] ECR I-799, para. 57.

[162] Waterfield, 'Polish workers protest against French bosses' *EUPolitix.com*, 4 October 2005, 1. France was not alone. The Swedish trade minister, Thomas Ostros, was reported as saying 'There cannot be a service directive, unless there is also a protection against social dumping': Küchler, 'McCreevy locks horns with Swedish unions' *euobserver.com*, 10 October 2005.

[163] This section draws on Barnard, *EC Employment Law*, (3rd edn, Oxford, OUP, 2006), ch. 5

provider means better value for money for the public purse. However, to the host state's labour unions such 'contracting-out' has raised the spectre of 'social dumping'—that service providers take advantage of cheaper labour standards in their own states to win a contract in the host state,[164] to the detriment of employment in the host state. This was the nub of the issue in *Rush Portuguesa*.[165]

Rush Portuguesa, a Portuguese company, entered into a subcontract with a French company to carry out rail construction work in France. It used its own third country national workforce,[166] contravening French rules which provided that only the French Office d'Immigration could recruit non-Community workers. The Court ruled that Articles 49 and 50[167]:

preclude a Member State from prohibiting a person providing services established in another Member State from moving freely on its territory *with all his staff* and preclude that Member State from making the movement of staff in question subject to restrictions such as a condition as to engagement *in situ* or an obligation to obtain a work permit.

The Court said the imposition of such conditions discriminated against guest service providers in relation to their competitors established in the host country who were able to use their own staff without restrictions.

Thus, in *Rush Portuguesa* (and other cases) the Court appeared to be taking an important step to opening up the market in services and allowing companies from countries with cheaper labour costs, primarily the southern and eastern European states, to profit from their comparative advantage to win contracts in other states (primarily the northern states with higher labour costs) and to take their own workforce with them to do the job. The reason why they can afford to win contracts is that the conditions of employment of temporary staff are usually governed by the labour law rules applicable in the country where the company is established and where the individual habitually carries out his work. The only limitation by the case law is that the service provider's workforce (ie the posted workers) must return to the country of origin after completing the task: they cannot join the labour market of the host state.[168]

Germany, like France, was also concerned about the threat posed by the Treaty provision on services to its labour law system and it was especially anxious to preserve the local system of wage setting and collectively negotiated, levy-based

---

[164] This point was also noted by the Commission which talked of the risk that 'in addition to disadvantages for workers this will give rise to distortions of competition between undertakings' (Social Charter Action Programme, s. 4).

[165] Case C-113/89 *Rush Portuguesa v Office national d'immigration* [1990] ECR I-1417.

[166] The workforce was actually Portuguese but at the time the transitional arrangements for Portuguese accession to the EC were in place which meant that the rules on freedom to provide services were in force but not those relating to the free movement of workers. Therefore, Portuguese workers did not enjoy the rights of free movement and so for our purposes the Portuguese workers constitute third country nationals (see para. 4 of the judgment).

[167] Para. 12, emphasis added.

[168] Case C-445/03 *Commission v Luxembourg* [2004] ECR I-10191, para. 38.

'social funds' in the German construction industry[169] from the threats posed by cheap migrant labour. In recognition of these concerns, the Court ruled in *Rush Portuguesa* that[170]:

Community law does not preclude Member States from extending their legislation, or collective labour agreements entered into by both sides of industry, to any person who is employed, even temporarily, within their territory, no matter in which country the employer is established; nor does Community law prohibit Member States from enforcing those rules by appropriate means.[171]

Thus, in one (unreasoned) paragraph the Court put a stop to a threat of social dumping by allowing the host state to extend its labour laws and conditions to the staff employed by service providers working in its country.

In subsequent cases, the Court has more fully articulated its reasoning. It has looked to see (1) whether the requirements imposed by the host state on the service provider restrict the freedom to provide services (the answer is usually yes). It then examines (2) whether the measure can be justified on the grounds of, for example, worker protection,[172] especially the interests of the posted workers,[173] or even to stop social dumping[174] or unfair competition[175]; (again the answer is usually yes); (3) whether the same interest is already protected in the state of establishment (this is usually left to the national court to decide); and finally (4) whether the steps taken are proportionate.[176]

Not that long after *Rush Portuguesa*, Germany passed a law, the AEntG, which stipulated that all employers based outside the country and sending one or more employees to work in Germany had to abide by provisions laid out in the relevant collective agreement, relating to minimum pay and certain conditions of employment, such as minimum holiday pay. These employers also had to make payments into the relevant social security funds unless they were already paying into social security funds in their own country or had already done so. Employers with headquarters outside Germany but which were sending employees to work in the country had to register in writing with the relevant local authorities in Germany

---

[169] See Streeck, 'Neo-voluntarism: A New Social Policy Regime' (1995) 1 *ELJ* 31, 42, and Simitis, 'Dismantling or Strengthening Labour Law: the Case of the European Court of Justice' (1996) 2 *ELJ* 156, 163.

[170] Para. 18.

[171] Citing Joined Cases 62/81 and 63/81 *Seco SA and Another* [1982] ECR 223.

[172] Joined Cases C-49, 50, 52, 54, 68 & 71/98 *Finalarte Sociedade de Construçâo Civil Ld^a* [2001] ECR I-7831, paras. 41–9, for a careful scrutiny of the worker protection justification and that the national measures did actually confer a genuine benefit on the posted worker. See also Case C-164/99 *Portugaia Construçôes Ld^a* [2002] ECR I-787, paras. 28–9.

[173] Joined Cases C-49, 50, 52, 54, 68 & 71/98 *Finalarte* [2001] ECR I-7831, para. 41.

[174] Case C-244/04 *Commission v Germany* [2006] ECR I-000, para. 61.

[175] Case C-60/03 *Wolff & Müller v Pereira Félix* [2004] ECR I-9553, para. 41.

[176] See e.g. Joined Cases C-369 & 376/96 *Criminal Proceedings against Jean-Claude Arblade and Arblade & Fils SARL and against Bernard Leloup and others* [1999] ECR I-8453.

before work commenced. Employers also had to supply the name of the employee concerned, the commencement and expected duration of the employment and the location of the site where the work was to be carried out.

In *Finalarte*[177] and *Portugaia Construções*,[178] the Court had to consider whether the German AEntG could be justified. The Court particularly looked at the expressed economic aim of protecting 'the German construction industry from competition in the European internal market, and thus from foreign providers of services, and reducing unemployment to avoid social tensions'.[179] As the Court put it, the law was aimed at combating the 'allegedly unfair practice of European businesses engaged in low-pay competition' [180] ie 'social dumping'.[181] Generally, the Court rejects wholly 'economic' justifications for the existence of national legislation. However, in these cases the Court said that while the political debates might indicate the intention of the legislature, it was not conclusive.[182] It was for the national court to check whether, viewed objectively, the rules in fact conferred a genuine benefit on the workers which significantly added to their social protection.[183]

The Posted Workers' Directive

This softly, softly approach to Northern European labour standards gave the green light to the enactment of the Directive 96/71 on Posted Workers.[184] Directive 96/71 on the posting of workers in the framework of the provision of services,[185] based on Articles 47(2) and 55, is intended to promote the transnational provision of services which requires a 'climate of fair competition and measures guaranteeing respect for the rights of workers'.[186] As Vladimir Špidla, EU Employment, Social Affairs and Equal Opportunities Commissioner bluntly put it, 'This Directive is a key instrument both to ensure freedom to provide services and to prevent social dumping'.[187] It aims to coordinate the legislation in the Member States and to lay down and give detail of the hard core of mandatory EC rules which *must* be respected by undertakings assigning their employees to work in another Member State. In this way, the Directive goes further than *Rush Portuguesa* which merely permitted (as opposed to requiring) Member States to extend certain rules to employees posted to their territory and did not specify which rules could be extended.

---

[177] Joined Cases C-49, 50, 52, 54, 68 & 71/98 *Finalarte Sociedade de Construção Civil Ld*[a] [2001] ECR I-7831.

[178] Case C-164/99 *Portugaia Construções Lda* [2002] ECR I-787.

[179] Ibid.

[180] *Finalarte*, para. 38.

[181] See AG Mischo's Opinion in Case C-164/99 *Portugaia Construções Lda* [2002] ECR I-787, para. 15.

[182] Para. 40.

[183] Para. 42.

[184] Directive 96/71/EC ([1996] OJ L18/1). See P. Davies, 'Posted Workers: Single Market or Protection of National Labour Law Systems' (1997) 34 *CMLRev.* 571.

[185] [1996] OJ L18/1. See also COM(93) 225 final—SYN 346.

[186] Preambular, para. 5.

[187] IP/06/423.

In essence, the Directive allows host states to apply to posted workers certain key labour law rules, in particular relating to minimum wages, working time and equal treatment, even in the case of short-term postings. However, since the Directive has the effect of requiring the out-of-state service provider to adapt its terms and conditions of employment each time it posts workers to another Member State, some argue that it interferes with, rather than promotes, the provision of services.[188] The Posted Workers' Directive does not try to harmonize the rules of the Member States categorized as mandatory. It merely identifies those employment conditions which the guest undertaking must respect. Thus, the Directive is based on coordination rather than harmonization, although the disparity between the rules of the different Member States in these core areas will be reduced as the Community passes further legislation in the social field. Significantly, those working conditions which this Directive identifies as important largely correspond to the areas in which Community legislation has already been passed or proposed.

The Laval case

The importance of these provisions, especially those concerning collective agreements, are highlighted by an important case referred to the Court of Justice, *Laval un Partneri*.[189] The reference itself goes to the heart of the Swedish model of industrial relations, based as it is on voluntary collective agreements without *erga omnes* procedures: is it compatible with rules of the EC Treaty on the freedom to provide services and with the provisions of Directive 96/71/EC for trade unions to attempt, by means of industrial action in the form of a blockade, to force a foreign (Latvian) service provider to sign a collective agreement in respect of terms and conditions of employment, if the situation in the host country (Sweden) is such that the legislation intended to implement Directive 96/71 has no express provisions concerning the application of terms and conditions of employment in collective agreements?

The dispute itself goes to the heart of the 'social dumping' debate.[190] A Latvian company, Laval, won a contract to refurbish and extend a school in the Stockholm suburb of Vaxholm. Laval was not a signatory to the Swedish Construction Federation collective agreements with Byggnads, the major Swedish construction trade union. Laval used its own Latvian workers to fulfil the contract. These workers earned about 40 per cent less per hour than comparable Swedish workers. Byggnads wanted Laval to apply the Swedish national agreement but, after some prevarication, Laval decided against doing so. This led to a union picket at the school site and a blockade by construction workers, and sympathy industrial action was

---

[188] See eg P. Davies, 'The Posted Workers Directive and the EC Treaty' (2002) 31 *ILJ* 298, 300.

[189] Case C-341/05 *Laval un Partneri Ltd v Svenska Byggnadsarbetareförbundet*. An application for the case to be heard by the accelerated procedure was refused: Order of 15 November 2005. See Eklund, 'The *Laval* Case' (2006) 35 *ILJ*. 202.

[190] For a full description of the dispute, from which the following draws, see Woolfson and Sommers, 'Labour Mobility in Construction: European Implications of the Laval un Partneri Dispute with Swedish Labour' (2006) 12 *EJIR*. 49.

taken by the electricians unions who boycotted Swedish companies operating at the site. Laval brought proceedings in the Swedish labour court, claiming that the industrial action and blockade were illegal, as was the sympathy strike. In an interim ruling, the court said that actions like this, aimed at pushing through an add-on to the leading collective agreement within the industry, could not be seen as going against good labour market practices.[191] Subsequently, the 10 million strong International Federation of Building and Wood Workers launched a solidarity campaign and the trade unions intensified their boycott. However, the Internal Market Commissioner, Charlie McCreevy, spoke out against Scandinavian collective agreements and said they breached EC law on free movement.[192] His remarks caused consternation in some quarters, in particular with the European Parliament where Martin Schulz MEP demanded that Mr Barroso 'disown this unacceptable attack on a social model that is universally recognised as being one of the most successful in the world'.[193] But for Laval, McCreevy's interventions came too late: it announced its withdrawal from Sweden[194] and its Swedish subsidiary filed for bankruptcy.

The Services Directive

While the Posted Workers' Directive appeared to plug one hole in the Northern European damn protecting their own labour markets from the 'flood' of cheap migrant labour, the Services Directive seemed to open up a potentially calamitous breach in the damn.

The Bolkestein proposal

The Services Directive aimed at providing a legal framework that would eliminate the obstacles to, (1) the freedom of establishment for service providers, and (2) the free movement of services between the Member States. In order to eliminate the first type of obstacles—those connected with the freedom of *establishment*—the initial Bolkestein proposal provided for administrative simplification and the prohibition of certain particularly restrictive legal requirements.[195] In order to eliminate the obstacles to the free movement of *services*, the proposal provided for:

- the application of the country of origin principle, according to which a service provider was subject only to the law of the country in which he is established and Member States could not restrict services from a provider established in another Member State. This principle was accompanied by derogations which are either general, or temporary or which may be applied on a case-by-case basis;

[191] Ibid, 56.
[192] Küchler, 'McCreevy locks horns with Swedish unions' *euobserver.com*, 10 October 2005.
[193] Mahoney, 'Barroso and Mc Creevy called to account in Swedish social model row' *euobserver.com*, 13 October 2005. His appearance is reported by Kubosova, 'Scandinavian model must comply with EU rules, says McCreevy' *euobserver.com*, 26 October 2005.
[194] Ibid, 57.
[195] COM(2004) 2 final/3, 3–4.

- in the case of posting of workers, the proposed Directive provided that Directive 96/71 applied and, so Article 17 of the original proposal contained a derogation from the country of origin principle where those rules were concerned. However, in order to facilitate the free movement of services and the application of Directive 96/71 the original draft clarified the allocation of tasks between the country of origin and the Member State of posting, and the administrative supervisory procedure.[196] Specific provision was also made for the posting of TCNs.[197] In particular, the proposed Directive wished to scrap certain administrative obligations concerning the posting of workers, accompanied by measures to reinforce administrative cooperation between states.

In some quarters, these two aspects of the Bolkestein proposal caused particular consternation. Opponents of the Directive feared that it would lead to social dumping thereby undermining the European social model.[198]

---

[196] Art. 24. This provided: 'Where a provider posts a worker to another Member State in order to provide a service, the Member State of posting shall carry out in its territory the checks, inspections and investigations necessary to ensure compliance with the employment and working conditions applicable under Directive 96/71/EC and shall take, in accordance with Community law, measures in respect of a service provider who fails to comply with those conditions.

1. However, the Member State of posting may not make the provider or the posted worker subject to any of the following obligations, as regards the matters referred to in point (5) of Article 17:
   (a) to obtain authorisation from, or to be registered with, its own competent authorities, or to satisfy any other equivalent requirement;
   (b) to make a declaration, other than declarations relating to an activity referred to in the Annex to Directive 96/71/EC which may be maintained until 31 December 2008;
   (c) to have a representative in its territory;
   (d) to hold and keep employment documents in its territory or in accordance with the conditions applicable in its territory.

2. In the circumstances referred to in paragraph 1, the Member State of origin shall ensure that the provider takes all measures necessary to be able to communicate the following information, both to its competent authorities and to those of the Member State of posting, within two years of the end of the posting:
   (a) the identity of the posted worker;
   (b) his position and the nature of the tasks attributed to him;
   (c) the contact details of the recipient;
   (d) the place of posting;
   (e) the start and end dates for the posting;
   (f) the employment and working conditions applied to the posted worker.

In the circumstances referred to in paragraph 1, the Member State of origin shall assist the Member State of posting to ensure compliance with the employment and working conditions applicable under Directive 96/71/EC and shall, on its own initiative, communicate to the Member State of posting the information specified in the first subparagraph where the Member State of origin is aware of specific facts which indicate possible irregularities on the part of the provider in relation to employment and working conditions'.

[197] Art. 25.

[198] See the remarks made by Evelyne Gebhardt, Socialist MEP, with responsibility for steering the Services Directive through the EP. Writing in *Parliament Magazine* and reported in *EUPolitix.com*, 4

The McCreevy package

Eventually, the European Parliament, at first reading, put forward a watered-down measure,[199] and the Commission then drafted a revised proposal.[200] This 'McCreevy' draft was narrower in scope than its Bolkenstein predecessor and shorn of both the country of origin principle[201] (but not the derogations which went with it) and the social provisions.[202] It has now been adopted as Directive 2006/123[202A] At the same time, the Commission issued a Communication on the Posted Workers' Directive[203] aimed at strengthening the position of service providers wishing to use their own workforce to fulfil contracts in other Member States. In his speech to the European Parliament,[204] McCreevy said that the decision to remove all interaction between the Services Proposal and labour law was one of the most important elements in creating a more positive atmosphere around this new draft. He continued that 'This has allowed us to move on from allegations of lowering of social standards and threats to the European social model', adding that 'While this perception was wrong it did not go away and poisoned the debate'.

The Communication on Posted Workers[205] draws on the provisions of the Bolkestein Directive and the case law of the Court which will continue to apply. Essentially, it rules out three types of requirements and permits another two.[206] Those requirements which are prohibited are:

- The obligation for a service provider to have a permanent representative on the territory of the host Member State: the appointment of a person from among the posted workers, such as the site foreman, to act as a link between the foreign company and the labour inspectorate is sufficient.

October 2004, 1, she said the Bolkestein proposal 'constitutes a threat to consumer protection, the European social model and public services'. The Prime Minister and then president of the European Council, Jean-Claude Juncker, said (http://www.eu2005.lu, 24 March 2005) that any new draft of the Directive's text will 'take into account the double imperative of the opening of the services market as well as respect for the European social model in accordance with the motto: Yes to the liberalisation of services, no to social dumping. Those who wish the services directive to be fashioned in such a way that employees lose all their rights, thereby bringing unhealthy pressure to bear on the level of salaries and diminishing employees' rights through the opening up of markets, are sadly mistaken'.

[199] A6–0409/2005 FINAL.

[200] COM(2006) 160.

[201] Only a year before, Commission President Barroso is quoted as saying that 'The directive just wouldn't work without' the country of origin principle: The Services Directive and the European Constitution' *Eu.observer.com*, 21 March 2005.

[202] Arts. 24 and 25 of the original proposal were removed.

[202A] [2006] OJ L376/36.

[203] 'Guidance on the posting of workers in the framework of the provision of services': COM(2006) 159. This is accompanied by a report SEC(2006) 439. It also issued a Communication, *Social services of general interest in the European Union* COM(2006) 177. It is beyond the scope of this work to consider this.

[204] SPEECH/06/220, 4 April 2006.

[205] COM(2006) 159.

[206] Although see the ETUC's criticisms of this: 'Commission is sending out contradictory messages on enforcement of posting directive' http://www.etuc.org, press release 5 April 2006.

- No prior authorization can be required as a general rule by the host country for the posting of workers,[207] but service companies may have to obtain a specific authorisation in certain sectors (eg temporary employment agents) when rendering services in another Member State provided this requirement is justified, proportionate and account is taken of the controls already carried out in the home state.
- The host state cannot impose administrative formalities or additional conditions on posted workers form third countries when they are lawfully employed by a service provider established in another Member State, without prejudice to the right of the host state to check that these conditions are complied with in the state where the service provider is established.[208]

Those requirements which are permitted are:

- The possibility for host states to ask for a *declaration* (which is less restrictive than a prior authorization) from the service provider by the time the work starts which contains information on the workers who have been posted, the type of service they will provide, where and how long the work will take is compatible with Community law.[209] In respect of TCNs, the declaration can specify that they are in a 'lawful situation' in the home state (ie the state in which the service provider is established), including in respect of visa requirements, and that they are legally employed in the home states.[210]
- The host state can require service providers to keep social documents such as time-sheets or documents related to health and safety conditions at the place of work. However, the host state cannot require a second set of documents if the documents required under the legislation of the Member States of establishment, taken as a whole, already provide sufficient information to allow the host state to carry out the checks required.

In addition, the Communication makes clear that the national authorities of the countries of origin have to cooperate loyally with the authorities in the host Member States and to provide them with all the required information, in order to enable these to perform their controlling duties and fight illegal practices. Liaison offices and the monitoring authorities have to be sufficiently equipped and resourced in order to be able to reply correctly and swiftly to any kind of demand. Appropriate measures must be in place to sanction foreign service providers when the correct terms and conditions of employment as set out in the Directive are not complied with.

---

[207] Relying on Case C-43/93 *Vander Elst* [1994] ECR I-3803.

[208] See the discussion of Case C-244/04 *Commission v Germany* [2006] ECR I-000 and Case C-445/03 *Commission v Luxembourg* [2004] ECR I-10191 above.

[209] See the discussion of Case C-244/04 *Commission v Germany* [2006] ECR I-000 and Case C-445/03 *Commission v Luxembourg* [2004] ECR I-10191 above.

[210] See the discussion of Case C-43/93 *Vander Elst* [1994] ECR I-3803 above.

Viking

The other case which highlights this tension between the economic freedoms of the Treaty and workers' rights is *Viking*.[211] Viking Line, a Finnish company and one of the largest passenger ferry operators in the world, wanted to reflag its vessel, the Rosella which traded the loss-making route between Helsinki and Tallinn in Estonia, under the Estonian flag so that it could man the ship with an Estonian crew to be paid considerably less than the existing Finnish crew.[212] The International Transport Workers' Federation (ITF), which had been running a Flag of Convenience (FOC) campaign trying to stop ship owners from taking such action, told its affiliates in the jurisdictions which the Rosella visited, to boycott the Rosella and to take other solidarity industrial action against both the Rosella and other Viking vessels. The Finnish Seaman's Union (FSU) threatened strike action. *Viking* therefore sought an injunction in the English High Court (ITF had its base in London and so jurisdiction was established pursuant to the Brussels Regulation 44/2001[213]), restraining the ITF and the FSU from breaching, *inter alia*, Articles 43 on freedom of establishment and Article 49 on services.

In the High Court, Gloster J ruled that reflagging of a vessel in a Member State involved the exercise of establishment[214]; and that the ITF/FSU's proposed actions amounted to a restriction on the freedom of establishment under Article 43.[215] Applying *Gebhard*[216] and *Guiot*,[217] the judge ruled that 'Any measure which places an additional financial burden on a person so as to make the exercise of a free movement right more difficult constitutes a restriction on that free movement right'. She also thought that Article 43 applied to organizations like ITF/FSU which intended to create 'obstacles resulting from the exercise of their legal autonomy by associations or organisation not governed by public law'.[218] Indeed, she went so far as to say that the ruling in *Angonese*,[219] that Article 39 had full horizontal direct effect, was not confined to workers' cases and applied equally to Article 43.[220]

The judge then ruled that the FOC policy was directly discriminatory: it prevented the owner of a Finnish vessel from re-flagging so as to employ a crew of another Member State, and compelled the owner to retain its Finnish crew. Even if the policy was not directly discriminatory, it was, she said, indirectly discriminatory. She then considered whether the directly discriminatory conduct could be

---

[211] *Viking Line ABP v The International transport Workers' Federation, the Finnish Seaman's Union* [2005] EWHC 1222 (QBD) and [2005] EWCA Civ. 1299 (Court of Appeal).

[212] For a full description of the facts, see Waller LJ in the Court of Appeal [2005] EWCA Civ. 1299.

[213] [2001] OJ L12/1.

[214] Para. 106.

[215] Para. 99.

[216] Case C-55/94 [1995] ECR I-4165.

[217] Case C-272/94 *Criminal proceedings against Guiot* [1996] ECR I-1905.

[218] Case C-415/93 *Bosman* [1995] ECR I-4921, paras. 82–84.

[219] Case C-281/98 [2000] ECR I-4139, considered in Ch 4.

[220] Para. 115.

saved by reference to one of the express derogations, namely public policy. She said[221]:

It is clear that the exercise of fundamental rights may fall within the scope of the public policy justification; . . . The right to take industrial action can, for present purposes, be characterized as part of the fundamental right of freedom of expression and of freedom of association and to take collective action.

However, since the express derogations must also be appraised by reference to fundamental rights, Gloster J went on to find that the exercise of these fundamental rights could not, without more, authorize or justify discrimination on the grounds of nationality—or sex.[222] Thus, she said it was not compatible with Article 14 ECHR (prohibition against discrimination) that workers have a fundamental right to strike to prevent women from being employed on ferry boats. In the same way, the exercise or enjoyment of the right to take industrial action to prevent the reflagging of a vessel could also be characterized as a fundamental right.[223] She therefore concluded that fundamental rights could not be invoked to justify discrimination on the grounds of nationality.

Gloster J then considered whether the FOC rule, if considered to be *indirectly* discriminatory, could be objectively justified. While acknowledging that the protection of workers was an acceptable public interest justification, she required more of the social purpose of the justification. The first purpose offered, safeguarding the job opportunities of the FSU's members, was rejected by the judge on the grounds that Viking had given an undertaking that if it reflagged the Rosella none of its crew would be made redundant; they would be transferred elsewhere in the group.[224]

She also rejected the second purpose put forward by the unions, safeguarding the level of terms and condition of employment and the living standards of all seafarers working on vessels trading in the Baltic and Nordic area, regardless of their nationality, on the grounds first, that the primary purpose of the proposed action was to protect *Finnish* jobs; second that it would be disproportionate to insist that Finnish terms and conditions be applied to all workers on board the Rosella even though the vessel was reflagged in Estonia; and lastly, if the vessel was reflagged in

---

[221] Para. 123.

[222] Para. 124. See also AG Jacobs' Opinion in Case C-67/96 *Albany International BV v Stichting Bedrijfspensioenfonds Textielindustrie* [1999] ECR I-5751, where he said that while management and labour are in principle free to enter into such agreements as they see fit, they must, like any other economic actor, respect the limitations imposed by Community law, such as sex equality and free movement of workers. He continues that this could be seen as an application of the general rule that the exercise of a fundamental right may be restricted provided that the restriction in fact corresponds to objectives of general interest pursued by the Community and does not constitute in relation to the aim pursued a disproportionate and intolerable interference, impairing the very substance of the rights guaranteed.

[223] Para. 126.

[224] Paras. 133–134.

Estonia, the crew would be protected by an ITF affiliated Estonian trade union and Estonian collective bargaining. If due regard was given to the principle of mutual recognition, the judge said that it did not seem proportionate that the FSU and ITF should be entitled to insist that the interests of workers on board the Rosella be protected by the FSU, as opposed to an ITF affiliated trade union established in another Member State.[225] Thus, the judge concluded that the unions anticipated actions would not be objectively justified or were not appropriate or proportionate to secure the unions' purposes. As a result, she ordered interim relief in favour of Viking to restrain the unions from taking industrial action to deter Viking from, (1) reflagging the Rosella, and (2) if it did reflag, requiring Viking to continue paying its crew at Finnish rates negotiated with the FSU.

Gloster J's decision on interim relief was reversed by the Court of Appeal[226] which referred the case to the Court of Justice to rule on the issues considered by the judge at first instance. Before making the reference, Waller LJ, giving judgment on behalf of the court, expressed grave concerns about the view that Articles 43 and 49 applied to trade union acts.[227] While recognizing that there should not be a blanket exclusion of trade union activities from the free movement provisions, he thought the control mechanism should be the Social Policy Title of the Treaty ie 'if an activity plainly does not pursue a social object within Title XI, the free movement Articles will apply, whereas if it does they should not'.[228] He also suggested that if there was direct discrimination, the unions would be unlikely to justify any restriction but he thought it more likely that some indirect discrimination or other restriction would be found which, he recognized, might be justified by reference to fundamental rights. For these reasons, the Court of Appeal set aside Gloster J's decision and refused interim measures because, as Waller LJ said, granting the injunction to Viking would be close to giving Viking the remedy which should only be available to it after a full trial of the action.[229]

The unions see *Viking* as a case about unfair competition where ship owners used the rules on freedom of establishment to cut costs and lower labour standards. Mr Zitting, chairman of the FSU is quoted by Gloster J as saying that 'this is a fight against social dumping'[230] and that social dumping is 'the idea that you replace an employee with a cheaper one coming from somewhere else'.[231]

---

[225] Para. 138.
[226] [2005] EWCA Civ. 1299; [2006] IRLR 58. The reference is Case C-483/05. See Davies (2006) 35 *ILJ*. 75 and and Novitz, 'The right to strike and reflagging in the European Union: free movement and human rights' [2006] *LMCLQ* 242.
[227] Para. 62.
[228] Para. 44.
[229] Para. 64.
[230] Para. 119.
[231] Para. 137.

CONCLUSION

The renaissance of the Treaty provisions on services in the last 15 or so years has helped to open up the market in services. When terms and conditions of employment did not differ so substantially between the original 6 Member States, the free market did not pose a significant threat to the integrity of national social orders. But as the EU began to expand, first to the south (Portugal, Spain and Greece) and, more importantly to the east, the tensions between the free market and the preservation of national social models began to resurface. The *Viking* and *Laval* cases have brought these tensions into sharp focus and, indirectly, they have influenced public perception of the Services Directive. The Court, inevitably, has become caught up in this debate. It will have to decide *Viking* and *Laval*, and other cases like them, but it has already started to pin its colours to the mast. With its (uncritical) recognition of 'social dumping' as a public interest requirement in *Commission v Germany*, it has disregarded the bigger social picture of the benefits to the Latvian and Estonian workers of having access to a much wider market for their services.

The Constitutional Treaty would not have helped resolve these challenges. It does, however, reinforce the tools that the Court has already equipped itself with to strike a balance between the interests of the internal market and the interests of individual workers. In that respect the second Treaty of Rome offers greater balance and a more rounded view than the first.

6

The Area of Freedom, Security and Justice and the European Union's Constitutional Dialogue

DORA KOSTAKOPOULOU

Justice and Home Affairs (JHA), which is now known as the Area of Freedom, Security and Justice (AFSJ), has been a rapidly developing policy field. Although the development of JHA exhibits the gradualism and incrementalism that characterize the process of European integration in general, one cannot ignore its distinctive features. First, because policing, criminal law and immigration policy are areas of 'high politics', that is, they are intimately linked with national sovereignty and statehood, the Member States' perception that closer cooperation in this area comes at the cost of compromising state sovereignty has functioned as a brake to adopting integrationist solutions. Accordingly, cooperation in JHA has developed in various stages, evolved at variable speeds and has blended intergovernmental and integrationist elements in a unique way.[1] Secondly, as law and order issues have traditionally been the prerogative of the executive in all Member States, politicians and bureaucratic elites have been eager to maintain this control in the European arena. For this reason, JHA cooperation has been executive driven, secretive and, until the mid-1990s, insulated from the input of parliaments, NGOs and from media scrutiny. The third distinctive feature follows closely from the above two. In a terrain where perceptions about security threats, be they real or imagined, ideological orientations and political expediency blend and shape choices and policy options, one finds that more often than not politics and rhetoric, be it about open borders, influxes of migrants and security deficits, subjugates policy. As a result, JHA cooperation has been characterized by complex and confused institutional arrangements, ad hoc reactions to issues and external events, institutional crowding and, until 1999, by the absence of comprehensive planning and clear objectives.[2]

---

[1] See S. Peers, *EU Justice and Home Affairs Law* (2000), chapters 1–3; Den Boer and W. Wallace, 'Justice and Home Affairs', in H. Wallace and W. Wallace (eds.), *Policy-Making in the European Union* (2000).

[2] N. Walker, 'In Search of the Area of Freedom, Security and Justice: A Constitutional Odyssey', in N. Walker (ed.), *Europe's Area of Freedom, Security and Justice* (2004).

However, European integration has been a process of learning by doing and JHA cooperation is no exception. Throughout its 30 year history (1975–2005), national executives have had to reflect upon larger contexts and transnational challenges, be they terrorism, drugs trafficking, international crime and human mobility, to interrogate the doctrine of sovereignty, to learn to trust each other and to search for improved institutional arrangements. Accordingly, a distinctive trait of JHA cooperation is institutional restlessness. Lacking a robust institutional framework and the clearly defined goals that characterize other EU policy fields, JHA cooperation has always been in transition in some form or another.

The Constitutional Convention's deliberations concerning the area of freedom, security and justice and the Constitutional Treaty that sprung from the Convention's work are good cases in point.[3] The Constitutional Treaty completed the process of transition from intergovernmentalism to supranationalism and opened up the possibility for better and more efficient law-making in JHA matters and for a more open and accountable EU. The infrastructure has also been laid down for a more proactive and better coordinated JHA cooperation, and the principle of mutual recognition clearly enhances the array of policy options at the Union's disposal. Although the ratification crisis prompted by the French and Dutch referenda has stalled progress and has sparked lively debates, such as whether the Treaty is 'dead' or 'in a coma',[4] simply relying on the Nice settlement is unlikely to be a viable option for the Area of Freedom, Security and Justice. Nor can it be argued that the key reforms in the institutional framework and procedures in this area introduced by the Constitutional Treaty can be adopted by a series of inter-institutional agreements.[5]

---

[3] On the Convention on the Future of Europe and the Constitutional Treaty, see K. Lenaerts and M. Desomer, 'Bricks for a Constitutional Treaty of the European Union: values, objectives and means', *European Law Review* (2002) 377; P. Magnette and C. Nicolaïdes, 'The European Convention: Bargaining in the shadow of rhetoric', 27 *West European Politics* (2004) 381; J. Temple Lang, 'The main issues after the Convention on the Constitutional Treaty for Europe', 27 *Fordham International Law Journal* (2004) 544; P. Craig, 'Constitutional Process and Reform in the EU: Nice, Laeken, the Convention and the IGC', 10(4) *European Public Law* (2004) 653; M. Dougan, The Convention's Draft Constitutional Treaty: A 'Tidying-Up Exercise' That Needs Some Tidying-Up Of Its Own, *Federal Trust Online Constitutional Essay*, 27/2003; A. Dashwood, 'The Draft EU Constitution—First Impressions', 5 *Cambridge Yearbook of European Legal Studies* (2002/2003) 419; G. de Búrca, 'The Constitutional Challenge of New Governance in the European Union', 28 *European Law Review* (2003); B. de Witte, 'Simplification and Reorganisation of the European Union', 39 *Common Market Law Review* (2002) 1244; *Ten Reflections on the Constitutional Treaty for Europe* (2003); M. Dougan, 'The Convention's draft Constitutional Treaty: bringing Europe closer to its lawyers?', 28 *European Law Review* (2003) 763; A. Arnull, 'Member States of the European Union and Giscard's Blueprint for its Future', 27 *Fordham International Law Journal* (2004) 503; P. Birkinshaw, 'A Constitution for the European Union?—A Letter from Home', 10 *European Public Law* (2004) 57.

[4] See the briefing papers for the European Parliament Committee on Constitutional Affairs on the occasion of the Symposium 13/14 October 2005 (http://www.europarl.eu.int/meetdocs/2004_2009/organes/afco).

[5] Such inter-institutional agreements could ensure the implementation of other institutional innovations of the Constitutional Treaty, such as, for example, the provisions concerning the increased input

But irrespective of whether one concedes that the Constitutional Treaty is unlikely to be salvaged in its current form and that some kind of Treaty amendment will be needed in the near future, both the evolution of JHA and the present debate about the constitutional future of the EU are poignant reminders of the fact that EU constitutionalism is, essentially, an ongoing discursive engagement with the principles and terms of European governance and with institutional design.[6] In this respect, old and new debates, such as whether the Constitutional Treaty was a treaty or a constitution; or whether it represented 'a critical moment' for shaking off the institutional past[7] or constituted an exercise in simplification and consolidation[8]; or whether the Constitutional Treaty could be salvaged as a whole or in parts (Part I and II), and the merits and demerits of a second referendum in France and the Netherlands, all make important contributions to the European constitutional dialogue.

More importantly, irrespective of the form that institutional reform takes and of whether the constitutional language and symbolism are retained in the future,[9] it is important to bear in mind that any future revision of the provisions concerning the Area of Freedom, Security and Justice (AFSJ), as indeed any other revision that has preceded it, will be both a consolidating and transformative project. Provisions that

from national parliaments in relation to the subsidiarity principle; see Jo Shaw's contribution to the symposium on 13/14 October 2005.

   [6] Compare Bruno de Witte, 'The Closest Thing to a Constitutional Conversation in Europe: The Semi-Permanent Treaty Revision Process', in P. Beaumont, C. Lyons and N. Walker (eds.), *Convergence and Divergence in European Law* (Oxford: Hart Publishing, 2002); N. Walker, 'Constitutionalising Enlargement, Enlarging Constitutionalism', 9 *European Law Journal* (2003) 365; P. Craig, 'Constitutions, Constitutionalism and the European Union', 7(2) *European Law Journal* (2001) 125; J. Weiler, 'A Constitution for Europe? Some Hard Choices', 40(4) *Journal of Common Market Studies* (2002) 563; J. Shaw, *The Legal and Political sources of the Treaty establishing a Constitution for Europe*, Working Paper, Manchester University.

   [7] Critical moments represent opportunities for significant change and complete departure from previously established patterns. The retention of the existing institutional balance in the legislative process, the making of the co-decision procedure as the ordinary legislative procedure, the extension of the EU's competence to new areas, the abolition of the pillared structure, the incorporation of the EU Charter into the Treaty and the enhanced role of national parliaments in the EU decision-making process, all could taken to be reforms endowed with deep transformative effects.

   [8] According to the minimalist view, the Constitutional treaty does not substantially alter the constitutional balance between the MS and the EU. Nor does it signal a new supranational direction for the Union. Adherents of this perspective would pinpoint the attribution of formal institutional status to the European Council and the strategic role it enjoys in JHA issues, the provisions on the double Presidency, that is, the Chair of the European Council, elected by qualified majority, and the President of the Commission, who is chosen by the European Council and elected by the European Parliament by majority voting, the appointment of the Foreign Affairs Minister by the European Council by qualified majority with the agreement of the Commission President, the omission of references to 'an ever closer Union' and 'the acquis communitaire being an express objective of the Union' and the explicit reference to the possibility of states' withdrawal from the Union.

   [9] This refers to the possibility of giving the next European Parliament the explicit mandate to draft the European constitution. On the importance of constitutional symbolism, see N. Walker, *After the Constitutional Moment*, Federal Trust Online Constitutional Essay, (2003).

preserve the institutional balance and consolidate existing relations will thus be interwoven with provisions that destabilize and generate new openings. For institutional change in the EU is neither a process of simple iteration nor the result of radical breaks. It is, instead, incremental-transformative, that is, the product of a complex mix of consolidation and transformation, of a vision and a compromise. European integration has been a journey in institutional experimentation, reflection and critique, and, gradients, be they ascending or descending, by and large, make journeys interesting.

The discussion in this chapter maps the evolution of justice and home affairs cooperation since 1975. In this 'constitutional odyssey',[10] attention will be paid to the process of incremental-transformative change culminating in the provisions of the Constitutional Treaty. By bringing JHA cooperation in line with the Community method, the Constitutional Treaty brought about the most significant institutional innovations in this area. And although it is true that JHA cooperation will not be marked by stagnation in the absence of the Constitutional Treaty, it is equally true that the Constitutional Treaty's provisions are bound to be the point of departure for any future discussion about institutional reform and Treaty amendment in this area.

MAPPING THE EVOLUTION OF JUSTICE AND HOME AFFAIRS

Phase 1 (−1985): Ad hoc and Loose Intergovernmental Cooperation

Because policing and criminal law strike at the core of statehood, it is often assumed that states' natural stance in this area is one of non-cooperation. And yet as early as 1914 the First International Police Congress in Monaco endorsed the idea of centralized international criminal records and standardized extradition procedures. Subsequent initiatives, such as the establishment of the International Criminal Police Commission in 1923 and the International Criminal Police Organization (Interpol) in 1946, showed states' willingness to move beyond loose forms of cooperation by developing common institutions in order to combat crime. In the field of criminal law too, a network of treaties under the aegis of the UN and the Council of Europe have brought about the 'internationalization' of criminal procedure. In the context of the European Union, the origins of JHA cooperation can be traced back to attempts to tackle fraud in the Community finances following the design of the Common Agricultural Policy in the 1960s, advance civil judicial cooperation and promote mutual assistance among customs authorities in 1967.

Against this background, and in an attempt to tackle political extremism in the 1970s, the Trevi Group was established in Rome in 1975 as a forum for enhancing intergovernmental cooperation in counterterrorism. Drawing on the experience of European Political Cooperation, the Member States (MS) believed that regular

---

[10] The term is borrowed from Walker, *supra* n. 2.

meetings of ministers and senior civil servants would advance European police cooperation. The Ministerial Group initially met semi-regularly and, following 1984, once every six months under the chairmanship of the country that held the Council Presidency. TREVI also involved senior officials and civil servants of justice and interior ministries and, on occasions, senior police officers, taking part in three working groups (Terrorism, Technical Forum and Drugs, and Serious Organised Crime) and later on in ad hoc working groups. In 1985 the scope of TREVI included football hooliganism, serious international organized crime, especially drugs trafficking, and in 1988 a fourth working group on the abolition of border controls, TREVI 1992, was established.[11] By that time, police and customs officers had successfully established 'a chain of equivalence' between the single market, free movement and security deficits, whereby the abolition of internal border controls was seen to require compensatory measures of tightened external border controls and internal surveillance. The Paris Declaration of the TREVI Ministers on 15 December 1989 and the Schengen project are manifestations of this discursive formation.

Phase 2 (1985–1992): Advanced Intergovernmental Cooperation

Although JHA cooperation preceded the single market project, the Single European Act gave it much impetus. In anticipation of the internal market, which had to be achieved by the beginning of 1993, France, Germany and the Benelux countries signed the Schengen agreement on the abolition of border controls in the small village of Schengen in 1985. Owing to protracted negotiations, the reunification of Germany and fears of mass migration from Central and Eastern Europe, the implementing measures were not agreed until mid-June 1990.[12]

Lacking an input from national parliaments, Community institutions and the civil society, national executives saw the Schengen project as dependent on: (a) the design of an external frontiers policy and the harmonization of visa policies (Articles 1–27 of the Schengen Implementing Agreement); (b) common rules on asylum and migration-related issues (Articles 28–38); (c) other forms of operational cooperation, hot pursuit by police and customs officers, cross border observations, controlled deliveries of drug shipments (Articles 39–91); and (d) the establishment of a central information database (SIS) in Strasbourg which would link the various databases in

---

[11] See R. Bieber and J. Morgan (eds.), *Justice and Home Affairs in the European Union: The Development of the Third Pillar* (1995); E. Ucarer, 'Cooperation in Justice and Home Affairs', in Cram *et al.* (eds.), *Developments in the European Union* (1999), 247–65.

[12] Its entry into force was delayed for another five years owing to political reasons and the difficulties associated with the Schengen Information System (SIS), a computerized database at the disposal of police and customs officers in the Schengen countries. By that time all Member States, with the exception of UK and Ireland, had either acceded to or were progressing towards full membership; Italy joined in 1990, Portugal and Spain in 1991 and Greece in 1992. On 1 May 1996 Denmark, Sweden and Finland became observers.

the MS, national sections (NSIS), thereby allowing law enforcement authorities to exchange and obtain personal identification data and descriptions of lost or stolen objects (Articles 92–119). Entries of information in the national databanks would be copied to all other NSIS by the central computer within a few minutes.[13] Schengen's leading institutional body was the Schengen Executive Committee, consisting of national ministers and secretaries of state. The Committee was assisted by the Central Group, consisting of 120 senior civil servants and police officers, which directed and supervised the work of several committees, working groups and subsidiary working groups. The complexity of Schengen's institutional structure, coupled with the secretive character of the meetings of the various groups, highlighted the accountability deficit of the Schengen vision of JHA cooperation. At the same time, it showed that that national preference formation did not precede interstate cooperation, as liberal intergovernmentalism claims. Rather, the formulation of objectives and the pursuit of strategies were the product of discussions at the European level, and these were as much influenced by ideology and embedded beliefs as domestic policy-making.

The alleged link between the abolition of internal frontiers and increased crime rates and levels of migration was neither called into question nor verified by risk assessment analyses and empirical research. Many doubted whether borders make a difference to the overall level of serious organized crime and its international networks of operation. Similarly, despite rhetoric about 'drugs flowing to Europe', experts argued that drug trafficking could only be combated through intelligence operations, and not incidental seizures of drugs at the border. In addition, the 1990 report of the House of Commons Home Affairs Committee commented on the terrorists' ability to circumvent border controls and made it clear that an effective anti-terrorist policy would have to rely on police intelligence rather than the apprehension of terrorists at borders. After all, despite its symbolic political attraction, the idea of creating a 'hard outer shell' (Fortress Europe) can never be fully operationalized given the porosity of Europe's many points of exit and entry. Furthermore, although restrictive migration and asylum policies were presented as an inevitable consequence of the internal market, in reality they had very little to do with it. The trend towards restriction and control of migration had begun in the early 1970s in Western Europe, as racist concerns about the social costs of 'coloured migration' and fears of 'being swamped by alien cultures' resulted in the ideological reframing of migration, be it voluntary or forced, as a problem and a 'law and order' issue.

Instead of responding to any externalities associated with single market, national executives thus sought to anticipate security risks associated with speculative transnational flows and levels of crime, thereby generating moral panics. The single market became the pretext and the justification for restrictive measures of migration

---

[13] SIS went online on 26 March 1995, and was complemented by SIReNE, a communication system which enables law enforcement agencies to exchange information in relation to specific queries.

control and increasing internal surveillance. In a paradoxical way, the abolition of internal border controls gave rise to mobile controls internally and the erection of new barriers externally. The creation of what Bigo has termed 'an internal security continuum',[14] that is, the perception of a security deficit in a Europe without frontiers, furthered the interests of senior bureaucrats in justice and interior ministries, and security agencies were able to maintain their levels of public funding despite the removal of border controls.

It also precipitated a proliferation of working groups on a wide range of JHA issues. Monar estimates that from 1986 to 1991, the Member States created over 20 new intergovernmental bodies,[15] the most prominent of which was the Ad Hoc Working Group on Immigration. Set up at a meeting of Interior Ministers in London in 1986, the Group drafted the Dublin Convention (15 June 1990), aimed at preventing alleged 'asylum shopping', and was involved in the drafting of the External Frontiers Convention (1994), which never entered into force owing to differences concerning sovereignty and a territorial dispute between Britain and Spain over Gibraltar. In an attempt to provide some organizational infrastructure and coordination in the work of these groups, the European Council set up a Group of National Coordinators in 1988, consisting of senior civil servants from national interior and justice ministries. Following the Rhodes European Council, the Group of Coordinators compiled the so-called Palma document which entailed a set of 'compensatory measures' required by the abolition of border controls.

The concentration of power in the hands of national executives and their civil servants, which acted as quasi-legislators, coupled with the absence of parliamentary oversight and judicial scrutiny, exacerbated the democratic deficit and aroused fears about the creation of 'an authoritarian Europe'. The Schengen institutional framework was criticized for the undue concentration of power in the hands of the Schengen executive committee; for increasing police and surveillance powers at the expense of human rights; for failing to protect personal data; for lacking a dispute settlement mechanism; and for compromising international law obligations towards refugees and asylum seekers. Similar concerns arose with respect to the Dublin Convention, which superseded the Schengen provisions on asylum. Notwithstanding these criticisms, however, European institutions viewed Schengen as the laboratory for European JHA cooperation. The principal perceived advantage of the Schengen initiative (and equally, in the view of others, a major weakness), was its flexibility, that is, it enabled the five MS to continue their integrative efforts outside of, but in parallel with, the framework of EC. The benefits of enhancing cooperation and fostering a culture of trust among the MS were therefore seen to outweigh the accountability and transparency deficits associated with intergovernmental cooperation. Perhaps, the Commission believed a more appropriate institutional design creating linkages with EC institutions would remedy these deficiencies.[16]

---

[14] D. Bigo and R. Leveau, *L'Europe de la securitite interieure* (1992).
[15] 'The Dynamics of JHA: Laboratories, Driving Factors, Costs', 39(4) *JCMS* (2001), 747–64.
[16] Commission Communication SEC(91) 1855 final.

Phase 3 (1993–1998): The Maastricht Third Pillar

In line with the institutional form of pure intergovernmentalism state cooperation in JHA was loose, ad hoc and outside the Community's formal structure. National executives conducted negotiations in accordance with international law which, on occasions, culminated in conventions. The secrecy that surrounded deliberations, the insufficient input by the relevant stakeholders in this process, the lack of coordination among the various workings groups which often resulted in the duplication of activity, the difficulty in agreeing binding measures and monitoring their implementation all led to increased calls for the establishment of formal linkages with the Community process. While some states favoured this reform during the Intergovernmental Conference, which culminated in the Treaty of the European Union or Maastricht Treaty in 1992 (in force in November 1993), other states believed that removal of migration, asylum, judicial and police cooperation from their exclusive domain of jurisdiction would make them less sovereign. The ensuing compromise was the making of nine areas of JHA cooperation matters of common interest located into a separate intergovernmental pillar (the so-called Third pillar): asylum policy, rules on the crossing of external borders, immigration policy and policy regarding nationals of third countries, combating drug addiction, combating international fraud; judicial cooperation in civil matters, judicial cooperation in criminal matters, customs cooperation and police cooperation (Article K. 1 TEU).[17] Resembling a Greek temple, the European Union's architecture encompassed the Community pillar, consisting of the EC, ECSC and Euratom Treaties, and two intergovernmental pillars on common foreign and security policy, and justice and home affairs respectively. Notwithstanding its usefulness, however, the Greek temple simile concealed areas of overlap between the first and third pillars which gave rise to jurisdictional conflicts: the articulation of common rules governing the crossing of the external border of the EU (K.1(2)) and visa policy (Article 100c EC); the Community policy on public health and action to combat drug addiction; fraud affecting the financial interests of the Community and action to combat fraud on an international scale under Article K1(5) EU.

JHA Organizational actors

The Commission. Although the MS were eager to maintain their sovereign prerogatives with regard to the maintenance of law and order and the safeguarding of internal security at Maastricht, the Commission for the first time had to be fully associated with the work in justice and home affairs. However, the Commission did not have an exclusive right of initiating legislation; it had a shared right of initiative in the first six areas of common interest and no right of initiative in the remaining three areas of police, customs and criminal judicial cooperation.

[17] See J. Monar and R. Morgan (eds.), *The Third Pillar of the European Union: Cooperation in the Fields of Justice and Home Affairs* (1995); T. Kostakopoulou, *Citizenship, Identity and Immigration in the European Union: Between Past and Future* (2001).

In Maastricht Europe, the Commission exercised its shared right of initiative in a pragmatic and strategic way. Following an initial cautious approach owing to states' sensitivities about sovereignty, the Commission became more active. Aided by the establishment of a JHA policy portfolio with the Social Affairs Commissioner and the new division in the Secretariat General monitoring and supporting the third pillar, it proposed both legislative instruments and funding programmes. The latter secured the Council's agreement. The Commission also used the overlap between the first and third pillars in order to propose measures concerning the Community's financial interests, a list of (129) countries whose nationals required a visa when crossing the external borders of the MS and a uniform format for visas under Article 100c(3) EC. In 1994 the Commission also issued a Communication on immigration and asylum policies, laying down a framework for a European Immigration and Asylum Policy. By taking such initiatives and developing credible policy ideas, the Commission was signaling to the MS the potential benefits of granting agenda-setting power to it in the future.

The Parliament. While in the Community pillar the European Parliament (EP) plays an important and ever increasing role in the adoption of Community legislation by means of the co-decision procedure which was introduced at Maastricht; in the third pillar it had only to be 'regularly informed' of JHA discussions and 'consulted' by the Presidency of the Council on the 'principal aspects of activities' (Article K.6). In practice, consultation took the form of documents submitted to it ex post facto.[18] The Council's failure to consult the EP over the Europol convention led it to initiate an examination of the measure ex post facto in 1996. The institutional circumscription of its role, coupled with the culture of secrecy that accompanied the JHA Council's meetings, led the EP to voice its concerns about the lack of democratic accountability in JHA cooperation. Similar concerns were expressed by national parliaments which complained about the lack of transparency and about persistent delays in depositing documents in Parliaments for scrutiny.

The Court of Justice. Whereas in the Community pillar the Court has far reaching jurisdiction over preliminary rulings, judicial review of Community law, infringements of Community law and the EC institutions' failure to act where they have an obligation to do so, in the third pillar the ECJ had no mandatory jurisdiction. A system of judicial review by the ECJ was only optionally provided for third pillar conventions under Article K.3(2) EU.

The Council. In line with the institutional form of intergovernmentalism, the Council of Ministers had leading actor status. While in the first pillar qualified majority voting was widespread, unanimity prevailed in the third pillar. The JHA Council, which replaced the General Affairs Council after Maastricht, was assisted by the Coordinating Committee under Article K.4(1) EU. The latter's role was to prepare JHA Council meetings (three to four a year) in conjunction with the

---

[18] For a critique, see D. O'Keeffe, 'Recasting the Third Pillar', 32 *Common Market Law Review* (1995) 893.

Committee of Permanent Representatives (COREPER) and to give opinions for the attention of Council. In reality, however, the K.4 Committee, which absorbed the Coordinators' Group, ensured that COREPER played a limited role in JHA cooperation. The K.4 Committee's substructure was far from novel; it formalized the Trevi structure, thereby confirming the historical institutionalist insight about the long-term implications of past institutional choices (path dependence). The structures of the Trevi process had been firmly locked into place as attested by the K.4 Committee's three Steering Groups. Steering Group I oversaw working groups on migration, asylum, visas, external borders, CIREA (asylum statistics), CIREFI (immigration statistics), and false documents. Steering Group II encompassed working groups on police cooperation, Europol, terrorism, customs cooperation, drugs and organized crime. Under Steering Group III there existed working groups on extradition, the Brussels II Convention, service of documents, criminal law, and Community law. There also existed horizontal working parties on the European Information System and drugs which reported directly to the K.4 Committee. The existence of such a complex, five-tiered, decision-making structure (JHA Council, COREPER, K.4, Steering Groups and Working Groups) gave rise to coordination problems which undermined effectiveness. For this reason, the Irish Presidency introduced reforms in the second half of 1996 and the UK Presidency abolished the Steering Groups altogether in 1998. It is worth noting here that in Maastricht Europe, new working groups were created to deal with specific issues (eg on Eurodac, mutual criminal assistance) and ad hoc groups, such as the group which drew the Organised Crime Action Plan in 1997, sometimes had a limited life span. The latter led to the establishment of a new high level multidisciplinary working group on organized crime and the secondment of eight specialists from the MS to form a policy-making unit within the Council Secretariat.

Instruments

In contrast to the traditional Community legal instruments, the main third pillar instruments were joint positions, joint actions and Council Decisions establishing Conventions. Joint Positions were used in order to promote cooperation contributing to the Union's objectives and fell into desuetude in the post-Maastricht era. Joint Actions, on the other hand, were circumscribed by reference to the principle of subsidiarity, that is, they were used if the Union's objectives could be better achieved by joint action than by unilateral action.

Legal effect

The legal effect of Joint Actions and Joint Positions was not clarified by the Treaty on European Union. According to the Council's Legal Service, joint actions were legally binding. Although soft law instruments, such as resolutions, recommendations and conclusions, were favoured by the ministers, conventions remained the main 'hard law' instrument in the third pillar. However, conventions had to be agreed unanimously, epitomised the lowest common denominator approach, that is, the reduction of provisions to a bare minimum acceptable to all, and were followed by long and slow periods of ratification. The Dublin Convention, for example, entered into force seven years following its agreement in 1997. As the Council could not impose any time limits or compel ratification, Dublin, Rome and Schengen were the only three out of 11 conventions agreed during the first phase (1985–1992) that had been ratified by 1999.[19] Another problem associated with convention law-making is the possibility of national opt-outs from particular legal obligations. The Europol convention is a case in point. Britain and Denmark opposed any involvement by the ECJ in Europol affairs, while Germany and the Benelux countries considered it necessary. Despite attempts made by France to resolve the matter in 1995, the dispute became bound up politically with the row over the EU's ban on exports of British beef owing to BSE (bovine spongiform encephalopathy), before a complex compromise on the ECJ's preliminary ruling reference procedure was agreed at the Florence summit in June 1996. The latter culminated in a Protocol to the Europol Convention, giving the MS wide discretion to opt-out of the preliminary rulings jurisdiction and modify the procedure at will, at the price of undermining the uniform application of rules and threatening to create 'security gaps'.

Differentiated integration

Article K.7 EU authorized bilateral or multilateral action outside the framework of the EU or EC in so far as it 'did not conflict with or impede' third pillar cooperation, thereby giving status to differentiated integration arrangements, such as Schengen.

Whereas in the first phase of JHA cooperation the same forces that had induced the 'intenationalization' of cooperation, that is, transnational challenges and growing interdependence, led to European intergovernmental cooperation, in the second phase these functioned more as background conditions for interstate cooperation. The TEU's third pillar design can thus be explained on the basis of the combined effect of the single market programme, that was seen to engender significant spill over expectations,[20] and national governmental elites' desire for more optimal outcomes that would not damage national sovereignty.

It is noteworthy here that although the institutional architecture of 'diluted intergovernmentalism' appeased national executives' concerns about national sovereignty, it, nevertheless, entailed a fundamental ambiguity; namely, intergovernmental negotiations had to be conducted under the shadow of future Community competence. The 'passerelle' provision of K.9 opened the possibility of the transfer of all areas of JHA cooperation with the exception of customs, police and criminal judicial cooperation into the Community pillar, thereby functioning as a bridge between the first and third pillars. True, the transfer required the Council's unanimous approval and ratifications in accordance with national constitutional

[19] Peers, *supra* n. 1, at 16.

[20] Contrary to the neofunctionalist assumption concerning the expected shift of loyalties to 'Europe', however, national elites continued to be favourably disposed towards intergovernmentalism.

requirements (the 'double lock' procedure). However, the unthinkable had already happened. The inclusion within the third pillar of the possibility of its own transcendence fuelled supranationalist aspirations and paved the way for the partial Communitarization of the third pillar at Amsterdam.

Phase 4 (1999–): The Area of Freedom, Security and Justice

The *modus operandi* of the third pillar revealed the deficiencies of the intergovern-mentalist institutional framework: ineffectiveness of policy-making due to the prevalence of unanimity, convention law-making and the over-cumbersome five-tier decision-making structure; the absence of clearly defined objectives; lack of enforcement mechanisms; the growth of a culture of secrecy; the absence of effective Parliamentary involvement and judicial supervision; and the substantive rights deficit of the policies agreed. Correcting the deficiencies of JHA cooperation and meeting increasing transnational challenges required a different institutional format.[21] During the 1996 Intergovernmental Conference, the calls for the partial transfer of migration-related areas and civil cooperation to the Community pillar increased.[22] The Commission had prepared the ground for a gradual shift to Communitarization, a position endorsed by the Irish Presidency (December 1996) which suggested a new title on Free Movement, Asylum and Immigration without incorporating it into the Community pillar. The Benelux countries, Italy, Germany, Spain and Austria also favoured the incorporation of the Schengen acquis, that is, of the Schengen Convention and the associated implementing acts, into the Treaty. The EP, non-governmental and quasi-governmental actors, such as the European Council of Refugees and Exiles, Migrants Forum, the Starting Line Group, the Migration Policy Group, the Dutch Standing Committee of Experts on International Immigration, Refugee and Criminal Law and so on, all supported such reforms, hoping for more accountability, transparency and qualitative better policy-making on migration-related issues.

The Amsterdam Treaty (in force on 1 May 1999) transferred to the Community pillar responsibility for external border controls, the rights of third country nationals, migration, asylum and judicial civil cooperation. Police and judicial cooperation in criminal matters remained within a reformed third pillar which also included action against racism and xenophobia and offences against children. Customs cooperation and the protection of the financial interests of the Community were transferred to other parts of the EC Treaty. Although there existed neither a divergence in the definition of problems and security threats nor substantial disagreements over the

---

[21] S. Hix, *The 1996 Intergovernmental Conference and the Future of the Third Pillar*, Churches Commission for Migrants in Europe, (1995); S. Hix and J. Niessen, *Reconsidering European Migration Policies: the 1996 Intergovernmental Pillar and the Reform of the Maastricht Treaty*, Churches Commission for Migrants in Europe (1996).

[22] Reflection Group, *Progress Report on the 1996 Intergovernmental Conference*, (1995). See also M. Petit, The Treaty of Amsterdam, *Harvard Jean Monnet Working Paper Series*, 2 (1998).

general orientation of the policies agreed among the MS, Britain and Denmark resisted any erosion of national sovereignty, while Ireland opposed the reforms due to its commitment to maintaining a common travel area with Britain. The ensuing compromise increased significantly the complexity of the institutional arrangements at Amsterdam which rendered the traditional supranational/intergovernmental dualism which captured the Maastricht pillared structure outdated.

At Amsterdam the concept of justice and home affairs was replaced by the discursive utterance of 'creating an area of freedom, security and justice' (AFSJ) which became an objective of the Union. AFSJ is defined as an area 'in which the free movement of persons is assured in conjunction with appropriate measures with respect to external border controls, asylum, immigration and the prevention and combating of crime'. Article 29 EU further elaborates on this objective, and Articles 30 and 31 EU specify the scope of common action in relation to police cooperation and judicial cooperation in criminal matters respectively, thereby lending credence to the logic of functional spill over.

Although the AFSJ pertained to both first pillar and third pillar (the mutual interdependence among the different aspects of this overall objective is confirmed by Art. 61 EC which mentions Art. 31(e) EU), the role and relations of the EU institutions in the new Title IV EC and the reformed Third Pillar (Title VI EU) were very different, as follows:

JHA organizational actors

The Commission. Although the Council continued to have leading actor status in Title VI EU (the third pillar), the Commission gained a shared right of initiative in all areas. Title IV EC, on the other hand, weaves together Community and intergovernmental features: it set out a five-year transitional period from the entry into force of the Treaty during which the Council would take decisions by unanimity (with the exception of visa matters under Article 100c EC) on an initiative put forward by either the Commission or a MS after consultation with the EP. Following the end of the five-year transitional period (1 May 2004), the Community method replaced the intergovernmental institutional framework: the Commission assumed its exclusive right of initiative, but had an obligation to consider any request by a MS for a legislative proposal, and the Council would decide by unanimous vote to switch to co-decision and qualified majority voting. The Treaty of Nice inserted a fifth paragraph in Article 67 EC which allowed for measures relating to civil judicial cooperation and asylum to be adopted by using the co-decision procedure, under certain conditions. In December 2004, co-decision and qualified majority voting was extended to all Title IV measures, with the exception of legal migration, as of 1 January 2005.[23] Although the requirement of unanimity in migration-related

---

[23] Council Decision 2004/927/EC of 22 December 2004 providing for certain areas covered by Title IV of Part Three of the Treaty establishing the European Community to be governed by the procedure set out in Art. 251 of that Treaty, OJ 2004 L396/45.

areas hampered progress in post-Amsterdam Europe, the Commission did not hesitate to initiate a number of important legislative proposals (eg on family reunification, long-term resident third country nationals and asylum). The creation of a new Commission-level portfolio for justice and home affairs contributed to the Commission's high profile role. To support the Commissioner, the Justice and Home Affairs Task force was turned into a full scale Directorate General, thereby boosting the Commission's administrative and agenda-setting capacity. Concerned about the dilution of its proposals owing to the Council's tendency to adopt the lowest common denominator approach, the Commission suggested the standardization of the co-decision procedure as a means of enhancing the Union's legitimacy during the EU Convention.[24]

The Parliament. As earlier noted, the powers of the European Parliament were strengthened in Title IV EC, particularly following the end of the transitional period. By contrast, in Title VI EU the Parliament saw a modest increase in its old powers by means of a right to be consulted before the adoption of framework decisions, decisions, conventions and measures implementing decisions and conventions. National Parliaments gained increased opportunities to scrutinize draft proposals at Amsterdam. Protocol 13 establishes an obligation on the part of the Commission to deposit all legislative proposals to national parliaments and provides that six weeks must lapse between a Commission proposal under the EC Treaty or Title VI EU and the placing of that proposal on the Council agenda for decision. Articles 5 and 6 of the Protocol make provision for the involvement of COSAC, the Conference of European Affairs Committees, on matters including the AFSJ.

The European Court of Justice. The input of the Court was enhanced in both Titles (contained intergovernmentalism). In Title IV EC the ECJ obtained jurisdiction over enforcement actions, annulment, failure to act and non-contractual liability. As regards its jurisdiction to rule on a preliminary reference request by a national court, however, national delegations decided to circumscribe the ECJ's role by limiting preliminary ruling requests to courts of last instance, which tend to be more sensitive to the concerns of the executive, and by making such requests discretionary. The Court also has no jurisdiction to review measures or decisions as regards a MS' unilateral decision to reinstate border controls relating to the maintenance of law and order and the safeguarding of internal security. Finally, the Council, the Commission or a MS may request the ECJ to give a ruling on a question of interpretation of this title or of secondary legislation but the ECJ's ruling shall not apply to judgments of national courts or tribunals that have become *res judicata*. As a consequence, individuals cannot benefit retroactively from the Court's decisions.

In Title VI EU, the ECJ was given jurisdiction to give preliminary rulings on the validity and interpretation of framework decisions and decisions, the interpretation of conventions and on the validity and interpretation of measures implementing them, provided that a MS decided to opt-in the ECJ's jurisdiction by means of a

---

[24] Commission Communication on the Institutional Structure, COM(2002) 728, Brussels 11 December 2002.

declaration made at the time of signature of the Treaty of Amsterdam. In the declaration a MS had to specify whether it would allow only its appellate courts to refer questions to the ECJ or whether any court or tribunal would have such capacity. Most MS have made such declarations.[25] The 'permissive jurisdiction by declaration' was not a novel idea; it formalized a pre-existing compromise which had been devised in order to end states' disputes over the jurisdiction of the ECJ in a number of conventions, including Europol. Although the institutionalization of a pattern of variation in preliminary rulings reference procedure could be seen as a manifestation of state power, in reality it reveals states' anxieties about the ECJ's possible expansive jurisdiction to third pillar instruments which would effectively undermine their control and empower individuals in the area of data protection.[26]

The Court was also excluded from reviewing the validity or proportionality of operations carried out by the police or other law enforcement services of a MS or MS' acts relating to the maintenance of law and order and the safeguarding of internal security. However, for the first time the Court was given powers of judicial review of framework decisions and decisions, akin to those it has under the EC Treaty, and wider jurisdiction in the settlement of disputes among the MS regarding the interpretation of all acts under the third pillar.

The Council. As already noted, unanimity remained the rule in Title VI EU; special qualified majority voting (62 votes in favour cast by at least 10 members) was provided for the implementation of third pillar decisions and a majority of two thirds of the states was required for the adoption of measures implementing conventions. COREPER II was assisted by 'JHA Counsellors', that is, experts from the national ministries who often met as an informal group.[27] The K.4 Committee became 'Article 36 Committee' and its remit was confined to third pillar matters. The Committee coordinated the activity of working groups on police and customs cooperation, criminal judicial cooperation and on organized crime. The Committee worked closely with the Strategic Group on Immigration, Frontiers and Asylum established on 16 March 1999 and a new Civil Law Committee.

Instruments

While the Community legal instruments (regulations, directives, decisions, recommendations and opinions) apply to Title IV EC, the third pillar; Title VI EU, envisages a different set of instruments: common positions, framework decisions, decisions and conventions. Article 34(2)(a) EU provides that common positions define the approach of the EU to a particular matter. The main instrument for the approximation of national laws or administrative provisions is the framework

---

[25] The UK, Ireland and Denmark have not submitted declarations. As regards the new members, only Hungary and the Czech Republic have submitted declarations.

[26] E. Guild and S. Peers, 'Deference or Defiance? The Court of Justice's Jurisdiction over Immigration and Asylum', in E. Guild and C. Harlow (eds.), *Implementing Amsterdam*.

[27] J. Monar, 'Justice and Home Affairs in the Treaty of Amsterdam: Reform at the Price of Fragmentation', 23 *European Law Review* (1998) 230.

decision. Resembling the Community directive, this instrument is binding on the MS with regard to the result to be achieved, thereby leaving them with the choice of forms and methods. Unlike Community directives, however, framework decisions are incapable of having vertical direct effect, that is, of creating rights for individuals that are enforceable before national courts. Similarly, decisions, which can be used for any other purpose designed to achieve the objectives of Title VI except approximating national laws and regulations, do not entail direct effect. However, in the first reference for a preliminary ruling under Article 35 EU, the ECJ stated that framework decisions can have indirect effect, that is to say, national authorities are under the obligation to interpret national law as far as possible in the light of the wording and purpose of the framework decision.[28] As the Court stated, '[its] jurisdiction would be deprived of most of its useful effect if individuals were not entitled to invoke framework decisions in order to obtain a conforming interpretation of national law before the courts of the Member States',[29] and Article 10 EC creates obligations on the part of the MS in the area of police and criminal judicial cooperation.[30] Concerning Conventions, the Amsterdam Treaty stipulated that they enter into force once they have been ratified by at least half of the MS that adopted them.

Legal effect

The legal effect of common positions was left unclear by the Treaty. Framework decisions and decisions, on the other hand, are binding on the MS, but do not entail direct effect. Overall, the binding nature of Framework decisions, decisions and conventions was a positive step towards enhancing legal certainty and effectiveness in JHA matters.

Differentiated integration

Britain, Ireland and Denmark opted-out from Title IV EC by means of protocols; namely, the protocols on the position of the UK and Ireland, on the application of Article 14 EC to the 'Common Travel Area', and on the position of Denmark. Britain and Denmark opted-out owing to their longstanding reservations about border controls and sovereignty respectively, while Ireland wished to maintain a Common Travel Area with Britain. Although Britain and Ireland were given the option of opting-in either the adoption or the implementation of a proposed measure and have widely availed of their opt-in powers, Denmark can opt-in only by accepting Title IV legislation in its entirety.[31]

The Amsterdam Treaty also integrated the Schengen acquis into the EC/EU. This process entailed the identification of the correct legal basis for each of the provisions

---

[28] Case C-105/03, *Criminal Proceedings against Maria Pupino*, Judgment of the Court of 16 June 2005. This is considered further by S. Prechal in this volume.

[29] ibid para 38.

[30] ibid paras 39–42.

[31] For a more detailed account, see K. Hailbronner, 'European Immigration and Asylum Law under the Amsterdam Treaty', 35 *Common Market Law Review* (1998) 1047; M. Hedemann-Robinson, 'The

and decisions in accordance with their subject-matter and was completed in May 1999. Although the acquis is not binding on the UK and Ireland, both states were offered the possibility of taking part in some or all of the agreements under the Schengen acquis and have already done so with respect to measures relating to police cooperation and criminal judicial cooperation. As a Schengen member, Denmark, on the other hand, could decide to opt-in to measures adopted by the Council which 'build upon the Schengen acquis', but the incorporation of any such decision into national law would create public international law obligations only. Finally, the interests of Iceland and Norway were accommodated by the conclusion by the Council of two separate agreements outside the institutional framework of the Union. Notwithstanding its advantages in terms of enhancing democratic account-ability, transparency and judicial scrutiny, the integration of the Schengen acquis increased the complexity of the JHA institutional framework and created the spectre of inconsistent application of rules in the Community.

The final instance of differentiated integration was Article 40 EU. This article, which was one of the specific procedural provisions for closer cooperation, provided for the possibility of closer cooperation among the MS by using the institutions, procedures and mechanisms laid down by the Treaties, provided that such cooper-ation does not encroach on the powers and objectives of the Community and the objectives laid down by Title VI aims at enabling the Union to develop more rapidly into an area of freedom, security and justice. These provisions, which were made less stringent, more operational and were renamed as 'enhanced cooperation' by the Treaty of Nice, have not been invoked yet.

The creation of such a complex institutional framework, coupled with the institutionalization of 'variable geometry', should be seen as neither a sign of state retreat in the face of vocal and concerted opposition nor a manifestation of state power. Rather, it shows that national governments have not behaved as rational and strategic actors in the JHA area,[32] in opposition to liberal intergovernmentalist and neorealist assertions. Lacking clear objectives, a well thought through strategy and comprehensive forward planning, national governments have often adopted what Wessels has termed 'parallel strategies', that is, incoherent approaches reflecting short-term interests.[33] Examples of parallel strategies are: having an interest in increasing efficiency in decision-making and enhancing coordination in JHA and 'retaining a national say on the outcome of day to day politics'; dogmatic adherence to outdated templates of sovereignty for certain MS in 'history-making decisions' and a pragmatic interest in taking part and adopting policies and measures; viewing

---

Area of Freedom, Security and Justice with Regard to the UK, Ireland and Denmark: The "Opt-In Opt-Outs" under the Treaty of Amsterdam', in D. O'Keefe and P. Twomey (eds.), *Legal Issues of the Amsterdam Treaty* (1999).

[32] den Boer and Wallace, *supra* n. 1, 518; N. Walker, 'Justice and Home Affairs', 47 *International and Comparative Law* Quarterly (1998) 231.

[33] W. Wessels, 'The Nice Results: The Millennium IGC in the EU's Evolution', 39(2) *JCMS* (2000) 197, at 201.

the free movement of Community nationals and their family members as a right while regarding the movement of non-EU nationals as a problem.

Whereas federalists would view the partial Communitarization of the Third Pillar as a step closer to (future) supranational statehood, neofunctionalists would regard it as an incremental spillover effect of the internal market and as evidence of the Community's structural evolution. However, the fact that the spillover did not extend to criminal judicial cooperation and policing shows both the continuing salience of politics and the non-linear and uneven character of transformative institutional change. And although the Amsterdam Treaty did not displace the inter-governmentalism of the third pillar, it, nevertheless, showed that the MS' dream of the continued dominance of intergovernmental reflexes can only have intermittent fulfilment, since in the long-run it is impossible to escape from the dominance of the practical. This, perhaps, explains why at the very heart of the revised third pillar one finds again the 'Communitarization constant', that is, the possibility of trans-ferring third pillar matters to Title IV EC by a unanimous vote in the Council (Article 42 EU). Although Article 42 EU reflected a mere possibility, it, neverthe-less, exerted a serious gravitational pull which, as we shall see below, had to be taken seriously.

Framing the Area of Freedom, Security and Justice

As we have seen, at Amsterdam, justice and home affairs cooperation was replaced by the notion of creating 'an area of freedom, security and justice'. The amended Article 2 EU states that one of the objectives of the Union is 'to maintain and develop the Union as an area of freedom, security and justice'. This is defined as an area 'in which the free movement of persons is assured in conjunction with appropriate measures with respect to external border controls, asylum, immigration and the prevention and combating of crime'. Article 29 EU further elaborates on this objective by stating that the Union's objective is to provide citizens with a high level of safety within an area of freedom, security and justice by developing common action among the MS in the fields of police and judicial cooperation in criminal matters and by preventing and combating racism and xenophobia. This objective is to be achieved by preventing and combating crime, organized or otherwise, in particular terrorism, trafficking in persons and offences against children, illicit drug trafficking and illicit arms trafficking, corruption, and fraud. Articles 30 and 31 EU specify the scope of common action in relation to police cooperation and judicial cooperation in criminal matters respectively. As the concept of freedom, security and justice applies to both Titles IV EC and VI EU, the mutual interdependence among the different aspects of this overall objective is confirmed by Article 61 EC which mentions Article 31(e) EU.

Asserting a leadership role in JHA matters, the Cardiff European Council (15/16 June 1998) called for an action plan to implement the area of freedom, security and justice (AFSJ). Responding to this call, the Commission issued a communication furnishing an analysis of the conception of an area of freedom, security and justice, and outlining the various routes that would lead to its realization in July 1998.[34] In December 1998, the Vienna European Council adopted the Action Plan *on how best to implement the provisions of the Treaty of Amsterdam on an area of freedom, security and justice*, which entailed a list of measures which had to be adopted within a time frame of two years and five years, respectively.[35] These ranged from the development of Europol and the incorporation of the Schengen acquis regarding police and customs cooperation to the adoption of a European migration strategy based on the reduction of migration pressure at the source, on combating of undocumented migration, the control of legal entry of people and so on. The Tampere European Council (15 and 16 October 1999) diluted the restrictive character of the above objectives and set out a number of policy orientations and priorities which would make the AFSJ a reality. A scoreboard was set up to monitor progress towards its implementation. At Tampere, the principle of mutual recognition of judicial decisions in both civil and criminal matters was endorsed as the basis of judicial cooperation within the Union. To reinforce the fight against serious organized crime, it was decided to set up Eurojust, a body that would facilitate the proper coordination of national prosecuting authorities and support cross-border criminal investigations in this area.

The association of the concept of freedom with security and justice is neither accidental nor purely conjunctive, bearing in mind the securitization ethos[36] that has characterized justice and home affairs cooperation since the mid-1970s. As we saw in the previous section, official discourses had constructed a chain of equivalence between the single market project, free movement of persons and security, whereby the abolition of internal controls was seen to necessitate compensatory measures of tightened external border controls and internal surveillance, prior to the Maastricht Treaty. The Schengen project was a clear manifestation of the institutionalization of this discursive formation. Although the Schengen project run in parallel with intergovernmental cooperation within the context of the Union, the Schengen objectives and provisions eventually found their way into the JHA framework.[37] The assumption that a security problem exists in a Europe without internal border controls was well-embedded within policy circles.[38] Accordingly, the MS demanded compensatory

---

[34] COM (1998) 459.

[35] OJ 1999 C 19 of 23 January 1999.

[36] The term securitization refers to the removal of an issue from the normal political arena and to its articulation as an issue of national security and/or as an existential threat justifying measures outside the normal bounds of political procedure; on this, see B. Buzan, O. Waever and J. de Wilde, *Security. A New Framework for Analysis* (1998); O. Waever, Securitisation and Desecuritisation, Working Paper 5/1993, Centre for Peace and Conflict Research. Also published in Lipschutz (ed.), *On Security* (1995). When the agenda is dominated by security concerns, then the range of policy options becomes quite narrow.

[37] For a discussion on how prior institutional commitments condition further action and limit the scope of change, see P. Pierson, *Politics in Time: History, Institutions and Social Analysis* (2004).

[38] S. Lavenex, 'The Europeanisation of Refugee Policies: Normative Challenges and Institutional Legacies', 39(5) *Journal of Common Market Studies* (2002) 851; P. Boeles, 'Introduction: Freedom,

powers of control at the external frontiers and gave police and customs agencies the opportunity to craft a new role for themselves within an enlarged Europe, by identifying specific categories of security risk.[39]

This created the paradoxical situation whereby freedom of movement of EU nationals was celebrated as a fundamental right, while the EU's policy towards extra-EC migration became increasingly controlled and restrictive. In pre-Amsterdam Europe, these parallel (albeit contradictory) trends were kept apart. In theory, both are instrumental in creating an area without internal frontiers within which the free movement of goods, persons, capital and services is ensured (Article 14 EC). However, the general approach and philosophy underpinning them are very different. Indeed, it was this endemic incoherence of European migration policy (ie, the securitization ethos characterizing extra-EU migration policy v. the liberalization ethos of intra-EU movement) that provided ammunition for the critique of the intergovernmental methodology, and had raised normative expectations that 'more Europe' may yield more liberal migration policies and the inclusion of long-term resident third country nationals in the Euro-polity.

The Amsterdam Treaty did not only rupture the membrane separating the two migration policies (extra- and intra- EU migration), but it also laid down irreversible linkages between the two. The Communitarized areas of the third pillar came to support the first pillar: they were indispensable flanking measures to the abolition of internal border controls and to the maintenance of security. The Council and the Commission's Action Plan on how best to implement these provisions of the Amsterdam Treaty stated[40]:

Freedom loses much of its meaning if it cannot be enjoyed in a secure environment and with the full backing of a system of justice in which all Union citizens and residents can have confidence. These three inseparable concepts have one common denominator—people—and one cannot be achieved in full without the other two. Maintaining the right balance between them must be the guiding thread for Union action. It should be noted in this context that the treaty instituting the European Communities (article 61 ex article 73I a), makes a direct link between measures establishing freedom of movement of persons and the specific measures seeking to combat and prevent crime (article 31 e EU), thus creating a conditional link between the two areas.

The concept of security underpinning the notion of an area of freedom, security and justice necessitated measures designed to ensure that the citizens of Europe are

---

Security and Justice for All', in E. Guild and C. Harlow (eds.), *Implementing Amsterdam* (2001); A, Geddes, *Immigration and European Integration: Towards Fortress Europe* (2000).

[39] Risk analysis found a clear expression in the Presidency conclusions of the Seville European Council in June 2002. On this and on the subsequent project on Common Integrated Risk Analysis model (CIRAM), see E. Guild, *The Legal Elements of a European Identity; EU Citizenship and Migration Law* (2004), at 179.

[40] *Supra* n. 33, at 1–2.

free from risk or danger and from anxiety or fear.[41] 'Security' thus obtained an individual dimension. While neither the order of the state nor the ability of a society to persist in its essential character under changing conditions was under threat, Union citizens were, allegedly, vulnerable to threats and thus in need of security.[42] In post-Amsterdam Europe, the term security thus underwent an expansion; it migrated from defence and international security matters under the Common Foreign and Security Policy to migration-related matters.[43]

In the 'freedom, security and justice' configuration, neither 'security' nor 'justice' are neutral additions and mere complements to 'freedom'. Rather, they become closely connected with freedom. As stated above, it is alleged that 'freedom loses much of its meaning if it is not enjoyed in a secure environment' and, further, that freedom of movement requires an accessible system of justice which can contain and deter all those who seek to deny and abuse this freedom. According to the Action Plan, 'freedom of movement of people within the Union remains a fundamental objective of the Treaty, and one to which the flanking measures associated with the concepts of security and justice make their essential contribution. Security is not a subsidiary consideration, but a principle equal in weight with freedom of movement.' In such a discursive articulation, the security paradigm, that has traditionally underpinned justice and home affairs cooperation, becomes more prominent, and the inclusion of justice in the triad 'freedom, security and justice . . . marks a step beyond the old Schengen rationale with its focus on free movement and "mere compensatory measures." '[44]

The framing of 'security' as a supplement of freedom, however, has produced two successive dislocations which affect policy-making; namely, the conceptual widening of freedom and the promotion of security at the expense of freedom. As regards the former dislocation, it is interesting that freedom is no longer confined to free movement across the MS. It takes on the meaning of freedom from fear, violence and deception.

According Mrs Anita Gradin, former EU Commissioner:

freedom must mean considerably more that simply the absence of internal border controls. In our opinion it also means that people will avoid being subjected to abuse, deception, discrimination and every form of violence . . . But liberty signifies a lot more than freedom of movement. It also implies the right to live in a society which takes effective action against

---

[41] The Commission's Report on the functioning of the TEU had stated that security at home and abroad are legitimate concerns for every citizen: Bul. EU 5-1995, at 92.

[42] In her speech at the Tampere European Council, the President of the European Parliament, she noted that the EC must take into account people's day-to-day feelings of insecurity (http://www.europarl. eu.int/president/speeches/en/sp0003en.htm).

[43] J. van Selm-Thorburn, 'Asylum in the Amsterdam Treaty: A Harmonious Future?', 24(4) *Journal of Ethnic and Migration Studies* (1998) 627, at 635.

[44] J. Monar, 'Justice and Home Affairs', Annual Review, 37 *JCMS* (1999) 155, at 167.

those who place themselves above the law. The concept of Europe therefore requires that all MS have confidence in each other's ability to deal with serious organised crime.[45]

The second important dislocation in the discursive chain of freedom, security and justice concerns the emergence of a value laden hierarchy, whereby security was promoted at the expense of freedom.[46] While in the past security cooperation was a spillover effect of the internal market, it now becomes an enabling condition of free movement. Free movement is thus seen to require a common security space, which guarantees the absence of threats and the unimpeded exercise of free movement rights. But as Huysmans has argued, 'security policy is not simply a practice of protecting and/or limiting a pre-given freedom. It is a governmental practice that translates the abstract notion of freedom into a concrete practice through shaping and moulding practical modalities of the legitimate and optimal conduct of freedom within a society.'[47] The primacy and centrality attributed to security signals not only the sedimentation of the securitization ethos in discourse and policy, but also the framing of security as the condition of possibility for both freedom of movement and the enjoyment of liberty in general. This conception, however, is deeply flawed since it is based on a self-referential logic whereby what is supposed to help realize free movement, namely, security, can only be realized by policies of security.

Previously competing organizational actors, such as the Council and the Commission, now jointly take part in the institutional dynamics of shaping a new form of political order. By so doing, they not only legitimize the institutional output of JHA cooperation, but they also produce a unified discursive structure which shapes identities and policy orientations. Drawing on a populist repertoire, EU official discourses justify the creation of an area of freedom, security and justice on the basis that it safeguards the 'European citizen and his/her interests wherever he/she may be in the EU'. In this way, it creates a European public space in which citizens feel that 'a proper sense of "European Public Order" has taken shape and is actually visible today in their daily lives.'[48]

But such a framing of justice and home affairs matters is problematic on several grounds. First, it creates an endemic incoherence in legal and political discourse which, ultimately, can undermine the validity of European collective action in this area. The conceptual linkage between free movement and security is based on the incorrect assumption that those who take advantage of the free movement rights

---

[45] *Liberty, Security and Justice: an Agenda for Europe*, PE168.396, 14–15.

[46] On this, see J. Huysmans, 'Security! What do you Mean? From Concept to thick Signifier', 4(2) *European Journal of International Relations* (1998) 226; 'The European Union and the Securitisation of Migration', 38(5) *Journal of Common Market Studies* (2002) 751; D. Bigo, 'Çriminalisation of "Migrants": the Side Effect of the Will to Control the Frontiers and the Sovereign Illusion', in Bogusz *et al.* (eds.), *Irregular Migration and Human Rights: Theoretical, European and International Perspectives* (2004).

[47] J. Huysmans, *Security and Freedom*, Paper presented at the UACES Workshop on the Evolving European Migration Law and Policy, University of Manchester (2002).

[48] Working Group X, Freedom, Security and Justice Final Report WD 18 REV.

are more exposed to security threats. Secondly, the supplement 'security' is prone to the logic of perversion; that is, it leads to policies that may exacerbate the conditions they seek to remedy. Since all supplements are 'dangerous' in the sense that they tend to threaten that which they supplement, the basic risk entailed by this reframing of the JHA cooperation is that security becomes an overriding policy goal which may redefine the terms of the free movement of persons in Community law.[49] Accordingly, the pursuit of security may make Europeans insecure by threatening or depriving the authenticity of their fundamental right of free movement. This, of course, does not mean that the connection of freedom and security has no functionality; rather, its functionality is to define issues and preordain the policy responses that seem appropriate. This process is facilitated by the remarkable elasticity that characterizes such abstract and imprecise terms as freedom, security and justice. The political act of filling the meaning of such signifiers is particularly important, and both the Commission and the Council are jointly involved in the process of framing and enlarging their meaning. It is noteworthy, for example, that freedom has not been defined to include the protection of fundamental freedoms, and justice is confined to giving citizens access to justice and to enhancing judicial cooperation in the EU. Thirdly, the reframing of justice and home affairs cooperation can result in a rather narrow policy-agenda. It is often the case that when the policy agenda is dominated by security concerns, then the range of policy options becomes more limited, means and ends become confused and it is difficult to strike a balance among competing interests. Although it is true that the AFSJ can make a contribution to enhancing the Union's social legitimacy, the Community does not have to imitate the 'protective state'. For in the eyes of the public, a protective Union may well be a defective Union, particularly if it fails to respect human rights and civil liberties and provide adequate protection of personal data.

Recasting the Institutional Design: the Constitutional Treaty

The Convention and the ensuing Constitutional Treaty initiated a 'deeper and wider debate' about European governance; they addressed issues that strike at the heart of the EU's constitutional framework, including the pillared architecture of the Union. Introduced by the Treaty on European Union (1992), the pillared structure has resulted in unnecessarily complex institutional configurations, has hindered effective policy-making and the implementation of law, has preserved executive domination at the expense of democratic accountability and judicial scrutiny, and has given rise to jurisdictional conflicts owing to divergent positions about the correct legal base for an act.[50]

---

[49] T. Kostakopoulou, 'The "Protective Union": Change and continuity in Migration Law and Policy in Post-Amsterdam Europe', 38(3) *Journal of Common Market Studies* 497.

[50] In Case C-176/03 *Commission v Council* (Judgment of 13 September 2005), the Grand Chamber annulled Council Framework Decision 2003/80/JHA on the protection of the environment through criminal law (OJ 2003 L 29/55) on the ground that it was established law that acts adopted under Title

The Convention's Working Group on Justice and Home Affairs (Working Group X 'Freedom, Security and Justice') produced its final report on 28 November 2002.[51] The report was followed by a lively plenary debate and, following various amendments, it culminated in a revised draft. The latter entailed a number of reforms based on two 'golden rules'; namely, (a) the formal abolition of the pillared structure and the unification of the legal framework in justice and home affairs matters, and (b) the separation between 'legislative' and 'operational' tasks within the Union and reinforced coordination of operational collaboration at Union level. The latter could be achieved by the creation of a more efficient structure for the coordination of operational cooperation at high technical level within the Council; namely, a new standing Committee which would coordinate the activities of the various bodies dealing with (broadly defined) 'internal security'. The report also suggested the standardization of co-decision and qualified majority voting in JHA matters, that is, its application to all areas in Title IV EC, with the exception of measures concerning family law with cross border implications, and to most areas of the revised third pillar.[52] Following the Tampere 'milestones', the Report also recommended the inclusion of the principle of mutual recognition of judicial and extra-judicial decisions in the Constitutional Treaty and suggested further progress in the field of the approximation of certain elements of criminal procedure and substantive criminal law.

The Brussels European Council managed to secure agreement on the Constitutional Treaty on 18 June 2004, which was then signed on 29 October 2004 in Rome. The Constitutional Treaty abolishes the pillared structure, thereby placing all justice and home affairs matters under a single institutional framework. The unification of law-making will result in a simpler institutional configuration. The distinctive third pillar instruments (ie, common positions, framework decisions, decisions and conventions) will be replaced by European laws (directly applicable regulations) and framework laws (directives). Co-decision will be standardized, and unanimity will be replaced by qualified majority voting, at least in those areas where there are not divergent national positions. The Commission's exclusive right of initiative is strengthened and the ECJ assumes full jurisdiction in all JHA matters, with the exception of the validity and proportionality of policing actions.

VI were not to encroach on powers conferred by the EC Treaty on the Community, and there was such encroachment in the present case as Articles 1 to 7 of the Framework Decision had as their main purpose the protection of the environment and so could properly have been adopted on the basis of Article 175 EC. On the implications of this judgment, see Commission Communication COM (2005) 583 final/2, Brussels, 24 November 2005.

[51] CONV 426/02, Brussels, 2 December 2002.

[52] The exceptions were legislation on the establishment of a European Public Prosecutor's office; cross-border actions by police; operational police measures; the establishment of minimum rules concerning not explicitly mentioned aspects of criminal procedure; and the identification of new areas of serious crime for which minimum rules concerning the definition of criminal offences may be introduced.

One of the new objectives of the Union is to offer its citizens 'an area of freedom, security and justice without internal frontiers, and a single market where competition is free and undistorted' (Article I-3(2)). Although the specific objectives of this policy area are defined in greater detail in Part III of the Treaty and in Article I-42 which states that 'the Union shall constitute an area of freedom, security and justice', Article I-3(2) will, nevertheless, function as an interpretational aid to the definition and implementation of AFSJ. According to Article I-42, the AFSJ will be achieved by combining positive and negative integration and by enhancing the operational cooperation among the competent authorities of the MS, including the police, customs and other authorities specializing in the prevention and detection of criminal offences (Article I-42). It may be observed, here, that the above means are not novel; legislative harmonization and operational cooperation were envisaged by the Treaty of Amsterdam (Articles 29, 34(2) and 30(1)(a) EU), while mutual recognition, which was first included in the Presidency Conclusions of the Cardiff European Council in June 1998, was explicitly endorsed by the Tampere European Council (October 1999).[53] Interestingly, the Treaty does not envisage the creation of federal agencies endowed with executive power. It relies, instead, on the horizontal cooperation of law enforcement authorities. In addition, the AFSJ is expressly stated to be an area of shared competence, while new legal bases have been created concerning the integrated management of external borders (Article III-265), criminal procedure (Article III-270(2)) and the establishment of a European Public Prosecutor's Office (Article III-274).

The Constitutional Treaty strengthens the Commission's right of initiative by giving it exclusive power to propose legislation in migration and asylum-related matters.[54] This will shield the Community interest against possible resurgence of intergovernmentalism. However, the Constitutional Treaty also preserves the MS's right to bring forward legislative initiatives in the fields of police and criminal judicial cooperation (Article I-42(3)). While at present any MS can propose legislation in this area, Working Group X had suggested the introduction of a threshold of either 1/3 or 1/4 or even 1/5 of the Member States for a MS initiative to be admissible. Following this suggestion, the Treaty (Article III-264) states that a quarter of MS can bring forward legislative initiatives in criminal matters including the operational cooperation between administrative and police bodies of the MS. The imposition of this threshold will prevent governments from taking politically expedient decisions reflecting national political situations and the perceptions or interests of national elites. The exercise of a MS initiative would thus have to reflect a wider European interest and to promote the development of the Union.

---

[53] The importance of this principle has also been reaffirmed by the ECJ in *Gozutok and Brugge*; Joined Cases C-187/01 and C-385/01, [2003] ECR I-1345 at para 33.

[54] The Commission already had an exclusive right of initiative in judicial cooperation in civil matters under the Treaty of Nice.

The Constitutional Treaty increased the EP's powers. Co-decision is stated to be the 'ordinary legislative procedure'; the traditional consultation and consent procedures are 'special legislative procedures'. The reach of the co-decision procedure has also been extended to cover more areas than hitherto (from 37 to 80 to 90 domains), thereby enhancing the democratic credentials of European legislation. Important too is the extension of co-decision to police and criminal judicial cooperation matters where the EP has currently only a consultative role. Making the EP a genuine co-legislator will bring about greater accountability in this policy field and will facilitate effective scrutiny.

The scope of qualified majority voting has also been extended from about 35 to 70 policy areas. Police and criminal judicial cooperation have, generally speaking, been removed from the domain of unanimity. The areas that still require unanimity are family law (Article III-269(3)); Article III-270(2)(d) on the establishment of minimum rules on specific aspects of criminal procedure; Article III-271(1) on the identification of new areas of serious crime for which minimum rules concerning the definition of criminal offences may be introduced; Article II-274(1) concerning the adoption of a European law on the establishment of a European public prosecutor; Article III-275(3) on the adoption of legislative measures regarding operational cooperation between law enforcement officers; and Article III-277 concerning the adoption of legislative measures laying down the conditions and limitations under which law enforcement authorities may operate in the territory of another MS. Assuming the Treaty comes into force, from 1 November 2009 qualified majority voting will require the support of 55 per cent of the MS representing at least three fifths of the population of the Union. When the constitution does not require the European Council or the Council of Ministers to act on the basis of a proposal of the Commission, the required qualified majority consists of two thirds of the MS representing at least three fifths of the population of the Union (Article III-25(2)). It may be noted, here, that the President of the European Council and the President of the Commission are not voting members.

The Treaty also formalizes the institutional role of the European Council; the latter shall 'define the strategic guidelines for legislative and operational planning within the area of freedom, security and justice' (Article III-258). Reflecting on and institutionalizing the Council's leadership role since the Treaty of Amsterdam, the Treaty opens up the opportunity for the European Council to continue to provide special impetus in the institutionalization of the AFSJ by defining its general political direction and strategic priorities. The election of a Council President for a period of two and half years, renewable once, will aid this process by ensuring policy continuity and by bridging legislative and operational programmes. The European Council could also contribute to enhancing the effectiveness of JHA cooperation by influencing the Council to adopt legislative instruments. Although the Treaty is silent on the issue of judicial review of the European Council's acts (except for the case of the suspension of voting rights of the MS), it is plausible to argue that the provisions concerning the capacity to bring an action for failure to act and preliminary rulings apply to it. Likewise, the provisions concerning access to documents and the jurisdiction of the Ombudsman apply to the European Council.

The Constitutional Treaty also envisages the establishment of a new standing committee on 'internal security', the Article III-261 standing committee, which replaces the Article 36 Committee. The new committee will be endowed with the task of coordinating the action of national police, customs and civil protection authorities. Although the reinforced coordination of operational collaboration might enhance the effectiveness of EU action in this area, and the Committee does not appear to have powers of directing the actions of national police and other authorities in relation to specific actions, the all embracing concept of 'internal security', coupled with the fact that the committee will not be accountable to parliaments, be they European or national, gives rise to concern.[55]

The Constitutional Treaty foresees greater transparency in JHA matters. Article I-50 reaffirms the link between transparency and participatory democracy by stating that 'in order to promote good governance and ensure the participation of civil society, the Union's institutions, bodies and agencies shall conduct their work as openly as possible'. To this end, the updated and amended text of Article 255 (Article I-49) extends the citizens' right of access to documents of the Union's institutions, bodies and agencies. Although each institution, body or agency shall determine in its own rules of procedure specific provisions regarding access to documents, Article I-50(3), which is specified in Article III-399, encapsulates the centrality of the principle of transparency in the new constitutional order. In addition to the constitutional guarantee of openness, that is, the obligation on the part of the Union to act as openly as possible, a European law which will lay down the general principles and limits which govern the right of access and finally, the institutions' own rules of procedure which will entail the specific provisions for public access to documents in accordance with the relevant European law (Article I-50(4) and (5)). Given the chronic lack of democratic control and oversight in JHA, the promise of increased transparency and the constitutionalization of the openness of legislative proceedings in the Council are welcome reforms. More specifically, Article I-50 on 'transparency in the proceedings of Union institutions, bodies, offices and agencies' states that all the above bodies shall work as openly as possible and that the European Parliament and the Council (when it considers and votes on a draft legislative act) shall meet in public. And under Article III-399(2), the European Parliament and the Council of Ministers shall ensure publication of the documents relating to the legislative procedures'.[56]

---

[55] In light of the Praesidium's note that the Committee would coordinate operational cooperation in the 'event of a major catastrophe, attacks and events and demonstrations on a European scale', it is plausible to argue that 'internal security' was not confined to police matters.

[56] The Amsterdam Treaty required the Council, when acting a legislator, to publish the results of its votes, but not its deliberations (Art. 207 (3) EC). The Seville European Council (June 2002) obliged

The general extension of the European Court of Justice's jurisdiction is a welcome reform.[57] The restrictions in the Court's jurisdiction under Titles IV EC and VI EU, including the intergovernmentalist modifications of the preliminary ruling reference procedure in Article 68(1) EC and Article 35 EU, have not found their way into the European Constitution. This means that any national court or tribunal will be able to activate the preliminary reference procedure. The only limitation in the Court's jurisdiction that has been preserved is Article 35(5) EU in relation to police and criminal judicial cooperation; that is, the exclusion of the Court from reviewing 'the validity or proportionality of operations carried out by national police or other law enforcement authorities or the exercise of responsibilities incumbent upon MS with regard to the maintenance of law and order and the safeguarding of internal security, where such action is a matter of national law' (Article III-377).

Crucial for the AFSJ and the judicial protection of individuals is also Article III-365(5) which expands the scope of judicial review to acts of bodies and agencies that produce legal effects; 'acts setting up bodies and agencies of the Union may lay down specific conditions and arrangements concerning actions brought by natural or legal persons against acts of these bodies or agencies intended to produce legal effects'. By so doing, Article III-365(5) grafts flesh onto the principle of judicial protection enshrined in Article II-107 of the EU Charter. The need for ensuring adequate protection for individuals in this area has been made apparent by the reasoning of the Constitutional courts in Germany and Poland concerning the European Arrest Warrant, which found that national implementing legislation does not conform to the constitutional guarantee of recourse to a court (Articles 19(4) and 55(1) of the German and Polish Constitutions, respectively).[58]

Concerning the restrictive *locus standi* under Article 230(4) EC, the Discussion Circle on the European Court of Justice addressed the issue in detail without reaching a decision on the appropriate reform. Some members did not favour a reformulation of Article 230 on the grounds that private litigants were afforded effective judicial protection by activating the preliminary ruling reference procedure at national courts. Critics of the strict interpretation of direct and individual concern requirements argued for a liberalization of the conditions by allowing private litigants to challenge at least some acts of direct concern to them which do not entail implementing measures without the need to prove individual concern, on the grounds that this would enhance access to justice. The compromise solution put forward by the Chairman, Antonio Vittorino, found its way into the Constitution;

---

the Council to open its legislative meetings to the public. Implementing the conclusions of the Seville European Council, the new rules of procedure for the Council state deliberations on acts to be adopted in accordance with the co-decision procedure shall be open to the public.

[57] Compare also the novel provision of Article I-29(1) which reinforces the dialogic and decentralized pattern of enforcement of Community law; 'the MS shall provide rights of appeal sufficient to ensure effective legal protection in the field of Union law'.

[58] Judgment of 18 July 2005, 2 BvR 2236/04, Bundesverfassungsgericht and Judgement of the Polish Constitutional Tribunal, 27 April 2005, p1/05.

namely, according to Article III-365(4), any natural or legal person can challenge legislative and regulatory acts which are of direct and individual concern to him/her and regulatory acts which do not entail implementing measures if he/she is able to prove direct concern. True, such a modest liberalization of standing rules for non-privileged applicants does not address in depth the problems raised by the restrictive rules of standing and the need for providing sufficient legal protection for individuals as highlighted by Advocate General Jacobs in the *UPA*[59] case and may be seen to contradict the principle of effective judicial protection underpinning Article I-29.

Enhanced cooperation

The Treaty has simplified the enhanced cooperation procedure by changing the minimum number of participating states from eight to one third of the total membership, replacing unanimity by qualified majority in the Council and by bringing third pillar flexibility within the ambit of first pillar rules. According to the Constitutional Treaty's provisions on flexibility (Article I-44 and Articles III-416 to III-423), authorization to proceed with enhanced cooperation, which must further the objectives of the Union, protect its interests and reinforce the integration process, must be granted by the Council of Ministers as a last resort, provided that the objectives of such cooperation cannot be attained within a reasonable period by the Union as a whole and provided that it brings together at least one third of the MS.[60] The MS' request is addressed to the Commission which must either submit a proposal to the Council of Ministers or justify its refusal to put forward a cooperation initiative. Should the Commission decide to give the go-ahead to the cooperation initiative, the Council must provide its authorization by means of a formal decision and must obtain the consent of the EP before adopting the decision. The exception will be the common foreign and security policy where Council authorization for enhanced cooperation will still require unanimity. In those policy areas where the Council acts by unanimity, Member States participating in enhanced cooperation may use qualified majority voting and introduce co-decision when adopting measures. Although acts adopted within the framework of enhanced cooperation, which still applies only to areas of joint competence, bind the participating states, cooperation can be extended to all MS at any time in accordance with the procedure laid down in Article III-418.

In the field of AFSJ, the Treaty also envisages an 'emergency brake' mechanism which will allow any MS to refrain from participating in framework laws that approximate criminal procedure or the definition of criminal offences or sanctions

---

[59] Case C-50/00 *Union de Pequenos Agricultores v Council* [2002] ECR I-6677.

[60] In light of the para-Communitarian experience of Schengen in which only five out of the 15 MS participated and national sensitivities about JHA matters, it is true to say that the requirement of one third of the MS remains high for this policy area.

where it considers that they would affect fundamental aspects of its criminal justice system. Under this mechanism, any MS can suspend the legislative procedure and refer the matter to the European Council which, within four months, must decide either to send the measure back to the Council for adoption by qualified majority voting or request a new draft measure from the Commission or the group of MS that proposed the draft framework law. If the European Council has taken no action within the four-month deadline or no decision is taken after a further 12 months those states that so wish (at least one third) may establish enhanced cooperation in the area concerned. The general Treaty provisions on enhanced cooperation then apply (Articles I-44 and III-416 to III-423), and the MS that objected to the draft framework law would not be bound by the enhanced cooperation. The emergency break mechanism represents a compromise aimed at allowing MS, such as the UK, to preserve national sovereignty over criminal procedural law without hindering progress among MS wishing to pursue greater cooperation.

Democratic infusions

The increasing involvement of National Parliaments

According to the Constitutional Treaty, national parliaments may 'participate in the evaluation mechanisms foreseen in Article III-260' and shall be involved in the political monitoring of Europol and the evaluation of Eurojust's activities in accordance with Articles III-273 and 276 (Article I-42(2)). It is unfortunate that national parliaments' participation in the mutual evaluation of the MS' implementation of Union policies in the AFSJ is discretionary. The enhanced position of national parliaments is also attested by a new provision, Article III-259, which provides a special role for national parliaments monitoring the principle of subsidiarity in the area of freedom, security and justice, and the amended protocols on the role of the national parliaments in the European Union and on the application of the principles of subsidiarity and proportionality.[61]

In line with the Laeken Declaration, the Constitutional Treaty improved the provisions for the transmission of documents and established an early warning system for monitoring the application of the subsidiarity principle. As regards the former, the amended Protocol on the role of National Parliaments states that all legislative proposals forwarded by the Commission to the Council and the EP shall be sent simultaneously to national parliaments, and that 10 days must elapse between the placing of a proposal on the agenda for a Council meeting and the adoption of a position by the Council. In addition to draft legislative acts and amended drafts, and all Commission consultation documents, national parliaments shall receive a wider

---

[61] National parliaments have witnessed an incremental increase in their involvement in EU affairs initially by Declaration 13 appended to the Treaty on European Union, and later on by the Amsterdam provisions concerning the prompt forwarding of consultation papers and legislative proposals, or a proposal for a measure to be adopted under Title VI TEU to national parliaments within six weeks before the item is placed on the Council's agenda for decision (subject to exceptions on the ground of urgency).

range of non-legislative documents, ranging from the Commission's annual legislative programme, any other instrument of legislative planning or policy strategy and the annual report of the Court of Auditors to the agendas for and the outcome of meetings of the Council of Ministers, including the minutes of Council's deliberations on legislative proposals. Welcome as this provision may be, one cannot underestimate the risk of information overload which may hinder adequate scrutiny.

The Constitutional Treaty also introduces a formal role for national parliaments in monitoring compliance of legislation with the principle of subsidiarity. More specifically, it envisages an early warning system whereby any national parliament or any chamber of a national parliament of a MS may, within six weeks of the date of the transmission of a Commission's legislative proposal, send to the Presidents of the EP, the Council of Ministers and the Commission, a reasoned opinion stating why it considers that the proposal contravenes the principle of subsidiarity. If a sufficient number of parliaments object to a proposal (at least of one third of all the votes allocated to national parliaments and their chambers) the Commission must review its draft legislation. This threshold shall be at least a quarter in the case of a Commission proposal or an initiative emanating from a group of MS under the provisions of Article II-264 of the Constitution on the area of freedom, security and justice. Although the Commission is neither obliged to carry forward the national parliaments' objection nor to withdraw its proposal, this provision, nevertheless, enhances national parliaments' direct involvement in the EU policy process by inducing the Commission or a group of MS to provide more detailed justifications about the conformity of proposed legislation with subsidiarity and to give reasons concerning their decision about the objection. Under Article III-365 (currently Article 230 EC), the ECJ shall have jurisdiction to hear actions on grounds of infringement of the principle of subsidiarity brought by a MS on behalf of its national parliament. Although the early warning system falls short of being a brake to the adoption of legislation, it, nevertheless, empowers national parliaments and enhances democratic accountability. It strengthens the democratic credentials of the European governance and the increased visibility of national parliaments in the EU policy process is likely to appease concerns about the 'creeping competence' of the Community. Additionally, the enhanced role of national parliaments will complement the EP's involvement in JHA matters, and is likely to trigger further reforms in the future, such as national parliamentary involvement in the definition of strategic guidelines and priorities by the European Council, and the European Parliament's mandatory consultation in relation to actions plans.

The increasing involvement of civil society
The enshrinement of the principle of participatory democracy in the Constitutional Treaty enhances the dialogue between EU institutions and civil society, thereby furnishing the preconditions for the creation of European public sphere. According to Article I-47(1), the Union institutions shall 'give citizens and representative associations the opportunity to make known and publicly exchange their views in

all areas of Union action', while the second paragraph of Article I-47 states that 'the Union institutions shall maintain an open, transparent and regular dialogue with representative associations and civil society'. Although it has been pointed out that it is not for the EU institutions to establish an elitist system for determining representative organizations, and EU agencies are not covered by this provision, the emphasis given to the process of public deliberation is very welcome. In addition, the principle of participatory democracy may lead to the institutionalization of formal consultation rights in the future, such as to specific obligations on the part of all Union institutions to make proposals and background documents available to the public and/or include a compulsory consultation process before the articulation of a proposal. Notably, according to Article I-47(3) only the Commission has an obligation to carry out broad consultations with parties concerned in order to ensure that the Union's actions are coherent and transparent.

Constitutionalizing rights

The insertion of the Charter of Fundamental Rights[62] in the Constitutional Treaty represented a constitutional choice.[63] The Charter becomes legally binding, and its incorporation in Part II, rather than in a Protocol, reflects the importance attributed to rights protection in the new constitutional order. While certain MS, such as the UK, had opposed the straightforward insertion of the Charter into the Constitutional Treaty, most MS saw it as an indispensable part of the new Treaty and a means of enhancing both the legitimacy and the democratic credentials of the European constitution. The British Government had thus to be contented with 'a series of safeguarding arm locks around it', including the preamblic reference that 'the Charter will be interpreted by the courts of the Union and the Member States with due regard to the explanations prepared at the instigation of the Praesidium of the Convention which drafted the Charter'.[64]

The Treaty also envisaged possible accession to the ECHR by the EU, thereby ameliorating the ECJ's prior concerns on this subject.[65] In the case of accession, individuals wishing to challenge a measure of EU law or some national measure which falls within the scope of EU law would have to activate first the preliminary ruling reference procedure and then pursue their claim before the European Court

[62] OJ 2000 C364/1 of 18 December 2000.

[63] See, P. Craig, *What Constitution Europe Needs? The House that Giscard Built: Constitutional norms with a View*, Federal Trust Online Constitutional Essay, 26/2003; Kokott and Ruth, 'The European Convention and its Draft Treaty Establishing a Constitution for Europe: Appropriate Answers to the Laeken Questions?', 40 *Common Market Law Review* (2003) 1315; J. Dutheil de la Rochère, 'The EU and the Individual: Fundamental Rights in the Draft Constitutional Treaty', 41 *Common Market Law Review* (2004) 345; D Phinnemore, *The Treaty Establishing a Constitution for Europe: An Overview*, RIIA EP BN 04–01, www.chathamhouse.org.uk.

[64] Peter Hain's response to Q31, House of Lords, Forty first report, paras 255–156, http://www.parliament.the-stationary-office.co.uk.

[65] See Opinion 2/94 [1996] ECR I-1759.

of Human Rights (ECtHR). Accession is not automatic; the Member States' unanimous decision will be required. Admittedly, such a multi-tiered constitutional framework for rights protection will not only be ridden with complexity, but it will also reveal the lack of a perfect congruence between ECHR and the EU Charter. It is noteworthy, for example, that the ECJ has interpreted Article 8 ECHR more widely that the ECtHR as regards the rights of the family members of Union citizens, and Article II-65 goes beyond the ECHR by expressly prohibiting trafficking in human beings. It is perhaps for this reason that Article II-112(2) states that rights recognized by the Charter for which provisions is made in other parts of the Constitution shall be exercised under the conditions and within the limits defined by these relevant parts. In addition, Article II-112(3) and (4) provide that those Charter rights that correspond to rights guaranteed by the ECHR or result from the constitutional traditions common to the MS shall be given the same scope and meaning as those in the ECHR or should be interpreted in harmony those traditions. But this shall not prevent Union law from providing more extensive protection.

It is the latter provision that has given rise to fears that the Charter will provide a platform for a more expansive interpretation of Union law and policy and may even extend the legal basis for Community action, despite the fact that Article II-111(2) states that 'the Charter does not extend the field of application of Union law beyond the powers of the Union or establish any new power or task for the Union, or modify powers and tasks defined in the other parts of the Constitution'. In addition, Article II-112(5) appeases such fears by distinguishing between rights and principles and by stating that the latter shall be judicially cognisable only when acts implementing the principles are interpreted or reviewed. Furthermore, Article II-112(6) states that full account shall be taken of national laws and practices as specified in the Charter. Notwithstanding these provisions, few would dispute the importance of a fully-binding and justiciable Charter for justice and home affairs matters.

The evolving area of freedom, security and justice

Article III-257, which replaces Articles 29 EU and 61 EC, states that 'the Union shall constitute an area of freedom, security and justice with respect for fundamental rights and the different legal traditions and systems of the Member States'. Although it was suggested during the Convention's deliberations that the AFSJ should apply to 'everyone within its jurisdiction irrespective of nationality legal status and the place they are' this suggestion did not find its way into the text. Article III-257, nevertheless, contains explicit references to the need to respect fundamental rights, an acknowledgement of the different legal traditions and systems of the MS, the application of the mutual recognition principle to both civil and criminal judicial cooperation and the framing of 'a common policy on asylum, immigration and external border control, based on solidarity between the MS, which is fair towards third country nationals'. Article III-257(3) strengthens the legal basis for taking action concerning crime prevention.

Concerning migration-related matters (Articles III-265 to III-268), the Treaty establishes a legal basis for the gradual introduction of an integrated management system for external borders without explicitly referring to the establishment of a European Border Guard which featured in the Conclusions of the Seville and Thessaloniki European Council meetings in June 2002 and 2003 respectively. Although the provision concerning the integrated management system for external borders builds on the momentum created by the incorporation of the Schengen acquis into the EC/EU and the Tampere conclusions, the suggestion that any measure in this area must give 'due regard to the necessary safeguards for democratic control and the rights of individuals' was not adopted. Reflecting national executives' anxieties, the third paragraph of Article III-265 states that the Community's competence in this area shall not impinge upon MS' sovereign powers concerning the geographical demarcation of their borders, in accordance with international law.

A welcome development in the field of asylum is the reference to a uniform status of subsidiary protection for nationals of third countries requiring international protection. A provision that has given rise to many concerns, however, is Article III-266(2)(g) which refers to measures concerning partnership and cooperation with third countries with a view to managing inflows of asylum seekers—a provision that was not included in the Working Group's report and was especially supported by the British Government. NGOs have criticized this provision for legitimizing attempts to 'sub-contract' the MS asylum obligations to third countries via the establishment of reception centres or even resettlement schemes. Explicit references have been added concerning the combating of trafficking in persons and readmission agreements, thereby delineating the key aspects of the Union's policy in this area.[66] In addition, the EU has now express power to act against unauthorized residence, in addition to illegal immigration, including removal and repatriation of persons residing without authorization. However, the Tampere commitment to the equal treatment of long-term resident third country nationals has not found its way into the Treaty. In addition, Article III-267(4) establishes a legal basis for 'measures to provide incentives and support for the action of MS with a view to promoting the integration of third country nationals residing legally in their territories, excluding any harmonisation of the laws and regulations of the MS'. Article III-267(5), nevertheless, limits the Community's competence in the field of migration by stating that 'this article shall not affect the right of the MS to determine volumes of admission of third country nationals coming from third countries to their territory to seek work, whether employed or self-employed'.

The enshrinement of the principle of solidarity and fair sharing of responsibility (including its financial implications) between the MS in the areas of immigration,

---

[66] The Hague Programme envisages the appointment of a Special Representative for a common readmission policy.

asylum and border controls into the Treaty creates a specific legal basis for the adoption of appropriate measures in this area (Article III-268), thereby replacing the existing Community competence to adopt measures on burden-sharing related to asylum (Article 63(2)(b)).

Section 3 of the chapter on the AFSJ deals with civil judicial cooperation. Building upon the existing acquis in this area, the Treaty amends Article 65 EC by deleting the sentence 'insofar as necessary for the proper functioning of the internal market' contained in Article 65 EC, thereby laying the foundation for the extension of the Union's competence to non-economic matters. The enshrining of the principle of mutual recognition of judgments and decisions in extra-judicial cases, the development of measures of preventive justice and alternative methods of dispute settlement, support for the training of the judiciary and judicial staff and the application of the co-decision procedure for measures concerning parental authority, the only sector of family law governed by unanimity, are noteworthy provisions. Finally, in line with the Tampere conclusions, the Treaty envisages the adoption of measures designed to ensure a high level of access to justice. This cannot but have implications for the future establishment of minimum standards guaranteeing an appropriate level of legal aid for cross-border cases throughout the Union, and special common procedural rules in order to simplify and speed up the settlement of cross-border disputes concerning small commercial claims under consumer legislation, or to establish minimum common standards for multilingual forms or documents in cross-border proceedings.

Section 4 of Chapter IV deals with criminal judicial cooperation while section 5 deals with police cooperation. More specifically, Article III-270 formalizes the close link between negative and positive integration. As regards the former, the principle of mutual recognition of judgments and decisions, which was proclaimed to be 'the cornerstone for judicial cooperation' at Tampere receives explicit reference in Article III-270(1). As regards the latter, mutual recognition is accompanied by the approximation of substantive and procedural criminal laws. According to Article III-270(2), European framework laws may establish minimum rules on: (a) the mutual admissibility of evidence among the MS, (b) the rights of individuals in criminal procedure, (c) the rights of victims of crime, and (d) any other specific aspects of a criminal procedure identified by the Council in advance. The important criteria for the approximation of legislation in procedural criminal law are: the facilitation of the mutual recognition of judgments and judicial decisions, and police and criminal cooperation in criminal matters having a cross-border dimension. The explicit acknowledgement of the need for such provisions echoes previous commitments made at Tampere. In addition to the principle of mutual recognition, certain MS, such as the UK and Ireland, insisted on the inclusion of an explicit reference to the principle of respect for the diversity of the MS' legal systems, thereby alleviating concerns about the implications of the harmonization of criminal procedural law. In addition, an emergency break mechanism is envisaged in the case where a MS believes that harmonization of certain elements of criminal procedure 'would affect fundamental aspects of its criminal justice system'. Under Article III-270(3), a MS can request the referral of the draft framework law to the European Council, which has the obligation to either refer the draft back to the Council or request the submission of a new draft. As earlier noted, a failure to take action on the part of the European Council can always activate the enhanced cooperation procedures.

The extension of the Union's competence regarding criminal procedural law also applies to substantive criminal law (Article III-271). As regards the approximation of substantive criminal law, European framework laws can be used in two instances. First, European framework laws may establish the minimum rules concerning the definition of offences and sanctions in 12 listed areas of serious crime with a cross-border direction, ranging from terrorism and trafficking in human beings to tackling computer crime and organized crime (Article III-172(1)). It has been suggested that organized crime should be deleted from this list, since there is no common understanding of this category of criminal offence within the EU. Secondly, the second paragraph of Article III-271 refers to the minimum harmonization of criminal legislation in order to ensure the effective implementation of a Union policy in an area which has been subject to harmonization measures, such as fraud affecting the financial interests of the Union, counterfeiting of euro, facilitation of unauthorized entry and residence, counterfeiting and piracy of products, environmental crime and also racism and xenophobia. What is noteworthy here, is that the Union may define minimum rules with regard to the definition of criminal offences and sanctions, irrespective of whether or not they are of a cross-border nature. Article III-271(3) *et seq* also entails an emergency brake mechanism and the referral of a legislative measure to the European Council, thereby providing a safeguard of last resort. In addition, the new clause Article III-272 gives specific legal basis for measures concerning crime prevention.[67] Community action in this area, however, can only promote and support the action of MS and excludes the approximation of legislation.

The remaining two articles of section 4, namely, Articles III-273 and III-274 deal with Eurojust and the creation of a European Public Prosecutor respectively. The former article outlines Eurojust's mission and expands its powers, which now include the initiation of criminal investigations and proposing the initiation of prosecutions to be conducted by the competent national authorities, particularly those relating to offences against the financial interests of the Union, and the resolution of conflicts of jurisdiction. According to Article III-273(2), 'European laws shall determine Eurojust' structures, workings, scope of action and tasks' and that 'European laws shall determine arrangements for involving the European Parliament and Member States national parliaments in the evaluation of Eurojust's activities'. It remains to be seen whether Eurojust will be endowed with supervisory

---

[67] Notably, crime prevention was mentioned in Art. 29 EU, but it was not included in the specific legal bases of Arts. 30 and 31 EU.

powers over Europol, thereby subordinating the latter to the former. It has also been suggested that Eurojust should not have the open-ended brief provided for under Article III-273. Instead, it would have been preferable to define Eurojust's mandate on the basis of specifically enumerated offences.

The Constitutional Treaty has extended further the Union's JHA acquis by establishing a legal basis for a European Public Prosecutor's Office within Eurojust. Drawing on the Commission's green paper on the establishment of a European Public Prosecutor in the field of the Community financial interests,[68] the Constitutional Treaty stipulates that the EPP shall be responsible for investigating, prosecuting and bringing to judgment, the perpetrators of and accomplices in offences against the financial interests of the Union. The powers of the EPP may be extended to include serious crime having a cross-border dimension by the European Council acting by unanimity after obtaining the consent of the EP. Although the structural and functional relations between the EPP and Eurojust are unclear, as indeed are the details concerning its *modus operandi*, it, nevertheless, remains the case that the extension of judicial criminal cooperation into the field of law enforcement has generated anxieties about the Union's creeping competence or federalizing tendencies.

The EU's powers concerning police cooperation remain broadly unchanged. European laws and or framework laws could be used to establish rules concerning: (a) the collection, storage, analysis and exchange of relevant information, (b) support for the training of staff, and cooperation on the exchange of staff, on equipment and on research into crime detection, and (c) common investigative techniques in relation to the detection of serious forms of organized crime (Article III-275). Concerning Europol, the Constitutional Treaty extended its powers to carry out investigations and to participate in operational actions carried out jointly with the MS's competent authorities or in the context of joint investigative teams where appropriate in liaison with Eurojust. According to Article III-276(3), any operational action by Europol must be carried out in liaison and in agreement with the authorities of the MS whose territory is concerned. The application of coercive measures would remain the exclusive responsibility of the competent national authorities. Although Article III-276 delineates Europol's broad areas of action, rather than providing an exhaustive list of Europol's tasks, the last indent of this paragraph ensures the accountability of Europol by stating that European laws shall also lay down the procedures for scrutiny of Europol's activities by the European Parliament, together with the MS' national parliaments. Finally, Article III-277 on operations on the territory of another MS does not make any substantive amendments to Article 32 EU.

---

[68] COM(2001) 715 final.

CONCLUSIONS

Taking an overall view, it may be said that the Constitutional Treaty entails significant innovations.[69] It has redesigned Justice and Home Affairs, boosted the efficiency and effectiveness of cooperation and has addressed important deficits with regard to democracy, judicial supervision, transparency, coherence and complexity. More importantly, it did so in line with the model of multilevel and reflexive constitutionalism that characterizes the EU, thereby steering clear of the federalization of the area of freedom, security and justice.

Although the ratification of the Constitutional Treaty has stalled, it is, nevertheless, the case that its provisions have made an important contribution to the constitutional dialogue surrounding the area of freedom, security and justice. It is highly unlikely that the dynamism entailed by such a constitutional dialogue will evaporate. After all, a unique characteristic of European constitutionalism is that it does not seek to fix the institutional landscape once and for all, thereby freezing the conversation about the terms of political association and institutional design. The European Union legal order remains incomplete and restless, and as the European Union's *modus operandi* over the years has revealed, incompleteness and restlessness are not necessarily weaknesses.

It is, however, true to say that preserving these institutional innovations will not be easy. Nor could possible activation of Article 42 EU provide a comprehensive and viable solution,[70] and although it would be wrong to assume that the absence of a Constitutional Treaty will lead to either stagnation or inaction in this area,[71] its provisions are bound to exert a deep influence on the continuing conversation about institutional reform in the area of freedom, security and justice. By setting up

---

[69] Compare S. Peers, *The EU Constitution and Justice and Home Affairs: the Accountability Gap*, Statewatch (2004); S. White, *European Constitution: What is New in the Area of Judicial Cooperation in Criminal Matters and Police Cooperation*, Federal Trust Online Constitutional Essay, 27/2003.

[70] See, E. Guild and S. Carrera, *No Constitutional Treaty? Implications for the Area of Freedom, Security and Justice*, CEPS Working Document, No. 231 (2005).

[71] On 4 November 2004, the European Council adopted the Hague Programme which set the objectives to be implemented in the area of freedom, security and justice for the period 2005–2010. This was followed by the Commission's Action Plan (May 2005), which outlined 10 priorities for action, a set of implementing measures and a timetable for their adoption. The priorities cover: fundamental rights and citizenship, counter-terrorism, a common asylum area, migration management, integration, internal borders, external borders and visas, privacy and security, organized crime, civil and criminal justice, sharing responsibility, and solidarity. The Commission's effort to strike a better balance between freedom and security is evident in the Action Plan, which was approved by the Council on 2 June 2005. See European Commission Communication to the Council and the European Parliament, *The Hague Programme: Ten Priorities for the next five years—the Partnership for European Renewal in the filed of Freedom, Security and Justice*, COM(2005) 184 final, Brussels 10 May 2005.

a pattern of institutional reform within the bounds of possibility, the Constitutional Treaty is very likely to prompt a close reflection on the procedural, institutional and substantive weaknesses of AFSJ, thereby making the retention of the Treaty of Nice framework a problematic option. Whether these ideas and institutional reforms will find their fullest and lasting expression in a treaty amendment or a constitutional treaty in the future remains to be seen.

7

Unity and Pluralism in the EU's Foreign Relations Power

ENZO CANNIZZARO*

INTRODUCTION

In the ambitious programme of vesting the European Union with a written constitution, the reform of the current system of foreign relations deserved a prominent
place. One of the tasks assigned to the Convention, set up on the basis of the Laeken
Declaration, was to make proposals concerning the simplification of the architec-
tural structure of the Union and the definition of a unitary personality of the Union.
Both of these objectives were plainly aimed at giving unity and comprehensiveness
in the Union's external action, conceived as a necessary condition for a Constitutional
legal order. Consistently with such an aim, the new Constitutional Treaty made a
serious attempt—the most serious endeavoured thus far—to merge in a unitary set
of rules the main provisions concerning the external aspects of European integration.
Indeed, the achievement of these objectives—the 'de-pillarization' of the European
construction, and the acknowledgement of the Union as a unitary international
actor—seems to entail the re-unification of the vast array of powers and prerogatives
which are currently distributed in a disorderly and random bundle of competences.

By no means, however, is such a task easy to accomplish. Quite the contrary, it
is one of the most complex projects imaginable, as it entails untying knots which
resulted hitherto in insurmountable hurdles towards the unity of the EU foreign
affairs power. Indeed, the present, fragmented state of the EU system of foreign

* Professor of International Law, University of Macerata, cannizzaro@unimc.it. This chapter presents, in a systematic and expanded version, the topic dealt with in a course given at the summer school
of the Academy of European Law, at the European University Institute of Florence, in the Summer of
2005. Subsequently, I held a seminar at the University of Michigan Law School, in the Fall term of
2005, on 'The European Union in the International Arena'. These teaching experiences gave me the
opportunity to rethink a topic which has constantly fascinated me: the governance of international relations of a non-unitary entity. In finalizing what is nothing more than a tentative conclusion of an ongoing reflection on this topic, I wish to acknowledge gratefully the contribution given by the students of
both the course and the seminar, who continuously challenged my certainties. A valuable contribution
to the drafting of this work was given by Eugenia Bartoloni and Mel Marquis, Research Fellows at the
Institute of International and EU Law of the University of Macerata. All errors and infelicities remain,
of course, attributable only to me.

relations is not due to misfortune or to the failure of the architects of European integration. Rather, it is the result of the particular balance of power within the Union—with, on the one hand, the Member States constantly playing down the consequence of the transfer of competence to the EU/EC on the international plane; and, on the other, the European institutions tending to assert themselves as actors autonomous from the Member States.

To complicate the picture further, the legal regime of the European foreign relations system also suffers from the disorderly fashion in which it developed, with a continuous overlapping among provisions originally included in the Treaties, supervening revisions, case law of the ECJ and institutional practice, which create an intertwined situation which is difficult to disentangle even for the most gifted lawyers. The difficulty of construing these various elements in a consistent picture might have dissuaded the European scholarship from going beyond the technical difficulties and from inquiring more closely into the far-reaching implications of such a system.

All in all, the transfer of competence to the EU/EC has created a strange situation where no entity—neither the EU nor the EC or the Member States—possesses the plenitude of the foreign relations power, which is instead deeply segmented in a plurality of actors, objectives and decision-making procedures. This seems to be at variance with most contemporary experiences with federalism, in which the jealous defence of the powers and prerogatives of sub-state units on the internal plane goes hand in hand with the attempt to secure unity in external relations and to allow the federal entity to assert itself as a unitary actor in the international arena. Even for the most zealous custodian of the 'sovereign' rights of the component parts, the need for unity has represented the lighthouse for navigating the perilous waters of international relations: plurality inwards, but unity outwards.[1]

Not all of the questions arising out of this situation will be treated in the present chapter. Its objectives are less ambitious by far. It aims, first, at highlighting the internal fragmentation of the EU foreign relations power deriving from the distribution of competences between the EC and the EU, and second, at analysing the attempt to lend unity and coherence to the EU foreign relations power. Consistently with these narrow objectives, only the 'internal' fragmentation of the EU foreign affairs power, which results from the lack of unity within the EU system, will be considered in detail. Less attention will be devoted to the 'external' fragmentation, which results from the sharing of international powers and prerogatives between the Member States and the EU. Although this latter subject is highly interesting, and only rarely considered by the international literature, this aspect is logically autonomous and too broad, taken as a whole, to be squeezed into the quantitative terms of this chapter.[2] Beyond some cursory remarks, it must, in its comprehensiveness, remain outside the scope of the present analysis.

---

[1] See M. Farrell, 'EU External Relations: Exporting the EU Model of Governance?', 4 *European Foreign Affairs Review* (2005), 451, at 453.

[2] To this topic, I have elsewhere devoted extensive analysis. See 'Fragmented Sovereignty', 13 *The Italian Yearbook of International Law* (2003), 35.

Turning now to describe more closely the structure of this contribution, it seems opportune to devote the first section to a preliminary look at the main models of organization of the foreign relations power. This inquiry can help to explain the theoretical implications of the different models and their constitutional dimension.[3]

The second and third sections will focus respectively on the external relations system of the EC and on the system of the CFSP of the EU. The main aim of these two sections, which touch upon fields covered by an extensive literature, is to highlight the difficulty of ensuring that the regime governing the foreign affairs power of the EC remains separate from the one governing the foreign policy of the EU. This will in turn pave the way for an analysis concerning the practical devices employed in order to achieve mutual communication between these two sub-systems. This analysis will constitute the fourth section of this contribution.

In a further section, closer inquiry will be devoted to the new provisions on the EU's external action incorporated in the Constitutional Treaty, which have the express aim of establishing a comprehensive system of external action for the Union. Although, at the time of writing, the entry into force of the Constitutional Treaty seems far from certain—indeed, it rather seems doomed to failure—a legal analysis of the new integrated system of the Union's external action is a useful exercise, as its importance goes beyond mere cultural relevance. Apart from its historical contingencies, the new provisions represent the most sophisticated attempt, thus far, to set up a new integrated system of external action that could remedy (at least partially) the current fragmentation and establish unity in the Union's foreign relations power. In spite of the many misgivings such a system provokes, its technical study is worthwhile precisely because it may offer some guidance for future elaboration.

UNITY AND PLURALISM OF THE FOREIGN RELATIONS POWER IN A COMPARATIVE OVERVIEW

It is interesting, at the outset, to dedicate a brief overview to the main models of organization of the foreign relations power in composite entities. The aim of this section is to provide an illustration of the conceptual evolution which occurred in

---

[3] On the constitutional dimension of the European foreign affaire system, and on the impact of that dimension on the works of the Convention, see B. de Witte, 'The Constitutional Law of External Relations', in Pernice and Poiares Maduro (eds), *A Constitution for the European Union: First Comments on the 2003—Draft of the European Convention* (2004), 95; M. Cremona, 'Values in the EU Constitution: the External Dimension', in M. Aziz, S. Millns (eds), *Values in the Constitution of Europe* (2005); Id., 'The Draft Constitutional Treaty: External Relations and External Action', 40 *CMLRev* (2003), 1347; R.A. Wessel, 'Fragmentation in the Governance of EU External Relations: Legal Institutional Dilemmas and the New Constitution for Europe', in J.W. de Zwaan *et al*, (eds.), *The European Union—An Ongoing Process of Integration*, (Liber Amicorum Fred Kellermann (2004)), 123; E.-U. Petersmann, 'The 2004 Treaty Establishing a Constitution for Europe and Foreign Policy: a New Constitutional Paradigm?', in C. Gaitanides, S. Kadelbach, G.C. Rodriguez Iglesias (eds), *Europa und seine Verfassung: Festschrift für Manfred Zuleeg zum siebzigsten Geburtstag* (2005); M. Krajewski, 'Foreign Policy and the European Constitution', in 22 *Yearbook of European Law* (2003), 436.

this area, from the first examples, in which the sharing of competence in the internal sphere did not touch upon the unity of the entity in international affairs, to the most recent developments, in which the existence of a plurality of entities sharing powers and prerogatives in the international arena is more widely accepted.

In the classical process of federal integration, the organization of the foreign relations power has not generally been the subject of much dispute. The rights and prerogatives of the State in the international sphere were generally regarded as a corollary of sovereignty and even as an essential part of that notion. Consequently, they were considered to be indivisible and necessarily allocated in the governmental organs or entities which represented the State in its international relations.

Both elements, the unitary character of the foreign relations power and the need to assign it to the bearer of sovereignty, emerge clearly in the classical work on federalism which provided the theoretical foundation for the establishment of the US Federation. In Federalist Paper n. 42, Madison wrote:

The second class of powers, lodged in the general government, consists of those which regulate the intercourse with foreign nations, to wit: to make treaties; to send and receive ambassadors, other public ministers, and consuls; to define and punish piracies and felonies committed on the high seas, and offenses against the law of nations; to regulate foreign commerce (. . .). This class of powers forms an obvious and essential branch of the federal administration. If we are to be one nation in any respect, it clearly ought to be in respect to other nations.

This statement does not explain in plain terms why those powers, instead of being shared among different level of government, are reserved for the federal administration. It simply says that this solution is obvious. The obviousness derives from the fact that the nation would not be 'one' *vis-à-vis* other nations if it did not have the plenitude of the foreign relations power. Consequently, it must have been seen by the author, and in fact it has consistently been seen by many readers, as self-explanatory.[4] The foreign relations power is the one that outwardly (and symbolically) depicts the essence of the nation. To split up the foreign affairs power would clearly have been inconsistent with the goal of national unity, and indeed could have resulted in the various units acting externally at cross-purposes.

The assignment of the foreign relations power in its entirety to the centralized unit creates a clear asymmetry between the internal and the external normative dimension. The internal sphere is dominated by an institutional pluralism and distinguished by the principle of distribution of powers among different organs and levels of governance. Conversely, the external sphere is dominated by the opposite principle of the preservation of the unity of the course of the 'nation'.[5]

---

[4] Besides the logical, and perhaps ideological, argument in favour of the unity of the foreign relations power, one can also find scattered around the Federalist papers other arguments of a more practical tenor. Generally, they refer to the need to establish authoritativeness and coherence in the governance of foreign affairs and to ensure that irresolute or inconsistent behaviour on the foreign relations front does not obstruct the taking of decisions for the good of the nation as a whole.

[5] This asymmetry has created, and in fact continues to create, overlaps and inconsistencies between internal and external action and is a recurrent cause of disharmony and conflicts. Indeed, in a system in

The US system represents one of the most coherent applications of a model which can be plausibly be named 'unitary'.[6] In this model, both the treaty-making power and the foreign policy are concentrated in the hands of the central unit.[7] The consequences for the decentralized units are obviously very heavy. Not only are they precluded from entering into any treaty or any other form of international compact, they must also accept that the treaties concluded by the federal entity are applicable within their legal order and that such treaties take priority over their internal acts. Furthermore, the ability of the decentralized units to enact internal legislation having an impact on the federal foreign policy is severely impaired. This is the far-reaching effect of the 'dormant foreign policy clause', which has been re-asserted even recently by the US Supreme Court to the detriment of the internal competence of the States.[8]

The unitary model, so well embodied by the US constitutional system, is thus one in which the foreign relations power is entirely entrusted to the centralized entity, and in which the latter's pre-eminence interferes in a variety of ways with the sharing of competences on the internal plane. It is thus rooted in the premise that the external sovereignty is unitary and must be 'unitarily' held and exercised— a conception which reigned in multiple forms over the legal thought of the nineteenth and the first half of the twentieth century.

which certain entities possess internal powers only, a concern arises with respect to maintaining untouched the principle of the internal distribution of competence, and to avoid any overlapping foreign relations powers that might jeopardise it. This concern also has historical importance. Indeed, the assignment to a sole entity of the foreign relations power tends inevitably to simplify, as far as international affairs are concerned, the rich articulation of competence on the internal plane and can even be seen as a threat to the internal balance of power, unless there are no adequate safeguards for the internal level of government. It is precisely the need to safeguard the sphere of competence recognized internally from the interference produced on the internal plane by the exercise of the foreign relations power which prompted the first theoretical elaborations that ultimately opened the way to the full-fledged dualistic conception of the relation between international law and municipal law. I have dealt with this topic in my study 'Trattato internazionale (adattamento al)', in *Enciclopedia del diritto*, vol. XLIV (1991), 1393.

[6] The obvious reference is to the classic work by L. Henkin, *Foreign Affairs and the United States Constitution* (2nd ed., 1997).

[7] The wording of Art. I, sec. 10 ('No State shall, without the Consent of Congress, (. . .) enter into any Agreement or Compact with another State, or with a foreign Power . . .') might appear to suggest that the Constitution intended to assign the treaty-making power to the states, subject to the consent of the Congress. However, the prevailing opinion in the literature and the well-settled stance in jurisprudence tend to uphold the view that in foreign affairs, the US is virtually a unitary State (see L. Henkin, *Foreign Affairs and the United States Constitution, supra*, n. 6; E. Stein (in collaboration with L. Henkin), 'Towards a European Foreign Policy? The European Foreign Affairs System from the Perspective of the United States Constitution; in M. Cappelleti, M. Seccombe and J. H. H. Weiler (eds.), *Integration Through Law: Europe and the American Federal Experience*, vol. 1, *Methods, Tools and Institutions* (1986), book 3.

[8] The Supreme Court held in *Garamendi*, (*American Insurance Association v John Garamendi, Insurance Commissioner, State of California*, 539 U.S. 396 (2003)), that, '[t]here is, of course, no question that at some point an exercise of state power that touches on foreign relations must yield to the National Government's policy, given the 'concern for uniformity in this country's dealings with foreign nations' that animated the Constitution's allocation of the foreign relations power to the National Government in the first place'. See also *Zchernig v Miller*, 389 U.S. 429 (1968).

In recent times, however, the monolithic nature of federal entities in international affairs seems to be increasingly questioned, with sub-state entities which tend to vindicate their autonomy not only on the internal plane, but also, albeit in limited forms, in international relations.

A small, but not insignificant, number of federal States (or other non-federal States that nevertheless exhibit some degree of decentralization) now tend to adopt a more liberal approach towards the external power of the sub-State units. The most limited application of this approach consists of assigning to such units the power to conclude treaties in some of the fields in which they have internal competence. This is an asymmetrical model of 'treaty-making power sharing'. Generally, this power to conclude treaties extends only to minor forms of international engagements, within limits strictly marked by the federal Constitutions and subjected to strict procedural restraints aimed at securing the consistency of the treaty-making power with the federal foreign policy.[9]

With different nuances, such a solution seems to have been adopted in various legal systems. Traditionally, in the Swiss federal system the Cantons enjoy a limited international capacity, which extends to the power to conclude treaties in specified fields.[10] The foreign relations power of the Cantons has been even enlarged by the 1999 Constitutional reform, as we will see soon. Recently, an analogous tendency is discernible in Austria,[11] Italy[12] and even France,[13] for centuries considered to be among the most visible examples of a unitary State.

[9] For a general reconsideration, see C. Tomuschat, 'Component Territorial Units of States under International Law', in L. Daniele (ed.), *Regioni e autonomie territoriali nel diritto internazionale ed europeo* (2005), 31. There is no need to trace back some famous historical examples of disguised autonomy assigned to sub-State units, deprived however of practical significance. It is well known that Ukraine and Belarus were among the original signatories of the UN Charter, despite the fact that their autonomy was in practice reduced to nil. For a study of these precedents, see K. Ginther, 'Article 4', in B. Simma (ed.), *The Charter of the United Nations. A Commentary* (1995) 158; H.-J Schütz, 'Membership', in R. Wolfrum (ed.), *United Nations: Law, Policies and Practice* (1995), 877.

[10] See L. Wildhaber, 'External Relations of the Swiss Cantons', in 12 *Canadian Yearbook of International Law* (1974), 211.

[11] See Art. 16, para. (1) of the Austrian Constitution according to which, '(I)n matters within their own sphere of competence the Laender can conclude treaties with States, or their constituent States, bordering on Austria'.

[12] See Art. 117, para. 9 of the Italian Constitution, as amended in 2003. Although this provision seems to attribute unequivocally a certain form of treaty-making power to the Regions, its impact has been severely curtailed by the corresponding implementing legislation, apparently without appreciable reactions by the Regions. It may be worthwhile to note that the Italian system tends to attribute primacy to treaties concluded by the Regions over national laws, so as to ensure that any inconsistency between a regional treaty and national law does not prevent the Region in question from observing its commitments. This would solve the problems experienced in other legal systems, such as Switzerland, where the primacy attributed to federal law over treaties concluded by the Cantons can make it difficult to find residual areas in which such treaties might be feasible. Indeed, supervening federal law could even make it impossible for the Cantons to comply with treaties already concluded. See *infra* n. 15.

[13] Such unusual treaties in the case of France relate to the activities of the *territoire d'autre-mer* (TOM) and of the *Départements d'autre-mer* (DOM). See various contributions collected in *Les*

It is more rare to find examples of a symmetrical share of competence, where, both the centralized unit and the decentralized units are assigned the power to conclude treaties corresponding to the full range of the competences they possess internally. Notoriously, the German Basic Law of 1949 contains a provision of the kind, although its implementation has been strongly influenced by political events.[14] Ultimately, the *s.c. Lindauer* agreement, concluded in 1957 by the Federation and the Länder, settled the respective views and established a *modus vivendi* which tends, on the one hand, to limit the competence of the Länder to conclude treaties and assigns, on the other hand, to them the power to veto the conclusion of treaties by the Federation which might affect their internal competence.

An example of the symmetrical share of the treaty-making power, one which apparently brings into harmony the internal and the external sphere of autonomy, is the current Swiss system. The 1999 revision of the Swiss Constitution radically transformed the Swiss system and assigned to the Cantons a treaty-making power that is symmetrical to that of the federal Government for all the matters which are assigned internally to the Cantons' competence.[15]

In spite of its symbolical character, the recognition of sub-State units as internationally active entities is generally not perceived as a threat to the comprehensiveness of the foreign relations power of the centralized entity. The reason for this is twofold. First, the power assigned to sub-State units is generally concurrent with that of the State, meaning that the latter maintains the power to intrude upon the prerogatives of those sub-units by concluding treaties in matters internally reserved to their

---

collectivités territoriales non-étatiques dans le système juridique international: journée d'études organisée avec le concours du Centre de Recherche sur les Pouvoirs locaux dans la Caraïbe de l'Université des Antilles et de la Guyane, Colloque de la Société française pour le droit international (2002).

[14] Art. 32, para. 3 of the German Basic Law provides that, '[i]nsofar as the Länder have power to legislate, they may conclude treaties with foreign states with the consent of the Federal Government'. However, the wording of this provision allows room for different views as to the scope of the power of the Länder to conclude and to implement treaties in the fields which are internally assigned to their competence. This difference of opinion has never been settled legally, but a mode of practice has been developed, in a way that is typical of German federalism, which allows both sides to hold their respective views without disturbing the conduct of business. See recently B. Fassbender, 'The Weight of Tradition and the Challenges of Political, Economic and Legal Convergence: The *Status* of the German *Länder* in International and European Law', in *Regioni e autonomie territoriali nel diritto internazionale ed europeo*, supra, n. 9, at 339.

[15] Art. 56 of the 1999 Swiss Constitution provides that:

'(1) The Cantons may conclude treaties with foreign countries within the scope of their powers.

(2) These treaties may not be contrary to the law nor to the interests of the Federation nor to the laws of other Cantons. Before concluding a treaty, the Cantons must inform the Federation.

(3) The Cantons may deal directly with lower ranking foreign authorities; in other cases, the relations of the Cantons with foreign countries are conducted by the Federation acting on their behalf.'

The system adopted by Switzerland provides an example of the difficulties entailed in the attribution of the sharing of the treaty-making power. In particular, the ambiguous wording of Art. 56, para. 3, makes it difficult to identify the entity which is the international party to a treaty concluded by the Federation on the Cantons' behalf.

competence. As already pointed out, in most, if not all, of these systems, the treaty-making power of sub-State units is conceived merely as an internal articulation of the unitary treaty-making power of that entity, which does not touch upon its unitary international actorship.

Second, and perhaps more importantly, even where the treaty-making power is vertically shared, foreign policy remains strictly in the hands of the Federation. The consistency between external activities of sub-State entities and the foreign policy of the State is secured through complex mechanisms which, in a variety of manners, tend to limit the autonomy of the non-sovereign entities. The presence of these mechanisms tends to assuage the impact of the sharing of the treaty-making power, which is not perceived as jeopardizing the Madisonian principle of the unity of the 'nation' in international affairs.[16]

All of this changes where an assignment of the treaty-making power is accompanied by guarantees of exclusivity, all the more so when that power is, expressly or impliedly, recognized as a political power which bestows on its bearer the quality of a political actor. Belgium is, to my knowledge, the only system in which not only is the treaty-making power symmetrically distributed, but the decentralized treaty-making power is also exclusive. Moreover, there seem to be no limits in the Belgian system as to the objectives which the sub-state units can pursue by concluding agreements, which, therefore, can be inspired also by purely political considerations.[17]

A further possible example is the unique position of Quebec in the Canadian legal system, where Quebec seems *de facto* to have acquired significant powers in the external sphere which, in practice, give it the possibility of carrying out its own foreign policy.[18]

---

[16] Thus, the assignment to sub-State entities of the power to conclude treaties in enumerated fields only seems to replicate, in a reverse form, the assignment to international organizations of the power to conclude treaties in some of the fields of competence assigned to them. Indeed, such a power is often conceived as the possibility to discharge the mission entrusted to these organizations by availing themselves of certain powers of action in the international sphere.

[17] Art. 167 of the Belgian Constitution reads:

'(1) The King manages international relations, without prejudice to the ability of communities and regions to engage in international co-operation, including the signature of treaties, for those matters within their responsibilities as established by the Constitution and in virtue thereof. [. . .]

(2) The King concludes treaties, with the exception of those described in §3. These treaties may take effect only following approval of the Chambers.

(3) Those Communities and Regional Governments described in Article 121 conclude, in matters that concern them, treaties regarding matters that are in the scope of the responsibilities of their Councils. These treaties may take effect only following approval by the Council.

See W. Pas, 'The Role of the Belgian Regions and Communities in International and European Law', in *Regioni e autonomie territoriali nel diritto internazionale ed europeo*, supra, n. 9, at 313.

[18] Regarding to the matter of treaty-making, Canadian Constitutional Law … itself provides little guidance and has given rise to different interpretations (for an analysis of the relevant constitutional passages and their history, see I. Bernier, *International Legal Aspects of Federalism* (1973), at 51 ff.). Absent

It may be seen that we are now approaching the outer limits of federalism. While the attribution to sub-State units of limited forms of treaty-making power, appropriately depoliticized and concurrent with the national treaty-making power, does not jeopardise the comprehensiveness of the State's external unity, the flat-out sharing of the foreign relations power is clearly at variance with the essence of the State's sovereignty.

Beyond its limited practical impact, the growing tendency to accept the possibility of a shared external relations power shows the far-reaching implications of the issue. It reveals the existence of a number of possible models of distribution of that power, from a very restrictive one which tends to preserve the unity of the foreign relations power (considered to be the essence of statehood) to more permissive models which seem to allow for a distribution of powers that touches on the most intimate aspects of state sovereignty. Although one can readily see a certain logical development in the unfolding of the various models, it is not easy to foretell the outcome of this process. In particular, it is not easy to determine whether the expansive tendency can be regarded as transitory and destined to recede with the increasing difficulty of coping with a plurality of political actors expressing different voices in the international arena, or whether this tendency will instead gain momentum and further complicate the international landscape. If this is the case, this raises the question of how to coordinate the activities of a plurality of entities possessing powers of action on the external sphere. In turn, this might require an adaptation of a number of doctrines of international law which are premised on the principle of the unity of its international actors.

The previous pages offer a useful background for a closer inquiry into the EU foreign relations power and into the possible determination of its nature and its functioning, to which it is now time to turn our attention.

THE EC FOREIGN AFFAIRS POWER

I will now examine briefly the main lines of the development of the foreign relations power of the EC. Originally restricted to the power to conclude agreements in very limited fields, this power has undergone a complex and turbulent process of development in both quantitative and qualitative terms, right up to its current, highly unstable state.

---

explicit provisions in the Constitution, the Federal Government has defended the view that treaty-making power, as part of the executive power, was unitarily transferred to Canada by the Crown. But Quebec argues that there is no constitutional authority to support an exclusive federal treaty-making power, and since the late 1960s, has consistently asserted its competence to conclude treaties on matters falling within its legislative competence. Quebec's position has never been formally accepted by the federal government. Notwithstanding constitutional muddles, in practice Quebec concluded a number of agreements with foreign jurisdictions. The Federal Government generally made acquiescence to this practice, though sometimes expressing its approval to the conclusion of agreements by the Provinces (see P.W. Hogg, *Constitutional Law of Canada*[3] (1992), at 298; L. Di Marzo, *Component Units of Federal States and International Agreements* (1980), at 84.

This analysis will not claim to provide a comprehensive picture of this system, which is very complex indeed. Rather, I will look at the system from a particular angle: I will try to highlight the difficulties arising from the existence of an entity endowed with the treaty-making power in vast areas of competence but devoid of the foreign policy power (which, in the EU context, is not extended to the Community but reserved to the second pillar). In accordance with this very narrow purpose, I will eschew many of the questions which abound in this intricate field but which are unrelated to the purpose of the current study. Moreover, reference to the abundant literature and case law in this field must remain confined to what is strictly demanded by the argument. For a more thorough analysis of the EC system of external relations, and for more extensive and systematic references to case law and scholarly contributions, the reader can refer to the many excellent systematic treatises on this topic.[19]

The EC Treaty, when originally adopted (as the EEC Treaty), endowed the EC with broad competence in the internal sphere but with a very narrow class of powers on the external plane. The powers expressly assigned to the EC were basically limited to the fields of commercial policy and association agreements with third States. Other powers were referred to in sparse provisions of the Treaty, such as that of establishing and maintaining contacts with the UN and with other international organizations (IOs).[20] The Treaty also proclaims emphatically, in Article 281, that the EC has legal personality. Although this provision was probably drafted with only the internal personality in mind, it was to play a major role in the process of transformation of the EC treaty-making power.

Not unlike its internal powers, furthermore, the foreign power of the EC was restricted to the pursuit of enumerated purposes. Due both to the asymmetrical share of external power between the EC and its Member States and to the duty to exercise the few external powers originally put at its disposal for the objectives

---

[19] Just to indicate a few among the most recent contributions, see P. Koutrakos, *EU International Relations Law* (2006); J.-V. Louis, M. Dony (eds.), *Commentaire J. Mégret—Le droit de la CE et de l'Union européenne, Relations extérieures* vol. 12 (2005); I. Govaere, 'The External Relations of EU: Legal Aspects', in D. Mahncke, A. Ambos and C. Reynolds (eds), *European Foreign Policy: from Rhetoric to Reality?* (2004); P. Eeckhout, *External Relations of the European Union. Legal and Constitutional Foundations* (2004); M. Knodt, S. Princen (eds.), *Understanding the European Union's External Relations* (2003); M. Cremona, 'External Relations end External Competence: The Emergence of an Integrated Policy', in P. Craig, g. De Búrca (eds), *The Evolution of EU Law* (1999). See also the contributions collected in H. Wallace, W. Wallace and M.A. Pollack (eds), *Policy-Making in the European Union* (2005); T. Tridimas, P. Nebbia (eds), *European Union Law for the Twenty-First Century: Rethinking the New Legal Order*, Vol. 1, Constitutional and Public Law, External Relations (2004); E. Cannizzaro (ed.), *The European Union as an Actor in International Relations* (2002); S. Griller, B. Weidel (eds), *External Economic Relations and Foreign Policy in the European Union* (2002); A. Dashwood, C. Hillion (eds), *The General Law of E.C. External Relations* (2000); M. Koskenniemi (ed.), *International Law Aspects of the European Union* (1998); I. Mcleod, I.D. Hendry, S. Hyett (eds), *The External Relations of the European Community* (1998).

[20] Art. 302 EC.

expressly stated in the Treaty, the international action of the EC represented the exception rather than the rule.

However, it is well known that this situation changed very rapidly by virtue of a resolute stance adopted by the European Court of Justice (ECJ), which radically altered the scope of the EC foreign power. As a result of this process of expansion, the EC passed from an entity possessing only enumerated powers to one having at its disposal an open catalogue of competences on the international sphere, corresponding to (although not necessarily limited by) its competences in the internal sphere. However, this momentous process of expansion has been limited to the *means of action* put at the disposal of the EC, without extending to the set of aims which it could pursue. In other words, this process of development of the EC competence was seen by the ECJ as a process by which the EC acquired more means to achieve the objectives assigned to it by the Treaty, but not as a process aimed at transforming the EC from an entity empowered to act only for enumerated purposes to one which can pursue an open catalogue of purposes. This process was made possible by the tacit acceptance of the Member States, which acquiesced in the expansion of the EC's means of action on condition that they remained the 'Lords' over the aims of that action.

Express Powers

In the original system of the Treaty, only few provisions referred expressly to external powers of the EC. Among them, a prominent role was to be acquired by Article 133 (originally Article 113), which conferred to the EC the power to adopt acts and to conclude treaties in the field of commercial policy. The provision was drafted so as to give the impression that the Member States still retained significant external competence in that field, whereas the competence of the EC was limited to 'uniform principles'. In Opinion 1/75, however, the ECJ held that the objective of the Treaty to secure the unity of the commercial policy was inconsistent with the Member States retaining significant powers in this area. In other words, the need to secure the unity of the EC actions would pre-empt the Member States from exercising powers in this area, and in particular from undertaking international obligations which could impair the objectives of the commercial policy.[21] In consequence

---

[21] Opinion 1/75, 'Understanding on a Local Cost Standard' [1975] ECR 1355. See the famous definition of exclusivity in the Opinion: 'the exclusive nature of the community's powers . . . depends, on the one hand, on the objective of the understanding in question and, on the other hand, on the manner in which the common commercial policy is conceived in the treaty. (. . .) Such a policy is conceived in that article in the context of the operation of the common market, for the defence of the common interests of the Community, within which the particular interests of the Member States must endeavour to adapt to each other. Quite clearly, this conception is incompatible with the freedom to which the member states could lay claim by invoking a concurrent power, so as to ensure that their own interests were separately satisfied in external relations, at the risk of compromising the effective defence of the common interests of the community' (para. 2).

of this 'functional' notion of exclusivity the Court concluded that the competence of the EC in the field of commercial policy was to be considered as exclusive.[22]

The scope of the EC commercial power was further expanded, first by shaping the idea that the presence of ancillary clauses in commercial agreements did not affect the characterization of the agreement. This means that the power of the EC under commercial policy may also extend to encompass provisions which, individually considered, would not fall within the EC trade competence, if their presence is instrumental to the functioning of the agreement.[23] This doctrine seemed to have come to an end in Opinion 1/78,[24] on the rubber agreement, where the ECJ failed to consider as ancillary the provisions concerning the financing of the system of stabilization set up by the agreement, and accepted that their financing by the Member States entailed their participation in the agreement, with the consequence that the agreement had to be concluded in mixed form.[25]

A fortunate doctrine employed in order to enlarge substantially the scope of the EC foreign power was that of the evolutionary interpretation of certain notions of the Treaty, in particular, the notion of commercial policy.[26] Although mainly

[22] This functional conception of exclusivity was applied, in its purity, only to the field of commercial policy and was probably due to the will of the ECJ to depart from the wording of Art. 113 in construing the foreign power of the EC in the field of commercial policy. If the ECJ also adopted an analogous definition in regard to purely internal powers, the nature of a vast part of the EC's competence on the internal plane would be transformed accordingly.

[23] See again Opinion 1/75, *supra* n. 22, para. 2, where one can read: 'It is of little importance that the obligations and financial burdens inherent in the execution of the agreement envisaged are borne directly by the Member States. The "internal" and "external" measures adopted by the Community within the framework of the common commercial policy do not necessarily involve, in order to ensure their compatibility with the treaty, a transfer to the institutions of the Community of the obligations and financial burdens which they may involve: such measures are solely concerned to substitute for the unilateral action of the Member States, in the field under consideration, a common action based upon uniform principles on behalf of the whole of the Community'. The Court did not have many other occasions for using such a theory in order to allocate competence between the EC and the Member States. Conversely, such a doctrine was amply used in order to allocate the EC competence among the various legal bases provided for by the Treaty. See, for a clear indication, Case C-268/94, *Portuguese Republic v Council* [1996] ECR I-6177 and Opinion 2/00 'Cartagena Protocol on Biosafety' [2001] ECR I-9713.

[24] See Opinion 1/78, 'International Agreement on Natural Rubber' [1979] ECR 2871. If one accepted that the scope of the EC external power extended to provisions of a treaty having an accessory character, it would seem logical to conclude that, correspondingly, the Member States have no competence. However, this would entail the impossibility to predetermine the borders of the EC competence. In a different perspective, it would not seem completely illogical to assume that the competence of the EC generated by the doctrine of the ancillary clauses is not exclusive. Indeed, the entire theory of the ancillary clauses is not among the most clear in the Court's jurisprudence.

[25] Opinion 1/78, 'International Agreement on Natural Rubber', *supra* n. 24, para. 60.

[26] Opinion 1/78, 'International Agreement on Natural Rubber', *supra* n. 24, para. 44. This paragraph reads: 'following the impulse given by UNCTAD to the development of this type of control it seems that it would no longer be possible to carry on any worthwhile common commercial policy if the Community were not in a position to avail itself also of more elaborate means devised with a view to

referred to in the field of trade, this doctrine was also applied silently by the ECJ in other fields.[27] However, the expanding effect of this conception, which the Court never explicitly abandoned, was carefully delimited in the subsequent development of the jurisprudence. In particular, in Opinion 1/94, the effects of that doctrine were counter-balanced with the adoption of a strict approach to the scope of the EC competence.[28]

In the original setting of the Treaty, the only other provision which expressly assigned to the EC the power to conclude agreements was Article 310 (originally Article 238). The EC made large use of this power, and concluded a number of association agreements.[29] Due to the presence of provisions which fell indisputably within the competence of the Member States, these agreements have been concluded in mixed form.

The nature and the scope of the power conferred to the EC by Article 310 remained, thus, largely undetermined. Article 310 does not assign new fields to the competence of the EC and seems only to empower the EC to use the external competence it already possesses under the Treaty in order to set up institutionalized forms of cooperation with third States and with IO. Were it so, Article 310 could not be viewed as a provision assigning to the EC new means of action, as rather as one enlarging the gamut of the objectives for which the EC can make use of the external powers of which it disposes under the Treaty.

The ECJ took, however, a different course. In *Demirel*, it was asked to determine the scope of the respective competence of the EC and Member States under the Association agreement with Turkey. The Court said: 'Since the agreement in question is an association agreement creating special, privileged links with a non-member country which must, at least to a certain extent, take part in the community system, article 238 must necessarily empower the Community to guarantee commitments towards non-member countries in all the fields covered by the treaty'.[30]

---

furthering the development of international trade. It is therefore not possible to lay down, for article 113 of the EEC Treaty, an interpretation the effect of which would be to restrict the common commercial policy to the use of instruments intended to have an effect only on the traditional aspects of external trade to the exclusion of more highly developed mechanisms such as appear in the agreement envisaged. A "commercial policy" understood in that sense would be destined to become nugatory in the course of time.' Analogies can be drawn between this argument and the argument unfolded by the Court in Opinion 1/75 (*supra* n. 22) in order to determine the exclusive nature of the EC competence under Art. 113.

[27] A good example is Case C-268/94, *Portuguese Republic v Council, supra* n. 23, at para. 23, where the Court found that human rights clauses could be covered by an evolutionary conception of the competence of the EC in the field of development cooperation.

[28] Opinion 1/94 'WTO' [1994] ECR I-5267. See in particular paras. 43 ff. and 59 ff.

[29] See P. Eeckhout, *External Relations of the European Union*, supra, n. 19, at 103.

[30] Case 12/86, *Demirel v Stadt Schwäbisch Gmünd* [1987] ECR 3719, para. 9. In the decisions, the Court went on to state: 'Since freedom of movement for workers is, by virtue of article 48 et seq. of the EEC Treaty, one of the fields covered by that Treaty, it follows that commitments regarding freedom of movement fall within the powers conferred on the Community by article 238.' The construction of

This conclusion entails clearly that Article 310 has the effect of attributing to the EC fresh external powers. Indeed, using Article 310 as the legal basis of its action, the EC is empowered to undertake obligations with third parties in all the fields covered by the Treaty, to the extent that they are necessary in order to set up an association agreement. This means that the power of the EC under Article 310 is co-extensive with all the areas in which the Treaty assigns competence to the EC. The potentially intrusive effect of this new competence on the delicate balance of power between the EC and the Member States can be hardly overshadowed. Indeed, the conclusion of an association agreement in mixed form can be viewed as an exercise of EC competence in regard to all the provisions included in that agreement which fall within the range of the actual or the potential competence of the EC.[31] Indeed, in *Demirel* the Court considered that provisions governing the treatment of non-national workers, for which one could hardly find *ad hoc* legal basis in the Treaty, constituted in effect an exercise of the EC competence distinctly assigned to it by Article 310.

Over the years, starting with the Maastricht Treaty, new provisions have been included in the Treaty which aim to bestow fresh powers on the European Community in the field of external relations. With the notable exception of the competence in the field of monetary policy[32], in other fields the competence is explicitly labelled as concurrent. This is the case with Articles 170, 174 and 181 EC, dealing respectively with research and technological development, the environment and development cooperation.

The implications of express concurrent competence in the field of external relations are not entirely clear and the success of this formula is probably due to political reasons. Beyond speculation, two kinds of consequences can be discerned. The first is that the conclusion of agreements by the EC does not have pre-emptive effect. In other words, the treaty-making power of the EC does not become exclusive even after being exercised.[33] Clearly, however, agreements concluded by the EC enjoy

---

Art. 238 as the legal basis of an instrumental competence of the EC to include in association agreements provisions in all the fields covered by the Treaty opened the door to the competence of the Court to interpret those provisions.

[31] Of course, the power of the EC to conclude association agreements cannot have, by itself, pre-emptive effect in regard to all the possible substantive provisions which can potentially be included therein. Thus, until an association agreement is concluded, the Member States retain the substantive competence that they possess internally. It follows that the presence in an association agreement concluded in mixed form of provisions falling within an area of concurrent competence is not an element pointing unequivocally to the competence of the EC.

[32] In this field, the external action of the EC is governed by specific treaty rules, which raise distinctive, and very complex, interpretative issues which must remain outside the scope of the present work. See, for all the extensive literature, J.-V. Louis, 'Les relations extérieures de l'Union économique et monétaire', in E. Cannizzaro (ed.), *The European Union as an Actor in International Relations, supra* n. 19, at 77.

[33] This marks off the express concurrent power from the implied concurrent power, in accordance with Opinion 1/76. In the latter case, as will be seen below, the actual exercise of the power has the

primacy over all Member State legislation. This means that the Member States are nonetheless precluded from concluding agreements whose effect would be to undertake obligations inconsistent with the implementation of EC law. The nature and content of this limitation, and the way it differs from the effect produced by implied concurrent competence, will hopefully become clear in the following pages.

The second, and probably more important, effect lies in the fact that EC action based on an express concurrent competence does not need further justification. In particular, in order to conclude agreements in these fields the EC does not have to demonstrate that the conclusion of agreement is necessary for achieving the objectives of the Treaty. This effect, which indeed did not emerge clearly from previous cases, was ultimately upheld by the ECJ in *Mox Plant*.[34]

effect of transforming it from concurrent to exclusive, with the consequence that the Member States cannot conclude agreements affecting agreements already concluded by the EC. This effect does not occur when an agreement is concluded under those express provisions of the Treaty which give to the EC the power to conclude agreements 'without prejudice to Member States' competence to negotiate in international bodies and to conclude international agreements'. The without-prejudice clause seems to refer to the possibility that an agreement concluded by the EC does not pre-empt the conclusion of agreements by the Member States so long as they do not require the Member States to act inconsistently with their obligation to comply with the agreements concluded by the EC.

[34] Judgment of 30 May 2006, Case C-459/03, *Commission v United Kingdom*, n.y.r. Paragraph 95 reads: 'The Community can enter into agreements in the area of environmental protection even if the specific matters covered by those agreements are not yet, or are very partially, the subject of rules at community level, which, by reason of that fact, are not likely to be affected.' Although the Court quotes in support of this finding the authority of Opinion 2/00, *supra* n. 23, this reference does not seem fully appropriate. Indeed, the reading of Opinion 2/00 does not leave the impression that the scope of the EC external power in the field of environmental protection is much different from that of the implied powers. On a careful reading, it even seems doubtful that the Court in that Opinion had identified the power to conclude the Cartagena Convention on the express external power of the EC to conclude agreement in the field of environmental cooperation. The ambiguous wording of the relevant passage of the Opinion (paras. 43–46) seem rather to indicate that the Convention was to be concluded on the basis of the implied external power and, more precisely, on the basis of the power produced by the existence of internal legislation in the field of the environment. Indeed, in Opinion 2/00 the Court was not asked to determine the scope of the external competence in environmental matters. The question concerned the identification of the most appropriate legal basis for the conclusion of the Cartagena Convention. In *Mox Plant*, the question was quite different, and concerned rather the identification of which entity, the EC or the Member States, was the proper addressee of certain obligations in the field of the environmental protection deriving from a mixed agreement: the UN Convention on the law of the sea. Thus, the Court, once stated that the EC, 'by becoming a party to the Convention, elected to exercise its external competence in matters of environmental protection' (paras. 96–97), concluded that 'a transfer of areas of shared competence, in particular in regard to the prevention of marine pollution, took place within the framework of the Convention, and without any of the Community rules concerned being affected, within the terms of the principle set out in the AETR judgment' (para. 105). According to the terms of the declaration of competence, such a transfer was 'subject to the existence of Community rules, even though it is not necessary that those rules be affected' (para. 106). Thus, the Member States retained their competence only in areas in which there were no Community rules (para. 107).

The conclusion of the judgment does not appear fully convincing. In particular, the wording of the declaration of Community competence seems to indicate precisely that in areas of shared competence the competence rests primarily with the Member States, unless Community internal rules existed

Implied Powers

Although a strictly textual reading of the Treaty might give the impression that the EC treaty-making power is limited to only some of the competences transferred to it internally, that impression is quickly dispelled when one considers the momentous development that has occurred by recourse to the implied powers doctrine. The rationale of the development lies in the search for consistency between internal and external action of the EC.

Although sometimes presented as a purely internal, constitutional doctrine, the implied powers doctrine is, in the present context, based on the implications of the sharing of competence on the external plane. The premise underlying it is the finding that the Treaty did not establish the EC as a means for coordinating the international activities of the Member States but rather as a separate entity, endowed with its own legal personality. The existence of a separate legal personality pleads in favour of a symmetrical sharing of competence in order to avoid inconsistencies between the obligations deriving from the exercise of competence on the external plane by one entity (ie a Member State) and the exercise of competence on the internal plane by the other (the EC).[35]

The basic rationale of the existence of a 'dormant foreign affairs clause' underlying the system of the competence assigned to the EC is the need to ensure that the Member States do not assume obligations with which they cannot comply due to a previously enacted EC norm.[36] Thus, the exercise of power on the internal plane by the EC pre-empts the Member States from acting externally insofar as they might otherwise incur obligations whose implementation could affect pre-existing EC norm. The scope of the external competence of the EC depends not on the mere existence of an internal competence but rather on its actual exercise. It is the

which could have been affected by the Convention. The interpretation of the relevant passage of the declaration by the Court seems to reverse that principle and to affirm instead the opposite principle, according to which, in the presence of Community rules, the Community must be presumed to have exercised its external competence, even if these rules are not affected by the Convention provisions. Be that as it may, it emerges that, in the conception of the Court, the express power of the Community to conclude environmental agreements is quite independent from both the conditions which, alternatively, justify the exercise of implied powers, ie from the existence of internal legislation likely to be affected by the agreement, under the *ERTA* doctrine; and the 'necessity' test, under the *Opinion 1/76* doctrine.

[35] See, in particular, paras. 12 ff. of the *ERTA* judgment, Case 22/70 *Commission v Council* [1971] ECR 263.

[36] One can wonder whether the same logical argument, applied in the reverse sense, could not support an implied power of the EC to assume obligations which it has the power to abide by. For example, this consideration could justify, contrary to the finding of the ECJ in Opinion 2/94, 'Accession by the Communities to the Convention for the Protection of Human Rights and Fundamental Freedoms' [1996] ECR I-1759, the power of the EC to conclude treaties on human rights containing obligations which the EC has the capacity to abide by or, respectively, to violate, through the exercise of its internal competence. I developed this line of reasoning more at length in my contribution 'The Scope of the EU Foreign Power', in E. Cannizzaro (ed.), *The European Union as an Actor in International Relations, supra*, n. 19.

existence of an EC act that triggers the pre-emption of the 'normative space' on the external plane.[37] So long as the EC's internal competence is not exercised, there is no need to pre-empt the Member States from concluding agreements whose implementation does not affect pre-existing EC norms.

This conclusion is politically wise. It would be unthinkable for the mere existence of a concurrent competence, which could remain quiescent forever, to indefinitely bar the external powers of the Member States. It is therefore not the abstract competence but its materialization which pre-empts the powers of the Member States. The emphasis on the actual exercise of internal competence as the factor producing EC's treaty-making power pleads in favour of a certain symmetry between the internal and the external planes.

The price to be paid for this is to make the scope of the EC external power very uncertain and likely to change in time. The instability of the legal basis of implied external powers might even prevent a 'perfect' symmetry between internal and external sphere from arising. Since it is only the exercise of the internal competence of the EC which has pre-emptive effect,[38] international obligations assumed by the Member States prior to the later enactment of EC norms might prove inconsistent with these subsequently adopted norms. Thus, the possibility of inconsistency between the external competence of the Member States and the internal competence of the EC remains and has not been completely swept away by the further developments of the jurisprudence, although the ECJ has recognized the existence of an obligation for the Member States to avoid concluding treaties without cooperating or consulting with the EC if they concern fields in which the latter has manifested an intention to act.[39]

Moreover, if the EC's treaty-making power is to follow the contours of the internal legislation, agreements to be concluded may frequently fall only partly within the competence of the EC and partly within the competence of the Member States. Such agreements therefore require the participation of both. In other words, the need for the external power to follow the 'sinuosity' of the internal legislation renders more and more frequent the occurrence of mixity, an issue which only indirectly affects the purpose of this study and which must therefore be left to one side.

Although the early jurisprudence could give the impression that the pre-emptive effect was triggered by the existence of an actual conflict between internal EC acts

---

[37] See paras. 17 ff. of the ERTA judgment, *supra*, n. 35.

[38] In the absence of internal rules, the EC can claim competence only if: its competence is exclusive (see Opinion 2/91, 'ILO Convention N. 170 Concerning the Use of the Chemicals at Work' [1993] ECR I-1061, para.8, where the Court said that the existence of an exclusive competence 'arising from a Treaty provision excludes any competence on the part of Member States which is concurrent with that of the Community, in the Community sphere and in the international sphere'); or the exercise of the external competence is necessary for the achievement of the objectives of the treaty (see the relevant passages in Opinion 1/76, 'Draft Agreements Establishing a European Laying-Up Fund for Inland Waterway Vessels' [1977] ECR 741 and, more recently, in Opinion 1/94 *supra* n. 28).

[39] See recently Case C-433/03, *Commission v Germany* [2005] ECR I-6985. The legal basis and the limits of this obligation are pointed out by AG Tizzano, at paras. 59 ff. of his Opinion.

and the Member States' international engagements, the ECJ has gradually developed a more nuanced concept of 'potential interference'. According to this concept, Member States are pre-empted from undertaking engagements which, while not necessarily involving a conflict with pre-existing EC acts, may nonetheless have the effect of interfering in a variety of manners with the scope of those acts.[40]

The foreign affairs power impliedly conferred to the EC by the exercise of its internal competence was from the origins conceived by the ECJ as exclusive. The *ERTA* judgment made it clear that the enactment of internal rules has a pre-emptive effect on the international power of the Member States.

However, the EC may have concurrent implied powers and may therefore conclude agreements, absent internal legislation, if their conclusion is necessary for the achievement of the objectives of the EC Treaty. This occurs, presumably, when the objectives of the Treaty cannot be achieved, or cannot be satisfactorily achieved, through unilateral EC action and an international instrument is therefore necessary. This principle was first established by the ECJ in Opinion 1/76,[41] and it was refined in the Court's subsequent case law.[42]

In principle, these two sets of external powers, deriving respectively from the application of the *ERTA* doctrine and from the *Opinion 1/76* doctrine, are distinct, although they are based on analogous reasoning. To bestow on the EC exclusive

---

[40] See the *Open Skies* judgments of 5 November 2005, (Cases C-466/98, C-467/98, C-468/98, C-469/98, C-471/98, C-472/98, C-475/98, C-476/98, in particular paras. 108 ff. of Case C-476/98, *Commission v Germany*, [2002] ECR I-9427) containing a restatement of the cases in which the internal action of the EC has a pre-emptive effect on the treaty-making power of its Member States. In *Open Skies*, the Court has substantially followed the Opinion of AG Tizzano, who also seems to foreshadow subsequent developments in the case law (paras. 72 ff. of his Opinion). See below in the text and accompanying footnotes.

In light of the foregoing discussion, it may be useful to highlight some differences between the treaty-making powers of the EC and those of the EU. Since the doctrine of implied powers has been developed in regard to the EC system, it cannot be applied to the EU, where Arts. 24 and 38 TEU confer upon the EU a concurrent power to conclude treaties for the full range of its activities. This is an express power, which does not depend neither on the existence of an internal act nor on the necessity test under the Opinion 1/76 doctrine. Since this power has been bestowed independently of the existence of an internal act, it covers the full range of the EU's activities. Consequently, there is no need for an implied powers doctrine in order to enlarge the scope of the EU's treaty-making power. Conversely, the presence of an internal EU act does not seem to preclude further external action by the Member States. Due to the vagueness of content and scope of most EU acts, a pre-emption would otherwise have a dramatic effect on the capacity of the Member States to act as independent political actors in the international arena. See Declaration n. 4, attached to the Amsterdam Treaty, which refers to Arts. 24 and 38 TEU as provisions which do not entail a transfer of competence from the Member States to the EU. The wording of the declaration does not seem fully proper, as one could speculate about whether the treaty-making power constitutes an instrument or a competence. Be that as it may, the express provision of a power to conclude treaties for the full range of the EU activities makes it superfluous to inquiry about the existence of implied external powers in the TUE.

[41] Opinion 1/76, *supra* n. 38, para. 4.

[42] Opinion 1/94, *supra* n. 28 and Opinion 2/92, 'Third Revised Decision of the OECD on National Treatment' [1995] ECR I-521, para. 7.

external power to the extent necessary to preserve the scope of the EC internal legislation is not the same as bestowing on the EC a concurrent external power to the extent necessary to pursue the objectives of the Treaty. However, there are certain overlaps. In particular, there are many situations in which the two doctrines can be invoked alternatively as a basis for the Community's external competence. In those situations, trends in the case law seem to give priority to the application of the *ERTA* doctrine. This led to a particularly narrow approach to the necessity test under Opinion 1/76 and, conversely, to a broad application of *ERTA*.

Thus, in Opinion 1/94, the Court said that the need to conclude an agreement, absent previous internal legislation, occurs only insofar as the objectives of the Treaty are 'inextricably linked to the conclusion of a Treaty',[43] and this restrictive approach was maintained in the subsequent case law.[44]

The restrictive approach adopted in regard to the necessity test stands out when assessed against the recent development in the case law concerning the *ERTA* test. This development culminated in Opinion 1/03, where the Court developed the idea that the EC has exclusive external powers even if these are not strictly necessary in order to prevent an actual or a potential interference with common rules, if such powers are exercised with a view to ensuring 'a uniform and consistent application of community rules and the proper functioning of the system which they establish in order to preserve the effectiveness of community law'.[45]

This development thus seems to sever the link between external exclusive powers and internal rules, on which the entire doctrine of the parallelism of competence rested, and seems to embrace a new, much more extreme functional conception of the EC external powers. According to this scheme, the Treaty prevents the Member States from acting, and assigns exclusive powers to the EC, not only when there is an incumbent risk of interference with actual or foreseeable common rules but also in those cases in which the independent action of the Member States might jeopardise the proper functioning of the Community system. The scope of the implied external power of the EC thus extends to vast areas where the EC has only concurrent competence, and possibly also to areas where it has no competence at all, if there is the danger that the conclusion of that agreement might even remotely interfere with the functioning of internal rules. Absent any indication as to the kind of interference required in order to trigger the pre-emptive effect, this amounts to a radical transformation of the scope and nature of the EC's external competence. It does not seem hazardous to conclude that this new functional conception tends to merge together the two sets of implied external powers: the exclusive external

---

[43] Opinion 1/94, para. 86.

[44] See the *Open Skies* judgments, and, in particular, Case C-476/98, mentioned above, n. 38, at paras. 82 ff. For a thorough analysis of the difficulties surrounding the necessity test, see the Opinion of AG Tizzano, at paras. 51 ff.

[45] Opinion 1/03 of 7 February 2006 on the 'Competence of the Community to conclude the new Lugano Convention on jurisdiction and the recognition and enforcement of judgments in civil and commercial matters', n.y.r., paras. 128 ff.

powers, based on the *ERTA* doctrine and its progeny, and the concurrent powers, based on the *Opinion 1/76* doctrine.

So far, we have looked at the momentous process of expansion of the EC's foreign power, which has substantially transformed the system of the external EC competence and which now tends to correspond symmetrically to its competences on the internal plane. As seen above, the scope of the external competence might even be broader than those held on the internal plane by virtue of the doctrine of potential interference, which might prove to extend significantly the boundaries of the EC external power. The EC, in turn, has made ample use of this power, so as to enlarge its influence in world affairs progressively. Nowadays, the EC is a member of a large number of IOs, and is a party to important multilateral treaties related to its activities.

Although it sometimes operates at the borders of its competence, the EC's international role is nevertheless severely impaired by its inability to assert itself as a political actor. This is due to the limitation of the aims assigned to it by the EC Treaty, which coincide substantially with those assigned to purely internal action. The objectives assigned to the different EC policies only sporadically encompass objectives of a political character, such as the protection of human rights in the fields of development cooperation policy and economic, financial and technical cooperation with third countries.[46] However, with a few notable exceptions, the external action of the EC is confined to the pursuit of economic or social objectives related to the functioning of the common market.

The view has repeatedly been put forward that the EC can escape these narrow aims and have recourse to a wider and even unlimited set of aims. This view, expressed in particular in regard to the EC's common commercial policy, was fed initially with the idea that this competence was to be seen as eminently instrumental. If one accepted this position, EC measures affecting, for any purpose whatever, the commercial flows between the EC and third States would have the nature of trade measures and would fall under Article 133 EC. Nowhere has this position been upheld by the ECJ. Some equivocal expressions, contained in a late jurisprudential pattern, might suggest that the scope of the commercial competence also encompasses trade measures enacted for non trade-related purposes.[47] However, this stance seems simply aimed at upholding the competence of the EC to implement, through commercial measures, political decisions taken at the political cooperation level according to a scheme which was later embodied in the provisions of

---

[46] See Articles 177(2) and 181A.(1), which, with identical wording, read: 'Community policy in this area shall contribute to the general objective of developing and consolidating democracy and the rule of law, and to that of respecting human rights and fundamental freedoms'. See the decision of the ECJ in Case C-268/94, *Portuguese Republic v Council*, *supra*, n. 23.

[47] As the Court said in the *Centro-com* judgment, Case C-124/95, *The Queen v HM Treasury and Bank of England ex parte Centro-Com* [1997] ECR I-81, 'the Member States cannot treat national measures whose effect is to prevent or restrict the export of certain products as falling outside the scope of the common commercial policy on the ground that they have foreign and security objectives' (para. 26).

Article 301 EC.[48] In any case, any possible doubt about the scope of the EC's foreign power, and in particular about the possibility of construing the EC's competence to adopt trade measures so broadly as to include every measure affecting international trade, even if it is not designed to 'promote, facilitate or govern trade', has been swept away by Opinion 2/00.[49]

This should also dispel the idea that functional and structural ties between the EU and the EC make it possible for EC measures to pursue the aims of the Treaty on European Union (TEU). Such an idea does not find support in the TEU, unless one construes in very broad terms those vague provisions which call for coherence and consistency between the action of the Union and that of its single parts.[50] Those provisions suggest that consistency in the Union's external action is to be secured by the Institutions, who should avail themselves, in this regard, of the margin of manoeuvre left by the Treaties. Nowhere is it suggested that this otherwise salutary result can be achieved at the cost of setting aside specific provisions of the EC Treaty which govern the conduct of the Institutions in that frame and determine the limits of their action. A further argument supporting this conclusion comes from the consideration of the very particular role assigned to Article 301 EC in the system of the relationship between the EC and the EU. This provision sets up an exceptional procedure for the Member States to bypass the functional limits placed on the EC's action and to use the substantive competence of the EC for achieving political aims. This provision would be superfluous if the EC could act on its behalf in the pursuit of objectives of the TEU.

It is true (and some examples will also emerge from the following analysis) that certain actions undertaken by the Community do not fit squarely within the limits set up by the Treaty, and that, quite to the contrary, they show a certain readiness to overcome these limits and to adapt the abstract principles to the needs of the international reality. It is much more doubtful that this flexible and casuistic approach can be converted into a coherent and full-fledged legal doctrine aimed at

---

[48] It is open to doubt whether, prior to the adoption of Art. 301, the EC had competence to implement at community level a political decision taken by the Member States. A positive answer seems to be given by AG Jacobs in his Opinion in Case C-124/95, *Centro-Com, supra* n. 47. See para. 42 of the Opinion. For an overall study of these issues, see A. Davì, *Comunità europee e sanzioni economiche internazionali* (1993).

[49] The Court ruled out the possibility that the Cartagena Protocol could be concluded on the basis of Art. 133 EC by virtue of its provisions concerning trade in living modified organisms (see Opinion 2/00, *supra* n. 23, paras. 35 ff). In the same vein, the Court concluded, in its judgment of 10 January 2006, Case C-94/03, *Commission v Council*, n.y.r., that the Rotterdam Convention on international trade of hazardous chemicals and pesticides could not be concluded on the sole basis of Art. 133 EC.

[50] Art. 3 TEU states: 'The Union shall be served by a single institutional framework which shall ensure the consistency and the continuity of the activities carried out in order to attain its objectives while respecting and building upon the acquis communautaire.

The Union shall in particular ensure the consistency of its external activities as a whole in the context of its external relations, security, economic and development policies. The Council and the Commission shall be responsible for ensuring such consistency and shall cooperate to this end. They shall ensure the implementation of these policies, each in accordance with its respective powers.'

overcoming the limits of the principle of conferral, which is still to be considered as one of the cornerstones of the European legal system.

The existence of the EC's foreign power, running parallel with its internal competence but bound to pursue objectives narrowly assigned to it by its Member States, thus creates an unusual situation in the landscape of modern federalist structures: that of an entity possessing vast, unprecedented competence in external relations, substantially eroding its Member States' sovereign powers, which is however incapable of pursuing an open set of purposes in the international arena. The assignment of external power to the EC has thus 'dismembered' the otherwise unitary foreign-relations power of the Member States and has created a distinct class of powers which can be exercised only for integration purposes.[51] I will refer to this process as the 'de-politicization' of the EC's external power.[52]

THE FOREIGN POLICY OF THE EU

This section will be devoted to a brief analysis of the nature and scope of the foreign policy of the European Union. This policy has been conceived as detached from the substantive EC policies and, in particular, from the EC's external power. Yet these two fields interfere continuously and create a thick network of legal relations. Once again, it must be stressed that no attempt will be made to lay down a comprehensive analysis of the CFSP; the legal regime applying to this field will be considered only insofar as necessary to stress the lack of unity of the EU's foreign relations system.

To begin with, what is the CFSP? From its name, it can reasonably be inferred that it is a common policy, not so dissimilar from other common policies which, in a different context, have been established by the EC Treaty. However, stepping beyond this rather misleading terminology, the CFSP is not a 'policy' in the same sense as the others. The main difference lies in the fact that, unlike the vast majority of the EC's substantive policies, the CFSP has no pre-determined material content.

---

[51] It is an open question whether these restraints are purely *internal* restraints, which the Member States are bound to observe only in their relations with the other Member States and with the EC (but not *vis-à-vis* third States), or whether the transfer of powers to the EC created an objective situation in which the Member States, when acting externally, cannot exercise powers that have been transferred to the EC. See G. Gaja, 'Restraints Imposed by European Law on the Treaty-Making Power of the Member States', in I. Cameron and A. Simoni (eds), *Dealing with Integration*, vol. II: *Perspectives from Seminars on European Law 1996*-1998 (1998), 97; J. Klabbers, 'Restraints on the Treaty-Making Powers of Member States Deriving from EU Law: Towards a Framework for Analysis', in E. Cannizzaro (ed.), *The European Union as an Actor in International Relations, supra* n. 19, at 151.

[52] Nowhere has the idea been suggested that the EC can enlarge the aims of its action by recourse to, as it were, an 'implied purposes' doctrine. It was only in the recent judgments of *Kadi* (Case T-315/01, *Yassin Abdullah Kadi v Council and Commission* [2005], n.y.r.) and *Yusuf* (Case T-306/01, *Ahmed Ali Yusuf e Al Barakaat International Foundation v Council and Commission* [2005], n.y.r) that the CFI advanced the idea that an interplay between Arts 301 and 307 of the EC Treaty can have the effect of enlarging the aims (and means) of EC action. See paras. 196 ff. of the *Kadi* judgment. For a more detailed discussion of these decisions see below, n. 68.

The scope of the EU's foreign policy is defined by Article 11(1) of the TEU:

The Union shall define and implement a common foreign and security policy covering all areas of foreign and security policy, the objectives of which shall be:

- to safeguard the common values, fundamental interests, independence and integrity of the Union in conformity with the principles of the United Nations Charter,
- to strengthen the security of the Union in all ways,
- to preserve peace and strengthen international security, in accordance with the principles of the United Nations Charter, as well as the principles of the Helsinki Final Act and the objectives of the Paris Charter, including those on external borders,
- to promote international cooperation,
- to develop and consolidate democracy and the rule of law, and respect for human rights and fundamental freedoms.

As can be seen, this definition is strikingly tautological. As set forth by the introductory clause, the CFSP encompasses all actions which pursue the aims of the CFSP. The CFSP is thus defined in purely functional terms, which is very rare in the landscape of the competences transferred from the Member States. Potentially, its scope is very wide, as it extends to all kinds of material conduct or acts inspired by one of the objectives laid down in that provision, and can interfere materially with the other policies of the Union as well as those of the EC or of the Member States. The aims of Article 11(1) are also very broadly worded. It would thus appear to follow that the borders of this 'policy' are virtually unlimited.[53]

However, upon closer inspection, this impression proves to be fallacious. Indeed, although the TEU lays down only one limit to the scope of the CFSP, it is a very potent one. Article 47 TEU reads:

Subject to the provisions amending the Treaty establishing the European Economic Community with a view to establishing the European Community, the Treaty establishing the European Coal and Steel Community and the Treaty establishing the European Atomic Energy Community, and to these final provisions, nothing in this Treaty shall affect the Treaties establishing the European Communities or the subsequent Treaties and Acts modifying or supplementing them.

While this provision has rarely been referred to explicitly in the jurisprudence of the ECJ,[54] its importance can hardly be understated. At first glance, this provision seems to lay down a mere clause of subordination, in the classical sense in which

---

[53] See P. Koutrakos, 'Which Policy for Which Europe? The Emerging Security and Defence Policy of the European Union', in T. Tridimas, P. Nebbia (eds), *European Union Law for the Twenty-first Century. Rethinking the New Legal Order*, supra, n. 21, 273 at 278.

[54] See the two judgments of the ECJ, Case C-170/96, *Commission v Council* [1998] ECR I-2763, and recently, Case C-176/03, *Commission v Council* [2005] ECR I-7879, concerning both the relationship between actions conducted under the third pillar and EC action. In regard to interference between CFSP and EC action, see the action brought on 21 February 2005 by the European Commission against the Council of the European Union for annulment of Council Decision 2004/833/CFSP of 2 December 2004, implementing Joint Action 2002/589/CFSP with a view to a EU contribution to ECOWAS in the framework of the Moratorium on Small Arms and Light Weapons (Case C-91/05, *Commission v Council*, OJ 2005 C115/10). See also the decision of the CFI in Case T-338/02 *Segi and others v Council*

this notion is understood under the international law of treaties. If that were the case, inconsistency between obligations deriving from the TEU and obligations deriving from the EC Treaty would be solved in favour of the latter.

However, the broad wording of this provision suggests a wider effect. The provision does not refer only to the possibility of inconsistencies between measures adopted respectively under the two Treaties. Rather, it provides that the obligations deriving from the TEU must not 'affect' the EC Treaty. There are good reasons to assume that the term 'affect' must be understood in a broad sense, so as to prevent the EU from entering the normative space assigned, even only potentially, to the EC.[55] In particular, the Member States, acting under the CFSP, cannot take measures which the Community has the power to adopt. This view seems to have been upheld by the ECJ, which has treated the mechanism of Article 47 (and of Article 29) TEU as requiring an inquiry into whether the EC Treaty provides a proper legal basis for a measure which was taken instead under the second or the third pillar, without regard to the existence of an actual conflict between inconsistent provisions. Thus, if the EC Treaty provides for an appropriate legal basis for a certain measure, it would be illegal to adopt it under the TEU.

This jurisprudential pattern has two effects. First, it points out that it is not the actual conflict with a pre-existing EC norm which makes a CFSP measure illegal but the existence of a competence of the EC, regardless of its exclusive or concurrent character.[56] Thus, it would be improper to draw any analogy between the effect of Article 47 and the pre-emption of the Member States' treaty-making powers resulting from the transfer of powers to the EC.

[2004] ECR II-1647, para. 41. An indirect application of the mechanism of Art. 47 can also be seen in a jurisprudential pattern aimed at protecting the EC competence from intrusive action by Member States taken on the basis of their competence in the field of foreign policy. The most clear example in that direction comes from the judgments of the Court of 17 October 1995 (Case C-83/94, *Criminal proceedings against Leifer and others* [1995] ECR I-3231; Case C-70/94, *Werner v Bundesrepublik Deutschland* [1995] ECR I-3189) and of 14 January 1997 (Case C-124/95, *The Queen v HM Treasury and Bank of England ex parte Centro-Com, supra* n. 47). See, recently, M.-G. Carbagnati Ketvel, 'The Jurisdiction of the European Court of Justice in Respect of the Common Foreign and Security Policy', 55 *The International and Comparative Law Quarterly* (2005), 77 ff.

[55] This not only means that the Member States are prevented from taking measures, through the CFSP, which the EC has the power to take, but also that an act of CFSP cannot enlarge the scope of the EC competence. An example of this latter case is the improper use of Art. 308 to take measures aimed at the interruption or reduction of payments or movements of capital and of economic relations with regard to individual persons not directly linked to the government of a third country (see, for instance, Council Regulation (EC) No 1183/2005 of 18 July 2005, imposing certain specific restrictive measures directed against persons acting in violation of the arms embargo with regard to the Democratic Republic of the Congo, OJ 2005 L 193/1).

[56] At first sight, it might not seem totally logical to prevent the Member States from adopting, collectively through the CFSP, measures which they were fully entitled to adopt individually, if the competence assigned to the EC is concurrent and it has not been previously exercised. However, a CFSP act is much more liable to prejudice the EC's potential competence than measures adopted individually by the Member States. Indeed, CFSP acts have a pre-emptive effect on EC action which individual actions of the Member States do not have.

Second, it emerges from the ECJ's case law that the relevant element which triggers the prohibitory effect of Article 47 is the content of a certain measure which has been taken under the CFSP, and which instead could have been taken under one of the substantive EC policies.[57] The focus on the identity in content of the actual CFSP measure and a potential EC measure implies that Member States are not prevented from taking CFSP measures for the full range of EC competences, provided that the content of such measures is not susceptible of being the object of EC measures. This means that the CFSP could interfere with a competence transferred to the EC in a more subtle and nuanced way by, for example, soliciting the adoption of a certain measure on the part of the EC, or discouraging the EC from acting. Although, in a certain sense, this would 'interfere' with the EC's action, the CFSP measure could not be said to 'affect' the EC's competence in a proper sense. This might be legally explained on the basis of a systemic interpretation of the Treaties. Indeed, as noted above, the objectives of the CFSP are broadly drafted so that they undoubtedly overlap with the objectives assigned to the EC. This makes it possible for the EU to enact rules in the same fields assigned to the EC competence for the attainment of the EU's objectives, having care not to intrude substantively in the sphere of the EC competences or to alter their scope. In other words, the adoption of CFSP acts aimed at determining the political direction along which the EC can exercise its competence seems to be entirely consistent with Article 47 TEU. All things considered, this conclusion appears to be an acceptable compromise between the need to assign a guiding role to the CFSP in determining the aims of the EU's external action, on the one hand, and the need to protect the autonomy of the EC's supranational political process from the pervasive influence of the Member States, on the other.

However, with these notable exceptions, the main aim of Article 47 is that of insulating the EC's institutional and normative framework and of maintaining a principle of mutual exclusivity with the CFSP. Therefore, in the fields covered by the EC Treaty, the CFSP cannot have a substantive content which would otherwise affect the competence assigned to the EC. Nor can it enact rules aimed at altering the scope of the EC's competence. The 'de-politicization' of the EC's activities is thus matched by the 'de-materialization' of those of the CFSP.[58]

---

[57] A somewhat restrictive reading of Art. 47 seems to have been embraced by the ECJ in its recent judgment concerning the relationship between EC action and EU action under the third pillar. In its judgment of 13 September 2005 (Case C-176/03 *Commission v Council, supra* n. 54), in which the Court annulled a framework decision on the protection of the environment through criminal law, which allegedly affected the EC competence, the Court stated: 'It is therefore necessary to ascertain whether Articles 1 to 7 of the framework decision affect the powers of the Community under Article 175 EC inasmuch as those articles could, as the Commission maintains, have been adopted on the basis of the last-mentioned provision.' However, the Court did not exclude that even milder forms of interference could fall within the scope of Art. 47.

[58] This may raise, and in fact has raised, a serious negative conflict between activities carried out respectively within the EC and within the CFSP, as both, for different reasons, can lack competence to take action. In my view, this is the essence of the ECJ's holding in *Centro-com* (*supra* n. 47), *Leifer* and *Werner* (*supra* n. 54), where the Court found that 'the Member States cannot treat national measures whose effect is to prevent or restrict the export of certain products as falling outside the scope of the

INTERCONNECTING THE PILLARS: OVERLAPS BETWEEN
THE EXTERNAL RELATIONS SYSTEM AND THE
FOREIGN POLICY COMPETENCE

So far, I have tried to point out the elements which call for a strict distinction between the EU's external action and that of the EC. It is now useful to look at the elements which go in the opposite direction and which in fact call for an interaction between these two spheres of European integration.

Indeed, in a model of strict separation between the CFSP and the EC competence, the contacts between foreign policy of the EU and the foreign power of the EC would be infrequent and occasional. However, this is highly unrealistic.[59] In the contemporary world, foreign policy is not confined to the traditional instruments of diplomacy and military might; quite to the contrary, it spills over its original borders and tends to materialize, in a variety of ways, in acts having their own substantive content.

Thus, although they are in principle independent, it is unavoidable for the CFSP and the EC foreign power likewise to interact in a number of ways, in order to deal with issues which do not fall in their entirety within the competence of either entity.[60] The set of possible practical situations is virtually unlimited and includes many ways in which the powers of the EU or the EC must be adjusted with each other in order to comply with the variety of situations offered by the daily life of international intercourse. Absent any instrument of coordination, with the notable but isolated exception mentioned above of Article 301 EC,[61] the interaction

common commercial policy on the ground that they have foreign and security objectives'. This finding seems to indicate that measures which substantively fall within the scope of the common commercial policy cannot be taken by the Member States on the ground that the objective of such measures concerns foreign policy or security. This can hardly be interpreted in the sense that such measures can be taken by the EC. Indeed, applying the rationale of the ECJ case-law in a reverse manner, it seems plausible to argue that measures having political objectives inconsistent with the objectives of the EC treaty cannot be treated by the EC as falling outside the functional scope of the CFSP on the basis of their substantive content.

   [59] See, among the many voices, F. Dehousse, 'La politique étrangère et de sécurité commune— L'identité européenne de sécurité et de défense', in J.-V. Louis, M. Dony (eds.), *Commentaire J. Mégret— Le droit de la CE et de l'Union européenne, Relations extérieures* vol. 12, *supra*, n. 19, 439, at 449; S. Griller, B. Weidel, *External Economic Relations and Foreign Policy in the European Union*, in Griller, B. Weidel (eds), *External Economic Relations and Foreign Policy in the European Union, supra* n. 19, at 5; R.A. Wessel, 'Fragmentation in the Governance of EU External Relations: Legal Institutional Dilemmas and the New Constitutions for Europe', *supra* n. 2, at 123; P. Koutrakos, 'The Elusive Quest for Uniformity in EC External Relations', 4 *The Cambridge Yearbook of European Legal Studies* (2002) 243; K.N. Schefer, 'The Use of Trade Instruments in the Pursuit of Human Rights: European Foreign Policy', in F.M. Abbott, C. Breining-Kaufmann, and T. Cotter (eds), *International Trade and Human Rights: Foundations and Conceptual Issues* (2006); C. Novi, *La politica di sicurezza esterna dell'Unione europea* (2005).
   [60] See E. Denza, *The Intergovernmental Pillars of the European Union* (2002); P. Gauttier, 'Horizontal Coherence and the External Competences of the European Union', 10 *European Law Journal* (2004), 23; R.A. Wessel, 'The Inside Looking Out: Consistency and Delimitation in EU External Relations', 37 *CMLRev.* (2000), 1135.
   [61] Notoriously, the ECJ, ruling after the entry into force of Art. 301 EC, had implicitly validated what appeared to be an early (anticipatory) application of that provision. In the well-known judgment

between these two sets of competences has been dealt with mainly through practical arrangements.

The multifarious set of instruments and devices used in practice can be grouped into two basic schemes. The first comprises the cases in which a distinct but inter-related action by both entities is required. This can be referred to as the model of coordination. A different scheme is one in which issues straddling over the competence of both entities are dealt with by the action of just one of them, either the EC or the EU. This latter scheme can be called the model of autonomy. Ultimately, the entire dynamics of the EC/EU external action can be described as the tension between autonomy and coordination.

In the following pages I will attempt to provide some insight as to the modalities of functioning of these two schemes, with a view to highlighting the tendency toward unity in the EU foreign relations system.

Cooperation

First, there are cases in which a CFSP act has been employed in order to give guidance to EC acts, which are therefore used in order to implement a legal framework designed by the Member States acting through the EU. One can distinguish two possible situations in which such a scheme has been employed. In the first, the CFSP act is adopted in order to give guidance to the EC action in situations in which the EC has competence to act on its own behalf. In such situations, the coordination between EU and EC action is not legally necessary but is nevertheless politically opportune in order to present the composite unit EU plus EC as a unitary entity. CFSP acts often call for EC implementing action, and such acts either indicate specific measures to be taken in regard to a certain issue or to a certain country, or, more frequently, they leave discretion to the EC as to the measures to be taken.[62]

---

of 30 July 1996 (Case C-84/95, *Bosphorus v Minister for Transport, Energy and Communications, Ireland and the Attorney General* [1996] ECR I-3953, para. 13, the Court considered that, 'Regulation no. 990/93 of the Council gave effect to the decision of the Community and its Member States meeting within the framework of political cooperation, to have recourse to a Community instrument to implement in the Community certain aspects of the sanction against the Federal Republic of Yugoslavia by the Security Council of the United Nations'.

[62] See, among other examples of the latter type, 2006/304/CFSP, Joint Action of 10 April 2006 on the establishment of an EU Planning Team (EUPT Kosovo) regarding a possible EU crisis management operation in the field of rule of law and possible other areas in Kosovo, OJ 2006 L112/19; 2005/826/CFSP, Joint Action of 24 November 2005 on the establishment of an EU Police Advisory Team (EUPAT) in the Former Yugoslav Republic of Macedonia (FYROM), OJ 2005 L307/61; 2005/889/CFSP, Joint Action of 12 December 2005 on establishing a European Union Border Assistance Mission for the Rafah Crossing Point (EU BAM Rafah), OJ 2005 L327/28; 2005/574/PESC, Joint Action of 18 July 2005 on support for IAEA activities in the areas of nuclear security and verification and in the framework of the implementation of the EU Strategy against Proliferation of Weapons of Mass Destruction, OJ 2005 L193/44; 2005/557/PESC, Joint Action of 18 July 2005 on the European Union civilian-military supporting action to the African Union mission in the Darfur region of Sudan, OJ 2005 L188/46; 2003/319/CFSP, Common Position of 8 May 2003 concerning European Union

On some occasions, the CFSP was used to secure a coordination in the combined action of the EC and of the Member States. A clear example of this way of addressing situations of common concern through a coordinated action is given by the response, by the EU, the EC and the Member States, to the enactment by the US of certain laws having extraterritorial effect. A CFSP act shaped the political frame within which the Member States and the EC adopted the countermeasures towards the US in their respective fields of competence.[63]

It is worth stressing that, in this case, the CFSP act carefully abstained from interfering with the scope of the EC competence. Indeed, both entities, the EC and the Member States, were fully entitled to use their competence in order to respond to unlawful conduct by the US in breach of its international prerogatives. What the CFSP did was simply to lay down a comprehensive framework for the combined action of the EC and the Member States. It thereby stressed the unity of the response by the EU and the EC as a single 'actor'—obtained through a combined, yet autonomous exercise of the respective competence of each entity. Another, more recent example, is Council Decision 2000/401/CFSP of 22 June 2000,[64] concerning the control of technical assistance related to certain military end-uses, which established a common legal frame implemented by the EC and the Member States, each acting within their own field of competence.[65]

---

support for the implementation of the Lusaka Ceasefire Agreement and the peace process in the Democratic Republic of Congo (DRC), OJ 2003 L115/87; 1999/479/PESC, Common Position of 19 July 1999 concerning support for the popular consultation of the East Timorese people, OJ 1999 L188/1; 98/735/PESC, Joint Action of 22 December 1998 in support of the democratic process in Nigeria, OJ 1998 L354/1. Examples of EU acts calling for more specific EC action might include 2000/420/PESC, Common Position of 29 June 2000, concerning EU support for the OAU peace process between Ethiopia and Eritrea, OJ 2000 L161/1; and 96/588/PESC Joint Action of 1st October 1996, on anti-personnel landmines, OJ 1996 L260/1.

[63] See 96/668/CFSP, Joint Action of 22 November 1996 adopted by the Council on the basis of Art J.3 and K.3 of the TEU concerning measures protecting against the effects of the extra-territorial application of legislation adopted by a third country, and actions based thereon or resulting therefrom, OJ 1996 L309/7; and Council Regulation (EC) No 2271/96 of 22 November 1996 protecting against the effects of the extra-territorial application of legislation adopted by a third country, and actions based thereon or resulting therefrom, OJ 1996 L309/1. This is by no means an exceptional situation. For a recent example, see 2004/796/PESC Joint Action of 22 November 2004 for the support of the physical protection of a nuclear site in the Russian Federation, which expressly states in the preamble that, '[t]o ensure coherence of the European Union's external actions, its activities should take place in a coordinated way with activities carried out by the European Community and Member States'. It might be worthwhile to add that the intent of this Joint Action to realize a common approach of the EC/EU to that issue is also evidenced by Art. 6, para. 2 of the document, which indicates that a failure by the Russian Federation to comply with its obligations under the Agreement on Partnership and Cooperation between the European Communities and their Member States and the Russian Federation may entail a suspension of the project of assistance established by the Joint Action.

[64] OJ 2000 L159/216.

[65] For the EC, see Council Regulation (EC) No 1334/2000 setting up a Community regime for the control of exports of dual-use items and technology, OJ 2000 L159/1, enacted on that same day.

In a second category of situations, the CFSP has been used in order to call for Community actions to be taken beyond the spectrum of the objectives assigned to it by the EC Treaty. Since this turns out to be a generalization (beyond the scenario of sanctions) of the mechanism envisaged by Article 301, in which the EC action is 'curved', bent to fit the needs of the CFSP, this variant of the cooperation model can be more appropriately indicated by the term 'subordination'.

As an example, it is worth mentioning the dual-use goods regime adopted in 1994,[66] although subsequently repealed.[67] That regime was based on the consideration that neither the CFSP nor any of the substantive EC policies could possibly be deemed to have the appropriate competence to set up a full-fledged legal regime for dual-use goods. Under those circumstances, the regime was established by combining the competence of the two entities. The EC substantive competence was thus enlarged in order to encompass a trade regime with the political goals of a CFSP decision.

Recently, this model was employed in the context of EU action against terrorism. In that context, certain CFSP acts provided for an act of the EC (namely, a Regulation) to implement Security Council resolutions calling for actions against individuals allegedly involved in terrorist acts.[68]

---

[66] See 94/942/CFSP Council Decision of 19 December 1994 on the Joint Action adopted by the Council of the basis of Art. J.3 of the Treaty on European Union concerning the control of exports of dual-use goods (OJ 1994 L367/8); and Council Regulation (EC) No 3381/94 of 19 December 1994 setting up a Community regime for the control of exports of dual-use goods (OJ 1994 L367/1).

[67] See 2000/401/CFSP, Council Decision repealing Decision 94/942/CFSP on the joint action concerning the control of exports of dual-use goods, *supra* n. 64; and Regulation (EC) No 1334/2000, *supra*, n. 65.

[68] The legal basis for EC action can hardly be traced back to Art. 301. Article 301 bestows upon the EC authority to sever economic ties with *third States* under the political umbrella provided by a CFSP act. It is therefore inappropriate to refer to that provision in order to adopt sanctioning measures against individuals. Nor does Art. 308, read in conjunction with Art. 301, add much in this regard. To the contrary, such an approach results in a vicious circle. Indeed, an action of the EC based on Art. 301 consists of using means already at the EC's disposal for goals not assigned to it by the Treaty. Conversely, an action based on Art. 308 consists of pursuing objectives assigned to the EC by the Treaty through means of action not expressly conferred to it. Thus, to have recourse to a joint legal basis composed of Arts 301 and 308 in order to justify a Community action whose means and goals are both outside the scope of the Treaty is essentially boot-strapping. For a more complete critique of the CFI's judgments in *Kadi* and *Yusuf*, where just such an approach is taken, I refer to my study, 'The Machiavellian Moment: The UN Security Council and the Rule of Law', 3 *International Organizations Law Review* (2006), forthcoming. In practice, Art. 301 is frequently referred to, in conjunction with Art. 308, as the legal basis for the adoption of measures targeting individual persons not directly linked to the government of a third country. For further examples, see Council Regulation (EC) No 305/2006 of 21 February 2006 imposing specific restrictive measures against certain persons suspected of involvement in the assassination of former Lebanese Prime Minister Rafiq Hariri, OJ 2006 L51/1; Council Regulation (EC) No 1183/2005 of 18 July 2005 imposing certain specific restrictive measures directed against persons acting in violation of the arms embargo with regard to the Democratic Republic of the Congo, OJ 2005 L193/1; Council Regulation (EC) No 1184/2005 of 18 July 2005 imposing certain specific restrictive measures directed against certain persons impeding the peace process and breaking international law in the conflict in the Darfur region in Sudan, OJ 2005 L193/9; Council Regulation (EC) No 560/2005 of 12 April 2005 imposing certain specific restrictive measures directed against certain persons and

In more general terms, the idea of a dual approach to political issues touching upon the EC competence has taken the form of 'common strategies' adopted by the EU on the basis of Article 13 TEU.[69] Common strategies are CFSP acts designed to promote an integrated approach in the relations between the EU, the EC and the Member States and a third State. Although this approach presents practical advantages, the legal nature of common strategies appears doubtful. Despite the call for coherence and consistency of the Union's external action, there seems to be nothing in the founding Treaties that gives formally to the Institutions authority to adopt acts having cross-pillar effects.

Autonomy

If the first model tends to achieve unity through coordination, the second stresses instead the capacity of one entity, the EC or the EU, to deal with complex issues stretching its competence, at the cost of producing interference with the competence of the other. This second model therefore purports to achieve unity through autonomy. It has been employed in situations very different with each other. The EU tends to act alone, and to 'drain' the competence of the EC, in politically sensitive issues where it is considered expedient to rely on intergovernmental decision-making mechanisms, for example to take advantage of the limited transparency that characterizes the adoption of CFSP acts. For its part, the EC tends to act alone in politically less sensitive fields.[70] Strikingly, however, the Member States tend to recognize an autonomous political role to the Community even for politically sensitive issues if they are already the object of political consent shared by the Member States and by the EU institutions.[71]

entities in view of the situation in Côte d'Ivoire, OJ 2005 L95/1; and Council Regulation (EC) No 1763/2004 of 11 October 2004 imposing certain restrictive measures in support of effective implementation of the mandate of the International Criminal Tribunal for the former Yugoslavia (ICTY), OJ 2004 L315/14.

[69] See 1999/414/CFSP Common Strategy of the European Union of 4 June 1999 on Russia (OJ 1999 L157/1); 1999/877/CFSP European Council Common Strategy of 11 December 1999 on Ukraine (OJ 1999 L331/1); and 2000/458/CFSP Common Strategy of the European Council of 19 June 2000 on the Mediterranean region, OJ 2000 L183/5.

[70] See K. E. Smith, _European Union Foreign Policy in a Changing World_ (2003), at 52 ff.

[71] See, for example, Council Regulation (EC) No 381/2001 of 26 February 2001 creating a rapid-reaction mechanism, OJ L57 of 27 February 2001. This Regulation establishes a Rapid Reaction Mechanism which 'may be triggered when in the beneficiary countries concerned there occur situations of crisis or emerging crisis, situations posing a threat to law and order, the security and safety of individuals, situations threatening to escalate into armed conflict or to destabilise the country and where such situations are likely to jeopardise the beneficial effects of assistance and cooperation policies and programmes, their effectiveness and/or conditions for their proper implementation' (Art. 3); Council Regulation No. (EC) 2666/2000 of 5 December 2000 on assistance for Albania, Bosnia and Herzegovina, Croatia, the Federal Republic of Yugoslavia and the Former Yugoslav Republic of Macedonia, OJ L306 of 7 December 2000; and the twin Council Regulations, (EC) No 975/1999 of 29 April 1999 and (EC) No 976/1999 of 29 April 1999, which lay down the requirements for the

This long-standing practice has been dealt with by extensive literature and I will not dwell on it further.[72] None of the two entities seems to have raised serious objections to this creeping process of competence-adjusting, which witnesses a certain mutual acquiescence, to the benefit of the entire EC/EU unit.

In the light of this consideration, it is worth noting that this scheme was also used in order to reduce the otherwise complex procedures for dealing with cross-pillar issues, which theoretically require action to be taken by all the entities involved, and which have sometimes been dealt with in a more simple way, by assigning competence to the principally competent entity. A notable example is the Agreement of 17 April 2002 concluded between the EU and Lebanon concerning cooperation in the fight against terrorism.[73] The agreement, concluded under Article 24 TEU, contains provisions which also concern the first and third pillars. An example in the opposite direction is the internal agreement by which the Member States agreed that it was for the Council to decide, by way of majority voting, that a third State had failed to abide by its obligations under Articles 96 and 97 of the Cotonou Agreement, and further to decide to start consultations and even to suspend parts of the agreement.[74] Article 3 of the Agreement makes clear that this procedure also applies in matters falling within the competence of the Member States.[75]

A typical field in which the competence of the EU and the competence of the supranational entity (in this case Euratom) overlap continuously is nuclear non-proliferation. In this field, one can find numerous examples of actions undertaken by one entity overlapping with the competence of the other.[76]

---

implementation of development cooperation operations, and, respectively, the requirements for the implementation of Community operations, other than those of development cooperation, which contribute to the general objective of developing and consolidating democracy and the rule of law and to that of respecting human rights and fundamental freedoms (OJ L 120 of 8 Mai 1999). Both Regulations contain recitals according to which 'it is necessary to ensure that these operations are consistent with the European Union's foreign policy as a whole, including the common foreign and security policy'. See below, n. 78. The dual role of development aid measures is highlighted by C. Santiso, 'Reforming European Foreign Aid: Development Cooperation as an Element of Foreign Policy', 7 *European Foreign Affairs Review* (2002), 401.

[72] See the thorough analysis of R. Baratta, 'Overlaps between EC Competence and EU Foreign Policy Activities', in E. Cannizzaro (ed.), *The EU as an Actor in International Relations, supra*, n. 19, at 51.

[73] The agreement, concluded in the form of an exchange of letters, has never, to my knowledge, been published in the OJ.

[74] Internal Agreement between the Representatives of the Governments of the Member States, meeting within the Council, on measures to be taken and procedures to be followed for the implementation of the ACP-EC Partnership Agreement, OJ 2000 L317/376.

[75] Article 3 reads: 'The position of the Member States for the implementation of Articles 96 and 97 of the ACP-EC Agreement shall, when that position concerns matters within their competence, be adopted by the Council, acting in accordance with the procedure set out in the Annex. If the planned measures concern matters falling within the competence of the Member States, the Council may also act on the initiative of a Member State'.

[76] See the Council Common Position 2001/869/CFSP of 6 December 2001 on participation by the EU in the Korean Peninsular Energy Development Organisation (KEDO), OJ 2001 L325/1. For a more comprehensive act on non-proliferation, see the European Security Strategy, 'A Secure Europe in

An example demonstrating the tolerance of the Member States for political action undertaken by the EC, absent any CFSP act but nonetheless supported by a wide political consent, is the creeping communitarization of human rights policy. In particular, the inclusion of human rights and democracy clauses in bilateral and multilateral agreements concluded by the Community with third States is striking.[77] This tendency is even more remarkable in the measures taken by the EC in order to promote and sustain political changes in Eastern Europe and presented as a first step towards the establishment of a partnership with the countries involved.[78]

a Better Word' adopted on 12 December 2003 by the European Council. This Strategy identifies a number of threats for the next decade, one of which is the proliferation of WMD. This strategy was implemented by certain CFSP decisions. See Council Joint Action 2006/243/CFSP of 20 March 2006 on support for activities of the Preparatory Commission of the Comprehensive Nuclear-Test-Ban Treaty Organisation (CTBTO) in the area of training and capacity building for verification and in the framework of the implementation of the EU Strategy against Proliferation of Weapons of Mass Destruction (OJ 2006 L88/68); Council Joint Action 2005/574/CFSP of 18 July 2005 on support for IAEA activities in the areas of nuclear security and verification and in the framework of the implementation of the EU Strategy against Proliferation of Weapons of Mass Destruction (OJ 2005 L193/44); Council Joint Action 2004/495/CFSP of 17 May 2004 on support for IAEA activities under its Nuclear Security Programme and in the framework of the implementation of the EU Strategy against Proliferation of Weapons of Mass Destruction (OJ 2004 L182/46).

In the opposite sense, see 1999/25/Euratom Council Decision of 14 December 1998 (OJ 1999 L7/31), which adopts a programme of actions relating to the transport of radioactive materials, safeguards and industrial cooperation with third countries. This decision also established a regime of export controls related to the nuclear sector and corresponding in many respects to the dual-use goods regime adopted under Regulation 1334/2000. This probably represents the best example of a 'creeping communitarization' of issues which, although they fall substantively within the EC competence, are politically sensitive and would normally be matters of prerogative for the EU.

[77] I refer to my study, 'The Scope of the EU Foreign Power. Is the EC Competent to Conclude Agreements with Third States including Human Rights Clauses?', in E. Cannizzaro (ed.), *The European Union as an Actor in International Relations, supra* n. 19, 297. See, among the most recent contributions, L. Bartels, *Human Rights Conditionality in the EU's international Agreements* (2005); P. Leino, 'European Universalism?—The EU and Human Rights Conditionality', 24 *Yearbook of European Law* (2005), 329; J. Harrison, *Human Rights and World Trade Agreements: Using General Exception Clauses to Protect Human Rights* (2005); C. Pippan, 'The Rocky Road to Europe: The EU's Stabilisation and Association Process for the Western Balkans and the Principles of Conditionality', 9 European Foreign Affairs Review, (2004) 214; E. Paasivirta, 'Human Rights, Diplomacy and Sanctions: Aspects to "Human Rights Clauses" in the External Agreements of the European Union', in J. Petman, J. Klabbers (eds), *Nordic cosmopolitanism* (2003); K. E. Smith, *European Union Foreign Policy in a Changing World, supra*, n. 70, at 134 ff.; P.A. Pillitu, *La tutela dei diritti dell'uomo e dei principi democratici nelle relazioni della Comunità e dell'Unione europea* (2003).

[78] The pre-existing practice in this regard has been codified by Council Regulation (EC) No 533/2004 of 22 March 2004 on the establishment of European partnerships in the framework of the stabilization and association process, OJ L86 of 24 March 2004, which was first implemented by the Council Decision of 14 June 2004 on the principles, priorities and conditions contained in the European Partnership with Serbia and Montenegro including Kosovo, as defined by the United Nations Security Council Resolution 1244 of 10 June 1999, OJ L227 of 26 June 2004. It is worth noting that Regulation

There have been other examples of EC measures inspired (in part or predominantly) by political aims. Here one can mention EC Regulation 2368/2002[79], which prescribes effective controls over the international trade in rough diamonds in order to prevent the trade in conflict diamonds from financing the efforts of rebel movements in Sierra Leone. The recitals make it clear that the Regulation also has the objective of maintaining international peace and security and to protect human rights, in spite of the absence of any CFSP decision.[80] The recently adopted Council Regulation 1236/2005/EC constitutes the apex of this tendency.[81] This Regulation bans the import to, and export from, the EC territory of equipment that can only be used for torture. Although import and export bans are typical measures used for regulating trade, there is little doubt that the only real motivation behind the Regulation is the protection of human rights. As no strictly commercial reason could possibly justify the adoption of such measures, it must be concluded that they fall outside the commercial policy competence of the EC.[82] Nor had any CFSP act been adopted with a view to calling for such a Regulation. Nevertheless, the Regulation

533 was based on Art. 181a TEC, incorporated in the TEC by the Treaty of Nice. This curiously worded provision assigned to the Community the competence to 'carry out, within its spheres of competence, economic, financial and technical cooperation measures with third countries'. According to the express terms of Art. 181a, activities undertaken under that provision can contribute to the 'general objective of developing and consolidating democracy and the rule of law, and to the objective of respecting human rights and fundamental freedoms'. Thus, in addition to its more specific competences, the Community can now establish cooperation frameworks with third States, and in this context, can pursue objectives having an undeniable political nature such as the protection of democracy and human rights. Presumably, this provision was added to the TEC in order to complement the analogous provision of Art. 181, which, having been established within the development cooperation competence, has a particularly narrow scope. The interpretation of Art. 181a raises a number of difficult issues concerning, in particular, the relationship between the new competence and the other substantive competences of the Treaty. In spite of its apparently all-embracing nature, there is a case to be made that, in principle, the new provision must be relied upon as a basis of competence only where other substantive policies fall short. Indeed, the first sentence of Art. 181a makes it clear that priority must be given, in case of an overlap, to the other provisions of the Treaty. These issues will not be further discussed. Suffice it to say, for present purposes, that Art. 181a seems to codify strains of previous practice and thus tends to recognise a political role in the international arena for the Community, albeit in limited fields, within a certain degree of autonomy from its Members States.

[79] Council Regulation (EC) No 2368/2002 of 20 December 2002 implementing the Kimberley Process certification scheme for the international trade in rough diamonds, OJ 2002 L358/28.

[80] See in particular recital 4 and Annex I of the Regulation. For another example, see Council Decision 2004/520/EC of 14 June 2004 (OJ 2004 L227/21), which provides that priorities and conditions in the European Partnership with Serbia and Montenegro including Kosovo are defined by the United Nations Security Council Resolution 1244 of June 1999. This decision, based on Art. 181a EC, refers to a UN Security Council Resolution, notwithstanding the absence of an CFSP act.

[81] Council Regulation (EC) No 1236/2005 of 27 June 2005 concerning trade in certain goods which could be used for capital punishment, torture or other cruel, inhuman or degrading treatment or punishment, OJ 2005 L200/1.

[82] See Arts. 131–134 EC.

is clearly in line with the political direction of the EU[83] and therefore enjoyed the broad support of the Member States.[84]

While the practice of the institutions has shown that a certain interconnection between the pillars is unavoidable, it has certainly not succeeded in shaping a coherent legal doctrine. In the recent past, much attention has been devoted by the European scholarship to the issue of the legal personality of the Union. Many different positions have been put forward, from those which recognize a unitary personality applying to the composite entity of 'EC plus EU', to those maintaining that the EC has its own legal personality but that the EU is not much more than a common agent of its Member States, with a variety of intermediate positions along the spectrum separating the two extremes.

In this study I have deliberately abstained from taking a position in a dispute for whose solution the fundamental elements are still, in my opinion, very uncertain. What is certain is that the question of the legal personality of the EU can hardly be resolved solely by interpreting the TEU's provisions, which are very ambiguous and do not lend support to either of the extreme positions just described. Only an analysis of how the EC/EU's powers have been concretely used can serve as an appropriate basis for solving this vexed issue. While it is indeed my intention to contribute to this analysis, the uncertainty of the results still makes me reluctant to draw definite conclusions.

The practice demonstrates a certain inclination of the EU and the EC to present themselves in the international arena as a unitary actor. This observation should lend some support to the idea that we are in the presence of one and the same entity.[85] This strangely configured entity would not dispose of the panoply of powers and prerogatives which are commonly referred to as the hallmark of statehood. Rather, it is vested with enumerated powers, transferred, moreover, not to one and the same unit, but rather to two different 'sub-units', the EC and the EU, and in an apparently

---

[83] The recitals to the Regulation (*supra*, n. 81) refer to Art. 6 TEU, which refers to human rights as one of the polestars of the European construction, and further reference is made to the Guidelines to the EU policy towards third countries on torture and other cruel, inhuman or degrading treatment or punishment, approved by the European Council in 2001, and to the UN Human Rights Commission's Resolution on torture and other cruel, inhuman and degrading treatment of 25 April 2001. However, while these acts, appropriately considered, might constitute a *limit* to the EC action, it is doubtful that they could ever be invoked as a *legal basis* for the EC competence.

[84] The creeping politicization of the external relations of the EC is highlighted by few contributions. See T. de Wilde d'Estmael, *La dimension politique des relations economiques extérieures de la Communauté européenne* (1998); recently, see F. Terpan, *La politique étrangére et de sécurité commune de l'Union européenne* (2003), at 33 ff.

[85] See, among the numerous contributions, A. Tizzano, 'La personalità internazionale dell'Unione europea', 3 *Il diritto dell'Unione europea* (1998) 377, at 404; A. Tizzano, 'The Foreign Relations Law of the EU between Supranationality and Intergovernmental Model', in E. Cannizzaro (ed.), *The European Union as an Actor in International Relations*, *supra* n. 19, 135, at 142; A. Von Bogdandy, 'The Legal Case for Unity: The European Union as a Single Organization with a Single Legal System', 36 *CMLR* (1999) 907; R. Wessel, *The European Union's Foreign and Security Policy. A Legal Institutional Perspective* (1999) at 315; and J. Klabbers, 'Presumptive Personality: The European Union in International Law', in M. Koskenniemi (ed.), *International Law Aspects of the European Union* (1998), at 249.

disorderly and inconsistent way. To the extent that these powers are exercised in coordination in the daily practice of international relations, the EU appears to be a unitary actor.[86]

To sum up briefly, the 'road towards unity' seems to be fraught with problematic issues. However, this should not preclude, in absolute terms, the possibility of interpreting the legal system erected by the founding Treaties in a coherent and consistent way.

ON THE ROAD TOWARDS UNITY: THE NEW CONSTITUTIONAL TREATY AND THE EU'S EXTERNAL ACTION

In the previous pages I have examined the main tools used in the inter-institutional practice to remedy the fragmentation of the external action inherent in the pillarization of the European construction. In this section I proceed further and analyse the provisions of the Constitutional Treaty aimed at establishing an external action of the EU. As already pointed out, the significance of this analysis is not merely historical and cultural. Yet while the chances for the entry into force of the Treaty are very slim, it is worthwhile inspecting this first attempt at establishing a unitary foreign relations system for the EU closely, with a view to determining its legal coherence and political propriety. Consistently with the purpose of this contribution, my analysis will focus on the substantive provisions of the Constitutional Treaty on the EU's external action, ie on those provisions which aim at grouping in a unitary legal setting competences and objectives which are, in the present system, distinctively assigned to the first or to the second pillar. In other words, I will look at those provisions which aim to lay down a bridge between the various competences of the Union in its external action and therefore to produce consistency through the normative dynamic. Little or no attention will be devoted to those provisions included in the Constitutional Treaty which aim to establish a unitary institutional frame and hence to produce consistency through the Union's institutional action.[87]

---

[86] That composite actor would thus have at its disposal the sum of the powers with which each 'sub-unit' was vested by the Member States, plus those powers which it acquires by virtue of its international 'actorship'. Indeed, the process of determining the complex of powers and prerogatives which the EC/EU wields internationally is not easy. In a different study, I suggested that the breadth of the international actorship of a certain entity vested with partial competence can be determined through a circular approach: the powers originally transferred to it by its constituent units generate the establishment upon it of rights and prerogatives by the international legal order by virtue of its international personality, which entails, in turn, a corresponding enlargement of its internal competence. See E. Cannizzaro, 'The Scope of the EU Foreign Power', supra, n. 77, at 297. Yet, if one accepts the idea that the international actorship of a certain entity tends to enlarge the set of powers of which it disposes by virtue of an internal transfer of competence, it does not seem illogical to argue that the scope of the international actorship of the composite entity EU/EC is in principle larger than the sum of powers and prerogatives possessed individually by each sub-unit.

[87] See Editorial, 'The CFSP under the EU Constitutional Treaty Issues of Depillarization', 42 *CMLR* (2005), 325.

The Main Features of the EU's External Action

The provisions which establish the EU's external action are extremely heterogeneous. Title V of the Constitutional Treaty regroups provisions concerning the CFSP of the Union and provisions concerning powers having an external impact which are, under the current system, assigned to the EC.[88] These two sets of provisions are kept together by norms which tend to establish a coordination between them. The result is an impressive number of provisions, many of which reproduce provisions already included in the TEU and the EC Treaty. Instead of passing to an analytical review of each individual provision, it seems more appropriate to illustrate the main features and the possible functioning of the new system. To that end, an analysis of the provisions which tend to ensure a coordination between the different policies is in order.

The first issue concerns the nature of the Union's external action. Even at a first reading, it is apparent that it is not a new policy but rather an attempt at regrouping and coordinating the exercise of a number of other autonomous policies, which therefore maintain their own nature and scope, and whose common hallmark is their external impact. This conclusion emerges clearly from Articles I-12 and I-16 of the Constitutional Treaty (CT).

A further question concerns the rationale for the inclusion or, respectively, exclusion of certain policies from the Union's external action. The answer is not as simple as it seems. One's first impression might be that the criterion for this relates to the possible effects of a certain policy on the external plane. However, since virtually all the substantive policies of the EU might have an external effect, the distinctive factor should lie in the main effect that a certain policy is designed to produce. Even from this perspective, however, the exclusion of policies such as border control, asylum and immigration, or environmental policy, which have a strong or even intrinsic external component, remains difficult to explain.[89] Moreover, it is hard to understand why Article III-292(3) CT extends the external action regime to the external aspects of other policies only as regards paragraphs (1) and (2) of that Article and not also, for example, as regards the application of other provisions,

---

[88] In the new Title V also provisions concerning the process of conclusion of agreements have been included, whose interpretation is not easy and whose coordination with other provisions included in the same title appears problematic. See B. de Witte, 'The Constitutional Law of External Relations', *supra*, n. 3.

[89] This mysterious plot thickens if one considers that environmental protection was in fact included among the aims of the external action enshrined in Art. III-292 CT. Nor is the decision as to the inclusion or exclusion of a certain policy in, or, respectively, from the external action without practical consequence. Indeed, Art. III-292(3) CT indicates that the legal regime of the external action applies to all other policies in their external aspects. However, it is highly controversial to determine precisely what are the 'external aspects' of a policy. Although the wording of this curious provision seems to allude to the conclusion of agreements, this would render the provision almost meaningless, as the conclusion of agreements is in fact governed by Art. III-325 CT, which is part of the external action. A different interpretation, according to which all aspects of a given policy having an external impact would be included in the external action regime, seems exceedingly broad since numerous actions undertaken under various policies might well have an external impact.

including, for example, the application of Article III-293 CT, which empowers the European Council to determine the Union's strategic interests and objectives.

CFSP and Substantive Policies as Part of a Unitary EU Foreign Affairs Power: Autonomy Versus Co-ordination

The case for autonomy

The main substantive novelty introduced by the Constitutional Treaty is the establishment of a common set of aims. In particular, Article III-292 merges, in a single provision, the objectives previously assigned to the CFSP with others currently assigned to EC policies. The effect of a common set of aims is to enable the EU external action to pursue simultaneously a plurality of objectives, some of which are unrelated to the common market and are aimed, rather, at asserting a political role for the EU in international relations. All in all, by establishing a plurality of heterogeneous aims, and by cumulatively assigning them to the diverse policies which constitute the EU's external action, Article III-292 CT subverts the principle of conferral, which requires that individual policies pursue the objectives distinctively assigned to each of them.

Is it then to be concluded that, in the system set up by the Constitutional Treaty, the principle of conferral is definitively abandoned in favour of a system of 'interchangeability' between the aims and means of the foreign power? There is a case to be made for adopting a more cautious attitude. First, the fact remains that, in addition to the general objectives of the external action laid down by Article III-292, several provisions assign specific aims to the substantive policies to which they correspond. For example, Article III-314 lays down the objectives specifically assigned to the common commercial policy. It would therefore be illogical to construe these two sets of provisions, containing respectively general and specific objectives, as clashing with each other. It seems more reasonable to argue that both have a binding effect and that, consequently, commercial measures of the Union must simultaneously conform to both. Thus, while the EU must take into account the political objectives of the Constitutional Treaty in the conduct of the commercial policy, it is more doubtful that it could adopt commercial measures inspired by purely political aims, not adequately supported by commercial considerations.

Another argument pointing toward a moderate interpretation of Article III-292 is the consideration that, if under the new system, individual EU substantive policies could pursue purely political aims, the very *raison d'être* of the CFSP would be seriously jeopardized. In other words, there would be little sense in establishing a complex machinery (based, moreover, on the common consent of the Member States) for adopting a stance on foreign policy if the EU, through its substantive policies and through a supranational method, could circumvent that machinery acting on its own initiative. The maintenance of a CFSP in parallel with other substantive policies can have no other meaning than to confirm and reinforce the primacy of the Member States on the political dimension of European integration.

The conclusion to be drawn from these considerations is that the establishment of a common set of aims in Article III-292 has the effect of enlarging the set of objectives of the EU substantive policies, without however making them completely interchangeable with those of the CFSP.

The case for subordination

If EU substantive policies are not conceived in the Constitutional Treaty as a substitute for the CFSP, and if instead the Treaty maintains a dual approach to the foreign power, questions arise as to their mutual relationship. In the new regime, one can certainly find elements suggesting a certain priority accorded to the CFSP to the detriment of the substantive policies, or, as it were, to the intergovernmental over the supranational dimension. An element in that direction is Article III-293(1), which provides for European decisions identifying the strategic interests and objectives of the Union. According to this provision, such decisions spell out the aims of Article III-292 in regard to a particular country or region (although they may also be more 'thematic' in approach) and establish an integrated frame for the harmonious and co-ordinated action developed by CFSP acts and by other substantive acts.

Thus, the Constitutional Treaty replaces the common strategies with a new kind of normative instrument which is truly 'cross-pillar' and which may provide guidance to all the activities undertaken by the Union in its external action. Article III-293(1), third paragraph, provides that the strategic interests and objectives of the Union are to be adopted under the arrangements laid down for each area. Therefore, if they include a foreign policy aspect, they must be adopted using the decision-making procedure established for the CFSP and are therefore subject to the intergovernmental voting procedure established for that policy. A hierarchy is thereby implicitly established between the CFSP and other external policies of the Constitutional Treaty. This normative hierarchy has important institutional implications, as it puts the supranational institutions under the direction and control of the intergovernmental decision-making mechanisms.[90]

Neither Autonomy Nor Subordination. A New, Creeping Pillarization?

In an integrated system that merges the CFSP and other external policies, there should be no room for a clause such as the one laid down in the current system by

---

[90] If the existence of this framework act serves the aim of coordinating the CFSP and the substantive policies so that the former has the power to give impetus and direction to the latter, it would nevertheless be a large step to think that the absence of this political umbrella prevents substantive EU policies from autonomously pursuing the aims of Art. III-292. In the provisions which laid down the legal regime of individual policies included in Title V CT, it is stated that these policies must be conducted 'in the context of the principles and objectives of the Union's external action' laid down by Art. III-292 (see, for example, Art. 315, para. 1). Thus, a political intermediation between the EU substantive policies and the political aims of the Treaty may be opportune, but it does not seem altogether necessary.

Article 47 TEU. However, the Constitutional Treaty contains a provision which indeed corresponds, with some significant change, to that Article. Ironically, this may in turn reintroduce the pillarization of the system, the abandonment of which was among the main aims of the Constitutional Treaty.

In order to explain this point, a brief analysis of the function discharged by Article 47 in the present system is in order. In the present, three-pillar system, the function of Article 47 is to 'protect' the EC policies from intrusion by a CFSP act. The provision has a unilateral structure insofar as it protects EC policies *vis-à-vis* the CFSP but not vice versa. At the present stage, this seems to be perfectly logical. There is a strong case for protecting the EC policies from the interference of the CFSP, a policy which is defined, as noted above, in purely functional terms. By contrast, there is no need to protect the CFSP from interference by the EC policies, precisely because these policies, as already pointed out, may only pursue the aims specifically assigned to them by the EC Treaty and are strictly excluded from pursuing the political aims assigned to the CFSP. Thus, the CFSP is sufficiently 'shielded' by the principle of conferral contained in the EC Treaty.

The establishment of a new, integrated normative system, and the merging of the two pre-existing systems, might raise the need to shield the CFSP from possible interference by substantive policies. This in turn would entail, one might conclude, the need to *bi-lateralize* the saving clause, which now, with a unilateral structure, is contained in Article 47 TEU. In this respect, Article III-322 would simply constitute an updated version of such a clause.

However, this conclusion would be simplistic, to say the least. A quick observation may reveal that, far from constituting an innocuous operation of adapting the pre-existing regime to the needs of new integrated system, the provision of Article III-322 represents the most vivid illustration of the difficulty of dismantling the normative barriers erected by the pillarization without, at the same time, reducing (lifting) the institutional barriers deriving from the existence of a plurality of decision-making procedures.

Protecting the Union's substantive policies from interference by the CFSP is technically possible, and indeed necessary to preserve the *acquis communitaire*. Since the scope of these policies is determined by reference to a material field, this aim is easily achieved by prohibiting CFSP measures from entering that field. This is, as seen above, the role of Article 47 TEU.

The inverse operation is more problematic. As the scope of the CFSP is determined by recourse not to a material field but only functionally, by reference to the objectives pursued by a certain measure, the only way to prevent substantive policies from interfering with the CFSP is to prohibit these policies from pursuing political objectives and to reserve the pursuit of these objectives to the CFSP.

Under the current regime, this function is discharged by the principle of conferral, without need for an express clause. Yet the novelty of the Constitutional Treaty resides in the establishment of a common set of aims assigned to the external action. Such a system implies that, in order to work properly, all the policies forming the external action must be able to pursue the common aims laid down by Article III-292. This effect would clearly be impaired if, by virtue of Article III-322, the Union's substantive policies could not intrude into the realm of the CFSP. Due to the purely functional nature of the CFSP, this prohibition would necessarily prevent the substantive policies from pursuing political objectives. In other words, as noted earlier, the undesired but inevitable effect of Article III-322 would be to re-erect the normative barrier between the CFSP and the substantive policies corresponding to the pillar structure that the Constitutional Treaty was meant to overcome.

The logical difficulty encountered in seeking a consistent construction to this strangely worded provision must not of course be overemphasized. There are certainly many possible interpretations which could avoid this patent contradiction and could soothe the impression of a new, creeping pillarization. However, in my view the foregoing discussion shows clearly just how tortuous the road toward unity is in the Union's foreign relations power.

CONCLUDING REMARKS: THE ASPIRATION TOWARD UNITY AND THE PERSISTENCE OF FRAGMENTATION IN THE EUROPEAN FOREIGN AFFAIRS POWER

At the outset, the question at the heart of this chapter is: 'Is there a unitary European foreign affairs power?' Or, put differently, can the various powers and prerogatives assigned to the different EU sub-units be composed in a legally unitary frame, or must we resign ourselves to having a multifarious gaggle of distinct powers and competences on the external plane, each detached from the others, which cannot be integrated within a single, comprehensive international 'actorship'?

In the preceding sections, an analysis was therefore undertaken with a view to answering that question. However, this analysis unfolded across a perilous path, fraught with technicalities making it easy to lose the thread that should give guidance to it. At the end of that path, one may be left with a sense of dissatisfaction and with the acute impression that no clear-cut answer can be given.

In particular, a tendency can be discerned to overcome the current state of fragmentation, and to ensure a coordinated exercise of the various powers assigned respectively to the EC and to the EU. Whereas in most cases such coordination is achieved at the expense of the Community pillar—as it entails superimposing the intergovernmental elements of the CFSP over the supranational elements of the EC—there are notable exceptions pointing in a different direction. From the institutional practice, some cases have emerged in which the EC has wandered beyond the limits to its action and adopted acts and policies having a clear political impact on the international arena. Indeed, at times the sole purpose of these acts and policies has been political.

The aspiration toward unity, which echoes in practice, makes abundantly clear the shortcoming inherent in the fragmentation of the European foreign relations system and creates a strong need for the creation of a new, integrated system of external action. This is essentially the conceptual ground on which the idea of an integrated external action took shape, and this finally materialized in Title V of the Constitutional Treaty. However, the analysis above has demonstrated the precariousness of the logic of the new system, which sought—unsuccessfully, in my view—to reconcile the need to attribute a political role to the supranational institutions with the strong will of the Member States to maintain their leading role in shaping the main lines of the European foreign policy. The many technical flaws of the system constitute the reflex, in legal terms, of the incapacity to balance these two incoherent objectives; to create a new integrated system while leaving the decision-making processes and the institutional features of the pre-existing ones untouched.

Indeed, the need to sustain the European integration at two different paces, one supranational and one intergovernmental, ultimately splits the external power into two parts, one political and one substantive. This essentially excludes unity and coherence in the foreign affairs power. The opposite path, the re-establishment of a unitary power, can be pursued via one of two alternatives: either to acknowledge the leading role of the CFSP, to the detriment of the autonomy of the supranational dimension, or to acknowledge the autonomy of the EU's substantive policies in pursuing foreign policy objectives. Given the lack of a *via media* between these two paths, the attempt of the Constitutional Treaty to set up an integrated external action for the EU seems to have been doomed to failure.

Thus, the analysis of the previous pages seems to offer some tentative results, which could be summarized as follows:

(a) The first conclusion concerns the difficulty of coordinating the external dimension of European economic integration, which logically and practically should be linked to the EC, with international political action, over which the Member States are keen to maintain control. This imbalance creates a clear asymmetry in the EU's foreign relations power, deriving basically from the fact that it is one thing to allocate competence on the internal plane between the EC and the EU, but that distributing between these entities the capacity to handle complex international issues is quite another matter. The 'impossible symmetry' between an entity's internal powers and its international powers, or rather the imperfect correspondence between the internal personality and international actorship of entities sharing powers and competence, is at the origin of the fragmentation of the legal system of the European foreign relations power.

(b) A second observation is that the drafters of the Constitutional Treaty were well aware of the problem just described. However, they sought to resolve this problem with the aid of the wrong utensils. As stated above, in order to remedy the lack of coordination in the international action of the EU and the EC, a previous determination of the nature and scope of the international actorship of the EC seems to be inescapable. Is the EC an entity which has the power to deal with politically sensitive issues using its competence and its supranational decision-making processes, or must it instead act, when political issues are at stake, only under the direction and control of its Member States? If a solution is to be found, the ship of the European integration must pass through the treacherous narrow waters between these two contradictory models, as in the legend of the two monsters at the strait of Messina, Scylla and Carybdis. However, the reading of the provisions on the EU's external action included in the Constitutional Treaty do not make it possible to untie this knot. They swing, with no apparent rationale, from cooperation to autonomy and betray a failure to reach any resolute decision in favour of one of the two models. In the end, the objective of de-pillarizing the Union's external action seems far from being attained.

(c) The difficulty of finding a proper solution through an adjustment of the normative process of the EU leads one to shift the course of the research and to ask whether a solution might not be found in the institutional practice. This hope is based on the fact that developments on the ground have often helped to work out feasible solutions to practical problems that could not adequately be solved through strictly legal techniques. Indeed, a global reading of the practice leaves the impression that, beyond the paralysing theoretical problems, a solution based on mutual understanding and tolerance has already taken place. This is based, on the one hand, on the acceptance that, with respect to certain issues in which political consent among the Member States and the European institutions is discernible, the EC feels confident to act as an autonomous political actor, even beyond the strict limits of the principle of conferral. For their part, the Member States exhibit a certain acquiescence to this expansion and tend to recognize the EC as a political actor, at least for low-level political issues. Conversely, where highly sensitive political issues are at stake, the EC seems to accept the EU giving guidance to its action not only by laying down general guidelines but also specific directives in the full spectrum of its competence. By gauging the effect of the basic principles which govern the interplay between supranational and intergovernmental action, the EU has been able to assert itself, in several situations, as a unitary political actor.

Among the virtues of practice there is the ability to adapt, on a case-by-case basis, the legal reality to the political reality, and hence the ability to find flexible solutions that cannot be expressed in 'hard' rules. A coordination based on mutual political arrangements and on a day-to-day search for the best practical solution can make it possible to work around the *impasse* created by the multi-speed pace of European integration. If there is a sense of dissatisfaction prompted by such a solution—which is the farthest thing from a coherent legal doctrine—this might be assuaged to some degree by the observation that the process of European integration has accustomed us to solutions which are at odds with the traditional premise of the coherence of legal orders, a premise which increasingly appears to be the myth of a bygone era.

8

'Euro-visions'? Some Thoughts on Prospects and Mechanisms for Future Constitutional Change in the European Union[†]

ANGUS JOHNSTON*

INTRODUCTION

On the last two occasions that any of the European electorate rejected the result of an Intergovernmental Conference ('IGC') that had agreed a Treaty to amend the founding Treaties of the European Community ('EC') and European Union ('EU'), the voters were given a second opportunity to change their minds and reach the 'correct' result. In Denmark in May 1993, the Maastricht Treaty was eventually accepted by the electorate in a second referendum after the subsequent adoption by the European Council of a Decision 'interpreting' the Maastricht Treaty. In September 2001 in Ireland, meanwhile, the addition of a Declaration to the Treaty on European Union guaranteeing Irish military neutrality provided the basis for a 'successful' referendum at the second attempt.

After agreement was reached on the Treaty Establishing a Constitution for Europe (hereinafter, 'TCE') under the Irish Presidency in June 2004, one editorial summed up the position of the governments of the Member States as follows:

The difficult task of the political leaders now is to explain in a clear way what they wanted to create, so that their citizens do not decide on the basis of propagandist clichés, but rather on the Union as they wanted it.[1]

[†] Sincere thanks are due to various friends and colleagues for comments on and discussions in connection with this paper, and in particular Albertina Albors-Llorens, Catherine Barnard, Alan Dashwood, Rebecca Williams and Bruno de Witte, but the author remains responsible for all views expressed and for any errors and inaccuracies that remain. I have endeavoured to cover events up to the start of July 2006, with some later developments included where possible. All internet references last visited 28 July 2006.

* M.A. (Oxon., Cantab.), LLM (Leiden), BCL (Oxon.), University Lecturer in Law, Faculty of Law, University of Cambridge, and Staff Fellow and Director of Studies in Law, Trinity Hall, University of Cambridge.

[1] Editorial, (2004) 41 *CMLRev* 899, 907. In the period leading up to the Spanish referendum, reports were widespread that adverts and flyers summarizing the content of the TCE were to be available

Whether or not this wise advice was heeded is a point that will no doubt be debated by historians, political scientists and lawyers (to say nothing of journalists) for many years to come. However, after a number of ratifications via national Parliamentary approval and a 'Yes' vote in a referendum in Spain, the early summer of 2005 saw the electorates of, first, France (29 May), and then the Netherlands (1 June) reject the ratification of the TCE. In spite of these 'No' votes, a number of other Member States have continued with their national ratification processes: indeed, a referendum in Luxembourg on 10 July 2005 returned a result in favour of the ratification of the TCE. The current state of play with regard to the ratification of the TCE is set out in Table 1, below: at the time of writing (early July 2006), 12 Member States have formally ratified the TCE, three have approved it at national level but have yet to lodge the formal instrument of ratification, two have rejected it in a referendum, seven seem to have suspended the ratification process indefinitely, and Finland expects to ratify by Parliamentary approval during the Finnish Presidency of the EU in the second half of 2006.

There is a serious danger that the history of previous ratifications may come back to haunt the EU and its Member States over the TCE. The statements by the European Council in June 2005 and June 2006, agreeing to continue a 'period of reflection' on the TCE could certainly be read as having left open the possibility of submitting the TCE to second referendums in both France and the Netherlands. However, the past practice with regard to Denmark and Ireland risks leading to angry reactions from press and populace alike, as the *Private Eye* cartoon illustrates presciently. A cynical saying has it that if 'the people don't like it, change the people', while the late Lord Williams of Mostyn (erstwhile Leader of the House of Lords) once opined that he believed that the people wanted a liberal democracy, and if they did not then 'they would be wrong'.[2] Even if only some account is taken of

at football stadiums around the country, in an attempt to publicize the document and the referendum: see reports on the internet at (eg) http://www.tsr.ch/tsr/index.html?siteSect=200002&sid=5453308 and http://www.robert-schuman.org/lettre/lettrean194.htm, and the Spanish government's 'Information Note' of 19 February 2005 on the referendum (available at http://www.es-ue.org/Documents/NOTA%20 ARTESANOS%20CAGRE.INGLES.doc). In the event, voter turnout was a somewhat disappointingly low 42.3% of those registered to vote, but no-one could argue that strenuous efforts had not been made to make the populace aware of the event and its source (although other reports suggested that one poll found that as many as nine out of ten Spaniards confessed to being unsure of what the TCE actually concerned, let alone what its provisions contained: see http://www.socialistworld.net/eng/2005/03/01europe. html). For a contemporary (and not entirely favourable) audit of the conduct of the Spanish referendum, see Madroñal (for Mas Democracia and Democracy International), 'Spanish Referendum on the EU Constitution—Monitoring Report' (20 February 2005, available at: http://europeanreferendum.org/ fileadmin/pdf/monitoring/di-spain.pdf).

  [2] The full quote reads: 'My Lords, given the alternative, I prefer a liberal democracy. I believe that that is what the overwhelming majority of countries, were the will of the people to be supreme at all times, would want—and if they did not, they would be wrong' (*Hansard*, 21 June 2001, Column 113; available at: http://www.publications.parliament.uk/pa/ld200102/ldhansrd/vo010621/text/10621-08.htm).

Table One *State of play on the ratification of the TCE (as of July 2006)*

Member State	Referendum?	Referendum Date	Referendum Result	Previous (European) Referendums?
Belgium	N	(Final approval from last regional Parliament, 8 February 2006)	(Y) (But yet to lodge formal instrument of ratification)	–
Czech Republic	Originally: Y; but later cancelled.	(Postponed (until end-2006/start of 2007?))	–	June 2003–Joining EU (Yes)
Denmark	Y	(Referendum indefinitely postponed)	–	1972–Joining EEC, etc (Yes) 1986–SEA (Yes) 1992–TEU (No) 1993–TEU (Yes) 1998–ToA (Yes) 2000–Euro (No)
Germany	N	(Parliamentary approval, 27 May 2005)	(Y) (Constitutional Court action has delayed ratification)	–
Estonia	N	(Parliamentary approval, 9 May 2006)	(Y)	September 2003– Joining EU (Yes)
Greece	N	(Parliamentary voting completed, 19 April 2005)	(Y)	–
Spain	Y	20 May 2005 (Parliamentary approval 18 May 2005)	Y (76.7% in favour; 42.3% turnout)	–
France	Y	29 May 2005	N (54.7% against; 69.3% turnout)	1972–Enlargement (Yes) 1992–TEU (Yes)
Ireland	Y	(Referendum Postponed indefinitely)	–	1972–Joining EEC (Yes) 1987–SEA (Yes) 1992–TEU (Yes) 1998–ToA (Yes) 2001–ToN (No) 2002–ToN (Yes)

Member State	Referendum?	Referendum Date	Referendum Result	Previous (European) Referendums?
Italy	N	(Parliamentary voting completed, 6 April 2005)	(Y)	1989–Consultative referendum on possible draft EC Constitution (Yes)
Cyprus	N	(Parliamentary approval, 30 June 2005)	(Y)	–
Latvia	N	(Parliamentary approval, 2 June 2005)	(Y)	September 2003– Joining EU (Yes)
Lithuania	N	(Parliamentary voting completed, 11 November 2004)	(Y)	May 2003–Joining EU (Yes)
Luxembourg	Y	10 July 2004 (Parliamentary approval 25 October 2005)	Y (56.52% in favour; 87.77% turnout)	–
Hungary	N	20 December 2004 (Parliamentary voting completed)	(Y)	April 2003–Joining EU (Yes)
Malta	N	(Parliamentary approval, 6 July 2005)	(Y)	March 2003–Joining EU (Yes)
Netherlands	Y	1 June 2005	N (61.6% against; 62.8% turnout)	–
Austria	N	(Parliamentary approval 25 May 2005)	(Y)	1994–Joining EU (Yes)
Poland	?	(Parliament failed to vote on ratification procedure, 5 July 2006)	–	June 2003–Joining EU (Yes)
Portugal	Y	(Planned for April 2005, but postponed after resignation of government and dissolution of Parliament in December 2004)	–	–

Table One *(Continued)*

Member State	Referendum?	Referendum Date	Referendum Result	Previous (European) Referendums?
Slovenia	N	(Parliamentary ratification, 1 February 2005)	(Y)	March 2003–Joining EU (Yes)
Slovakia	N	(Parliamentary ratification, 11 May 2005)	(Y) (Constitutional Court action has delayed ratification)	May 2003–Joining EU (Yes)
Finland	N	– (Parliamentary ratification expected during second half of 2006)	–	October 1994– Joining EU (Yes)
Sweden	N	(Ratification postponed indefinitely)	–	1994–Joining EU (Yes) 2003–Euro (No)
United Kingdom	Y	? (Was likely early 2006, but ratification process now indefinitely suspended)	–	1975–Remaining in the EEC, etc. (Yes)

[The relevant information concerning Member State ratifications is available at: http://europa.eu/ constitution/ratification_en.htm.]

the results in the French and Dutch referendums, neither of these approaches is open to the EU in the first decade of the 21st Century. So long as national ratification of any Treaty amendment is required, the same 'people' will have to be engaged: the key question is whether or not the position that they take in the future may change, and information and accountability will be key in any such development. Meanwhile, a commitment to representative democracy, coupled with some limitations upon what laws the representatives of the people can actually adopt, will clearly form an important part of any future EU developments, but the idea that any (political) elite can force this upon an unquestioning electorate, against their express will but paternalistically 'in their best interests' flies in the face of the forces unleashed by those same referendums.

This chapter is of necessity of a preliminary and incomplete nature, given the current status of the TCE and the ongoing 'period of reflection' in the aftermath of the French and Dutch referendum results in 2005. First, an outline will be given of possible ways of making changes of a constitutional nature within the EU. It will

Private Eye, Issue No. 1161
(June 2006), p. 9 (Reproduced here by kind
permission of Private Eye/Richard Jolley)

be suggested that careful matching of procedures to issues should be conducted to increase the chances of successful future constitutional reform. Second, strategies for coping with the results of the two negative referendums will be discussed, examining briefly the legal position of the TCE and some of the political moves made during the first part of the period of reflection, as well as seeking to unpack some of the reasons that lay behind the rejection of the TCE in France and the Netherlands. It will be argued that an understanding of these complexities is important to provide the necessary background to any future constitutional reform proposals, whether in the form of Treaty amendments or by other means. Third, two particular issues will be raised which, it is suggested, can safely and legitimately be pursued even in the absence of any (imminent) ratification of the TCE as it stands: these are the improvement of the transparency of EC proceedings (particularly those of the Council) and the application of the principle of subsidiarity in conjunction with national Parliaments. In conclusion, it will be suggested, first, that the raised profile for the EU and its workings that has resulted from the TCE ratification process will, in time, prove to be a highly beneficial development. Second, it is concluded that any moves to implement reforms that were embodied in the TCE, but do not require Treaty amendment to be brought about, must pay careful attention to the concerns raised throughout the EU and, crucially, seek to explain the reasons for such reforms clearly and straightforwardly, both to the citizenry and to national political representatives. Only in this way can the ground be prepared for future constitutional change via Treaty amendments in the years to come.

TYPOLOGY: APPROACHES TO EFFECTING CONSTITUTIONAL CHANGE IN THE EU

In making any assessment of how constitutional reform may move forward in the EU, it may be helpful to provide an outline of the various devices that might be employed by the EU and its Member States in the future. What follows is an attempt to provide a brief summary of the major methods that could be used, along with some discussion of the problems and prospects for the use of such methods, including a summary in tabular form (see Table 3, below). This will set the scene for the subsequent discussion of how the EU might attempt to deal with the situation that has arisen after the French and Dutch referendums (Section 3) and which particular areas might appropriately be addressed even without Treaty amendments (Section 4).

The 'Standard' Intergovernmental Conference Process

At an Igc where the reform of the existing EC and EU Treaties is on the agenda, the great bulk of the preparatory work is carried out, and much of the agreement reached, by representatives of national governments and national ministers from the relevant departments. However, issues of high sensitivity, dispute and controversy tend to be left to the Heads of State or Government at the final summit meeting. Such deliberations do not take place in public, although increasingly much of the relevant documentation is made available on the internet.[3]

It should not be forgotten that the IGC process has, over the history of the EU, secured many bold, innovative and far-reaching developments in the constitutional and institutional structure and operation of the EU: in particular, both the Single European Act and the Treaty of Maastricht made extensive contributions in this regard. At the same time, however, it was becoming clear that the nature of the IGC process also tended to create very complex compromises between Member States. The three pillar structure, various opt-outs, protocols on specific topics and areas of European-level activity in which some Member States did not participate were the price of such compromises, which were not always conducive to a clear understanding of the nature and functions of the EC and EU and were often heavily criticized.[4] Furthermore, and this is one of the main reasons behind the complex bargaining, the 'all or nothing' nature of the negotiations (requiring unanimous agreement among all Member States) allowed very robust defences of (perceived) national interests to stall, or at least exert very strong influence, over IGC discussions and ultimate agreements.

This complex bargaining process and defence of national interests was further facilitated by the secrecy of such inter-governmental deliberations, but this often

---

[3] J-C Piris, *The Constitution for Europe: A Legal Analysis* (Cambridge: CUP, 2006) (hereinafter, 'Piris (2006)'), at 50: see http://www.consilium.europa.eu/cms3_applications/Applications/igc/doc_register.asp? content=DOC&lang=EN&cmsid=900 for access to what has been made available from the 2003–2004 IGC that led to the adoption of the TCE.

[4] See, eg, the sustained and powerful critique of the outcome of the Maastricht Treaty provided by D Curtin, 'The Constitutional Structure of the Union: A Europe of Bits and Pieces' (1993) 30 *CMLRev* 17, and also JHH Weiler, 'Neither Unity Nor Three Pillars, The Trinity Structure of the Treaty on European Union' in: J Monar *et al.* (eds.), *The Maastricht Treaty on European Union, Legal Complexity and Political Dynamic* (Brussels: European Interuniversity Press, 1993) and A von Bogdandy and M Nettesheim, '*Ex Pluribus Unum*: Fusion of the European Communities into the European Union' (1996) 2 *ELJ* 267.

also led to speculation about horse-trading across issues and a general sense that the Member State governments did not wish there to be effective scrutiny of, or external input into, the IGC decision-making process.

On a substantive level, there was widespread dissatisfaction with the mismatch observed between, on the one hand, issues that it had been agreed needed to be resolved and, on the other hand, the actual (and rather limited) outcomes of the Amsterdam and Nice IGCs. Nice, for example, was explicitly convened to deal with the 'Amsterdam left-overs'[5] (and specifically the need to address the structure and operation of the EU institutions to improve their efficiency and effectiveness, and to prepare for the forthcoming substantial enlargement of the Union), yet few major improvements were achieved. Indeed, the Member State Heads of State and/or Government themselves recognized these shortcomings even as they signed the Treaty of Nice itself, as the inclusion of the 'Declaration on the Future of the Union' agreed by the IGC[6] made abundantly clear.

The Convention Process

Thus, there were dissatisfactions with the process and outcomes of Amsterdam and Nice,[7] alongside a sense that the issues that needed to be tackled by future constitutional reform in the EU would create an agenda too large and complex for an IGC to deal with satisfactorily under its normal procedures.

All of this led the European Council (in first the Nice[8] and then the Laeken[9] Declarations) to decide upon charging a Convention with responsibility for discussing the institutional reform questions that remained after Nice, so as to prepare the ground for the ensuing IGC envisaged under the Italian Presidency towards the end of 2004. This Convention seems consciously to have been modelled upon the group set up to draft the EU's Charter of Fundamental Rights, so a brief summary of that

---

[5] 'Protocol on the institutions with the prospect of enlargement of the European Union' annexed by the Final Act of the Amsterdam IGC to the EU, EC, ECSC and Euratom Treaties (1997) (available at: http://europa.eu/eur-lex/en/treaties/selected/livre545.html and http://europa.eu.int/eur-lex/en/treaties/dat/amsterdam.html).

[6] 'Declaration on the Future of the Union': Declaration 23, Treaty of Nice [2001] OJ C80/1 (hereinafter, 'Nice Declaration 23') (available at http://europa.eu.int/eur-lex/lex/en/treaties/dat/12001C/pdf/12001C_EN.pdf), 85–86.

[7] See, eg: J Lodge, 'Intergovernmental Conferences and European Integration: Negotiating the Amsterdam Treaty' (1998) 3 *International Negotiations* 345; W Wessels, 'Nice Results: The Millennium IGC in the EU's Evolution' (2001) 39 *JCMS* 197; and L Hoffmann, 'The Convention on the Future of Europe: Thoughts on the Convention Model', Jean Monnet Working Paper 11/02 (November 2002; available at: http://www.jeanmonnetprogram.org/papers/02/021101.html), 2–7.

[8] Nice Declaration 23 (n. 6, above).

[9] Laeken European Council, 'Declaration on the Future of the European Union' (Presidency Conclusions, SN 300/1/01 REV 1, 14–15 December 2001), paras. 3–4 and Annex I (hereinafter, 'Laeken Declaration') (available at: http://www.consilium.europa.eu/ueDocs/cms_Data/docs/pressData/en/ec/68827.pdf and http://europa.eu.int/constitution/futurum/documents/offtext/doc151201_en.htm).

group's structure and approach is apposite, to understand the benefits that the European Council hoped to bring to the work of preparing the 2004 IGC.

Charter of fundamental rights

In the Conclusions of the Cologne European Council in June 1999, the Member States agreed to set up:

a body composed of representatives of the Heads of State and Government and of the President of the Commission as well as of members of the European Parliament and national parliaments. Representatives of the European Court of Justice should participate as observers. Representatives of the Economic and Social Committee, the Committee of the Regions and social groups as well as experts should be invited to give their views. Secretariat services should be provided by the General Secretariat of the Council.[10]

Detailed provisions on the composition and working methods of this body were adopted by the European Council in the Conclusions from its Tampere meeting in October 1999[11]: there were to be 'Fifteen representatives of the Heads of State or Government of Member States, . . . [o]ne representative of the President of the European Commission, . . . [s]ixteen members of the European Parliament to be designated by itself, . . . and [t]hirty members of national Parliaments (two from each national Parliament) to be designated by national Parliaments themselves', making 62 in total (plus two observers from the Court of Justice and two from the Council of Europe, including one from the European Court of Human Rights).[12]

This body would draft 'a Charter of fundamental rights in order to make their overriding importance and relevance more visible to the Union's citizens'.[13] This rationale suggested that the exercise of drafting the Charter was focused more strongly upon explaining to the public what had been achieved by the EU in the field of fundamental rights (thereby securing support and legitimacy for EU activities) than on the substance of the rights enumerated.[14] In turn, this suggested that 'in many ways, and this is by now an obvious point, the process of drafting the Charter was always going to be at least as important—if indeed not more so—than the substantive document which eventually emerged'.[15] Here, too, the Tampere Conclusions were innovative, requiring that 'hearings held by the Body and

---

[10] Presidency Conclusions, Cologne European Council (3 and 4 June 1999) (hereinafter, 'Cologne Conclusions') (available at: http://europa.eu.int/council/off/conclu/june99/june99_en.htm), paras. 44–45 and Annex IV.

[11] Presidency Conclusions, Tampere European Council (15 and 16 October 1999) (hereinafter: 'Tampere Conclusions') (available at: http://www.consilium.europa.eu/ueDocs/cms_Data/docs/pressData/en/ec/00200-r1.en9.htm).

[12] *Ibid.*, Annex, paras. A(i) and (iii).

[13] Cologne Conclusions, Annex IV.

[14] See, eg, G de Búrca, 'The drafting of the European Union Charter of Fundamental Rights' (2001) 26 *ELRev* 126 (hereinafter, 'de Búrca (2001)').

[15] *Ibid.*, at 131.

documents submitted at such hearings should be public'[16] and suggesting that
'[o]ther bodies, social groups and experts may be invited by the Body to give their
views'[17]: a clear contrast with the criticisms of past IGCs as having lacked transparency and openness to popular contributions.

While acknowledging that there were limitations to the way in which the Charter
process operated, de Búrca has concluded that:

> It was established as a novel, experimental, relatively deliberative and open forum for consti-
> tutional debate, contrasting quite starkly with the traditional state-dominated IGC processes
> of tough bargaining and closed diplomacy as the means for Treaty change in the European
> Union.[18]

On the other hand, it is by no means clear that the public profile that the European
Council had sought to gain through this process was in fact achieved to any significant extent. Any potential great impact (itself perhaps somewhat wishful thinking)
of the proclamation of the Charter at the Nice IGC was dissipated by the Member
States' inability to agree upon how to deal with the Charter's legal status, and was
almost completely overshadowed by the duration, difficulty and controversy of the
Nice IGC negotiations and results on institutional reform.

With this background of the recent history of the EU prior to the discussions at
Nice and Laeken, we now have a greater insight into some of the reasons behind
the approach taken by the Nice IGC and the Laeken European Council to the
preparation of the 2004 IGC.

The Treaty establishing a Constitution for Europe

In the year leading up to the Laeken European Council, the combination of issues
post-Nice and the views of the Member States in the Council, the Commission and
the European Parliament had seemed to coalesce around the idea of setting up a
Convention process with a membership drawn from national Members of Parliament ('MPs'), Members of the European Parliament (MEPs), the Commission
and representatives of Member State governments.[19] Given the wide-ranging nature
of the issues on the agenda most protagonists were led to agree that the Convention
model would provide a 'democratic, transparent and credible mechanism for future
reform',[20] which was felt necessary given the matters at stake, and desirable given
the largely favourable reactions to the use of the model when drafting the Charter
(as discussed above). The eventual composition of the Convention on the Future
of Europe ('CFE'), as established by the Laeken Declaration, is illustrated in Table 2.
From these members, a 'Praesidium' was established, which was created to act as a

---

[16] Tampere Conclusions, Annex, para. B(ii).

[17] *Ibid.*, para. A(vi).

[18] de Búrca (2001) (n. 14, above), 138.

[19] PP Craig, 'Constitutional Process and Reform in the EU: Nice, Laeken, the Convention and the
IGC' (2004) 10 *EPL* 653 (hereinafter, 'Craig, (2004)'), 655–660.

[20] *Ibid.*, 657.

kind of steering board for the work of the CFE, preparing drafts to be presented to and discussed by the plenary Convention. It consisted of 13 members in total (again, the membership of the Praesidium is indicated in Table 2) and did not operate in public.

Table Two *Composition of the Convention on the Future of Europe*

Source	Details	Number	Alternates	Observers	Praesidium
European Council appointments	Chairman	1	–	–	1
	Vice-Chairmen	2		–	2
HSG* of the Member States		15	15	–	3**
HSG* of Accession States		10	10	–	1***
HSG* of the Candidate States		3	3	–	–
National Parliaments of the Member States		30	30	–	2
National Parliaments of Accession States		20	20	–	–
National Parliaments of Candidate States		6	6	–	–
European Parliament		16	16	–	2
European Commission		2	2	–	2
Economic and Social Committee		–	–	3	–
European Social Partners		–	–	3	–
Committee of the Regions		–	–	6	–
European Ombudsman	In person	–	–	1	–
		Total: 220 involved (118 at any one time)			

* HSG 5 Heads of State or Government.
** Drawn from the rotating Council Presidency (Spanish, Danish and Greek representatives).
*** An 'invitee': the Slovenian representative.

One group[21] of commentators has asked whether the composition of the CFE properly respected what it describes as the 'procedural aspect' of the subsidiarity principle. This, they argue:

implies that the burden of proof rests with those who want to centralise and that the decision whether to centralise or not must not be taken by those who have a vested interest in centralization.

The procedural dimension of the subsidiarity principle is a special case of the classical constitutional principle that the rules must not be made by those who later have to keep them. If those who will have to play by the rules are called to formulate these rules, they will not adopt the rules which are best for the citizens but those which are best for them.[22]

Thus, the CFE should not have contained any member who had a 'vested interest in centralization', so that it should have consisted 'only of representatives of the parliaments of the member states (including experts which they might have appointed). These representatives would not be eligible for public office or mandate in the European institutions in the future.'[23] At the same time, however, Rasmussen has commented that the lack of familiarity of many 'conventioneers' with 'the true nature and purpose of their new assignment and . . . with the working cultures of large EU-gatherings' created a malaise and necessitated many months of acclimatisation and 'learning by doing'.[24] There will thus always be costs and trade-offs to be made in the composition of any such body: reduction in expertise on the nature of the system and its operation to date may meet some legitimacy criteria (on input) and yet may endanger others (the output of any Convention process).

More generally, it is important that criticisms of Convention on the Future of Europe be placed in the practical context of what was possible to achieve in the circumstances, while not allowing pragmatic considerations to prevent us from raising concerns about how the process played out and the substantive outcome[25] of its deliberations.

It was probably inevitable that there would be some moves towards infusing the CFE process with intergovernmental elements (see, eg, the arrival of the German and

---

[21] 'The European Constitutional Group', which has a variety of members with legal, political science and economics backgrounds. A full list of members is published in the article cited in *n. 22, below.*

[22] 'The Constitutional Proposal of the European Convention: an Appraisal and an Explanation' (2004) 24 *Economic Affairs* 22, 26.

[23] *Ibid.* The Group applies this reasoning to the creation of Constitutional-level rules, but its strong decentralizing message would presumably also apply to the legislative process under any EC constitutional arrangements: see, eg, at 23, para. 12 of the Group's appraisal of the TCE, proposing the removal of the legislative initiative from the Commission on similar grounds of innate centralizing tendencies.

[24] H Rasmussen, 'The Convention Method' (2005) 1 *EuConst* 141 (hereinafter, "Rasmussen (2005)"), at 144. See also G Stuart, *The Making of Europe's Constitution* (London: Fabian Society, Fabian Ideas 609, December 2003) (hereinafter, 'Stuart (2003)'), 18–19.

[25] For an assessment of which see, eg, AA Dashwood and AC Johnston, 'The Institutions of the Enlarged EU under the regime of the Constitutional Treaty' (2004) 41 *CMLRev.* 1481, 1500 ff.) (hereinafter, 'Dashwood & Johnston (2004)').

French Foreign Ministers, Fischer and de Villepin respectively, in the late autumn of 2002), particularly once it became clear that the CFE intended to draw up an entire Treaty with constitutional character (rather than restrict itself to offering recommendations to the IGC).[26]

It is also clear that one key driver behind the increasing Praesidium control exercised over the drafting process towards the key submission date of the European Council meeting of 20 June was the very tightness of that submission deadline.[27] The Member States refused to allow the CFE any extra time for the delivery of its work, despite the fact that detailed discussions and drafting on the key institutional provisions had commenced so late in the Convention's work programme.[28] The control that the Praesidium was able to exert was further facilitated by the way in which working groups had been discharged once the final report on their respective topics had been submitted, and by the Praesidium Secretariat's drafting responsibilities.[29]

Further, a proper and careful treatment of the institutional questions would inevitably require some 'back and forth' with the views of key Member States: after all, there would have been little point in producing a draft of a Constitutional Treaty that would have been utterly unacceptable (even if only in parts) to certain Member States. This would have required issues to be reopened at the IGC stage, with the risk either of many more changes via horse-trading, or else unravelling the whole document. In this regard, the parallel with the acceptability to the European Council of Commission proposals under the EC's legislative procedures is a good one: while the European Council has no *formal institutional* role in the actual EC legislative process, nevertheless it is obvious that its members' positions on the Council (which can always prevent the adoption of EC legislation) require the broad political stance of the European Council to be taken seriously in the Commission's proposals for legislation. In the CFE, the Convention found itself in a not dissimilar position *vis-à-vis* the publicly expressed views of the larger Member States: this was naturally enhanced when such national political heavyweights as Fischer and de Villepin joined the Convention fray.

Nevertheless, one 'inside' account[30] of the Convention process has highlighted significant shortcomings of the way in which the enterprise was pursued, which deserve to be taken seriously given that the author (Gisela Stuart) was at the time both a UK MP and a member of the Praesidium of the CFE. Her basic criticisms related to a number of topics. First, they concerned presumptions that were made

---

[26] Craig, (2004) (n. 19, above), 668–669.

[27] *Ibid.*, 669.

[28] See, eg, Rasmussen (2005) (n. 24, above), 145: 'as late as May 2003, after 15 months of Convention-time and less than a month before the deadline, the Convention's crucial proposals about the institutional issues had not really reached the floor of the Convention'.

[29] For a similar conclusion concerning the role of the 'leadership' and Secretariat in the Convention that drafted the EU's Charter of Fundamental Rights (which could have served as a prescient prediction for the course of the CFE), see de Búrca (2001) (n. 14, above), 134–135.

[30] Stuart (2003) (n. 24, above).

in steering the discussions: of the inviolability of the *acquis communautaire*, of the need to find ways to do more on a European level and of the appropriateness of drafting a 'Constitution' to fulfil the mandate of the Laeken Declaration.[31] Second, she expressed misgivings about the power wielded by the 'elite' on the Praesidium, not least due to the difficulties in coordinating discussions among the national parliamentarians to try to come to some consensus view.[32] Third, the procedures and operation of the CFE came in for heavy criticism. In particular, the time frames involved in the receipt and consideration of documents, allied to the absence (until the closing stages of the CFE) of simultaneous translation led to the passage of 'large parts of the text . . . without detailed discussion', even in the Praesidium itself.[33] Also, the way in which 'consensus' was 'achieved' in both the Praesidium and the CFE seemed to have the character of having been 'declared' to exist by the President and recorded by the Secretariat, reflecting deals struck by various Member States in the late stages of the CFE rather than deliberations within the Praesidium or the full Convention.[34]

Thus, on the CFE itself, one may conclude that the method itself seemed to have much to commend it, building as it did on the generally well-received model of the body that had prepared the EU's Charter of Fundamental Rights. Certain aspects of the CFE's operation were encouraging, particularly with regard to the availability of documentation and the possibility for external contributions via the CFE's website. However, criticisms can be levelled at the practical operation of the CFE, and while some of the difficulties may be acknowledged to be inherent in the operation of a process involving such complex and finely balanced issues, others are less easy to explain away as the necessary price of this new way to prepare the ground for an IGC.

Convention plus referendum(s) plus IGC

The significance of the choice to set up a Convention to 'prepare' the ground for the IGC is clearly a topic that will continue to generate much debate and analysis[35] in the years to come, but Article 48 TEU meant that an IGC was required to give formal status to whatever came out of the CFE. As Piris has explained, subject

[31] *Ibid.*, 14–19.
[32] *Ibid.*, 17–18.
[33] *Ibid.*, 20–21.
[34] *Ibid.*, 23–25.
[35] For contributions on the topic to date, see (eg): G Milton and J Keller-Noëllet, with A Bartol-Saurel, *The European Constitution: its Origins, Negotiation and Meaning* (London: John Harper Publishing, 2005); P Norman, *The Accidental Constitution: the Making of Europe's Constitutional Treaty* (Brussels: EuroComment, 2nd edn., 2005); P Magnette and K Nicolaïdes, 'The European Convention: Bargaining in the Shadow of Rhetoric' (2004) 27 *West European Politics* 381; and J Jarlebring, 'Taking Stock of the European Convention: What Added Value does the Convention bring to the Process of Treaty Revision?' (2003) 4 *German Law Journal*, No. 8 (available at: http://www.germanlawjournal.com/pdf/Vol04No08/PDF_Vol_04_No_08_785-799_european_Jarlebring.pdf).

to 'a serious technical/legal review of the text',[36] the final IGC agreement in June 2004 'did not fundamentally modify the essential features of the draft proposed by the Convention'.[37] Indeed, there were strong voices throughout the IGC process that called for the CFE's draft to be left intact and discouraging attempts to re-open bargaining over the content of the Draft Constitutional Treaty.

However, perhaps the key issue (from both a practical and theoretical standpoint) is the marriage of the Convention method with the requirement of a further stage of approval of the output of the Convention. In particular, the significant element was in the form, not (just) of an IGC, but of national ratification processes which required (or adopted) a referendum to secure national constitutional approval for the TCE. It could be suggested that this was a further response to the Laeken goals of transparency, democracy and the involvement of EU citizens in the process, while also permitting the electorate a vote in a way that avoided the shackles of standard parliamentary democracy (executive-legislative connections and control over the political agenda) and specifically encouraging the citizenry to engage with the questions raised and fostering increased communication on the topics at stake, both to the electorate and between groups in different Member States.[38] All of this could be argued to enhance the legitimacy of the output of the CFE further, were such votes to secure agreement with its text, the TCE.

There are, however, those who have questioned whether choosing to pursue national ratification of the TCE via referendum would really bring substantial legitimacy benefits at all.[39] In part, this is argued to be due to the different legal force, legal bases and specific criteria (on matters such as minimum turnout requirements) that will arise from having referendums at Member State level,[40] rather than an EU-wide referendum. A further criticism is that most of the referendums were initiated and approved by the executive or by the majority in the relevant national Parliament, rather than 'bottom-up', as a result of a citizens' initiative or the actions of a Parliamentary minority: this is said to reduce the preventive function of such a referendum,[41] and it is interesting to note that in the Netherlands the Prime Minister was opposed to holding even a consultative referendum on the TCE, yet the Dutch Parliament insisted that a referendum be held and passed an *ad hoc* law to ensure that this would take place. Finally, if one accepts that the key determinant of the

---

[36] One problem which the Working Party of Legal Experts uncovered was that 'the Commission would have legally "disappeared" upon entry into force of the Constitution, due to the absence of proper transitional provisions' (!): Piris (2006), at 53.

[37] *Ibid.*, at 50.

[38] A Peters, 'Referendums on the Constitutional Treaty 2004: A Citizens' Voice?' (hereinafter 'Peters, (2005)') in D Curtin, AE Kellermann and S Blockmans (eds.), *The EU Constitution: The Best Way Forward?* (The Hague: TMC Asser Instituut, 2005) (hereinafter, 'Curtin *et al* (2005)'), 39–57, at 47–49.

[39] Peters, (2005) (n. 38, above).

[40] Including, of course, the point that citizens in some Member States will not have any such 'direct democratic voice' at all, due to their country's provisions and position on the ratification of the TCE.

[41] Peters, (2005) (n. 38, above), 53–56.

legitimacy of constitutional arrangements is their acceptance by society and the proof of the quality, efficacy and (perhaps) efficiency of their performance (output legitimacy),[42] then any number of referendums will not add to the overall legitimacy of the TCE.

Thus, while the ideas behind the composition of the CFE, the organization of its work and its output have attracted praise from many quarters, it should be noted that both the theoretical basis of the overall procedure for securing the relevant Treaty amendments and the practical putting into operation of the Convention method have also been subject to criticism as a mechanism for effecting future EU constitutional change. Criticisms have also been made of the next possible method for developing the EU's constitutional order—judgments issued by the European Court of Justice. Such concerns have been expressed both in theoretical terms and in the practical consequences of its judgments—it is to this method that we now turn.

Judicial Decisions

One clear possible device for the development and change of constitutional rules and principles is formed by court judgments. This mechanism is naturally one with which the English common lawyer is particularly familiar,[43] but it has also been a key element that has characterized the establishment and development of many important principles in the legal order of the European Community.[44] The principles of the supremacy and[45] the direct effect[46] (including the development of the so-called vertical direct effect of directives)[47] of Community law arose out of the interpretation by the European Court of Justice (hereinafter, 'ECJ') of the scope, wording and purpose of the E(E)C Treaty, as does the principle of Member State liability for sufficiently serious breaches of Community Law.[48] The doctrine of the

---

[42] *Ibid.*, 56–57.

[43] For a brief summary see, eg, AW Bradley & KR Ewing, *Constitutional and Administrative Law* (Harlow (England): Pearson Longman, 14th edn., 2006), at 16–17.

[44] See, generally, H Rasmussen, *The European Court of Justice* (Copenhagen: Gadjura, 1998), R Dehousse, *The European Court of Justice—The Politics of Judicial Integration* (Basingstoke: Macmillan, 1998), esp. Ch. 2, and AM Arnull, *The European Union and its Court of Justice* (Oxford: OUP, 2006).

[45] Case 6/64 *Costa v ENEL* [1964] ECR 1141 and Case 106/77 *Amministrazione delle Finanze dello Stato v Simmenthal SpA* [1978] ECR 629.

[46] Case 26/62 *NV Algemene Transport—en Expeditie Onderneming van Gend en Loos v Nederlandse Administratie der Belastingen* [1963] ECR 1. For detailed discussion, see (eg) S Prechal, *Directives in EC Law* (Oxford: OUP, 2nd edn., 2005) (hereinafter, 'Prechal, (2005)'), chs. 6, 7 and esp. 9.

[47] See, *inter alia*, Case 152/84 *Marshall v Southampton and South West Area Health Authority (Teaching) (Marshall (No. 1))* [1986] ECR 723, Case C-188/89 *Foster v British Gas plc* [1990] ECR I-3133 and Case C-91/92 *Dori v Recreb Srl* [1994] ECR I-3325: again, see Prechal (2005) (n. 46, above), chs. 6 and 9 and the references cited therein for discussion.

[48] Cases C-6 and 9/90 *Francovich and Bonifaci v Italy* [1991] ECR I-5357 and Cases C-24 and 48/93 *Brasserie du Pêcheur SA v Germany* and *R v Secretary of State for Transport ex parte Factortame Ltd.* [1996] ECR I-1029. For discussion, see (eg) Prechal (2005) (n. 46, above), Ch. 10.

pre-emption of Member State law by EC law has a similar history.[49] Overall, the 'constitutionalisation'[50] of the EC Treaty has been developed in no small part through the judgments of the ECJ.

An example *par excellence* of this mechanism of constitutional evolution is the infusion of the EC legal order with fundamental rights principles, via the case law of the ECJ and, latterly, the Court of First Instance (hereinafter, 'CFI'). While academic opinion has differed[51] on the reasons behind the ECJ's development of the EC fundamental rights jurisprudence, the effect of this case law has essentially been to incorporate fundamental rights principles in the EC legal order through the device of drawing inspiration from the 'constitutional traditions common to the Member States',[52] as well as various international human rights instruments,[53] including in particular the European Convention for the Protection of Human Rights and Fundamental Freedoms ('ECHR').[54] These principles have assumed significance for the interpretation of EC legislation and the provisions of the EC Treaty and play an increasingly important role in delimiting the scope of legitimate Member State action within the field of EC law (whether when implementing EC legislation or when derogating from EC rules, such as the free movement provisions). This constitutional evolution has continued since the adoption of the EU's Charter of Fundamental Rights in the year 2000. While the Charter has yet to be accorded any clear legal status (the Nice European Council in December 2001 merely 'proclaimed' the Charter) and the ECJ has yet to mention it in any judgment, both a number of Advocates General and the CFI have referred to the Charter, whether as indicative of a common agreed position among the Member

---

[49] See, eg, Opinion 1/75 *Re Understanding on a Local Costs Standard* [1975] ECR 1355 and Case 16/83 *Criminal Proceedings against Prantl* [1984] ECR 1299. For discussion, see E Cross, 'Pre-emption of Member State law in the European Economic Community: A Framework for Analysis' (1992) 29 *CMLRev.* 447 and S Weatherill, *Law and Integration in the European Union* (Oxford: Clarendon Press, 1995), Ch. 5 (esp. 135–144).

[50] GF Mancini, 'The Making of a Constitution for Europe' (1989) 26 *CMLRev.* 595 (reprinted in GF Mancini, *Democracy and Constitutionalism in the European Union* (Oxford: Hart Publishing, 2000), Ch. 1). See, also, on the ECJ's role in the infusion of the EC (legal) order with democratic principles, GF Mancini and D Keeling, 'Democracy and the European Court of Justice' (1994) 57 *MLR* 175.

[51] Compare, eg, J Coppel and A O'Neill, 'The European Court of Justice: Taking Rights Seriously?' (1992) 29 *CMLRev.* 669 and the response by JHH Weiler and N Lockhart, '"Taking Rights Seriously" Seriously: The European Court and its Fundamental Rights Jurisprudence' (1995) 32 *CMLRev.* 51 (Part I) and 579 (Part II); see, generally, FG Jacobs, 'Human rights in the European Union: the role of the Court of Justice' (2001) 26 *ELRev.* 331.

[52] Case 11/70 *Internationale Handelsgesellschat v Einfuhr—under Vorratstelle für Getreide under Futtermittel* [1970] ECR 1125, esp. para. 4.

[53] Case 4/73 *Nold v Commission* [1974] ECR 491. Particular reference has been made to the UN's International Covenant on Civil and Political Rights: see Case 374/87 *Orkem v Commission* [1989] ECR 3283.

[54] Case 36/75 *Rutili v Ministre de l'Intérieur* [1975] ECR 1219 and Case C-299/95 *Kremzow v Austria* [1997] ECR I-2629.

States on fundamental rights and values in the EC[55] or as even an indirect source for determining the relevant fundamental rights in the EC legal order.[56]

In providing a brief assessment of the use of judicial decisions as a means of constitutional development, let us take the example of the ECJ's jurisprudence on fundamental rights. Decisions by the courts can form a highly reactive and evolutionary process, particularly in terms of the recognition of (ranges of) such rights as 'fundamental' and the sufficiently authoritative nature of the relevant *source* of such rights (as discussed above). Formal *EC law* authority for such rights is then acquired by virtue of a declaration by the ECJ or CFI that they form a part of the EC legal order.

Yet, as a result of the incremental nature of this process, there will always be some degree of uncertainty as to exactly which rights were/are covered, and how 'fundamental' each right is (particularly in situations where such rights clash—eg internal market rights versus ECHR-inspired fundamental rights (such as freedom of assembly and expression).[57] These difficulties lead some[58] to conclude that the need for a written charter of such rights was strong, hence the creation of the EU Charter of Fundamental Rights—although its current legal status has done nothing to alleviate these uncertainties and has, indeed, merely added to them, providing as it has another source of 'inspiration' for the development of EC jurisprudence (for the CFI and the Advocates General, at least).

These issues of the judicial role in adopting and developing constitutional principles can naturally also be linked to broader debates concerning the desirability and legitimacy of the ECJ's so-called 'judicial activism', although this field of study also extends further to encompass other questions of pseudo-'policy-making' by the ECJ, particularly in fields of social and commercial relevance. It is beyond the scope of this Chapter to engage with this literature here, but it should simply be noted that the appropriateness of reliance upon the judicial role to establish and develop constitutional law at the EC/EU level must be assessed in this broader context.[59]

---

[55] See, eg, the Opinion of Advocate General Tizzano in Case C-173/99 *R v Secretary of State for Trade and Industry ex parte BECTU* [2001] ECR I-4881, paras. 26–28.

[56] Case T-177/01 *Jégo-Quéré v Commission* [2002] ECR II-2365, in which Art. 47 of the Charter was specifically invoked to bolster arguments in favour of providing an effective judicial remedy by relaxing the rules on *locus standi* under Art. 230(4) EC. The CFI's ruling was later overturned by the ECJ in Case C-263/02 P *Commission v Jégo-Quéré* [2004] ECR I-3425, which made no explicit reference to the Charter in its judgment. For discussion, see A Albors-Llorens, 'The Standing of Private Parties to Challenge Community Measures: Has the European Court of Justice Missed the Boat?' [2003] *CLJ* 72.

[57] See, eg, Case C112/00 *Eugen Schmidberger, Internationale Transporte und Planzüge v Austria* [2003] ECR I-5659 and Case C-36/02 *Spielhallen- und Automatenaufstellungs-GmbH v Oberbürgermeisterin der Bundesttadt Bonn* [2004] ECR I-9609.

[58] See, eg, T Eicke 'The European Charter of Fundamental Rights—unique opportunity or unwelcome distraction?' (2000) 5 *EHRLR* 280. Others, meanwhile, would continue to question whether the creation of such an EU Bill of Rights was such a high priority, when the alternative of facilitating accession to the ECHR could have been pursued: see, eg, JHH Weiler 'Does the European Union Truly Need a Charter of Rights?' (2000) 6 *ELJ* 95.

[59] From a wide literature, see: H Rasmussen, *On Law and Policy in the Court of Justice* (The Hague: Martinus Nijhoff, 1986); TC Hartley, 'The European Court, Judicial Objectivity and the Constitution

Ultimately, however, any constitutional development which is specifically precluded by Treaty provisions,[60] or requires an explicit Treaty basis to move forward,[61]
simply cannot be effected by means of judicial decisions on cases that come before
the EC courts. Furthermore, the courts must await cases before their pronouncements can have legal effect: they do not pick and choose particular issues that come
before them in the way that a politically-driven law-making process can and does.
Whether the ECJ (and CFI) have been too bold or too timid in identifying the
boundaries set by these kinds of constraints is a matter for conjecture, but this
methodological limitation means that EU constitutional reform via judicial decision will, in the future, be at best only an ancillary and/or residual (yet nevertheless important interstitial) device.

Inter-Institutional Agreements and Other Devices Adopted by the EC Institutions

There are numerous past examples in EEC, EC and EU practice of resort to Inter-
Institutional Agreements (IIAs)[62] and other institutional legal acts, declarations
and practices to put in place systems of great institutional and constitutional significance. For example, the early development of the principle of subsidiarity stems
from a fairly detailed specification of basic principles and guidelines laid down in
the Conclusions of the Presidency from the Edinburgh European Council (11–12
December 1992)[63] and was fleshed out by an Inter-Institutional Declaration of the
European Parliament, the Council and the Commission 10 months later.[64] Before
its entry into the Treaty framework (in what is now Article 255 EC), the question
of access to documents held by the European institutions was first raised by a
Declaration attached to the Treaty of Maastricht[65] and was then dealt with by means

---

of the European Union' (1996) 112 *LQR* 95 and *cf.* AM Arnull, 'The European Court of Justice and
Judicial Objectivity: A Reply to Professor Hartley' (1996) 112 *LQR* 411; A-M Slaughter, A Stone Sweet
and JHH Weiler, *The European Courts and National Courts: Doctrine and Jurisprudence* (Oxford: Hart
Publishing, 1997); and A Stone Sweet, *The Judicial Construction of Europe* (Oxford: OUP, 2004).

[60] This was the key reason given by the ECJ in its judgment in Case C-263/02 P *Commission v
Jégo-Quéré* (n. 56, above) for refusing to relax the criteria for *locus standi* under Art. 230 EC: see para. 36
of the judgment.

[61] Eg accession by the EC/EU to the ECHR: see Opinion 2/94 *Re Accession of the Community to
the European Human Rights Convention* [1996] ECR I-1759.

[62] For a useful recent analysis and many helpful references, see I Eiselt and P Slominski, 'Sub-
Constitutional Engineering: Negotiation, Content, and Legal Value of Interinstitutional Agreements in
the EU' (2006) 12 *ELJ* 209 (hereinafter, 'Eiselt and Slominski (2006)').

[63] Reproduced in D Pollard and M Ross, *European Community Law: Text and Materials* (London:
Butterworths, 1994), 52–56.

[64] Inter-Institutional Declaration of 25 October 1993 of the European Parliament, the Council
and the Commission on Democracy, Transparency and Subsidiarity [1993] OJ C329/133.

[65] Declaration 17 on the right of access to information, attached to the Final Act of the TEU
(7 February 1992, available at: http://europa.eu.int/en/record/mt/final.html).

of Code,[66] which was then enshrined in formal Decisions by both the Council[67] and the Commission.[68] Finally, and perhaps most significantly in practical terms, the budgetary arrangements of the EU rely heavily upon decisions reached at various European Councils[69] and IIAs[70] to ensure their (relatively) smooth operation.[71]

These developments are often subsequently enshrined in Treaty provisions (see Article 255 EC on transparency and access to documents and the current Protocol on the application of the principles of subsidiarity and proportionality)[72] or legal acts (see the legislation on access to documents)[73] by later constitutional changes. However, this does not prevent them from having some degree of constitutional significance in their own right, which can continue to be important even if not transformed into binding legal rules.

IIAs obviously may not amend primary or secondary EC legal provisions but they may have legal effects that bind the parties to such agreements and create potentially enforceable expectations as to the course of conduct to be adopted by the institution(s) in question,[74] although this latter effect will be easier to establish where there is clear intention on the part of the institutions to create a legally enforceable regime and/or where there is explicit Treaty authorization for the adoption of an IIA.[75] Such legal effects may also be felt by, and be of benefit to, third parties to the IIA in certain circumstances, although this will obviously be dependent upon the extent to which the IIA lays down clear and detailed provisions.

Using the device of an IIA (or other Inter-Institutional declaration or statement) has the advantage of allowing the institutions to put flesh on the bare bones of basic points agreed at an IGC, a European Council meeting or even *ad hoc* in response to particular developments. If they endeavour to achieve precisely specified goals,

---

[66] Developed by the Commission: see COM(1993) 258 [1993] OJ C166/5. For the current legislation in this field, see n. 158, below.

[67] Council Decision 93/731 of 20 December 1993 [1993] OJ L340/43.

[68] Commission Decision 94/90 of 8 February 1994 [1994] OJ L46/58.

[69] See, eg, the so-called 'Delors II' package agreed at the Edinburgh European Council: accessible from http://www.ena.lu/europe/european-union/conclusions-edinburgh-european-council-1992.htm.

[70] See the Inter-Institutional Agreements between the European Parliament, the Council and the Commission on budgetary discipline and improvement of the budgetary procedure of: 29 October 1993 [1993] OJ C331/1 and 6 May 1999 [1999] OJ C172/1 (also available at: http://europa.eu/eur-lex/en/treaties/selected/livre612.html). See also the Inter-Institutional Agreement of 13 October 1998 between the European Parliament, the Council and the Commission on legal bases and implementation of the budget [1998] OJ C344/1.

[71] For substantive discussion, see I Begg, 'Future Fiscal Arrangements of the European Union' (2004) 41 *CMLRev.* 775.

[72] Protocol 30 annexed to the EC Treaty (first adopted at the Amsterdam IGC): text available at [1997] OJ C340/1 and http://europa.eu/eur-lex/en/treaties/dat/amsterdam.html#0105010010.

[73] For the current legislation in this field, see n. 158, below.

[74] See, for discussion, F Snyder, 'Interinstitutional Agreements: Forms and Constitutional Limitations' in G Winter (ed.), *Sources and Categories of European Union Law* (Baden-Baden: Nomos, 1996), 453.

[75] Eiselt and Slominski (2006), 211–213, citing in particular (at 215–219) the establishment of the Ombudsman in the aftermath of the Maastricht Treaty.

then their outcome will often secure relatively clear and precise results that genuinely shape the future conduct of the institutions involved. Further, the negotiations between the institutions on the conclusion of IIAs are often relatively transparent and allow a fair grasp of the issues at stake to be clear to the outside observer. However, the ability of such outsiders to influence and contribute to such negotiations is clearly limited, while the impact of such IIAs may be far less striking where the relevant subject-matter lacks precision or is so controversial that reaching workable consensus between the institutions proves too difficult.

Having canvassed the basic possible methods by which constitutional change and reform might be developed in the EU, we can now try to draw together these strands to provide a framework for the analysis of future proposals for such reform.

A Possible Framework for Analysis

While this is not the place to define or analyse in detail the notion of legitimacy and its application to the decision-making and, indeed, constitution-making processes of the EU, it may be useful to set out one way in which we might approach the question of how legitimate each method for effecting constitutional change in the EU might be.[76] Clearly, other models can also be devised that give greater or less weight to various factors: here, it is assumed that each of the relevant methods satisfies the criterion of 'legality', in the sense that its appropriate procedures have been followed correctly. Broadly speaking, 'input legitimacy' refers to the source and quality of the inputs into the process in question,[77] 'output legitimacy' encompasses the question of whether or not the product of the process is acceptable and convincing to those subject to that product (here, the relevant rules)[78] and 'social legitimacy' embodies the idea of a direct linkage between the citizens in a society and the institutions and processes that apply to them.[79]

Table 3 (below) provides a representation of the range of some of the issues at stake, which may perhaps form a helpful framework to apply when considering the analysis of proposed constitutional changes. The content given to each cell in the table is merely the present author's indication of some of the ways in which the

---

[76] From the literature on the legitimacy of such techniques and processes, for a useful summary see D Beetham and C Lord, *Legitimacy and the European Union* (London: Longman, 1998), esp. Ch. 1.

[77] Including relatively direct democratic links in the form of Parliamentary representatives and their involvement in the process and indirect links via the role of Member State governments in the Council which were then democratically legitimised at their own domestic level. See, eg, H Abromeit and S Wolf, 'Will the Constitutional Treaty Contribute to the Legitimacy of the European Union?' (2005) 9 *EioP*, No. 11 (available at: http://eipo.or.at/eiop/texte/2005-011a.htm).

[78] Also sometimes known as 'technocratic legitimacy': for discussion, see, eg, C Lord and P Magnette, 'Notes Towards a General Theory of Legitimacy in the European Union' (ESRC 'One Europe or Several?' Working Paper 39/02, 2002; available at: http://www.one-europe.ac.uk/pdf/w39lord.pdf).

[79] See, eg, JHH Weiler, 'After Maastricht: Community legitimacy in post-1992 Europe' in WJ Adams (ed.), *Singular Europe: Economy and Polity of the European Community after 1992* (Ann Arbor: University of Michigan Press, 1992), 11–41.

Table Three *A framework for analyzing different methods for effecting constitutional reform in the European Union*

	Input legitimacy	Output legitimacy	Social legitimacy	'Pragmatics' – practical chances of success	Possible areas responding to methodology?
'Normal' Treaty amendment procedures (IGC, etc)	*Yes*: Role for MS governments *No*: Lack of transparency, accountability, input from other sources	*Yes*: If–quality, clarity, comprehensible *No*: If–unworkable, deviating from stated positions or goals, etc.	*Yes*: If high trust in national leaders *No*: If seen as a *fait accompli*, unclear and damaging national interests	Dependent upon issues involved, legitimacy (perceptions) and possible need for national referendums	Any now (after referendum experiences re TCE)? Perhaps re minor technical changes that can clearly be explained as such
Convention Process	*Yes*: Some enhancement over standard IGC *No*: Qs of composition, procedure, 'genuine' debate; still subject to IGC approval	*Yes*: Fair degree of praise for many key reforms *No*: Sheer bulk and complexity of full consolidated text, fears re clarity and direction of some reforms	*Yes*: Some clear input from national representatives *No*: Lack of profile, no widespread appreciation of function of CFE, still led to IGC	After a decent interval and with a clear mandate (possibly with reformed procedures), certainly a possibility	Drafting of a possible replacement for, or amendment to, the TCE (at some future date)

	Yes: Expertise / No: Democratic credentials	Yes: If–quality, clarity / No: If–usurping functions or perceived as over-'activist'	Yes: If–respect for judiciary / No: If– ECJ/CFI seen as empire-building or out of touch	Yes: Legal force / No: Reactive only	Many and varied: dependent upon cases that arise
Judicial decisions	*Yes*: Expertise *No*: Democratic credentials	*Yes*: If–quality, clarity *No*: If–usurping functions or perceived as over-'activist'	*Yes*: If–respect for judiciary *No*: If– ECJ/CFI seen as empire-building or out of touch	*Yes*: Legal force *No*: Reactive only	Many and varied: dependent upon cases that arise
Amending Institutional practice(s)	*Yes*: Response within institutions' own control *No*: No formal external input	*Yes*: If–reasons given are clearly present in the changes made *No*: If–changes are a sop or subject to many exceptions	*Yes*: If–clear reasons given why, and not major changes *No*: Lack of decision-making transparency		
– Inter-Institutional Agreements				Reasonable	National Parliaments and subsidiarity mechanism
– Rules of Procedure				Progress already made in this direction	Transparency in proceedings (eg Council)

methods (and the issues that they raise) might be analysed, while acknowledging that others may take a different view.

With this background in mind, the next questions that must be addressed concern how the situation after the French and Dutch referendums might be addressed in terms of legal options and political possibilities. The latter dimension also requires consideration of the various reasons given for concern about the TCE in those negative referendums—these reasons will help to inform any plans about what the EU should do to address questions of institutional and constitutional reform in the future.

' "CRISIS" MANAGEMENT' STRATEGIES IN THE LIGHT OF THE RESULTS IN THE FRENCH AND DUTCH REFERENDUMS

'Crisis Management' Approaches

Some form of 'crisis'[80] in the delicate process of ratifying the TCE was foreseen in a number of quarters, even during the CFE and certainly during the abortive attempts to conclude the 2003 IGC at the December European Council of that year. While most predicted that the UK's announcement that it would hold a referendum would be the toughest hurdle, there was open discussion of building a mechanism into the ratification process to ensure that the TCE would not be prevented from entering into force by its rejection by one or two 'difficult' Member States.[81] In the event, these proposals did not find their way into the TCE and the unanimous ratification requirement of Article 48 TEU has governed the TCE ratification process. The only caveat to this is Declaration 30 'on the ratification of the Treaty establishing a Constitution for Europe', annexed to the Final Act of the IGC:

The Conference notes that, if two years after the signature of the Treaty establishing a Constitution for Europe, four fifths of the Member States have ratified it and one or more Member States have encountered difficulties in proceeding with ratification, the matter will be referred to the European Council.[82]

This is clearly not a crisis management strategy in itself, but rather an acknowledgment that there may well be a crisis that will need to be addressed by the European Council. As Table 1 shows, the 'four fifths' threshold has yet to be

---

[80] See, eg, the editorials in (2005) 42 *CMLRev.* 905 and (2006) 33 *LIEI* 101, which both speak openly of the situation of 'crisis' after the votes in the French and Dutch Referendums, and N Eschke and T Malick (eds.), *The European Constitution and its Ratification Crisis: Constitutional Debates in the EU Member States* (Bonn: Zentrum für Europäische Integrationsforschung, Discussion Paper C156, 2006; also available at: http://www.zei.de/download/zei_dp/dp_c156_eschke_malick.pdf) (hereinafter, 'Eschke and Malick, (2006)').

[81] See, for a summary, B de Witte, 'The Process of Ratification and the Crisis Options: A Legal Perspective' in Curtin *et al.* (2005) (hereinafter, 'de Witte (2005)'), 21–38, at 21–27.

[82] See the Treaty establishing a Constitution for Europe [2004] OJ C310/1 (accessible at: http://www.eur-lex.europa.eu/JOHtml.do?uri=OJ:C:2004:310:SOM:EN:HTML), at 464.

met (12 Member States have ratified the TCE, three have completed the national procedures but have yet (for various reasons) to lodge a formal instrument of ratification, two have rejected it and eight have yet to complete the necessary procedures (of which six seem to have postponed their procedures indefinitely, pending the outcome of the period of reflection)).

Legal position

This issue has been discussed carefully and in detail elsewhere, so for present purposes only a brief summary of the legal options open will be provided.[83] Essentially, first, neither a partial entry into force of the TCE nor treating the TCE as a 'refoundation' of the EU would be a legal option open to the Member States—the fact that the TCE seeks to amend provisions relating to a pre-existing international organization, which would amend the rights and responsibilities of the current Member States, prevents both of these possibilities (unless agreed unanimously by all Member States).

Second, the Member States could acknowledge that the current Treaty regime will govern the EU for the foreseeable future and that the TCE will not enter into force. Thus, the founding Treaties, as last amended by the Treaty of Nice and the various Accession Treaties of 2004, will apply, and any amendments to their operation will have to be made within the limits and under the powers that those Treaties provide. Such amendments might proceed by way of changes to rules of procedure, by the adoption of agreements between the EC institutions to act in a particular manner or by seeking closer cooperation among those Member States that wished to move in the direction of the TCE provisions. This last approach could be achieved either by using the provisions in the EC Treaty on enhanced cooperation[84] or by cooperation between Member States outside the EU institutions and framework.[85]

The third obvious possibility is to pursue consensus by some sort of renegotiation of the TCE, by whatever means seem most appropriate. This could, as with Maastricht and Nice, simply be a case of minor reassurances to clear up difficulties or confusions (say by the addition of Protocols or Declarations), or it could stretch to the full-blown and genuine renegotiation of the TCE, leading to perhaps significant substantive changes to the text. This could be accompanied by some provisional application of the TCE, at least regarding those parts of the Treaty that were

---

[83] This section draws heavily on the work of previous writers, particularly de Witte (2005), (n. 81, above), 21–38, but also J Shaw, 'What happens if the Constitutional Treaty is not ratified?' in I Pernice and J Zemanek (eds.), *The Treaty on a Constitution for Europe: Perspectives after the IGC 2004* (Baden-Baden: Nomos, 2005) (also available at: http://www.arena.uio.no/cidel/Shaw.pdf); and C Grant, *What Happens if Britain Votes No?* (London: Centre for European Reform, 2005).

[84] Articles 11 EC and 43 and 45 TEU: see, for discussion of these provisions post-Nice, J Shaw, 'Enhancing Co-operation after Nice: Will the Treaty do the Trick?' in M Andenas and JA Usher (eds.), *The Treaty of Nice and Beyond: Enlargement and Constitutional Reform* (Oxford: Hart Publishing, 2003), 207–237.

[85] Eg by concluding international agreements between those vanguard Member States: see, for discussion, B de Witte, 'Old-fashioned flexibility: International Agreements between Member States of the European Union' in G de Búrca and J Scott (eds.), *Constitutional Change in the EU: From Uniformity to Flexibility?* (Oxford: Hart Publishing, 2000), 31–58.

relatively uncontroversial, although this would have to go hand-in-hand with negoti-ations to conclude a permanent Treaty. This last element could be seen to overlap with elements of the second suggested approach to 'crisis management', in that provisional application and changes to the existing practice may well cover the same ground.

Fourth, and perhaps most momentously, the possibility has been mooted that one or more Member States which simply cannot agree to the TCE may withdraw from the EU, whether voluntarily (if agreed to by the other Member States) or if forced to do so by the remaining Member States. This latter approach could not be effected via exclusion of the reluctant Member State(s), but rather by the collective withdrawal of the other Member States and the founding of a new organization.[86]

This was the legal background to the political discussions that developed after the French and Dutch referendums, leading up to the Brussels European Council I in mid-June 2006. Those discussions were certainly wide-ranging and had occa-sionally engaging moments, but were perhaps most striking for their lack of par-ticularly high profile in the media and at the national political level. It is to some brief observations on the political and diplomatic discussions to which we now turn.

Political angles

(a) *'Factum est illud, fieri infectum non potest'*[87]
One element which has cast a long shadow over political and diplomatic discussion and debate since early June 2005 is that there is no way to turn back the clock and do things differently. One horse has bolted and it is far too late to shut the stable door—ratifications which have already been completed by some Member States (whether by Parliamentary vote or popular referendum) cannot simply be deemed not to have occurred. Second, a cat has well and truly been let out of the bag—for those Member States with no tradition of (or constitutional requirement for) refer-endums on such matters,[88] new vistas have been opened up. This is either because a Member State decided itself to subject the TCE to popular ratification, or (even if not the former) because the citizenry have seen that other countries *did* adopt that route and may suggest that it would somehow be disenfranchisement not to offer the same chance to them as well in any future ratification process.

However, there were reports of French overtures to Germany in early 2006, sug-gesting that the EU Charter of Fundamental Rights might be dropped from the TCE framework, paving the way to focus upon a pared down version of the TCE, perhaps for agreement during 2007.[89] This was one instance where something already on paper, and indeed the original result of an earlier Convention process, seemed at least to be open to discussion (although there is no sign of this proposal

---

[86] See, eg, E Philippart and M Sie Dhian Ho, 'Flexibility and the New Constitutional Treaty of the European Union' in J Pelkmans *et al.* (eds.), *Nederland en de Europese grondwet* (Amsterdam: Amsterdam University Press, 2003), 137ff.

[87] 'Done is done, it cannot be made undone': TM Plautus, *Aulularia* (London: Penguin, 1965).

[88] For a helpful survey of the bases for referendums on the TCE in the various EU Member States, see Peters, (2005), (n. 38, above), 40–45.

[89] S Taylor, 'Sarkozy plots with Berlin to salvage constitution', *European Voice*, 6 April 2006.

in the eventual European Council conclusions from the Brussels summit on 15–16 June 2006).

(b) 'Aegroto, dum anima est, spes esse dicitur'[90]

As one Dutch journalist has wryly remarked, the '*grondwet wil maar niet sterven*',[91] despite (obviously premature, not to say exaggerated) proclamations of its death by various politicians and newspapers[92] in the time since the Dutch referendum result. In many ways, this should not be overly surprising—the motivations behind the creation of the CFE, identified by the European Council at Nice and Laeken, still resonate strongly and the amount of time, money and effort invested in the CFE and its output militate against simply ditching the various provisions of the TCE. While the TCE may ultimately prove very difficult to adopt in its present form without some amendments, subtractions or additions, much of what it has come to represent will be at the forefront of any future thinking, discussions and negotiations in this area. Life will not ebb away from what some have likened to a coma patient,[93] at least not while those in control of the life support instruments continue to reflect upon how to resolve what to do about the patient's legacy.

(c) 'Ich werde dieses Volk vor seinen Spiegel zwingen, sein Lachen wird ihm gefrieren'[94]

In periods of reflection, one is forced to take a good look at oneself, and it is clear that this was (on the face of it, at least) what the European Council intended when it proclaimed just such a period of reflection at its meeting on 17–18 June 2005.

In this case, however, it is not 'the people' who are being forced to take the hardest look at themselves, but rather the reactions of the French and Dutch people (at least) that have forced the political and bureaucratic 'elites' (ie the leaders of the Member States and their governments, the Commission and the European Parliament) to do so. In spite of the effort made to publicize the issues discussed by the CFE, in spite of the desire (expressly stated in the Laeken Declaration) to engage with the views and concerns of the citizens of the EU about its institutions and their operation, about future enlargement and about the EU's policies and role going forward, and in spite of the design of not one but two Conventions (on the Charter and the

---

[90] 'It is said that for a sick man, there is hope as long as there is life': MT Cicero, *Ad Atticum* (Cambridge (Mass.): Harvard University Press, 1999).

[91] 'Constitution just does not want to die': P de Hen, 'Grondwet wil maar niet sterven' (29 May 2006, available at http://www.elsevier.nl/opinie/commentaar-artikel/asp/artnr/100473/index.html).

[92] See, eg, *The Guardian*, 4 June 2005.

[93] See, eg, the editorial in (2006) 33 *LIEI* 101, and the recent publication of the House of Commons Foreign Affairs Committee, *Developments in the European Union* (Sixth Report of the Session 2005–2006, HC678, 26 July 2006; available at: http://www.publications.parliament.uk/pa/cm200506/cmselect/cmfaff/768/768.pdf), 20–24. The MPs on the Committee 'recommend that the Government encourage its European counterparts . . . explicitly to abandon the Treaty as a package, in the interest of making progress on some of the real and important issues which are at present caught up in the paralysis created by its rejection' (*ibid.*, para. 64).

[94] 'I will force these people [to stand] in front of their mirror[s]: their smile will freeze on their lips': M Frisch, *Andorra* (London: Methuen, 2001).

Table Four *Scenarios for a (new) (Constitutional) Treaty for the EU. (Based upon information in European Voice, with additions.)*

Year	2006		2007		2008		2009	
Presidency	Austria	Finland	Germany	Portugal	Slovenia	France	Czech Republic	Sweden
'Period of reflection'		**November:** Original deadline for report on ratification, etc.	Presidency to draw up road-map	Earliest date to start discussions for new negotiations for reform			General target to adopt and implement institutional reforms during this calendar year	
New accessions (#s of MEPs)				*Bulgaria and Romania join (at latest in 2008)* (# of MEPs up to 785)			European Elections (# of MEPs cut back to 736)	
National elections			**May:** French Presidential election; Dutch general election				**May:** Possible UK general election	
Plans:								
European Parliament		Parliamentary & citizens' fora to debate the way ahead	After results of the debate, take decision on the way ahead				Adoption of a New Treaty	
Barroso		Focus on policy issues	Messina II declaration on EU values and objectives		Review clause in EU budget		New Treaty adopted and ratified	
France [Sarkozy]		Apply changes that do not require new Treaty (JHA, Council Transparency)				[(Sarkozy) Negotiation of trimmed-down Treaty; secure better EU operation (QMV, co-decision, permanent Council President)]		

Merkel/Chirac	[Hints at dropping Charter of FRs and paring down TCE]	Review of the TCE	Concrete decision to be taken
PRESIDENCY CONCLUSIONS	– Pursue measures to enhance functioning of the under the existing Treaties;	– Presidency report to European Council (re TCE and future developments);	Steps to 'continue reform' (or at least decide on the basis therefore)
(16 June 2006)	– Debate on all aspects of further enlargements (Dec 2006).	– Adopt political declaration (Berlin 25–3–07) re Europe's values & ambitions.	to have been taken by the end of 2008.

CFE) that were intended to facilitate that engagement, the EU still seems some distance away from securing popular and public debate on, and support for, institutional change.

In the end, what must now be seen as the *first* 'period of reflection' led to a decision not to decide anything yet, but rather that something should be decided by a certain time (preferably, it seems, under the next German Presidency). In the interests of economy of space, Table 4 (above) provides a summary of the various options mooted and discussed and the basic outcome of the European Council in Brussels in June 2006.

'Lost among Echoes of Things Not There?'[95] Reasons behind the 'No' Votes and their Significance for the Road Ahead

It is obviously difficult to gain any robustly verifiable picture of the major driving forces behind the French and Dutch referendum 'No' votes, and in any assessment of the current position concerning views on the EU, one must also remember that significant proportions voted in favour of ratifying the TCE. However, if future constitutional changes are to be made (whether in the form of the TCE or in some other form (or by some other route(s)), an understanding of what needs to be explained, communicated and amended will be vital. This is especially important if (as seems the current trend) a number of the elements of the TCE are to be introduced by methods not requiring Treaty amendment (see heading 'Key Substantive Topics for Consideration' below). This is because a clear answer must be prepared to the question: 'why are the EU institutions simply going ahead and implementing the TCE's provisions anyway, even in the absence of ratification by all Member States?' (This ratification will, of course, in a number of cases also require popular consent.) Any answer to this question must be able to show that the decision to make such changes is based upon introducing those elements from the TCE that specifically *address* the concerns raised by those who were opposed to the EU that they felt would result from accepting the changes to be made by the TCE. Otherwise, the EU and its institutions run the serious risk of appearing to be treating the 'No' votes in the French and Dutch referendums as simply the 'wrong' answers to the question. Indeed, to appear to take this view flies in the face of the substance of the Laeken Declaration, which led to the Convention on the Future of Europe and the TCE in the first place:

Within the Union, the European institutions must be brought closer to its citizens. Citizens undoubtedly support the Union's broad aims,[96] but they . . . want the European institutions

---

[95] Peter Gabriel, 'Humdrum' (Track 5, *Peter Gabriel* (Atlantic/Wea, 1977)). The present author has used this description in a number of talks on the TCE, trying to clarify what the outcome of the CFE and the subsequent IGC had actually agreed, and what it had not. Perhaps, however, a modification is in order, to acknowledge that many concerns were in fact lost among echoes of things 'already there', in the sense that the vast bulk of the pre-existing Treaties would be left intact by the TCE.

[96] This claim would no doubt be castigated by some as presumptuous at best, even at the time of Laeken.

to be less unwieldy, rigid and, above all, more efficient and open. . . . [They] feel that deals are all too often cut out of their sight and they want better democratic scrutiny.[97]

As one might perhaps have predicted,[98] many of the concerns that were cited by those voters willing to state that they had voted 'No' related to matters that were only loosely related (if at all) to the TCE itself. They can be divided into a number of basic groups.

One group concerns the discovery of principles and rules that had long been a part of the EC legal order, whether explicitly laid down in the Treaties or developed by the ECJ as inherent to the system that the founding Treaties had created. For example, concerning the former, complaints have been made by some in France about the focus on economic liberalism and free trade at the expense of more 'social' concerns. Concerning the latter, meanwhile, the principle of the supremacy of EC law provides an excellent illustration: this was highlighted by the decision of the CFE to attempt to codify the principle in Article I-6 TCE, and which led to heated debate, both academic and journalistic, on the proper scope of the principle (both as developed by the case law and as recorded in the TCE).[99]

A second group relates to public perception about the consequences of both implemented EU projects (like the single currency and the recent 2004 enlargement) and EU future plans (like the next planned enlargement). Thus, the spectre of the proverbial Polish plumber hovered over the French referendum debate and vote, while in the Netherlands the possibility that Turkey might be admitted to the EU[100] assumed a similar role. In both countries, these issues received extensive media coverage in the lead up to the respective votes, which naturally intensified in the Netherlands in the immediate aftermath of the French 'No' vote. Similarly, there was widespread Dutch media coverage of the introduction of the Euro, both on technical matters such as the Stability and Growth Pact and on consumer perceptions that the introduction of the Euro[101] had led to a general increase in the prices of goods. Recent survey data and

---

[97] Laeken Declaration (n. 9, above), section I.

[98] Whether from even a cursory scan of the numerous press reports on the referendums in both France and the Netherlands or on the basis of earlier work on voting practices in previous elections to the European Parliament. Cf., however, the recent comments of A Tompkins, 'Why Europe needs a new, democratic convention' (27 July 2006, available at: http://euobserver.com/9/22158/?rk=1), arguing that the content of the TCE itself was indeed central to the referendum outcomes.

[99] For discussion, see M Dougan, 'The Convention's Draft Constitutional Treaty: A "Tidying-Up Exercise" That Needs Some Tidying Up Of Its Own' (Federal Trust Online Paper 27/03, August 2003, available at http://www.fedtrust.co.uk/default.asp?pageid=267&mpageid=67&subid=277&groupid=6), esp. 7–8 and P Cramér, 'Does the Codification of the Principle of Supremacy Matter?' (2004–2005) 7 *CYELS* 57 (Ch. 4).

[100] Although it should be noted that if one were to take the number of people who gave possible Turkish accession to the EU as a reason for voting 'No' in the French referendum then (in spite of the extensive coverage and emphasis that the point received at the time) it only in fact amounted to between 6 and 7% of the French electorate that actually expressed that point of view: see Eschke and Malick, (2006), (n. 80, above), 17.

[101] Key reasons for which appeared to be: (a) a feeling that the Dutch Guilder had been undervalued when the Netherlands joined the Euro; (b) concern that other Member States were not respecting

analysis[102] from the Netherlands shows a strong correlation between negative perceptions about the Euro and the possible future expansion of the EU, on the one hand, and a 'No' vote in the TCE referendum, on the other. This held true in spite of two interesting trends. First, survey data from the end of 2004[103] indicated that 75 per cent of Dutch citizens felt that EU membership was a 'good thing' and that 73 per cent of the Dutch supported a constitution for Europe. Second, in Dutch national elections an overwhelming majority of voters have consistently voted for political parties that were strongly in favour of the TCE: of the 150 seats in Parliament, 128 belonged to parties that supported the ratification of the TCE, yet the survey showed that between 37 per cent and 63 per cent of voters who had voted for each of those parties had in fact rejected the TCE in the referendum.

This data could be said to be consistent with the argument which suggests that European issues are of little or no significance to voting decisions in national elections: indeed, research suggests that voting behaviour in European elections tends instead to be actuated by the national political arena and its concerns, rather than by any conscious choice as to European-level considerations.[104] Arts and van der Kolk, the authors of the recent Dutch survey referred to above, conclude that the 'gap between voters and parties will probably not disappear after the referendum. Even after the lively referendum campaign, most . . . respondents indicated that they were only 'somewhat interested' in European affairs. . . . [National] political parties do not have incentives to adjust their position on this issue; it will not change their electoral prospects.'[105] This echoes a point[106] made by Moravcsik and Nicolaïdis about the politics of referendums, which process they argue is based upon the ('naïve') theory that:

greater publicity and participation encourages public education, which brings about greater support for sensible policies. . . . The central problem is that the EU will not . . . become

---

the Stability and Growth Pact; and (c) the aforementioned consumer perception that retailers had used the introduction of the Euro as an excuse to raise prices.

[102] K Aarts and H van der Kolk, 'Understanding the Dutch "No": The Euro, the East, and the Elite' (2006) 39 *PS: Political Science and Politics* 243 (hereinafter 'Aarts & van der Kolk, (2006)'). See also K Aarts and H van der Kolk, *Nederlanders en europa: het referendum over de Europese grondwet* (Amsterdam: Bert Bakker, 2005).

[103] Published in Eurobarometer 62 (December 2004) (available at http://europa.eu.int/comm/public_opinion/archives/eb/eb62/eb62first_en.pdf), which interestingly records that, at the same point in time, 70% of the French citizens questioned were also in favour of a constitution for Europe.

[104] See, eg, C van der Eijk *et al*, *Choosing Europe? The European Electorate and National Policies in the Face of Union* (Ann Arbor: University of Michigan Press, 1996) and E Oppenhuis, *Voting Behaviour in Europe* (Amsterdam: Het Spinhuis, 1995), esp. at 90. It should also be noted that a plausible alternative explanation could be sought more squarely within the recent and momentous developments in Dutch domestic politics (in the wake of the murders of Pim Fortuin and Theo van Gogh on 6 May 2002 and 2 November 2004 respectively), which may have changed the way in which the electorate relates to political elites and the various types of societal interests that they have long been seen to represent.

[105] Aarts & van der Kolk, (2006), (n. 102, above), 245.

[106] See also the discussion in AC Johnston, 'Democracy in the European System: Towards a Critical Approach' (1998) 9 *ELSA SPEL* 77, esp. the text accompanying n. 86–91.

the primary forum to address the issues that matter most to voters .... Thus, the common voter cannot be convinced to educate themselves, deliberate or vote on the basis of EU policies.

The recent referendums demonstrate what happens when voters are encouraged to participate actively in a debate about abstract matters unconnected with issues of concrete concern. They simply import into EU debates gripes about national policies, even when they have almost nothing to do with ongoing EU policies, let alone the substance of the constitution.[107]

This foray into opinion polls, and the explanatory analysis of the data gathered therefrom, also bridges the gap to the next set of reasons behind the rejection of the TCE in France and the Netherlands.

This third cluster of reasons can be grouped around issues arising at the *national* level that were not related to the EU or the TCE in any meaningful way at all. This phenomenon is familiar from the numerous studies of voting issues and behaviour in European elections since 1979[108] and has already emerged from the discussion of the second set of reasons, above. Particular trends that have been noted in various countries in the past have included the phenomenon of a safe 'protest vote' against the incumbent government or leader, particularly if recent domestic political developments have rendered the leader or government unpopular.[109] Recent strong Conservative performances in the European Parliament elections in the UK have often been ascribed in no small part to this phenomenon and similar suggestions have been made in attempts to explain the rejection of the TCE in the French

[107] A Moravcsik and K Nicolaïdes, 'The Future of the Constitutional Process of the European Union' (input to the European Parliament Symposium, 13–14 October 2005) (hereinafter, 'Moravcsik & Nicolaïdes (2005)'), section 1.

[108] See, eg, the long-running series of volumes edited by Juliet Lodge: *The 2004 Elections to the European Parliament* (Basingstoke: Palgrave Macmillan, 2005); *The 1999 Elections to the European Parliament* (Basingstoke: Palgrave Macmillan, 2001); *Euro-Elections 1994* (London: Continuum International Publishing Group—Academi, 1995); *The 1989 Election of the European Parliament* (Basingstoke: Palgrave Macmillan, 1990) and *Direct Elections to the European Parliament, 1984* (Basingstoke: Palgrave Macmillan, 1986). See also van der Eijk *et al* and Oppenhuis, n. 104, above; and the discussion in Johnston (n. 106, above) in the text accompanying nn. 71–84 (headed 'The Dangers of Democratic Supranationalism').

[109] See, eg, for a contemporary reaction to the reasons behind the French 'No' vote, the comments of L Pech, 'Non-sense: France's No to the European Constitution' (31 May 2005, available at: http://jurist.law.pitt.edu/forumy/2005/05/non-sense-frances-no-to-european.php). He suggested that 'it may be argued that the French No vote is the ultimate fruit of a degenerate politico-administrative elite, which simply cannot escape from its roots of intellectual constraints in a bureaucratic model of economic growth (read stagnation) and social organisation (read bankrupted model). With the end of the Cold War and subsequently, the EU's enlargement to 25 Member States, it [has] been necessary to explain the rationale and the continuing benefits of European integration. Unfortunately, the European Community has been constantly used as a convenient fig leaf to hide national incompetence in tackling national issues.' Again, the theme of national political elites and their failure to explain the (and their) activities on an EC level rears its head. Contemporary and subsequent events in France have led to the deep unpopularity of both the President, Jacques Chirac, and his beleaguered Prime Minister, Dominique de Villepin: see, most recently, 'France's president: The man who deserves a red card', *The Economist*, 15 July 2006, 41–42.

and Dutch referendums, in the face of the aforementioned survey data which suggested strong popular support both for EU membership and its benefits, and for the adoption of a constitution for the EU.[110]

This series of reasons for the rejection of the TCE in the French and Dutch referendums undoubtedly makes the explanatory task (suggested at the outset of both this contribution and this section) an extremely difficult and sensitive one. Seeking to communicate why any elements of the TCE should nevertheless be introduced into EC law and practice by means short of formal Treaty amendment will always run the risk of creating an impression of trying to by-pass the results of these referendum results (while at the same time receive support from those keen to emphasize the need not to marginalize the equally 'valid' choices made by those Member States who have already ratified the TCE). Before moving to consider two particular areas in which, it is argued, that the so-called 'cherry-picking' exercise should nevertheless be encouraged and adopted, it is important to gain a sense of how the EU's institutions reacted to the results of the referendums in France and the Netherlands. These reactions will play an important role in shaping debate and action, both during the ongoing period of reflection and in the longer term.

EU Institutional Reactions to the Results of the French and Dutch Referendums?

Citizenship initiatives

Some aspects of such programmes run a number of risks, in particular those of elitism and/or patronizing the citizenry. The warnings about these sorts of initiative provided a decade ago, in the aftermath of the Maastricht Treaty (see, eg, Ward),[111] seem equally apposite today, albeit from a slightly different perspective. The proposal of the Adonnino Committee to create a European flag has since been implemented, while the ideas of a European hymn, motto and 'Europe day' have found expression in the TCE itself (Article I-8 TCE).[112] The attempts to encourage the

---

[110] *Ibid.*, and see also his most recent comments, 'The future of the EU Constitution: Escaping the Ratification Maze' (11 July 2006, available at http://jurist.law.pitt.edu/forumy/2006/07/future-of-eu-constitution-escaping.php): 'Furthermore, it is manifest that the French and Dutch No votes cannot be understood as a simple No to the idea of a constitution for Europe or even the idea of further European integration . . . . There were certainly voters exclusively concerned with and ideologically favorable to the EU and who nonetheless rejected the Constitution. Above all, however, the French No was a patchwork of inconsistent claims: essentially a no to what is called there "Anglo-Saxon" Europe and its "neo-liberal" policies, a no to unemployment and social dumping and finally, a no to Turkey. With ideological absolutism on the left side of the political spectrum and a deeply unpopular government and President, these ingredients have proven fatal to the Constitution.' See also Aarts & van der Kolk, (2006) (n.102, above).

[111] I Ward, *The Margins of European Law* (Basingstoke: Macmillan, 1996) (hereinafter, 'Ward, (1996)').

[112] The statement in the fifth sentence of Article I-8 TCE that 'Europe day *shall* be celebrated on 9 May throughout the Union' (my emphasis) is perhaps a further illustration of the tendency to pursue

development of a cultural European identity have clearly moved with the times: Wistrich's pleas[113] (which chimed with ideas of the kind regularly backed by the Commission in the past) for a cultural space for the free movement of orchestras and fine art seem today to have been replaced by obsessions with football (perhaps forgivable in World Cup year, when the tournament was held in Germany) and the Eurovision song contest, particularly as the fiftieth anniversary of the founding of the EEC approaches. Indeed, among the many plans under discussion to mark this auspicious year, the Commission is reported to be pushing for the inclusion of a Eurovision-style singing contest,[114] while it seems that Germany will be going ahead with its plan (during its Presidency of the EU in the first half of 2007) 'to let "thousands" of its bakeries bake 50 sorts of cakes with recipes from all 25 Member States'.[115] The less said about such 'initiatives', the better. While earlier critiques of such proposals focused squarely upon the danger that this would lead to a situation in which 'European citizenship will . . . be restricted . . . to those who choose to spend what is left of their earnings on art galleries and orchestras',[116] some elements of these latest schemes seem to take the approach that 'any publicity is good publicity', although the recent 'straight bananas' and 'bent cucumbers' episodes would suggest that this orientation is something of a fallacy.

Nevertheless, other elements of the Commission's current approach towards such citizenship initiatives could well prove more promising. For example, the Commission recently adopted a proposal for a decision to establish a programme of 'Citizens for Europe',[117] whose adoption is still pending. While some of the actions

attempts to prescribe some 'European-ness' for the citizens of the EU. The cynic would add that far greater affinity might be secured through this route were 9 May each year to be granted public holiday status throughout the EU: nothing breeds positive feelings like an extra day's holiday.

[113] E Wistrich, *The United States of Europe* (London: Routledge, 1994), 90–91.

[114] M Beunderman, 'Commission pushes unpopular EU singing show idea' (14 July 2006, available at http://euobserver.com/9/22095/?rk=1). A direct link with the Eurovision song contest in its present format might prove tricky institutionally for the EU, if only because the countries involved in Eurovision include some candidate countries (Turkey, Bulgaria, Romania), some potential future members (Albania, Bosnia & Herzegovina, Croatia, FYR, Macedonia, Moldova) and many other non-EU Member States (Armenia, Israel, Norway, Russia, Switzerland and Ukraine). Furthermore, it has been suggested that voting practices within the Eurovision song contest exhibit a marked degree of regionalism and mutual back-scratching: see, eg, D Gatherer, 'Comparison of Eurovision Song Contest Simulation with Actual Results Reveals Shifting Patterns of Collusive Voting Alliances' (2006) 9 *Journal of Artificial Societies and Social Simulation*, No. 2 (available at: http://jasss.soc.surrey.ac.uk/9/2/1.html), and the references cited therein (I am indebted to Alex Mills for this reference). Some would suggest that this makes the model an inappropriate one for the EU to associate itself with, while others might take a different view. For the Eurovision song contest 2006, see http://www.eurovision.tv/english/index.htm.

[115] Beunderman, *ibid.*

[116] Ward, (1996), (n. 111, above), 7.

[117] Commission, 'Proposal for Decision of the European Parliament and of the Council establishing for the period 2007–2013 the programme "Citizens for Europe" to promote active European Citizenship' COM(2005) 116 final (6 April 2005) (available at: http://eur-lex.europa.eu/LexUriServ/site/en/com/2005/com2005_0116en01.pdf).

proposed run the risk of sounding either like rather wishful thinking[118] or even (unless very carefully organized) potentially favouring some groups over others in political debate and lobbying,[119] the focus on encouraging town-twinning activities has already won some support from a UK commentator.[120] The present author has benefited enormously from the opportunity to participate in such activities over many years, both in terms of improving linguistic competence and in terms of meeting, getting to know and understand the way in which colleagues (and now good friends) in other Member States approach issues of common interest.[121] Similar benefits of communication, experience and sharing of knowledge and ideas stem from the Erasmus and Socrates student exchange programmes, in which the present author has again been privileged to be a participant. In time, such understandings and linkages can help people to understand and appreciate those areas in which they may well face common problems that may warrant common solutions, but also where there are similar problems to which the best solutions are likelier to be reached by exchange of information, ideas and experience, rather than by centrally-mandated homogeneity. These kinds of issues will often be those that are of direct interest to the citizenry[122]: if the EU can become capable of assisting in facilitating such contacts and exchanges, its profile and reputation may well be revived in the medium-term. However, these proposals are no 'quick-fix' to the oft-bemoaned absence of a 'European identity' and, indeed, may foster only certain elements thereof over time on particular issues.

The Commission's 'Plan-D' and a 'Citizen's Agenda'

Both before and after the negative votes in the French and Dutch referendums, journalists and politicians were regularly heard to wonder whether the EU had a 'Plan

---

[118] Eg the organization of 'high-visibility' events 'by or in cooperation with the European Commission which are substantial in scale and scope, strike a significant chord with the peoples of Europe, help to increase their sense of belonging to the same community, make them aware of the history, achievements and values of the European Union, involve them in intercultural dialogue and contribute to the development of their European identity' (COM(2005) 116 final), para. 4.3.

[119] See 'Action 2: Active civil society in Europe', proposing the provision of structural support for both European public policy research organisations (ie think-tanks) and for organizations of civil society at European level (COM(2005) 116 final), para. 4.2.

[120] See, eg, P Sain ley Berry, 'Not singing but twinning' (28 July 2006, available at: http://euobserver.com/9/22174/?rk=1).

[121] On the occasion of the formal twinning of the towns of Newbury (Berkshire, UK) and Feltre (Belluno province, Italy) (held in Feltre, 2 August 2003: see http://www.newburytwintown.org.uk/Autumn%202003.pdf for a brief summary report of the ceremony), the author was fortunate to be given the opportunity to provide a personal view on the importance of such twinning and exchange activities for the future of the EU and its citizens.

[122] See the discussion under the heading above, ' "Lost among echoes of things not there?" Reasons behind the "No" votes and their significance for the road ahead', on the question of issues that are of genuine interest to citizens. It might also be suggested that, along with a role for national Parliaments (see heading below, 'National Parliaments and subsidiarity mechanism'), the Committee of the Regions may also be able to assist in facilitating such exchanges of practice and information.

B' to deal with the TCE ratification process. Equally regularly, the existence of any such Plan B was denied by the Commission and the Member States alike. On 13 October 2005, the Commission published its contribution to the period of reflection in a Communication, which was sub-headed 'Plan-D for Democracy, Dialogue and Debate'.[123] This was the Commission's response to the European Council's declaration on the ratification of the TCE,[124] which had suggested that the Commission should play a 'special role' in the organization of public debate during the period of reflection. Although prompted by the 'No' votes in the French and Dutch referendums, this plan was not presented as a rescue package for the TCE, but rather 'to stimulate wider debate between the European Union's democratic institutions an citizens'[125] and as 'a starting point for a long-term democratic reform process'.[126] Member States undertook to conduct 'broad-ranging national debates on the future of Europe',[127] while the Commission promised to conduct a wide range of actions on the European level to stimulate wider public debate, to promote citizens' participation in the democratic process and to use various tools to generate a dialogue on European policies.[128]

The Commission's 'A Citizen's Agenda for Europe',[129] adopted on 10 May 2006, stressed the need to shift to a 'policy agenda for citizens', drawing upon continued dialogue with the public via (*inter alia*) the implementation of Plan D. On the same day, the Commission published its report on its implementation of Plan D and how it fitted into the ongoing period of reflection.[130] The brief Annex to this Communication (described as a 'comprehensive stocktaking') indicated those actions pursued by the Commission, while the discussion of the various issues raised in the

[123] Communication from the Commission, 'The Commission's contribution to the period of reflection and beyond: Plan-D for Democracy, Dialogue and Debate' COM(2005) 494 final (available at http://ec.europa.eu/commission_barroso/wallstrom/pdf/communication_planD_en.pdf) (hereinafter, 'COM(2005) 494 final' or 'Plan-D'). The Committee of the Regions would have transformed this '3-D' Plan-D into one with a fourth dimension: that of Decentralization (see the Opinion of the Committee of the Regions of 15 June 2006 (CONST-IV-002, published on 27 June 2006) (available at http://coropinions.cor.europa.eu/coropiniondocument.aspx?language=en&docnr=52&year=2006).

[124] 'Declaration by the heads of State or Government of the Member States of the European Union on the Ratification of the Treaty Establishing a Constitution for Europe' (SN 117/05, 18 June 2005, available at: http://ue.eu.int/ueDocs/cms_Data/docs/pressData/en/ec/85325.pdf).

[125] COM(2005) 494 final, at 2.

[126] Communication from the Commission, 'The Period of reflection and Plan D' COM(2006) 212 final (10 May 2006) (hereinafter 'COM(2006) 212 final') (available at http://ec.europa.eu/commission_barroso/president/pdf/com_2006_212_en.pdf).

[127] COM(2005) 494 final, section 3.

[128] *Ibid.*, section 4: these actions were to include visits by Commissioners to Member States and their national Parliaments, creating a 'European Round Table for Democracy' (consisting of citizens from different backgrounds, to debate on common European issues), examining ways to increase levels of voter participation and the use of focus groups as a first step in policy-making processes.

[129] Commission Communication, 'A Citizen's Agenda: Delivering Results for Europe' COM (2006) 211 final (10 May 2006) (available at: http://eur-lex.europa.eu/LexUriServ/site/en/com/2006/com2006_0211en01.pdf).

[130] COM(2006) 212 final.

debates is presented as a 'synthesis' compiled by the Commission (although there is no reference to particular publications or other sources from which the synthesized material was drawn). The Presidency Conclusions after the Brussels meeting of the European Council on 16 June 2006 expressed the European Council's 'gratitude' for the Commission's contribution, which also formed part of the basis for the European Council's assessment of the 'reflection period'.[131] However, the experience of the Netherlands[132] in its attempts to organize some kind of national debate on European issues suggests that the idea of encouraging such activities is one which interests the EU and the Commission rather more than it engages either national politicians or their electorates. Indeed, the Commission itself noted (in the Annex to its report on Plan D) that while it 'sees itself mainly as a facilitator . . . it must be pointed out that the involvement of the Member States in the launch of national debates remains uneven'.[133] This, one fears, is putting it mildly.

KEY SUBSTANTIVE TOPICS FOR CONSIDERATION

Obviously, there are many interesting and significant institutional and substantive issues that may yet arise from what one might style the 'wreckage' of the TCE ratification process, but given the results of the recent Brussels European Council (and the Member States' decision to continue the 'period of reflection well into 2007'), it is premature to reach even interim conclusions on many of these matters. The status and future of the EU Charter of Fundamental Rights, for example, are questions that have featured in discussions between the Member States during the period of reflection to date,[134] but it is clear that any change in the status of the Charter will require much further discussion and a Treaty amendment to bring it beyond having merely been 'declared' and into legal effect.

One area, however, in which genuine and significant activity and progress has been visible in the year since the Dutch 'No' vote is that of increasing the degree of transparency in the activities of the Council, particularly during the legislative process. Proposals have also been forthcoming on transparency, information and communications from the European Commission and the European Parliament, which will be noted briefly below. Another topic worthy of brief consideration here is that of the principle of subsidiarity and the role of national Parliaments and the way in which their views and scrutiny can feed into the EC legislative process. This second issue is apposite here due both to recent EC-level initiatives and to the fact

---

[131] Presidency Conclusions, Brussels European Council, 15/16 June 2006 (Document 10633/06, 16 June 2006), paras. 2 and 3.

[132] After earlier bold declarations, September 2005 saw the Dutch government's attempts to put a national debate in place falter and then founder—see the series of online reports (in Dutch) at: http://:www.elsevier.nl/nieuws/europese_unie/nieuwsbericht/asp/artnr/63325/index.html; http://:www.elsevier.nl/nieuws/europese_unie/nieuwsbericht/asp/artnr/66469/index.html; and http://:www.elsevier.nl/nieuws/europese_unie/nieuwsbericht/asp/artnr/66611/index.html.

[133] COM(2006) 212 final, at 10.

[134] See, eg, S Taylor, 'Sarkozy plots with Berlin to salvage constitution', *European Voice*, 6 April 2006.

that it is another area from the TCE that may respond to implementation by means other than the adoption of a new Treaty (with all of the ratification questions that that would raise).

Improving the Transparency of EC Proceedings (Particularly in the Legislative Process)

Proceedings in the Council

One element of the TCE which received widespread praise[135] was the CFE's decision to recommend (and the IGC's approval) that Council legislative proceedings should be accessible to the public: see Article I-24(6) TCE. For many, the loss of this improvement in the transparency of a key aspect of the EC's legislative procedures was one of the sadder casualties of the failure to secure ratification of the TCE. It is thus unsurprising that the matter was prominent on the agenda after the European Council meeting of 16–17 June 2005 and has featured in reports, proposals and statements from a variety of EC institutional actors, national politicians and commentators.

The European Parliament has made a number of proposals and calls on the Council to open up its proceedings: as UK Labour MEP Gary Titley remarked in backing such calls, 'We're not trying to create Dallas or Big Brother, we just want to enhance scrutiny. The only legislative body that doesn't meet in public nowadays is North Korea'.[136] In December 2003, indeed, a complaint was made by a German MEP to the European Ombudsman, that the Council's then current rules of procedure unjustifiably limited how far the Council's legislative meetings could take place in public, to the extent that it amounted to an instance of maladministration, falling within the purview of the European Ombudsman under Article 195 EC. After careful consideration and passing reference to the provisions of the TCE, the Ombudsman concluded that the Council's refusal to amend its rules of procedure to facilitate greater transparency in its legislative proceedings did indeed amount to maladministration, on the basis of the exhortation in Article 1(2) TEU that EU decisions 'are taken as openly as possible and as closely as possible to the citizen'.[137] The key factor was that it was perfectly *possible* for the Council to amend its rules of procedure to provide for greater transparency in this regard, so that a

---

[135] The present writer has co-authored elsewhere on this topic (Dashwood & Johnston (2004), n. 25, above), while others have given a similar welcome to this proposed reform: see, eg: J Kokott and A Rüth, 'The European Convention and its Draft Treaty establishing a Constitution for Europe: Appropriate answers to the Laeken questions?' (2003) 40 *CMLRev.* 1315, at 1332; J Monar, 'Transparency in the Exercise of Power in the "Constitutionalized" Union: the problem of Diffused Leadership and Responsibility' in Curtin *et al* (2005), 209–220 (esp. 210–211); and Piris (2006) (n. 3, above), 34–35 and 181–183.

[136] Quoted in a news story on the BBC website (6 September 2005, available at: http://news.bbc.co.uk/1/hi/world/europe/4218776.stm).

[137] 'Special Report from the European Ombudsman to the European Parliament following the draft recommendation to the Council of the European Union in complaint 2395/2003/GG' (Strasbourg,

failure to do so amounted to 'a public body [failing] to act in accordance with a rule or principle which is binding upon it'—the definition of 'maladministration' adopted by the Ombudsman and welcomed by the European Parliament.[138]

In response to this finding, the Council decided at its meeting of 20–22 December 2005[139] to conduct in public meetings concerning legislative proposals under co-decision that were presented orally by the Commission and all final Council legislative deliberations under co-decision. However, these measures were subjected to criticism by both the European Parliament[140] and the European Ombudsman,[141] which intensified in the run up to the Brussels European Council of mid-June 2006.[142] The UK, however, despite having pushed the transparency issue very strongly itself during the UK Presidency in 2005,[143] seemed to acquire a serious case of cold feet on the topic during the Austrian Presidency.[144] Whatever the reasons for this change of heart,[145] it is clear that the UK's u-turn baffled many officials in

---

4 October 2005, available at: http://www.ombudsman.europa.eu/special/pdf/en/032395.pdf). (See also the Ombudsman's earlier 'Draft recommendation to the Council of the European Union in complaint 2395/2003/GG' (Strasbourg, 9 November 2004, available at: http://www.ombudsman.europa.eu/recommen/en/032395.htm), to which the Council responded on 17 February 2005 (rejecting the Ombudsman's finding of maladministration).) On the Ombudsman generally, see A Peters, 'The European Ombudsman and the European Constitution' (2005) 42 *CMLRev.* 697.

[138] See the Annual Report of the European Ombudsman for 2002 (10 February 2003, available at: http://www.ombudsman.europa.eu/report02/pdf/en/rap02_en.pdf), at 18.

[139] Council Press Release 15479/05 (Presse 349), concerning the 2702nd Council Meeting on Agriculture and Fisheries (20–22 December 2005), 53–54. See also the Information Sheet published by the General Secretariat of the Council of the EU, entitled 'Openness and transparency of Council proceedings' (TRA/00, December 2005, available at: http://ue.eu.int/ueDocs/newsWord/en/misc/87866.doc).

[140] For a summary, see http://www.europarl.europa.eu/news/public/story_page/008-7064-093-04-14-901-20060404STO07063-2006-03-04-2006/default_en.htm.

[141] Press Release EO/06/7 (5 April 2006, available at: http://www.ombudsman.europa.eu/release/en/2006-04-05.htm).

[142] See, eg, European Ombudsman Press Release EO/06/13 (13 June 2006, available at: http://www.ombudsman.europa.eu/release/en/2006-06-13.htm).

[143] See the documents considered in the House of Commons Select Committee on European Scrutiny, *Seventeenth Report of Session 2005–2006* (13 February 2006, available at: http://www.publications.parliament.uk/pa/cm200506/cmselect/cmeuleg/34-xvii/34-xvii.pdf), section 4, 'Transparency in the Council' (in which the then Minister for Europe, Douglas Alexander, made clear that the UK government had supported the wider option of having the Council meet in public for all stages of deliberation where the Council acts in a legislative capacity: see paras. 4.4–4.7 and 4.12); see also the earlier news story on the BBC website (http://news.bbc.co.uk/1/hi/world/europe/4218776.stm) on 6 September 2005 for details of the UK's initiative during its EU Presidency.

[144] See A Balzan, 'UK having second thoughts about transparency initiative' (8 June 2006, available at http://euobserver.com/9/21797/?rk=1).

[145] See the comments reported in Balzan (*ibid.*): the suggestion is that the views of the new UK Foreign Secretary (Margaret Beckett) on the matter are coloured by her previous experiences as Minister for Environment, Agriculture and Fisheries, particularly on the negotiation of fishing quotas. The fear, apparently, was that 'EU deal-making could be hampered if cameras are allowed into meetings as ministers would be more interested in their national audiences back home'.

Brussels[146] and MPs in the UK'[147] and may well have lost some of the goodwill that the UK had managed to generate on the matter during 2005.

Nevertheless, the European Council conclusions in June 2006 did indeed move to approve greater Council transparency: the Presidency conclusions from the Brussels European Council (16 June 2006)[148] are reproduced in Appendix 1 (below).[149] For present purposes, the key agreements reached were, first, that all Council deliberations on legislative acts under the co-decision procedure should take place in public (subject to the possibility of a decision by Council or Coreper to meet in private) and, second, that all public deliberations are to be broadcast on the internet and a recorded version must be available for at least a month after the meeting took place. The first point brings current Council practice a step closer to the position that would have been reached under the TCE (see Article I-24(6) TCE), although naturally any assessment of the significance of this step (and the other measures on transparency adopted by the European Council) will depend upon the frequency with which the Council has recourse to the clause allowing an opt-out from public deliberations. The Finnish Presidency has promised to use the possibilities provided by the new 'Overall Policy on Transparency' (such as deciding that subsequent discussions on non-co-decision legislation should take place in public, proposing that public debates be held on matters of importance to citizens and developing information provision, communications and mailing lists to give greater publicity to any Council public deliberations) to achieve marked improvements in the provision of information and the openness of the Council's procedures.[150] Essentially, as a result of these recent developments, the default position with regard to deliberations under the co-decision procedure is one of public accessibility, while under other procedures the Council's doors will remain closed, unless the Presidency proposes, and the Council agrees, otherwise.

On Tuesday 11 July 2006, the first Council (ECOFIN) meeting was televised on the web. It must be noted that there have been mixed reactions in the press coverage of this event,[151] particularly due to the decision to black out certain parts of

[146] And indeed satirical commentators back home: see 'Brussels Sprouts', *Private Eye*, Issue 1162 (4 July 2006), at 9.

[147] See, eg, the clear comments in favour of far-reaching transparency reforms in the House of Commons Select Committee on European Scrutiny, *Twenty-Third Report of Session 2005–2006* (11 April 2006, available at: http://www.publications.parliament.uk/pa/cm200506/cmselect/cmeuleg/34-xxiii/34-xxiii.pdf), paras. 21.6 and 21.12–21.14.

[148] Presidency Conclusions, Brussels European Council, 15–16 June 2006 (Document 10633/06, 16 June 2006), Annex I.

[149] Included at the end of this chapter.

[150] See, eg, Hill & Knowlton's *Guide to the Finnish Presidency of the European Union* (10 July 2006, available at: http://www.hillandknowlton.be/HK/pressoffice/presidency/Finnish2.pdf), at 16 ('Open the doors of the Council Meetings', by H Hautala, Finnish MP and Chair of the Finnish Green Parliamentary Group).

[151] For an immediate reaction, see M Beunderman, 'First EU ministers' webcast proves tedious' (11 July 2006, available at: http://euobserver.com/9/22066/?rk=1).

the meeting, which were deemed too sensitive for public consumption. As one commentator has argued,[152] what 'no-one seems to have [appreciated] is that immediately you black out a screen, ordinary viewers will be immediately convinced that all manner of corrupt, heathen and morally reprehensible practices are taking place behind it'. Only two items were held open to public view (the Finnish Presidency's economic and financial programme, and the mandate of the European Investment Bank), while discussions on the juicily controversial and sensitive topic of the operation of the Stability and Growth Pact (the basis for the Euro) were kept firmly under wraps. The Dutch Finance Minister, Gerrit Zalm, expressed concern that such debates on relatively technical matters would be highly unlikely to excite the interest of the citizenry: these topics, he said, were 'not attractive enough' to raise genuine public interest.[153] From a purely personal perspective, when the present author tried to access the webcast, he found that the media player chosen to run the broadcast on the Council's website was not easy to manipulate. There seemed to be no possibility to pause, rewind or skip ahead within the recording, which does not facilitate access for those minded to attempt to follow such matters. Still, the steps that are being taken are clearly ones in the right direction.

Other Transparency Developments and Initiatives in the EC Institutions[154]

It should not be forgotten that issues of the transparency of decision-making and the accessibility of information are not only raised in connection with the activities of the Council. Indeed, the European Ombudsman has recently reported that a quarter of all complaints received by his office in 2005 concerned transparency questions, and 68 per cent of all complaints were directed against the Commission (with 2.2 per cent targeting the Council, 9.2 per cent the European Parliament and 11.6 per cent the European Personnel Selection Office).[155]

The Commission launched its 'Transparency Initiative' in 2005,[156] which led to the publication of a Green Paper on a 'European Transparency Initiative' in the

---

[152] See, eg, the comment by P Sain ley Berry, 'A webcast full of black holes' (14 July 2006, available at http://euobserver.com/9/2207/?rk=1).

[153] See Beunderman, n. 151, above.

[154] Comitology remains a contentious area in this regard and one too complex to engage with in any detail here. For the current Comitology Decision, see Council Decision 1999/468/EC of 28 June 1999 [1999] OJ L184/23. From a large and burgeoning literature, see, eg, K St Clair Bradley, 'Comitology and the Law: Through a Glass, Darkly' (1992) 32 *CMLRev*. 693; E Vos, *Institutional Frameworks of Community Health and Safety Regulations* (Oxford: Hart Publishing, 1998); C Joerges and E Vos, *EU Committees: Social Regulation, Law and Politics* (Oxford: Hart Publishing, 1999); the House of Lords Select Committee on the European Union, *Reforming Comitology* (Session 2002–2003, 31st Report, HL Paper 135, 1 July 2003; also available at: http://www.publications.parliament.uk/pa/ld200203/ldselect/ldeucom/134/134.pdf); and M Savino, 'The Constitutional Legitimacy of the EU Committees' (Paris: Centre d'Études Européens, Cahiers Européens, No. 03/2005; available at: http://www.portedeurope. org/IMG/pdf/TheConstitutionalLegitimacySAVINO.pdf).

[155] Annual Report of the European Ombudsman 2005—Executive Summary and Statistics (13 March 2006, available at: http://www.ombudsman.europa.eu/report05/pdf/en/short05_en.pdf), esp. 28–29.

[156] See Commission Staff Working Document, 'Report of the Inter-departmental Working Group on a possible 'European Transparency Initiative' SEC(2005) 1300 final (November 2005, available at: http://ec.europa.eu/commission_barroso/kallas/doc/transp_report_en.pdf).

spring of 2006.[157] The consultation on the Green Paper ended on 31 August 2006. The issues to be covered are summarized as: 'fuller information about management and use of Community funds[,] professional ethics in the European institutions and the framework in which lobby groups and civil society organisations are operating'. In the first of these areas, the Commission will act to set up and develop a website covering the beneficiaries of EC projects and programmes, and to facilitate better scrutiny of the use of EU funds under centralized management. Other matters under review include: the possibility of requiring mandatory reporting of the beneficiaries of EU funds under shared Member State and EU management; a review of the legislation and practice on access to documents[158]; and the suggestion that there is a need for a more structured framework for the activities of lobbyists and interest group representatives when they engage with the EU institutions.[159]

Finally, on the issue of transparency and communication, it should be noted that the European Parliament has announced that it plans to launch its own internet TV channel.[160] An internal pilot programme will run from September 2006 and, if successful, the European Parliament hopes to launch a fully-fledged version in the second half of 2007.

In concluding on the topic of transparency, it must be acknowledged that some significant progress has been made in enhancing transparency in the legislative activities of the EC, even in the absence of the ratification of the TCE. Given the apparent success of pressure by the European Parliament in achieving improved Council transparency, it is to be expected that there will be more (and more regular) calls from the European Parliament, individual MEPs, national MPs and the press for further developments in this area, as well as scrutinizing ever more carefully other significant areas of policy-making and decision-taking which suffer from excessive opacity.[161]

---

[157] Commission Green Paper, 'European Transparency Initiative' COM(2006) 194 final (3 May 2006) (available at: http://ec.europa.eu/commission_barroso/kallas/doc/com2006_0194_4_en.pdf). For access to the consultation responses and other information, see: http://ec.europa.eu/commission_barroso/kallas/transparency_en.htm#1.

[158] Regulation 2001/1049/EC of the European Parliament and of the Council of 30 May 2001 regarding public access to European Parliament, Council and Commission documents [2001] OJ L145/43. Council Decision 1999/468/EC on access to Council committee documents, insofar as they are Council documents, see in particular Annex II ('Specific Provisions Regarding Public Access to Council Documents') to the Council's Decision of 22 July 2002 [2002] OJ L230/21. For recent discussion of the operation of the latest legislation, see B Driessen, 'The Council of the European Union and Access to Documents' (2005) 30 *ELRev.* 675 and D Chalmers, C Hadjiemmanuil, G Monti and A Tomkins, *European Union Law* (Cambridge: CUP, 2006), 317–329.

[159] See COM(2006) 194 final (n. 157, above), section I.

[160] M Beunderman, 'Parliament set to launch own web TV channel' (12 July 2006, available at http://euobserver.com/9/22073/?rk=1). Recordings and live broadcasts of European Parliament sessions are also now available on the European Parliament's website, at: http://www.europarl.europa.eu/eplive/public/default_en.htm?language=EN.

[161] For a recent example of further disquiet about the opacity of meetings relating to EU matters, see House of Lords European Union Committee, *Behind Closed Doors: the meeting of the G6 Interior Ministers at Heiligendamm* (40th Report of the 2005–2006 Session, HL Paper 221, 19 July 2006; available at: http://www.parliament.the-stationery-office.co.uk/pa/ld200506/ldselect/ldeucom/221/221.pdf), in which the Committee provides strong criticism of the UK government's failure to publicize and report

National Parliaments and the Subsidiarity Mechanism

The Presidency Conclusions from the Brussels European Council (16 June 2006) place great emphasis on the importance of these linked issues of the role of national Parliaments and the enhancement of the assessment of the principle of subsidiarity. Indeed, these topics are closely related to the transparency questions discussed under the heading Improving the transparency of EC proceedings (particularly in the legislative process), above: after all, if the Council deliberates and takes decisions in secret, then national Parliaments will lack any (let alone adequate) access to the information that they require if they are to hold their respective national governments to account for actions on the European level in the name of their particular Member State.[162] And the national electorate will have no means by which to judge national political parties on their performance on European issues. Thus, improvements in transparency of the kind canvassed in the immediately preceding paragraphs have a vital knock-on effect upon the extent to which national Parliaments can play a genuine and significant role by feeding their thoughts and concerns into the EC's legislative and policy-making processes.

Preliminaries: thoughts on the role of national Parliaments in the
implementation of EC law

One important element in framing the role of national Parliaments concerns the classic idea of EC directives as an instrument of subsidiarity, allowing a degree of national level discretion to be exercised, so as properly to incorporate the EC rules into the national legal system.

   Yet there are, it may be argued, flaws in this reasoning, at least when its operation is observed in practice. In general terms, the ECJ's case law under Article 226 EC concerning Member States' failure to implement such directives has often required such a degree of clarity in that implementation that verbatim adoption of the EC directive's wording in national law seems the only safe course.[163] More

---

to Parliament on the practice of the Interior Ministers from the G6 (France, Germany, the UK, Italy, Spain and Poland) of meeting at regular intervals to discuss how to take forward EU policy on security and justice and home affairs matters (in particular, on immigration). See, eg, paras. 12 and 13 of the Report: 'Ministers returning from Council meetings are expected to report back by written ministerial statement; the same should apply to meetings of the G6. The Home Office should publish the Conclusions of all G6 meetings—in English. We recommend that the results of subsequent G6 meetings should be fully publicized by the Home Office. A written ministerial statement should be made to Parliament. The papers should be sent to this Committee, and to the Commons European Scrutiny Committee and Home Affairs Committee'.

   [162] See, eg, M Höreth, *Die Europäische Union im Legitimationstrilemma: Zur Rechtfertigung des Regierens jenseits der Staatlichkeit* (Baden-Baden: Nomos, 1999) and I Pernice, 'The Role of National Parliaments in the European Union' in D Melissas and I Pernice (eds.), *Perspectives of the Nice Treaty and the Intergovernmental Conference in 2004* (Baden-Baden: Nomos, 2002) (also available at http://www.ecln. net/elements/constitutional_debate/perspective2004/content.html).

   [163] See T Weir, 'Difficulties in Transposing Directives' *ZEuP* 2004, 595 and AC Johnston and H Unberath, 'Law at, to or from the centre? The European Court of Justice and the Harmonisation of

specifically, concerning the role for national Parliaments, meanwhile, much will depend upon national constitutional arrangements and how they operate *vis-à-vis* EC law and its incorporation in the national legal order. For example, in the UK the vast majority of implementation takes place via secondary legislation adopted by the relevant Minister, under the auspices of the European Communities Act 1972, subject only to approval by Parliamentary resolution. This itself relies upon the interest and diligence of MPs in scrutinizing such use of these delegated legislative powers: this scrutiny is not always as rigorously conducted as it might be.[164]

On the other hand, for national Parliaments to be able to play their part in the system of dual legitimation, they have to be kept informed of the progress of legislation through the Council's decision-making process. Machinery was created for this purpose by a Protocol, which was annexed to the EC Treaty by the Treaty of Amsterdam. A Protocol on the application of the principles of subsidiarity and proportionality was annexed by the same Treaty to the EC Treaty. The TCE's wording significantly strengthened the two Protocols, which are discussed in the following paragraphs.

The TCE and national Parliaments[165]

It is worthwhile to remind ourselves of the provisions of the TCE that would have enhanced the role of national Parliaments, before moving to discuss whether, and if so how, similar developments might be brought about even in the absence of the ratification of the TCE.

(a) Protocol 1 to the TCE: the role of Member States' Parliaments in the European Union

The new version of the Protocol makes it a legal requirement that draft legislative acts originating from the Commission be 'forwarded to national Parliaments *directly* by the Commission, *at the same time as* to the European Parliament and the Council'.[166] It is further provided that '[t]he agendas for and the outcome of meetings of the Council, including the minutes of meetings where the Council is deliberating on draft European legislative acts, shall be forwarded directly to national Parliaments, at the same time as to Member States' governments'.[167] Adherence to these provisions should at least keep national Parliaments informed of EC

Private Law in the European Union', Ch. 5 in F Cafaggi (ed.), *The Europeanization of Private Law* (Oxford: OUP, 2006).

[164] See *Oakley Inc. v Animal Ltd.* Litigation: [2005] EWHC (Ch.) 210 and EWHC (Pat.) 419, [2005] Eu LR 713, overturned by the Court of Appeal: [2006] Ch 337, concerning a challenge made against use of s. 2(2) European Communities Act 1972. The issue was exactly what the government may do when implementing (eg not covering measures that are not *mandated* by an EC obligation): see M Howe, '*Oakley Inc v Animal Inc*: Designs Create a Constitutional Mess' (2006) 28 *EIPR* 192, for discussion of the Court of Appeal's judgment.

[165] These paragraphs are closely based upon Dashwood & Johnston (2004) (n. 25, above), 1487–1490.

[166] Protocol 1, Art. 2, third para. (emphases added): this is instead of leaving it to the Member States to pass on the information, as under Art. 2 of the current Protocol.

[167] Protocol, Art. 5.

legislative activity and better equip them to scrutinize matters in a careful and time-lier fashion.

(b) *Protocol 2 to the TCE: the application of the principles of subsidiarity and proportionality*

The main change to this Protocol is the establishment of a procedure giving national Parliaments a formal role in helping to ensure compliance with the subsidiarity principle. According to Article 5 of the Protocol, any national Parliament, or any chamber of a national Parliament which is bi-cameral, will have six weeks from the date of transmission of a draft European legislative act, in which to send to the Presidents of the European Parliament, the Council and the Commission a reasoned opinion stating why it considers the draft does not comply with the principle of subsidiarity. According to Article 6, second paragraph, for the purposes of this procedure, national Parliaments are to have two votes, one of which must go to each chamber of a bi-cameral Parliament, like that of the UK. If reasoned opinions challenging a measure's compatibility with the subsidiarity principle represent at least a third of all the votes allocated to the national Parliaments (currently, one third of 50, ie 17), the Institution which originated the draft is required to review it. Following such a review, the Institution concerned may decide to maintain, to amend or to withdraw the draft, and it must give reasons for its decision. If it opts to maintain the draft, and the measure is one that requires the approval of the Council (as legislative acts normally will), voting for its adoption would clearly entail a substantial political risk for any Minister from a Member State whose Parliament had sent in a written opinion on the issue of subsidiarity.

There is also an intriguing rider added by Article 7 of the Protocol to the jurisdiction of the Court of Justice under Article III-365 TCE, which is the provision equivalent to the present Article 230 EC. Judicial review is to be available, on grounds of infringement of the principle of subsidiarity by a European legislative act, not only in proceedings actually *brought* by Member States, but also in proceedings 'notified by them in accordance with their legal order *on behalf of their national Parliament or a chamber of it*'.[168] In other words, an action will be admissible in which the effective protagonist is not the government of the Member States concerned, but its Parliament or one of the chambers of the national Parliament (in which, perhaps, the government may not, for the time being, command a majority). The wording appears to have been carefully chosen, so as to avoid appearing to confer on national Parliaments a legal right under the TCE, which might conflict with constitutional arrangements in the Member States. However, governments would surely find it hard to deny their Parliaments the possibility of taking advantage of this facility, which the TCE would offer them.[169]

---

[168] Emphasis added.

[169] See the earlier, and fuller, discussion of the reinforcement of the subsidiarity principle in AA Dashwood, 'The Draft EU Constitution—First Impressions' (2002) 5 *CYELS* 395, 405–407.

It must be conceded that there are potential dangers in this proposed enhancement of the role of national Parliaments. For example, real or perceived fears of excessive (or excessively intensive/intrusive) action at EC level among the national electorate and/or parliamentarians may prompt increased mistrust of EC institutions and legal rules. The robust response to this must be that this risk must be run as the price of increased transparency and better communication of the EC's activities. On the other side of the same coin, it is possible that greater appreciation of the nature of the EC's powers and proposed activities may instead increase mistrust by national electorates of *national* political institutions: either because they seem powerless[170] to affect such matters or because they are seen as complicit in this process.

Procedural provisions (transparency, timing, judicial review?)

What if a national Parliament's view is at odds with that adopted and developed (even promoted) by its own government in negotiations concerning the proposed EC measure: how can the national Parliament get its view across? Can it force its own government to change tack? The current Danish approach to national Parliamentary scrutiny of such European matters effectively empowers the parliamentary scrutiny committee on EU affairs to direct the Danish government to act in a certain way—thus far, the Danish government has always followed such directions in its actions on the European level.[171]

A further question is: what if national Parliaments' views against a proposed EC measure reach the threshold required to force their concerns to be considered at the European level, and yet the EC institutions proceed with the measure anyway? Will the national Parliaments be able to get their respective governments to bring an action on the Parliaments' behalf against the EC measure(s) subsequently adopted? Possible alternative approaches might involve: a national MP seeking standing in a national court for a declaration that the national government should bring such an action before the ECJ; or a national MP seeking a declaration preventing the implementation of any EC measure adopted in the face of the concerns of the national Parliaments (which might involve the national court deciding to make an Article 234 EC reference to the ECJ on the matter). On the question of such legal avenues of redress, former European Commissioner Vitorino has stated that no judicial review was intended by the TCE so far as the *withdrawal* of draft acts was concerned: instead, it was to be available only concerning *ex post*

---

[170] Cf. F Duina and M Oliver, 'National Parliaments in the European Union: Are There Any Benefits to Integration?' (2005) 11 *ELJ* 173, for a more optimistic assessment of how the EC law-making and implementation process may have actually empowered national Parliaments in other areas: eg expanding the range and extent of topics within the reach of national Parliaments and facilitating cross-learning between national Parliaments, thus making the legislative process more efficient.

[171] See Art. 6(2) of the Danish Law on accession to the EC (11 October 1972) and, eg, the discussion in J Alboek Jensen, 'Prior Parliamentary Consent to Danish EU Policies', in E Smith (ed.), *National Parliaments as Cornerstones of European Integration* (The Hague: Kluwer Law International, 1996), generally and at 45.

challenges to the validity of legislation once adopted.[172] If the subsidiarity mechanism (whether via Treaty amendment or other constitutional reform process) is to convince electorates and national politicians alike that it is more than mere window-dressing, questions relating to the consequences of national Parliaments' concerns being raised and (possibly) not addressed must be given convincing answers. These answers must apply both at the stage that allows such concerns to feed into (and inform) the EC legislative process, and subsequent to the adoption of legislation which is challenged by national Parliaments on subsidiarity grounds.

EU Institutional commitments to involve national Parliaments

From the typology of methods for effecting constitutional change discussed under the heading 'Typology: Approaches to Effecting Constitutional Change in the EU', above, securing the possible introduction of an enhanced role for national Parliaments, in particular via the TCE-designed subsidiarity mechanism, seems well suited to the use of some form of EC institutional practice or commitment. Indeed, the Commission has already suggested that it wishes to take one step down the road of introducing the provisions of the TCE: in its 'Citizen's Agenda',[173] it clearly stated that it 'wishes to transmit directly all new proposals and consultation papers to national parliaments, inviting them to react so as to improve the process of policy formulation'. This, however, would provide less certainty that national Parliaments' views would be factored into the decision-making process than the TCE's mechanism, lacking as it does the formal requirement to review draft legislative proposals if sufficient weight of national Parliamentary opinion requires it. On the other hand, the Commission's proposals do extend more broadly in their coverage of consultation papers as well as draft legislative proposals.

One means for adding teeth to the potential role of national Parliaments would be for the EC institutions to adopt an Inter-Institutional Agreement ('IIA'), in which they would lay down the procedures for communicating with, *and*, importantly, how they intend to deal with contributions that they receive from, national Parliaments. This could form the basis for holding the EC institutions to these stated policies and procedures, by means of the enforcement of the procedural legitimate expectations[174] that would be raised in national Parliaments. Such an IIA could also adopt certain statements to clarify the answers to some of the questions raised under the heading above, 'Procedural Provisions (Transparency, Timing, Judicial Review?)'.

---

[172] Written evidence to the House of Lords Select Committee on the European Union on the Subsidiarity Early warning Mechanism (20 January 2005) (available on the internet at the following address: http://www.publications.parliament.uk/pa/ld200405/ldselect/ldeucom/999/999we01.htm).

[173] Commission Communication, 'A Citizen's Agenda: Delivering Results for Europe' COM(2006) 211 final (10 May 2006) (available at: http://eur-lex.europa.eu/LexUriServ/site/en/com/2006/com2006_0211en01.pdf), at 9.

[174] See, eg, Case 120/86 *Mulder v Minister van Landbouw en Viserij* [1988] ECR 2321 and the discussions in T Tridimas, *The General Principles of EC Law* (Oxford: OUP, 2nd edn., 2006), Ch. 5, and S Schønberg, *Legitimate Expectations in Administrative Law* (Oxford: OUP, 2000).

On a note of caution, however, perhaps one should not be over-optimistic about the degree of improvement that such reforms would bring to the law-making and policy-formulation processes in the EU, given the ECJ's approach to the scrutiny of subsidiarity arguments under the current Treaty arrangements[175] and the criticisms of how some EC legislation has been justified on subsidiarity grounds.[176] Nevertheless, the degree of communication and scrutiny that even the functioning of this process may bring with it are, it is submitted, sufficient reason to pursue the greater involvement of national politicians in this process.

Actions at national levels

It is hoped that the foregoing discussion has shown that some action can, and should, be taken at the EC level to enhance the role of national Parliaments. It would, however, be negligently unbalanced to present this topic without underlining that responsibility for helping this complex system of scrutiny, legislation and implementation to function effectively also lies squarely at the level of national Parliaments themselves.

(i) Information, scrutiny and accountability mechanisms in national Parliaments Those changes to the Protocols will only make a practical difference, however, if appropriate procedures for the scrutiny of EU legislative proposals are in place at the national level, and if parliamentarians are willing to invest the time and political energy necessary, in order to hold Ministers more effectively to account for Council decisions in which they have taken part. Experience to date of parliamentary scrutiny, in most of the Member States of long standing, gives scant cause for optimism[177]; and concern may be felt about the additional strain that coping with EU legislation will place on the young democratic institutions of some of the Union's recent Members, as well as those of the more established Member States, who risk being swamped by a torrent of EC documentation. Nevertheless, it may be hoped that members of national Parliaments will be spurred on to greater efforts by the enhanced role they are called upon to play under the TCE, more

---

[175] See, eg, Case C-84/94 *UK v Council* ('The *Working Time Directive* case') [1996] ECR I-5755 and Case C-491/01 *R. v Secretary of State* ex parte *BAT and Imperial Tobacco* [2002] ECR I-11543 and S Weatherill, 'Better Competence Monitoring' (2005) 30 *ELRev.* 23. Although cf. Case C-376/98 *Germany v Parliament and Council* ('*The Tobacco Advertising case*') [2000] ECR I-8419, for some possible indications of more careful ECJ scrutiny of EC competence.

[176] See, S Weatherill, 'Better Competence Monitoring' (2005) 30 *ELRev.* 23 and, further, the strong critique of G Davies, 'Subsidiarity: The Wrong Idea, in the Wrong Place, at the Wrong Time' (2006) 43 *CMLRev.* 63.

[177] In general, see C Harlow, *Accountability in the European Union* (2002), Ch. 4; A Cygan, *The United Kingdom Parliament and European Union legislation* (1998); E Smith (ed.), *National Parliaments as Cornerstones of Integration* (1996); V Bogdanor, 'Britain and the European Community' in J Jowell and D Oliver, *The Changing Constitution*, (3rd edn, 1994). See, for a relatively optimistic assessment of the prospects for reinforced scrutiny, T Raunio, 'Towards Tighter Scrutiny? National Legislatures in the EU Constitution', Federal Trust Online Paper No. 16/04 (available at: http://www.fedtrust.co.uk/default. asp?groupid=0&search=raunio).

particularly with respect to the subsidiarity principle: they, after all, have the most immediate interest in ensuring that complied with the principle is strictly enforced. It has even been argued that participation in the legislative process of the Union may reinvigorate a culture of government accountability at the national level.[178]

(ii) Coordination *between* National Parliaments

It is not only the 'vertical' relationship between national Parliaments and the decision-making institutions of the EU that is likely to prove increasingly important, but also the 'horizontal' relationship of national Parliaments *inter se*. A measure of mutual constitutional trust will be necessary, if the best use is to be made of the possibilities which have been created by strengthening the two Protocols, especially the introduction of the subsidiarity mechanism. The loose framework for inter-Parliamentary cooperation, which is provided by Title 2 of the Protocol on the role of Member States' national Parliaments in the EU, may be found to require further articulation.

Why are Reforms in the Areas of Transparency and National Parliaments and Subsidiarity Appropriate Issues to be 'Cherry-Picked' from the TCE?

The first and obvious point to make is that it is legally *possible* to make both sets of reforms (on transparency, national Parliaments and subsidiarity) within the current Treaty framework, whether via changes to the relevant procedural rules or by the adoption of new consultation, communication and publicity policies.

Second, and significantly in terms of linking proposed reforms to concerns voiced during the ratification process, a decision to enhance the transparency of the legislative process (and, indeed, of the activities of the other activities of the institutions) is fully consistent with a variety of possible visions for the future direction of the EU. A similar argument applies to the timelier and more consistent involvement of national Parliaments in the process of law- and policy-making in the EU.

Increased transparency can facilitate and enhance public, press and political scrutiny of the activities of the EU, which can be used both, on the one hand, to explain and justify more clearly what the EU does and how it does it and, on the other, to criticize those aspects of the EU and its operation that cause concern and consternation among citizens, politicians and interest groups alike. It may result in the enhancement of some kind of feeling of European identity across the borders of Member States (perhaps along interest or pressure group lines), but it may equally lead to greater scepticism of the utility of EU activity in a variety of areas. Equally, the greater involvement of national Parliaments via more rapid and intense communication of policy and legislative proposals, and particularly the opportunity

---

[178] See J Mather, *The European Union and British Democracy: Towards Convergence* (Basingstoke: Macmillan, 2000), who argues (*inter alia*) that the benefit may be felt not only *vis-à-vis* European policy issues but also in the overall conduct of policy-making, debate and government in the UK.

publicly to voice their concerns and even to trigger reconsideration of such proposals at European level, is likely to have a similar effect in raising awareness and even interest in such matters, with similarly potentially double-edged consequences. The point is that the choice to increase the transparency of the activities of the EU institutions, and to enhance the role of national Parliaments in their operation and scrutiny, does not prejudge such substantive questions, and may prove effective in facilitating better consultation and discussion of just such substantive concerns.

CONCLUSIONS

It is a truism of fruit harvesting that in any such process (whether picking cherries or otherwise) it is usually much easier and less time-consuming to pick the low-hanging fruit. The recent history of the EU 'after the "No"-s' has been an illustration of this basic truth, although even here the harvest has been fraught and subjected to occasionally unexpected interruptions from sharp storms in some areas and persistent droughts in others. This chapter has taken a necessarily interim, incomplete and selective look at events since the adoption of the TCE and has attempted to draw together some of the strands in the debate concerning how the EU might move its constitutional reform forward in the months and years to come.

One positive element to take from the results of the referendums in France and the Netherlands and subsequent events is that the profile of events relating to the EU and its activities has been raised. There are, naturally, some indications that this has not always had beneficial effects, whether viewed in terms of levels of support for the EU and its policies or in terms of the quality and accuracy of information being communicated. For example, a pair of Eurobarometer surveys on citizens' views on the EC's role in energy policy[179] suggests that support for the EC playing a key role in strategic energy decisions has waned markedly over the eight months to July 2006. The EC's approach in the energy sphere has come to the fore recently for a number of reasons, many of which relate to global political and economic developments outside the EC's control and influence. However, the Commission's scrutiny[180] of national government resistance in France and Spain to foreign take-overs of energy assets has highlighted the potential impact of the EC competition and the internal market rules upon national energy policy priorities and has

---

[179] See Special Eurobarometer 247, *Attitudes towards Energy* (January 2006, available at http://ec.europa.eu/public_opinion/archives/ebs/ebs_247_en.pdf) and the recent report by L Kubosova, 'Public support for EU energy policy wilts' (12 July 2006, available at http://euobserver.com/9/22078).

[180] See Commission Press Releases IP/06/802, 19 June 2006 (re Suez-GdF, available at: http://europa.eu/rapid/pressReleasesAction.do?reference=IP/06/802&format=HTML&aged=0&language=EN&guiLanguage=en), IP/06/437, 4 April 2006 (re Spanish legislation restricting foreign investment in energy companies, available at: http://europa.eu/rapid/pressReleasesAction.do?reference=IP/06/437&format=HTML&aged=0&language=EN&guiLanguage=en) and the recent report that the Commission has sent a letter to the Spanish government concerning the E-On-Endesa merger (see L Kirk, 'Energy merger pitches Spanish government against EU' (8 August 2006, available at: http://euobserver.com/9/22217/?rk=1)).

reinforced the profile of EC activity and its potential impact. This has been underlined by both the Sector Inquiry by DG COMP into the energy sector and the
Commission's Green Paper on 'A European Strategy for Sustainable, Competitive and
Secure Energy'.[181] At the same time, part of the reason for public attitudes towards
the desirability of an (expanded) EC role in this sphere may be based upon mis-
perceptions of what the EC currently has the power to do, whether as an absolute
matter of Treaty competence or due to inability to agree upon any given course of
action. As the same recent Eurobarometer survey reports, the 'EU does not have a
direct impact on taxes which are levied by member states on energy, in particular
petrol for cars', which is clearly a key energy concern of the vast majority of European
citizens, given rapidly rising petrol prices and increasing levels of car use.[182]

   This chimes with the proposal by Moravcsik and Nicolaïdes to focus future reform
efforts upon a combination of, on the one hand, clear policy development on concrete issues of genuine citizen interest and, on the other, the careful conduct of what
one might term 'expectation management'[183] on the part of the citizens of the EU.

European leaders should be as explicit as possible about the limits and constraints on the
European Union. . . . The unique genius of the EU lies precisely in its ability to lock in
intense interstate policy co-ordination while respecting the powerful rhetoric and symbols
that still adhere to national identity. Publics will be reassured if the EU is portrayed as
stable and successful in helping nation-states achieve their goals, rather than as an effort to
supplant them.[184]

It has been one of the purposes of this chapter to show, first, that such policy
initiatives and expectation management are aided by improved communication
concerning the nature of the Union, and of its powers and activities. It is submitted that the two specific areas discussed in the preceding section—of transparency
and the involvement of national Parliaments in assessing subsidiarity—are both
good illustrations of concrete steps forward that can be taken by the EU during the
period of reflection. Further, their implementation should assist in enhancing the
communication necessary between, on the one hand, the EU, its officials and parliamentarians and, on the other, institutions, representatives and citizens at national,
regional and local levels. Those who argue that pursuing action in these two areas
would somehow illegitimately amount to the implementation of the TCE by the

---

[181] COM(2006) 105 final (8 March 2006) (for details on the Green Paper and consultation thereon
see, generally, http://ec.europa.eu/energy/green-paper-energy/index_en.htm), although, somewhat ironically, the latest Eurobarometer report comments that 'during autumn 2005 and spring 2006, the action
of the EU was not visible' (see Kubosova, n. 179, above).

[182] See Kubosova, n. 179, above.

[183] See also on this point, and in similar vein, the contribution made by JQT Rood (available at:
http://www.europarl.europa.eu/meetdocs/2004_2009/documents/dv/rood_/rood_en.pdf) to the European
Parliament's *Symposium on the Future of the Constitutional Process of the European Union* (13 and 14 October
2005): available at http://www.europarl.europa.eu/meetdocs/2004_2009/organes/afco/afco_20051013_
1500_symposium.htm.

[184] Moravcsik & Nicolaïdes (2005), (n. 107, above), section 4.

back door should be mollified by the realization that increased transparency and scrutiny at national level of EU activities does not commit the EU, its Member States and citizens to any particular vision or theory of the EU and its future development. Instead, these measures are consistent with many approaches to the EU and may help to facilitate better understanding of the organization that we now have and how it came to take the form that it currently possesses, as well as to encourage informed debate about where it should go from here.

If this increased transparency, communication and explanation of what the EU is, what it does, and how and why it does it can be improved steadily in the coming years, then there is scope for some optimism about possible future Treaty changes. The current period of reflection may cause great scepticism about this claim, as it is currently hard to see exactly what the best route may be to achieve changes to the founding Treaties. However, if the procedures and substance of future negotiations leading to proposed amendments to those Treaties could better reflect some of the legitimacy criteria discussed under the heading above, 'Typology: Approaches to Effecting Constitutional Change in the EU', then an enhanced understanding of the EU by the electorate is by no means an impossible dream. The inevitable package deal which any such future Treaty amendment will have to embody will require clear explanation and justification, but if that is conducted in a climate of better information and understanding of what is (and, importantly, what is *not*) at stake, future referendums will have a greater chance of success.

As things stand, *grammatici certant, et adhuc sub iudice lis est*.[185] The consequences of the process that created the TCE, and the events that have followed its adoption by the Member States in 2004, have been, first, a substantial amount of quarrelling among scholars and others alike and, second, a realization that the judges who will rule on this case are likely to be greater in number than ever before in the history of the EU to date. The challenge of the years ahead will be to get them to deliver a verdict that is both workable and widely acceptable for the EU of the future.

Appendix 1: Extract from the Presidency Conclusions from the Brussels European Council (16 June 2006)

An Overall Policy on Transparency

With a view to further increase openness, transparency and accountability, the European Council agrees on the following measures aiming at a stronger involvement of citizens in the work of the Union:

- All Council deliberations on legislative acts to be adopted by co-decision shall be open to the public as shall the votes and the explanation of votes

---

[185] 'The scholars quarrel, and the case lies still undecided in the hands of the judge' (or, less prosaically, 'on that point the learned disagree'): Q Horatius, *Ars poetica* in *The Satires of Horace and Persius* (London: Penguin, 1974).

by Council Members. The Council or Coreper may decide in individual cases that a given deliberation should not be open to the public.

- The Council's first deliberations on legislative acts other than those adopted by co-decision, which given their importance are presented orally by the Commission in a Council session, shall be open to the public. The Presidency may decide in individual cases that the Council's subsequent deliberations on a particular act shall be open to the public, unless the Council or Coreper decide otherwise.
- The Council shall regularly hold public debates on important issues affecting the interests of the Union and its citizens. Such debates will be held further to a decision by the Council or Coreper, acting by qualified majority. Implementation of this commitment shall start during the incoming Presidency, which would submit proposals for such public debates taking into account the importance of the matter and its interest to citizens.
- The General Affairs and External Relations Council's deliberations on the 18 month programme shall be public, as shall other Council formations' deliberations on their priorities. The Commission's presentation of its five year programme, of its annual work programme and of its annual policy strategy, as well as the ensuing debate, shall be public.
- All public deliberations shall be broadcasted [*sic*] in all languages through video-streaming and there shall be an obligation for a recorded version to remain available for at least a month on the Council's internet site.
- The incoming Presidency is invited, together with the General Secretariat of the Council, to develop new means of giving more publicity to public deliberations, in particular through the Council's web site and mailing list, an easily accessible and constantly updated list of forthcoming debates, appropriate background material, as well as direct communication to target audiences. They will work closely together to provide the media and citizens with an open, rapid and technically advanced communication service.
- The General Secretariat of the Council shall inform the public in advance of the dates and approximate time on which public debates will take place and shall take all practical measures to ensure proper implementation of the rules of transparency.

Index